MANAGEMENT, ORGANIZATIONS, AND HUMAN RESOURCES: SELECTED READINGS

MANAGEMENT, ORGANIZATIONS, AND HUMAN RESOURCES: SELECTED READINGS

HERBERT G. HICKS
Professor of Management
Louisiana State University

McGRAW-HILL BOOK COMPANY

New York	*Kuala Lumpur*	*Panama*
St. Louis	*London*	*Rio de Janeiro*
San Francisco	*Mexico*	*Singapore*
Düsseldorf	*Montreal*	*Sydney*
Johannesburg	*New Delhi*	*Toronto*

MANAGEMENT, ORGANIZATIONS, AND
HUMAN RESOURCES: SELECTED READINGS

Library of Congress Catalog Card Number 77-178927

07-028732-5

1234567890 BPBP 7987654321

*This book was set in Theme by Allen-Wayne Technical
Corp., and printed and bound by The Book Press, Inc.
The designer was J. E. O'Connor; the drawings were
done by Allen-Wayne Technical Corp. The editors
were Richard F. Dojny, Hiag Akmakjian, and Sally
Mobley. Peter D. Guilmette supervised production.*

To the memory
of H. O. G.

CONTENTS

PREFACE

This book of readings is designed to serve as a text in courses on management and organizations. It may be used as a supplement in courses with regular texts or used alone in case-oriented courses. It can also serve as the main text in seminars, discussion groups, and managerial development programs. In addition, these readings may be helpful to practicing managers and students for their independent study. Courses for which this book is appropriate include basic management, organization theory, administrative practices, social organizations, and seminars in management. Instructors in the introduction to business courses, who wish to have a managerial emphasis in that course, may also find this book useful.

The articles included were selected from hundreds of possibilities. Special effort was made to include the article that best expressed the issues involved in each topic. Because an interdisciplinary approach was taken, articles from management theory, organization theory, psychology, sociology, and other fields are included. Articles were sought that are highly readable, in addition to being technically sound. Also, each article was evaluated on its ability to stimulate discussion of the issues.

The articles are arranged in chapters that parallel the second edition of *The Management of Organizations: A Systems and Human Resources Approach.* However, because the topics covered are similar, this book can also be used as a supplement to many other texts.

I appreciate the generosity of the authors and publishers who granted permission to reprint their materials.

Herbert G. Hicks

MANAGEMENT,
ORGANIZATIONS, AND HUMAN RESOURCES:
SELECTED READINGS

ORGANIZATIONS – AN OVERVIEW

Part I focuses on organizations — why they exist, what they are, how they relate to their environment, and how they live or die. In the first reading, Luther Gulick explains the advantages and limitations of specialization, or division of work. Because specialization requires organizations, it is a fundamental reason for their existence. However, as explained in the next article, specialization — such as on an assembly line — can be boring and monotonous and may cause a person to feel worthless. Baynard Hooper explains in his article that the abundance produced by modern, technological, specialized, and mass societies often causes the individual to feel overwhelmed by organizations. Taken together these three articles show that organizations are indispensable parts of modern civilization, but they also cause human problems.

Next, Peter M. Blau and W. Richard Scott suggest that the two basic aspects of social organizations are structure and shared beliefs of members. Rollin L. Burns then offers his view that the three basic components of organizations are people, products, and places.

In the next reading, Clifford E. Jurgensen gives research findings on the objectives or satisfactions persons say they want from their jobs. Hadley Cantril describes eleven basic sets of human needs. We can expect that persons would attempt to satisfy these individual objectives or needs in organizations.

Organizations also have objectives which are derived from but different from individual objectives. John F. Mee explains the importance of well-formulated organizational objectives in efficient organizations.

In recent years more and more emphasis has been placed on ecology, and Chas. F. Jones explains that a company must take responsibility for preserving the environment. Arthur W. Loring offers data showing that many corporate executives feel that their primary responsibility is not to society, as some persons have claimed.

In the last article in Part I, John W. Gardner gives nine rules whereby organizations can overcome "dry rot" and renew themselves.

THE DIVISION OF WORK*

Luther Gulick

It is appropriate at the outset of this discussion to consider the reasons for and the effect of the division of work. It is sufficient for our purpose to note the following factors.

WHY DIVIDE WORK?

Because men differ in nature, capacity and skill, and gain greatly in dexterity by specialization;

Because the same man cannot be at two places at the same time;

Because one man cannot do two things at the same time;

Because the range of knowledge and skill is so great that a man cannot within his life-span know more than a small fraction of it. In other words, it is a question of human nature, time, and space.

In a shoe factory it would be possible to have 1,000 men each assigned to making complete pairs of shoes. Each man would cut his leather, stamp in the eyelets, sew up the tops, sew on the bottoms, nail on the heels, put in the laces, and pack each pair in a box. It might take two days to do the job. One thousand men would make 500 pairs of shoes a day. It would also be possible to divide the work among these same men, using the identical hand methods, in an entirely different way. One group of men would be assigned to cut the leather, another to putting in the eyelets, another to stitching up the tops, another to sewing on the soles, another to nailing on the heels, another to inserting the laces and packing the pairs of shoes. We know from common sense and experience that there are two great gains in this latter process: first, it makes possible the better utilization of the varying skills and aptitudes of the different workmen, and encourages the development of specialization; and second, it eliminates the time that is lost when a workman turns from a knife, to a punch, to a needle and awl, to a hammer, and moves from table to bench, to anvil, to stool. Without any pressure on the workers, they could probably turn out twice as many shoes in a single day. There would be additional economies, because inserting laces and packing could be assigned to unskilled and low-

*Reprinted with permission from Luther Gulick and L. Urwick, *Papers on the Science of Administration*, Institute of Public Administration, New York, 1937, pp. 3-6.

paid workers. Moreover, in the cutting of the leather there would be less spoilage because the less skillful pattern cutters would all be eliminated and assigned to other work. It would also be possible to cut a dozen shoe tops at the same time from the same pattern with little additional effort. All of these advances would follow, without the introduction of new labor saving machinery.

The introduction of machinery accentuates the division of work. Even such a simple thing as a saw, a typewriter, or a transit requires increased specialization, and serves to divide workers into those who can and those who cannot use the particular instrument effectively. Division of work on the basis of the tools and machines used in work rests no doubt in part on aptitude, but primarily upon the development and maintenance of skill through continued manipulation.

Specialized skills are developed not alone in connection with machines and tools. They evolve naturally from the materials handled, like wood, or cattle, or paint, or cement. They arise similarly in activities which center in a complicated series of interrelated concepts, principles, and techniques. These are most clearly recognized in the professions, particularly those based on the application of scientific knowledge, as in engineering, medicine, and chemistry. They are none the less equally present in law, ministry, teaching, accountancy, navigation, aviation, and other fields.

The nature of these subdivisions is essentially pragmatic, in spite of the fact that there is an element of logic underlying them. They are therefore subject to a gradual evolution with the advance of science, the invention of new machines, the progress of technology and the change of the social system. In the last analysis, however, they appear to be based upon differences in individual human beings. But it is not to be concluded that the apparent stability of "human nature," whatever that may be, limits the probable development of specialization. The situation is quite the reverse. As each field of knowledge and work is advanced, constituting a continually larger and more complicated nexus of related principles, practices and skills, any individual will be less and less able to encompass it and maintain intimate knowledge and facility over the entire area, and there will thus arise a more minute specialization because knowledge and skill advance while man stands still. Division of work and integrated organization are the bootstraps by which mankind lifts itself in the process of civilization.

THE LIMITS OF DIVISION

There are three clear limitations beyond which the division of work cannot to advantage go. The first is practical and arises from the volume of work involved in man-hours. Nothing is gained by subdividing work if that further subdivision results in setting up a task which requires less than the full time of one man. This is too obvious to need demonstration. The only exception arises where space interferes, and in such cases the part-time expert must fill in his spare time at other tasks, so that as a matter of fact a new combination is introduced.

The second limitation arises from technology and custom at a given time and place. In some areas nothing would be gained by separating undertaking from the custody and cleaning of churches, because by custom the sexton is the undertaker; in building construction it is extraordinarily difficult to re-divide certain aspects of electrical and plumbing work and to combine them in a more effective way, because of the jurisdictional conflicts of craft unions; and it is clearly impracticable to establish a division of cost accounting in a field in which no technique of costing has yet been developed.

This second limitation is obviously elastic. It may be changed by invention and by education. If this were not the fact, we should face a static division of labor. It should be noted, however, that a marked change has two dangers. It greatly restricts the labor market from which workers may be drawn and greatly lessens the opportunities open to those who are trained for the particular specialization.

The third limitation is that the subdivision of work must not pass beyond physical division into organic division. It might seem far more efficient to have the front half of the cow in the pasture grazing and the rear half in the barn being milked all of the time, but this organic division would fail. Similarly there is no gain from splitting a single movement or gesture like licking an envelope, or tearing apart a series of intimately and intricately related activities.

It may be said that there is in this an element of reasoning in a circle; that the test here applied as to whether an activity is organic or not is whether it is divisible or not — which is what we set out to define. This charge is true. It must be a pragmatic test. Does the division work out? Is something vital destroyed and lost? Does it bleed?

THE WHOLE AND THE PARTS

It is axiomatic that the whole is equal to the sum of its parts. But in dividing up any "whole," one must be certain that every part, including unseen elements and relationships, is accounted for. The marble sand to which the Venus de Milo may be reduced by a vandal does not equal the statue, though every last grain be preserved; nor is a thrush just so much feathers, bones, flesh and blood; nor a typewriter merely so much steel, glass, paint and rubber. Similarly a piece of work to be done cannot be subdivided into the obvious component parts without great danger that the central design, the operating relationships, the imprisoned idea, will be lost.

A simple illustration will make this clear. One man can build a house. He can lay the foundation, cut the beams and boards, make the window frames and doors, lay the floors, raise the roof, plaster the walls, fit in the heating and water systems, install the electric wiring, hang the paper, and paint the structure. But if he did, most of the work would be done by hands unskilled in the work; much material would be spoiled, and the work would require many months of his time. On the other hand, the whole job of building the house might be divided among a group of men. One man could do the foundation, build the chimney, and plaster the walls; another could erect the frame, cut the timbers and the boards, raise the roof, and do all the carpentry; another all the plumbing; another all the paper hanging and painting; another all the electric wiring. But this would not make a house unless someone — an architect — made a plan for the house, so that each skilled worker could know what to do and when to do it.

When one man builds a house alone he plans as he works; he decides what to do first and what next, that is, he "co-ordinates the work." When many men work together to build a house this part of the work, the co-ordinating, must not be lost sight of.

In the "division of the work" among the various skilled specialists, a specialist in planning and co-ordination must be sought as well. Otherwise, a great deal of time may be lost, workers may get in each other's way, material may not be on hand when needed, things may be done in the wrong order, and there may even be a difference of opinion as to where the various doors and windows are to go. It is self-evident that the more the work is subdivided, the greater is the danger of confusion, and the greater is the need of overall supervision and co-ordination. Co-ordination is not something that develops by accident. It must be won by intelligent, vigorous, persistent and organized effort.

THE GRUELING LIFE ON THE LINE*

Anonymous

For eight hours every day, says Henry Belcher, a 40-year-old welder, "I am as much a machine as a punch press or a drill motor is." With that comment, he sums up a crucial reason for the auto-worker militancy that led to the strike against General Motors. Most of the men on the assembly line hate their jobs — with a bitterness that can hardly be understood by anybody who performs interesting tasks in comfortable surroundings. At best, reports *Time's* Correspondent David DeVoss, the auto worker's routine is a daily voyage from tedium to apathy, dominated by the feeling that he sheds his identity when he punches the time clock. At worst, in the industry's older plants, his life is one of physical discomfort as well.

Less than a minute. One such factory is the 60-year-old Dodge plant in Hamtramck, Mich., where Belcher works. Promptly at 6 a.m., the assembly line begins sending cars past his work station, and from then on Belcher is a part of the line, like the well-oiled gears and bearings. The noise is deafening; Belcher could not talk to the men at the next stations three feet away even if there were time. There never is. Partially assembled cars move past him at the rate of 62 an hour; in less than one minute he is expected to look over each auto, pound out a dent in a fender or reweld an improperly joined seam. Cars that cannot be fixed that quickly are taken off the line. In the winter, drafts from ill-caulked windows chill Belcher's chest, while hot air blasts from rust-proofing ovens 30 feet away singe his back. After two hours of standing on the concrete floor his legs ache, but the whistle does not blow for lunch until 10 a.m.

Then the line stops, and Belcher gets 30 unpaid minutes to eat. That is not long enough for him to walk down from his sixth-floor work station to the second-floor cafeteria, buy a hot meal and get back before the line starts again. So he munches a sandwich from a bag — often while standing at the back of one of the long lines of men waiting to use the urinals. The chance to visit the bathroom cannot be passed up, since Belcher can rarely leave the assembly line. Besides the lunch period, he gets breaks of eleven minutes in the morning and twelve minutes in the afternoon. After the lunch break, the whistle blows again at 10:30 a.m., and the men put in

---

four more hours of work until the shift changes at 2:30. Says Belcher, who makes $3.82 an hour: "Everything is regulated. No time to stop and think about what you are doing; your life is geared to the assembly line. I have lost my freedom."

Complaints like these have been heard almost from the days when the first assembly line started rolling. In fact, the conditions that so depress Belcher are not as bad as they once were. Under union pressure, companies have made some improvements. Shifts are a bit shorter now than the 3:30 p.m. to 1 a.m. stint that Walter Reuther worked at Ford in 1927. Over the years, the union has won regular relief breaks, the system of roving relief men and doors on toilets. Some workers who do especially dirty jobs such as painting, now get company-paid special clothing. Many plants now have enclaves away from the line where men on their breaks can sit down, smoke or get a cup of coffee from a vending machine.

For the workers, that is not enough. The amenities are greatest in the industry's newer plants, but a large proportion of union members labor in aged factories. The very nature of the work remains the worst problem. Auto managers concede that most assembly jobs are hard and boring, but they figure that little can be done about it. Managers commonly complain about shoddy workmanship. Union members vehemently retort that the line moves too fast for them to do as good a job as they would like to.

Welcome old age. For many workers, the only escape is retirement on a pension. Old age is not unwelcome in the auto plants; it is common to hear young men talk longingly of retirement. That is why the union's demand that workers be allowed to retire after 30 years, regardless of age, on minimum pensions of $500 a month, has become a key issue in the G.M. strike. Says Pete Tipton, 34, a welder for Cadillac: "All I have to look forward to is '30 and out!' I only have a ninth-grade education, so I can't do anything else, but my children are going to stay in school so that they will not have to subjected to this kind of life."

Some men, of course, work up to jobs that are free of much of the tough labor. Al Powarowski, 32, has advanced from loading boxcars for Ford to driving completed autos off the assembly line, at $3.72 an hour. Like many Ford workers, he believes that the company is more understanding than G.M. or Chrysler. But Powarowski feels insecure because of the un-steadiness of the work. He has spent 14 months of his seven years at Ford waiting out eight separate layoffs; the first, lasting one week, started on the 89th day of his 90-day probationary period as a new employee. "In the years when you are making money, you don't have time to spend it, and when sales go down and layoffs come, no one has any money at all," says Powarowski. His own annual income has dropped from $12,000 to $7,000 because his hours have been sharply reduced during this year's auto-sales slump. Besides, he finds the job maddeningly dull, if not physically taxing. "The only fun I have," he says, "is getting a few cold beers after work."

Richard Jankowski, 29, is happier — but only because he will soon realize the auto worker's dream of leaving the line for good. During the last three of his eleven years at G.M.'s Fisher Body plant in Ypsilanti, he went to night school, and this fall he will become a high school teacher. "I almost cry when I see kids coming into the shop today," he says. "Working in a factory is nothing to be ashamed of, but you look at men who are 35 and look 50 and you say, is that going to be me?"

As the nation's labor force becomes better educated, the automakers may run into trouble finding enough new men willing to enter the plants. Even before the strike, the once long queues outside plant hiring offices had disappeared, and for the first time in years in some factories, supervisors had begun hiring women for the line.

OUR ECONOMIC MIRACLE LEAVES MANY YOUTHS FEELING TRAPPED*

Baynard Hooper

Today the U.S. has more white-collar workers than blue, and technological expansion has long since shattered the economic myth that there are no new frontiers. Whole new fields such as aerospace, electronics and computers undermine that claim, as does a gross national product that has more than doubled in 20 years. And yet the very success and intensity of our economic miracle seem to have produced a counterreaction among many of the young people who will fall heir to it. "They see their lives laid out neatly before them," writes Irving Kristol.

They see themselves moving ahead sedately and more or less inexorably in their professional careers; they know that with a college degree even "failure" in their careers will represent no harsh punishment; they know "it's all laid on" — and they react against this bourgeois utopia their parents so ardently strove for.
One of the unforeseen consequences of the welfare state is that it leaves so little room for personal idealism; another is that it mutes the challenge to self-definition. All this is but another way of saying that it satisfies the anxieties of the middle-aged while stifling the creative energies of the young. . . . Indeed, many of these students simply dismiss American democracy as a sham, a game played by the "power structure" for its own amusement and in its own interests.

There is other evidence that the outward forms of American civilization conceal an inner restlessness and loss of faith in the old truths once held self-evident. The protest movements of today, whether the thin-lipped suspiciousness of the John Birch Society or the angry conformism of the New Left, are neither politics nor debate, as the men of reason who first founded this nation conceived those activities. On both sides, they are bare-faced attempts at coercion, a surrender to the feeling that in a mass society only mass movements count for anything.

The reaction has even reached that bumbling but well-meaning monster, the government bureaucracy: suddenly the welfare department has become "the enemy" to an increasing mass of welfare recipients, and the government frequently finds itself trying to ward off the anger of its beneficiaries by turning over its own programs to them — in effect, sponsoring an antigovernment movement.

ORGANIZATIONS, NOT INDIVIDUALS, CONTEND FOR POWER TODAY

Today, warns Professor Paul Kurtz, "it is organizations which contend for power, not individuals. Moral choices are largely within the context of an organizational structure. The individual thus becomes powerless, impotent and unable to affect the decision-making processes of his society."

As one result, many young people have turned inward. "The old ideologies and slogans leave these young people cold," management expert Peter Drucker has observed, "but there is a passionate groping for personal commitment to a philosophy of life. Above all, a new inner-directedness is all the rage."

Such an attitude can produce a paradox, and a dangerous one. On one side is an insecurity brought about in large part by an unprecedented opportunity to choose among many options — but in an environment where many of the established standards and traditions for making such choices have been discarded. On the other side is a sense of personal ineffectiveness and worthlessness in the face of massive systems and exploding knowledge. Feelings of worthlessness, as any psychologist will attest, are only a short distance from self-hate. Self-hate, in turn, is all too easily transformed into the hatred of others, which both the New Left and New Right so fervently enjoy.

The question, then, becomes: How shall our society reconcile the inner-directedness of people who feel impotent in the vastness of a society with the urgent problems that vastness has created? When the old verities seem hollow, how can we achieve a sense of national unity without slipping into some sort of benevolent despotism?

External changes will mean little unless they spring from, and are reinforced by, the convictions of millions of individuals that we can bring to our massive systems more flexibility, less impersonality, a less oppressive pace of growth and centralization. "If life is to be saved from boredom relieved only by disaster," Bertrand Russell once wrote, "means must be found of restoring individual initiative, not only in things that are trivial, but in the things that really matter.... It is in the individuals, not in the whole, that ultimate value is to be sought."

This is scarcely radical advice to us today. It echoes the ideals of the 18th Century philosophers who fathered our own revolution. It even reflects that ancient Greek admonition, "Know Thyself." None of this, of course, makes the precept any easier to follow, especially for an age which has largely discarded moral imperatives based on religious faith.

And yet Russell's dictum is both a beginning and an ending. A broad spectrum of individual commitment is both a definition of freedom and a defense of it. To relinquish the search, simply because the complexities of mass civilization make it too difficult, is to sacrifice all that has gone before.

THE CONCEPT OF FORMAL ORGANIZATION*

Peter M. Blau and W. Richard Scott

Social organization and formal organizations. Although a wide variety of organizations exists, when we speak of an organization it is generally quite clear what we mean and what we do not mean by this term. We may refer to the American Medical Association as an organization, or to a college fraternity; to the Bureau of Internal Revenue, or to a union; to General Motors, or to a church; to the Daughters of the American Revolution, or to an army. But we would not call a family an organization, nor would we so designate a friendship clique, or a community, or an economic market, or the political institutions of a society. What is the specific and differentiating criterion implicit in our intuitive distinction of organizations from other kinds of social groupings or institutions? It has something to do with how human conduct becomes socially organized, but it is not, as one might first suspect, whether or not social controls order and organize the conduct of individuals, since such social controls operate in both types of circumstances.

Before specifying what is meant by formal organization, let us clarify the general concept of social organization. "Social organization" refers to the ways in which human conduct becomes socially organized, that is, to the observed regularities in the behavior of people that are due to the social conditions in which they find themselves rather than to their physiological or psychological characteristics as individuals. The many social conditions that influence the conduct of people can be divided into two main types, which constitute the two basic aspects of social organizations: (1) the structure of social relations in a group or larger collectivity of people, and (2) the shared beliefs and orientations that unite the members of the collectivity and guide their conduct.

The conception of structure or system implies that the component units stand in some relation to one another and, as the popular expression "The whole is greater than the sum of its parts" suggests, that the relations between units add new elements to the situation.[1] This aphorism, like so

---

*Reprinted with permission from Peter M. Blau and W. Richard Scott, *Formal Organizations*, Chandler Publishing Company, San Francisco, 1962, pp. 2-8.

[1] For a discussion of some of the issues raised by this assertion, see Ernest Nagel, "On the Statement 'The Whole is More Than the Sum of Its Parts'," Paul F. Lazarsfeld and Morris Rosenberg (eds.), *The Language of Social Research*, Glencoe, Ill.: Free Press, 1955, pp. 519-527.

many others, is a half-truth. The sum of fifteen apples, for example, is no more than fifteen times one apple. But a block of ice is more than the sum of the atoms of hydrogen and oxygen that compose it. In the case of the apples, there exist no linkages or relations between the units comprising the whole. In the case of the ice, however, specific connections have been formed between H and O atoms and among H_2O molecules that distinguish ice from hydrogen and oxygen, on the one hand, and from water, on the other. Similarly, a busload of passengers does not constitute a group, since no social relations unify individuals into a common structure.[2] But a busload of club members on a Sunday outing is a group, because a network of social relations links the members into a social structure, a structure which is an emergent characteristic of the collectivity that cannot be reduced to the attributes of its individual members. In short, a network of social relations transforms an aggregate of individuals into a group (or an aggregate of groups into a larger social structure), and the group is more than the sum of the individuals composing it since the structure of social relations is an emergent element that influences the conduct of individuals.

To indicate the nature of social relations, we can briefly dissect this concept. Social relations involve, first, patterns of social interaction: the frequency and duration of the contacts between people, the tendency to initiate these contacts, the direction of influence between persons, the degree of cooperation, and so forth. Second, social relations entail people's sentiments to one another, such as feelings of attraction, respect, and hostility. The differential distribution of social relations in a group, finally, defines its status structure. Each member's status in the group depends on his relations with the others — their sentiments toward and interaction with him. As a result, integrated members become differentiated from isolates, those who are widely respected from those who are not highly regarded, and leaders from followers. In addition to these relations between individuals within groups, relations also develop between groups, relations that are a source of still another aspect of social status, since the standing of the group in the larger social system becomes part of the status of any of its members. An obvious example is the significance that membership in an ethnic minority, say, Puerto Rican, has for an individual's social status.

The networks of social relations between individuals and groups, and the status structure defined by them, constitute the core of the social organization of a collectivity, but not the whole of it. The other main dimension of social organization is a system of shared beliefs and orientations, which serve as standards for human conduct. In the course of social interaction common notions arise as to how people should act and interact and what objectives are worthy of attainment. First, common values crystallize, values that govern the goals for which men strive — their

---

[2] A purist may, concededly, point out that all individuals share the role of passenger and so are subject to certain generalized norms, courtesy for example.

ideals and their ideas of what is desirable — such as our belief in democracy or the importance financial success assumes in our thinking. Second, social norms develop — that is, common expectations concerning how people ought to behave — and social sanctions are used to discourage violations of these norms. These socially sanctioned rules of conduct vary in significance from moral principles or mores, as Sumner calls them, to mere customs of folkways. If values define the ends of human conduct, norms distinguish behavior that is a legitimate means for achieving these ends from behavior that is illegitimate. Finally, aside from the norms to which everybody is expected to conform, differential role expectations also emerge, expectations that become associated with various social positions. Only women in our society are expected to wear skirts, for example. Or, the respected leader of a group is expected to make suggestions, and the other members will turn to him in times of difficulties, whereas group members who have not earned the respect of others are expected to refrain from making suggestions and generally to participate little in group discussions.

These two dimensions of social organization — the networks of social relations and the shared orientations — are often referred to as the social structure and the culture, respectively.[3] Every society has a complex social structure and a complex culture, and every community within a society can be characterized by these two dimensions of social organization, and so can every group within a community (except that the specific term "culture" is reserved for the largest social systems). The prevailing cultural standards and the structure of social relations serve to organize human conduct in the collectivity. As people conform more or less closely to the expectations of their fellows, and as the degree of their conformity in turn influences their relations with others and their social status, and as their status in further turn affects their inclinations to adhere to social norms and their chances to achieve valued objectives, their patterns of behavior become socially organized.

In contrast to the social organization that emerges whenever men are living together, there are organizations that have been deliberately established for a certain purpose.[4] If the accomplishment of an objective requires collective effort, men set up an organization designed to coordinate the activities of many persons and to furnish incentives for others to join them for this purpose. For example, business concerns are established in order to produce goods that can be sold for a profit, and workers organize unions in order to increase their bargaining power with employers. In these cases, the goals to be achieved, the rules the

[3]See the recent discussion of these concepts by Kroeber and Parsons, who conclude by defining culture as "transmitted and created content and patterns of values, ideas, and other symbolic-meaningful systems" and social structure or system as "the specifically relational system of interaction among individuals and collectivities." A.L. Kroeber and Talcott Parsons, "The Concepts of Culture and of Social System," *American Sociological Review*, 23 (1958), p. 583.

[4]Sumner makes this distinction between, in his terms, "crescive" and "enacted" social institutions. William Graham Sumner, *Folkways*, Boston: Ginn, 1907, p. 54.

members of the organization are expected to follow, and the status structure that defines the relations between them (the organizational chart) have not spontaneously emerged in the course of social interaction but have been consciously designed a priori to anticipate and guide interaction and activities. Since the distinctive characteristic of these organizations is that they have been formally established for the explicit purpose of achieving certain goals, the term "formal organizations" is used to designate them. And this formal establishment for explicit purpose is the criterion that distinguishes our subject matter from the study of social organization in general.

Formal organization and informal organization. The fact that an organization has been formally established, however, does not mean that all activities and interactions of its members conform strictly to the official blueprint. Regardless of the time and effort devoted by management to designing a rational organization chart and elaborate procedure manuals, this official plan can never completely determine the conduct and social relations of the organization's members. Stephen Vincent Benét illustrates this limitation when he contrasts the military blueprint with military action:

If you take a flat map
And move wooden blocks upon it strategically,
The thing looks well, the blocks behave as they should.
The science of war is moving live men like blocks.
And getting the blocks into place at a fixed moment.
But it takes time to mold your men into blocks
And flat maps turn into country where creeks and gullies
Hamper your wooden squares. They stick in the brush,
They are tired and rest, they straggle after ripe blackberries,
And you cannot lift them up in your hand and move them.[5]

In every formal organization there arise informal organizations. The constituent groups of the organization, like all groups, develop their own practices, values, norms, and social relations as their members live and work together. The roots of these informal systems are embedded in the formal organization itself and nurtured by the very formality of its arrangements. Official rules must be general to have sufficient scope to cover the multitude of situations that may arise. But the application of these general rules to particular cases often poses problems of judgment, and informal practices tend to emerge that provide solutions for these problems. Decisions not anticipated by official regulations must frequently be made, particularly in times of change, and here again unofficial practices are likely to furnish guides for decisions long before the

[5] From *John Brown's Body*, Holt, Rinehart & Winston, Inc. Copyright, 1927, 1928, by Stephen Vincent Benét. Copyright renewed, 1955, 1956, by Rosemary Carr Benét.

formal rules have been adapted to the changing circumstances. Moreover, unofficial norms are apt to develop that regulate performance and productivity. Finally, complex networks of social relations and informal status structures emerge, within groups and between them, which are influenced by many factors besides the organizational chart, for example by the background characteristics of various persons, their abilities, their willingness to help others, and their conformity to group norms. But to say that these informal structures are not completely determined by the formal institution is not to say that they are entirely independent of it. For informal organizations develop in response to the opportunities created and the problems posed by their environment, and the formal organization constitutes the immediate environment of the groups within it.

When we speak of formal organizations in this book, we do not mean to imply that attention is confined to formally instituted patterns; quite the contrary. It is impossible to understand the nature of a formal organization without investigating the networks of informal relations and the unofficial norms as well as the formal hierarchy of authority and the official body of rules, since the formally instituted and the informally emerging patterns are inextricably intertwined. The distinction between the formal and the informal aspects of organizational life is only an analytical one and should not be reified; there is only one actual organization. Note also that one does not speak of the informal organization of a family or of a community. The term "informal organization" does not refer to all types of emergent patterns of social life but only to those that evolve within the framework of a formally established organization. Excluded from our purview are social institutions that have evolved without explicit design; included are the informally emerging as well as the formally instituted patterns within formally established organizations.

The decision of the members of a group to formalize their endeavors and relations by setting up a specific organization, say, a social and athletic club, is not fortuitous. If a group is small enough for all members to be in direct social contact, and if it has no objectives that require coordination of activities, there is little need for explicit procedures or a formal division of labor. But the larger the group and the more complex the task it seeks to accomplish, the greater are the pressures to become explicitly organized.[6] Once a group of boys who merely used to hang around a drugstore decide to participate in the local baseball league, they must organize a team. And the complex coordination of millions of soldiers with thousands of specialized duties in a modern army requires extensive formalized procedures and a clear-cut authority structure.

Since formal organizations are often very large and complex, some authors refer to them as "large-scale" or as "complex" organizations.

[6]For a discussion of size and its varied effects on the characteristics of social organization, see Theodore Caplow, "Organizational Size," *Administrative Science Quarterly*, 1 (1957), pp. 484-505.

But we have eschewed these terms as misleading in two respects. First, organizations vary in size and complexity, and using these variables as defining criteria would result in such odd expressions as "a small large-scale organization" or "a very complex complex organization." Second, although formal organizations often become very large and complex, their size and complexity do not rival those of the social organization of a modern society, which includes such organizations and their relations with one another in addition to other nonorganization patterns. (Perhaps the complexity of formal organizations is so much emphasized because it is man-made whereas the complexity of societal organization has slowly emerged, just as the complexity of modern computers is more impressive than that of the human brain. Complexity by design may be more conspicuous than complexity by growth or evolution.)

The term "bureaucratic organization," which also is often used, calls attention to the fact that organizations generally possess some sort of administrative machinery. In an organization that has been formally established, a specialized administrative staff usually exists that is responsible for maintaining the organization as a going concern and for coordinating the activities of its members. Large and complex organizations require an especially elaborate administrative apparatus. In a large factory, for example, there is not only an industrial work force directly engaged in production but also an administration composed of executive, supervisory, clerical, and other staff personnel. The case of a government agency is more complicated, because such an agency is part of the administrative arm of the nation. The entire personnel of, say, a law-enforcement agency is engaged in administration, but administration of different kinds; whereas operating officials administer the law and thereby help maintain social order in the society, their superiors and the auxiliary staff administer agency procedures and help maintain the organization itself.

One aspect of bureaucratization that has received much attention is the elaboration of detailed rules and regulations that the members of the organization are expected to faithfully follow. Rigid enforcement of the minutiae of extensive official procedures often impedes effective operations. Colloquially, the term "bureaucracy" connotes such rule-encumbered inefficiency. In sociology, however, the term is used neutrally to refer to the administrative aspects of organizations. If bureaucratization is defined as the amount of effort devoted to maintaining the organization rather than to directly achieving its objectives, all formal organizations have at least a minimum of bureaucracy — even if this bureaucracy involves no more than a secretary-treasurer who collects dues. But wide variations have been found in the degree of bureaucratization in organizations, as indicated by the amount of effort devoted to administrative personnel, the hierarchical character of the organization, or the strict enforcement of administrative procedures and rigid compliance with them.

ORGANIC ORGANIZATION*

Rollin L. Burns

An organization is composed of three basic components — *People* — organisms, *Products* — anything produced by labor, thought, or growth, and *Places* — locations where people and products merge in organic processes.

An organization is an organic medium composed of many organisms. Organisms are living, changing complex systems. Systems which do not change are considered lifeless, dead. Hence, if people, products, and places — the elements of an organization — do not change, they are not organic, but lifeless and essentially nonproductive.

Modifications vary with a total environment. In the stream of industrial progress, organicism has been influenced by political, social, economic, and ethical theories and practices. A reasonable balancing of theory and practice leads to a total environment providing creativity and innovation necessary in arriving at a pinnacle of productive effort.

In today's nuclear and space age only the organic organization appears capable of survival. Now the total environment is more conducive to rapid growth. Nothing appears impossible. A new philosophy of rapid change must be accepted by managers of organizations.

Failure to realize that the components of an organization are in a constant state of rapid change can only characterize the unsuccessful.

First, *People* change from day to day. Each organism is affected by a multitude of dynamic influences. Skills, capabilities, and attitudes are variable factors to be observed daily and to be considered by managers in the organic organization — the flexible organicism of effective and efficient management. When the individual organisms — the people — cease their growing, changing characteristics, they have no place in today's organic organization.

A possible failure of managers is the inability or unconcern for observance of changes in the basic ingredient of production — *People* — as biological organisms in a fluid state. Another weakness is apparent when managers are reluctant to rearrange structural features for greater attainment of projected action. Possibly the framed and often faded rectangular adornments of executive suites ought to be discarded, if a dynamic organization is desired. Obviously, change for its own sake is folly.

*Reprinted with permission from Rollin L. Burns, "Organic Organization," *Personnel Journal*, September, 1963.

The second basic component of the organic organization is *Product* — whether things, ideas, or services. The contemporary environment, highly competitive, has kept product alive. Most unchanged products have been short of life, and the producer as well. Little of that which does not change can live. The profit-takers are those saturated with a philosophy of change, improvement, and the new. Like people, products are organic; they must improve or the new must be created to effect a living organization.

The third component of an organic organization is *Places*. These tend to be the most changeless, lifeless. Are they? Should they be? It is almost axiomatic that if people and products are organic — in a constant state of flux as a result of inherent and environmental factors, places are also organic, and, if not, they may cause the disappearance of the other two components.

Organizations of the organisms of production no longer tolerate unpleasant places for productive effort. More of the things that please and satisfy — mechanical aids to supplant muscular effort, pleasant colors, enjoyable light and temperatures, as well as safe, modern tools of product are now demanded. The creative effort of producers is presumably thereby enhanced. Attention to location — places — may lead to more product, faster, improved services, important to producers and consumers.

In conclusion, the plea is for a living organization, characterized by current concepts of creativity, flexibility, mobility, and willingness to accept a management philosophy of organicism, unbound by stagnant, strait-jacket structures and concepts. Now, reasonable risks can be calculated quickly by mathematical models. Managers must realize that people are changing rapidly and need frequent re-alignment, that product competition demands quick changes, and that places must conform with the organic nature of people and product.

WHAT JOB APPLICANTS SAY THEY WANT*

Clifford E. Jurgensen

Within any community having a large number of employers, some have reputations as "good" companies and others are typically considered "poor" companies. Opinions which people have toward a company are important to that company. They do much to establish and maintain good or poor public relations, and they make it easy or hard to build up an adequate pool of job applicants from which to select satisfactory employees. An outstandingly good reputation may even permit a company to maintain an adequate pool of applicants, comprised of those currently working elsewhere but willing and anxious to shift their employment to the more desirable company. This type of situation not only reduces recruiting costs, but increases any competitive advantage resulting from hiring only the very best of employees. At the other extreme, a company with a "poor" reputation may have to run shorthanded because of an insufficient number of applicants, or hire underqualified applicants because "good" persons go elsewhere.

Similarly, certain departments and jobs within a single company have a reputation for being desirable or undesirable. What are the factors by which persons decide whether a job is a "good" job or a company is a "good" company? Discussion with executives, supervisors, union officials, employees, and job applicants frequently emphasizes the importance of the following ten factors:

1. *Advancement* (Opportunity for promotion.)
2. *Benefits* (Vacation, sick pay, insurance, etc.)
3. *Company* (Employment by company you are proud to work for.)
4. *Co-workers* (Fellow workers who are pleasant, agreeable, and good working companions.)
5. *Hours* (Good starting and quitting time, good number of hours per day or week, day or night work, etc.)
6. *Pay* (Large income during year.)
7. *Security* (Steady work, no layoffs, sureness of being able to keep your job.)
8. *Supervisor* (A good boss who is considerate and fair.)

*Reprinted with permission from Edwin A. Fleishman (ed.), *Studies in Personnel and Individual Psychology*, Dorsey Press, Homewood, Ill., 1967, pp. 18-22.

9. *Type of Work* (Work which is interesting and which you like.)
10. *Working Conditions* (Comfortable and clean – no objectionable noise, heat, cold, odors, etc.)

Few persons would deny that all these factors are important, but many disagreements arise regarding their *relative* importance. When executives or union officials are asked to rank these factors in order of their importance to workers, they frequently disagree widely. Lengthy discussions and conferences may be held in an attempt to reconcile the opinions of various individuals. Unfortunately, these attempts seldom reconcile divergent opinions. If a decision must be made, it usually reflects the view of the most verbally fluent person present or the individual having the highest status within the group.

HOW DO APPLICANTS RATE THESE FACTORS?

In 1945 the Minneapolis Gas Company decided to obtain data on what job applicants said they wanted rather than what executives thought they wanted. Little experimental data were available when the study was begun, and they consisted of specialized groups containing an exceedingly small number of cases and data collected during a brief period (e.g., 150 miscellaneous workers belonging to the Young Men's Department of a YMCA during the depression of the thirties). Since 1945 each job applicant has been given a questionnaire containing the ten job factors listed above and asked to rank the factors in order of importance to him. Each applicant was told that "All items are important, but people differ in the order in which they rank them. There are no right or wrong answers. Give *your* preferences, not what you believe others think." Applicants were not asked to sign their names, although for research purposes they were requested to give their sex, marital status, number of dependents, age, salary, extent of education, and main occupation.

Table 1 gives the average (median) rank assigned the ten job factors by 30,746 men and 12,783 women applicants. Factors are listed in order of their importance to men applicants. Inasmuch as the factor considered to be most important by the applicant was given a rank of one and the factor considered least important given a rank of 10, the smaller the average given in Table 1, the more important the factor was considered to be.

Security, advancement, type of work, and company were most important to men applicants. The next four factors received quite similar median ranks and consisted of pay, co-workers, supervisor, and benefits. At the bottom of the list were hours and working conditions. Data from women showed quite a different pattern than those obtained from men. With women, type of work stood alone as being most important. Benefits stood alone as being least important. The remaining factors were considered to be fairly close to each other.

In general, women were less interested than men in security, advancement, and benefits, and were more interested than men in type of work, working conditions, supervisor, co-workers, and hours. These differences form a definite pattern. Women were more interested in short-range or temporary factors which increase the pleasantness of work, whereas men were more interested in long-range factors which are important from a viewpoint of a lifetime of work to support themselves and their families.

Table 1
Average (median) ranks assigned job factors by applicants

Job factor	30,746 Men	12,783 Women
Security	2.3	4.6
Advancement	3.2	5.1
Type of work	3.3	1.6
Company	4.4	4.6
Pay	5.9	6.2
Co-workers	6.0	5.2
Supervisor	6.4	5.4
Benefits	6.9	8.1
Hours	7.6	6.9
Working conditions	7.8	6.4

SIGNIFICANCE OF FINDINGS

The emphasis given security is not surprising, for the importance of security has often been stressed by management, unions, and psychologists. These data indicate that such emphasis agrees with what workers say they want. As might be expected, security was more important to married men than to single men. Occupationally it was most important to physical workers and progressively less important to clerical, sales, managerial, and professional workers. Its importance decreased as extent of education increased.

The high rank of advancement also will be expected by many readers. The importance of advancement became greater as extent of education increased. Professional, managerial, sales, clerical, and skilled applicants were more interested in advancement than were semiskilled and unskilled persons.

The strong emphasis placed by applicants on type of work is surprising to many persons. Single men were more interested in type of work than were married men, and the importance of this factor decreased as number of dependents and age increased. Type of work decreased in importance as the job level decreased, the order from high to low being: professional, managerial, sales, clerical, skilled, semiskilled, and unskilled. It is interesting to note that the persons who worked on the least pleasant jobs were those least interested in type of work.

The emphasis placed on company is also surprising to many. It would appear that many companies could derive considerable benefit from increased attempts to "sell" the company to employees, job applicants, and residents of the community in which the company is located.

Relegation of pay to fifth position indicates considerable discrepancy between the importance pay is often believed to have and the position actually assigned it by applicants. Some persons will argue that these data are incorrect and will refer to the fact that a pay increase is usually the first demand of any union and that pay disputes are often the cause of strikes. However, this view is not supported by the fact that unionization frequently has taken first place in those companies paying the highest wage rates, and that the most intense labor strife often has been in those same companies and industries. Pay is obviously not a panacea which will solve all controversies.

Over 23,000 male job applicants and over 11,000 female job applicants who filled in the job preference blank, indicating what they wanted in a job, also ranked the factors on the basis of what they thought would be the preferences of others who were in the same type of work and who were similar in age, number of dependents, and education. Both men and women predicted that pay would be ranked most important by other persons. There seems to be sound reason to believe that most individuals consider that they are atypical in that they personally attach less importance to pay than do most persons. It appears that the importance attached to pay has been overemphasized by so many persons and in so many contexts that the overemphasis generally is accepted as applying to everyone except oneself!

Possible reasons for this overemphasis are many. In the first place, all employees would like to secure more pay than they have secured in the past, and if they believe they can get more, they try to do so. Further, demands for greater pay are often made in substitution of demands for other wants which may be either conscious or unconscious (e.g., lack of advancement opportunities, unpleasant boss, etc.). When employees go on strike, additional reasons enter into the picture. We can assume safely that no group of employees strikes against an employer unless there is intense feeling on both sides. This hostility may result in a desire to hit the opponent in a sensitive spot — and the pocketbook is such a sensitive spot. Striking employees may also overemphasize pay increases in order to arouse public sympathy in their favor. Sympathy is particularly easy to arouse if the public is made to believe that the workers are grossly underpaid. Use of this technique has resulted in serious public misconceptions regarding wages paid in particular industries or companies.

The fact that the factors of co-workers and supervisors were ranked almost the same as pay is further evidence that man does not live by bread alone. It would appear well worthwhile for management to give greater consideration to the personalities and backgrounds of employees who work together and to increase efforts in the area of supervisory training.

The relatively low rank assigned to benefits is misleading unless interpreted in light of a systematic change in importance to this factor during the past twenty years. Comparison of medians obtained for each single year indicates that benefits originally held the tenth position. It gradually has increased in importance until it is now in the eighth position for the entire period. Data collected during the past three years have given benefits a position almost identical with that given to supervisors and co-workers.

(Women, however, continue to place benefits in the tenth position, There have been no exceptions during the twenty-year period of the study.)

Hours of work and working conditions were factors which obtained low rank relative to the amount of effort generally expended toward their improvement. Considering the enormous improvement in hours and in working conditions during the past few decades, it would appear that the point of diminishing return has been reached and that time more profitably might be devoted to factors currently considered more important by the average job applicant. Current union emphasis on these factors may be a carry-over from employee needs a generation ago.

IMPLICATIONS FOR MANAGEMENT

These data have important implications in selecting, training, and supervising employees. For example, excellent results have been obtained by writing help-wanted advertisements which emphasize those factors ranked highest by job applicants. The job preference blank has been an exceedingly valuable tool when used in employment interviews.

These findings also have been valuable in determining personnel policies and in conducting union negotiations.

Although these data are based on job applicants, it must be remembered that future employees came from today's applicants.

Too much emphasis often has been given factors which, according to this study, are considered relatively unimportant by applicants. There would seem to be an excellent opportunity to devise principles and procedures that would result in greater job satisfaction on the part of the employees, and consequently in improved quality of work, increased quantity of output, and lower cost.

THE HUMAN DESIGN*

Hadley Cantril

With the mounting discussion of "existentialist" and "humanistic" psychology on both sides of the Atlantic, together with the search of political scientists for a psychological interpretation useful for their level of analysis, it seems appropriate to try to spell out what seem to be the demands human beings impose on any society or political culture because of their genetically built-in design. Furthermore, in bringing together recently in summary form the conclusions of a cross-national study of 13 different countries, I kept realizing anew that in describing differences found among people, it is all too easy to neglect basic functional uniformities which take diverse forms and to leave the accounting or explanation at that level. Differences are often dramatic and easier to detect than the similarities they may obscure. Here I shall try to orchestrate the diversities of mankind found in different societies into some systematic unity.

The aspects of "human nature" differentiated here are those that seem to me to be pointed to by the data of psychology and by the observations sensitive observers have made of the way people live their lives in a variety of circumstances. I shall try to use a level of accounting appropriate both to an understanding of people and to an understanding of social and political systems. In doing this some of the absurdities may be avoided that result when a single man-made abstraction, usually devised to account for some single aspect of behavior, is the sole theme song. As the different characteristics of the human design are reviewed here, it must be recognized and emphasized that they all overlap, intertwine and are interdependent. One must differentiate artificially in order to focus and describe.

1. Man requires the satisfaction of his survival needs. Any listing of the characteristics of any living organism must begin here. Neurophysiologists have located and described in a most general way two built-in appetitive systems found in higher animals: one system propelling them to seek satisfying and pleasurable experiences, the other protecting them from threatening or unpleasant experiences (2). These two systems together can

*Reprinted with permission from the *Journal of Individual Psychology*, November, 1964. This article is a somewhat revised version of the concluding chapter of a forthcoming book (1).

be thought of as the basic forces contained within all human beings which not only keep them and the species alive as their simple survival needs for food, shelter and sex are gratified, but that are involved in the desire for life itself.

These appetitive systems of course become enormously developed, refined and conditioned, especially in man, as new ways are learned to achieve satisfactions and avoid dangers and discomforts. It has often been noted that unless the survival needs are satisfied, a person devotes himself almost exclusively to a continued attempt to fulfill them, a pre-occupation which pre-empts his energies and repels any concern for other activities. Most people in the world today are still concerned with living a type of life that constitutes well-being on a relatively simple level with what amenities their culture can provide.

2. Man wants security both in its physical and its psychological meaning to protect gains already made and to assure a beachhead from which further advances may be staged. Man wants some surety that one action can lead to another, some definite prehension which provides an orientation and integration through time. People invariably become embittered if they nurse a dream for what they regard as a long time with no signs of it becoming a reality.

In this connection it should be recalled that the story of evolution seems to tell us that members of every species stake out some territory for themselves within which they can provide for their needs and carry on their living, the extent of this territory being dependent on what is required for the survival of the species and being extended if it will contribute to such survival. In the present era the territories human beings stake out for themselves are largely bounded by the nation-state, a territorial unit rapidly replacing narrower geographical and psychological identifications but doing so just at the time when it is becoming more and more apparent that the concept of nation itself limits and threatens man's development in an age of increasing interdependence and highly developed weaponry.

3. Man craves sufficient order and certainty in his life to enable him to judge with fair accuracy what will or will not occur if he does or does not act in certain ways. People want sufficient form and pattern in life to be sure that certain satisfactions already enjoyed will be repeatable and will provide a secure springboard for take-offs in new directions.

The conflict of old loyalties with emerging new loyalties in the case of developing people is bound to create uncertainties, doubts and hesitations. If people become frustrated and anxious enough, they will do almost anything in a desperate attempt to put some order into ap-parent chaos or rally around new symbols and abstractions that enable them to identify with a new order that promises to alleviate the uncertainties experienced in the here and now.

In stressing process and change, the desire of people to preserve the status quo when it has proved satisfying and rewarding and to protect existing forms against alteration must never be overlooked. And the craving for certainty would include the satisfactions that come from the sense of stability provided by our habitual behavior — including much of our social and political behavior.

4. *Human beings continuously seek to enlarge the range and to enrich the quality of their satisfactions.* There is a ceaseless quest impelling man to extend the range and quality of his satisfactions through the exercise of his creative and inventive capacities. This is, of course, a basic reason why order of any kind is constantly being upset. Whitehead expressed the point eloquently and repeatedly, for example, in his statements that "The essence of life is to be found in the frustrations of established order" (8, p. 119) and that "The art of progress is to preserve order amid change, and to preserve change amid order" (7, p. 515).

The distinguished British philosopher John Macmurray has used the phrase *The Self as Agent* as the title of his book (3) analyzing the role of action in man's constant search for value-satisfactions. And in a companion volume he has noted that "Human behavior cannot be understood, but only caricatured, if it is represented as an adaptation to environment" (4, p. 46). The search for an enlargement of satisfactions in transactions of living can also be phrased as the *desire for development in a direction*, the desire to do something which will bring a sense of accomplishment as we experience the consequences of successfully carrying out some intention, and thereby have an occasional feeling that our lives are continuous creations in which we can take an active part. During a conversation in Beirut, a wise man once remarked to me that "people are hungry for new and good experiences."

It seems worthwhile to differentiate this search for value-satisfactions into two varieties: *(a)* value-satisfactions that are essentially new, different, more efficient, more reliable, more pleasurable or more status-producing results of activity along familiar and tried dimensions, and *(b)* value-satisfactions that are new in the sense of being emergent, a new quality a person discovers or creates himself for the first time as does the child who tries out and relishes new experiences as his own developmental pattern unfolds. The former variety, like the growth on the limb of a tree, builds people out and extends their range, while the latter, like the new growth at the top of the tree, lets them attain new heights and see new vistas. The satisfactions sought by a newly developing people are at first most likely to be of the former type.

The particular value-satisfactions man acquires are the result of learning. Some of the values learned will serve as the operative ideals of a people, others will be chiefly instrumental. People in rich countries have learned to want and to expect many aspects of a good life that less favored people have not yet learned are possibilities. From this point of view one might say that the competition between social and political systems is a competition in teaching people what to want, what is potentially available to them and then proving to them in their own private experience that these wants are best attainable under the system described.

5. *Human beings are creatures of hope and are not genetically designed*

to resign themselves. This characteristic of man stems from the characteristic just described: that man is always likely to be dissatisfied and never fully "adapts" to his environment.

Man seems continually to hope that the world he encounters will correspond more and more to his vision of it as he acts within it to carry out his purposes, while the vision itself continuously unfolds in an irreversible direction. The whole process is a never-ending one. It is characteristic of man in his on-going experience to ask himself "Where do I go from here?" Only in his more reflective moods does a person ask "Where did I come from?" or "How did I get this way?" Most of the time, most people who are plugged into the changing world around them are future-oriented in their concerns.

6. *Human beings have the capacity to make choices and the desire to exercise this capacity.* Any mechanical model of man constructed by a psychologist or by anyone else is bound to leave out the crucially important characteristic of man as an "appetitive-perceptive agency." Perceptions are learned and utilized by people to provide prognoses or bets of a variety of kinds to weigh alternative courses of action to achieve purposes. Consciously or without conscious awareness, people are trying to perceive the probable relation between their potential acts and the consequences of these acts to the intentions that constitute their goals.

The human nervous system, including the brain, has the capacity to police its input, to determine what is and what is not significant for it and to pay attention to and to reinforce or otherwise modify its behavior as it transacts in the occasions of living (2). In this sense, the human being is a participant in and producer of his own value-satisfactions: people perceive only what is relevant to their purposes and make their choices accordingly.

7. *Human beings require freedom to exercise the choices they are capable of making.* This characteristic of man related to freedom is deliberately worded as it is, rather than as a blanket statement that "Human beings require freedom," since the freedom people want is so relative to their desires and the stage of development they have attained. Human beings, incidentally, apparently require more freedom than other species of animals because of their much greater capacity to move about and to engage in a much wider variety of behavior.

While it seems true that maximum freedom is a necessary condition if a highly developed individual is to obtain maximum value-satisfaction, it is equally true, as many people have pointed out, that too much freedom too soon can be an unbearable burden and a source of bondage if people, like children, are insufficiently developed to know what to do with it. For freedom clearly involves a learning of responsibility and an ability to take advantage of it wisely.

The concept of freedom is essentially a psychological and not a political concept. It describes the opportunity of an individual to make his own choices and act accordingly. Psychologically, freedom refers to the freedom to experience more of what is potentially available, the freedom to move about and ahead, to be and to become. Freedom is thus less and less determined and more of a reality as man evolves and develops; it emerges and flowers as people learn what it can mean to them in terms of resolving some frustrations under which they are living.

The authoritarian leadership sometimes required to bring about man's awakening and to start him on the road to his definition of progress appears to go against the grain of the human design once man is transformed into a self-conscious citizen who has the desire to exercise the capacity latent within him. The definition of freedom in the Soviet dictionary, *Ushakov*, as "the recognition of necessity" is limited to those periods in the life of an individual or a people when they are willing to let others define what is necessary and to submerge their own individuality.

8. *Human beings want to experience their own identity and integrity*, more popularly referred to as the need for *personal dignity*. Every human being craves a sense of his own self-constancy, an assurance of the repeatability of experience in which he is a determining participant. He obtains this from the transactions he has with other individuals.

People develop significances they share with others in their membership and reference groups. If the satisfaction and significance of participation with others ceases to confirm assumptions or to enrich values, then a person's sense of self-constancy becomes shaken or insecure, his loyalties become formalized and empty or are given up altogether. He becomes alienated or seeks new significances, new loyalties that are more operationally real.

9. *People want to experience a sense of their own worthwhileness.* This differentiation is made from the desire for personal identity and integrity to bring out the important relationship between this search for identity and the behavior and attitudes of others toward us. A human being wants to know he is valued by others and that others will somehow show through their behavior that his own behavior and its consequences make some sort of difference to them in ways that give him a sense of satisfaction. When this occurs, not only is a person's sense of identity confirmed, but he also experiences a sense of personal worth and self-respect. The process of extending the sense of Self both in space and in time appears also to involve the desire that one's "presence" shall not be limited merely to the here and now of existence but will extend into larger dimensions.

People acquire, maintain, and enrich their sense of worthwhileness only if they at least vaguely recognize the sources of what personal identity they have: from their family, their friends and neighbors, their associates or fellow workers, their group ties or their nations. The social, religious, intellectual, regional, or national loyalties formed play the important role of making it possible for individuals to extend themselves backward into the past, forward into the future and to identify themselves with others who live at more or less remote distances from them. This means the compounding of shared experiences into a bundle that can be conceptualized, felt, or somehow referred to in the here and now of daily living, thus making a person feel a functional part of a more enduring alliance. Man accomplishes such feats of self-extension largely through his capacity to create symbols, images, and myths which provide focal points for identification and self-expansion. After reviewing the lessons from history, Herbert Muller noted as one of the "forgotten simplicities" the fact that "Men have always been willing to sacrifice themselves for some larger cause, fighting and dying for their family, tribe, or community, with or without hope of eternal reward" (5, p. 392).

10. Human beings seek some value or system of beliefs to which they can commit themselves. In the midst of the probabilities and uncertainties that surround them, people want some anchoring points, some certainties, some faith that will serve either as a beacon light to guide them or a balm to assuage them during the inevitable frustrations and anxieties living engenders.

People who have long been frustrated and who have searched for means to alleviate their situations are, of course, particularly susceptible to a commitment to a new system of beliefs or an ideology that they feel holds promise of effective action.

Beliefs are confirmed in so far as action based on them brings satisfying consequences and they are denied with growing skepticism if disastrous results consistently occur because they are followed.

Commitment to a value or belief system becomes more difficult among well informed and sophisticated people who self-consciously try to reconcile what they believe with what they know and what they know with what they believe. In such circumstances, beliefs become more secular and less important as personal identifications.

11. Human beings want a sense of surety and confidence that the society of which they are a part holds out a fair degree of hope that their aspirations will be fulfilled. If people cannot experience the effectivity of social mechanisms to accomplish some of the potential goals they aspire to, then obviously their frustrations and anxieties mount, they search for new means to accomplish aims. On the other hand, they make any sacrifice required to protect a society they feel is fulfilling their needs but appears seriously threatened.

It cannot be stressed too strongly that any people will become apathetic toward or anxious about ultimate goals they would like to achieve through social organizations if they continually sense a lack of reliability in the means provided to accomplish these goals. Obviously any society that is to be viable must satisfy basic survival needs, must provide security, must insure the repeatability of value-satisfactions already attained and provide for new and emerging satisfactions. The effective society is one that enables the individual to develop personal loyalties and aspirations which overlap with and are congenial to social values and loyalties, and which at the same time take full account of the wide range of individual differences that exist.

Such a social organization must, too, become the repository of values, must provide symbols for people's aspirations, must comprise and contain customs, institutions, laws, economic arrangements and political forms which enable an individual in various ways to give concrete reference to his values in his day-to-day behavior. If the gap between what his society actually provides in terms of effective mechanisms for living and what it purports to provide becomes too great, the vacuum created will sooner or later engender the frustrations that urge people on to seek new social patterns and new symbols. Whitehead wrote:

The major advances in civilization are processes which all but wreck the societies in which they occur — like unto an arrow in the hand of a child. The art of free society consists first in the maintenance of the symbolic code; and secondly in fearlessness of revision, to secure that the code serves those purposes which satisfy an enlightened reason. Those societies which cannot combine reverence to their symbols with freedom of revision, must ultimately decay either from anarchy, or from the slow atrophy of a life stifled by useless shadows (6, p. 88).

Every social and political system can be regarded as an experiment in the broad perspective of time. Whatever the experiment, the human design will in the long run force any experiment to accommodate it. This has been the case throughout human history. And few would deny that the varied patterns of experiments going on today hold out more promise of satisfying the human condition for a greater number of people than ever before.

REFERENCES

1. Cantril, H. *The Pattern of Human Concerns.* New Brunswick, N.J.: Rutgers Univ. Press, 1965.
2. Cantril, H., & Livingston, W. K. The Concept of Transaction in Psychology and Neurology. *J. Indiv. Psychol.,* 1963, 19, 3-16.
3. Macmurray, J. *The Self as Agent.* New York: Harper, 1957.
4. Macmurray, J. *Persons in Relation.* London: Faber & Faber, 1961.
5. Muller, H. J. *The Uses of the Past.* New York: Mentor, 1954.
6. Whitehead, A. N. *Symbolism: Its Meaning and Effect.* New York: Macmillan, 1927.
7. Whitehead, A. N. *Process and Reality.* New York: Macmillan, 1929.
8. Whitehead, A. N. *Modes of Thought.* New York: Macmillan, 1938.

READING 8

OBJECTIVES*

John F. Mee

In current thinking and writing, the starting point for either a philosophy or the practice of management seems to center around predetermined objectives. The entire management process concerns itself with ways and means to realize predetermined results and with the intelligent use of people whose efforts must be properly motivated and guided. Objectives may be general or specific; they may concern the organization as a whole, a segment of it within a decentralized unit, or even a particular function such as production, sales, or personnel.

What are or should be the objectives of management in our industrial economy? A study of current management literature and the published objectives of business firms provide some revealing and interesting concepts from recognized authorities. Here are some selected statements:

- The goal of the organization must be this — to make a better and better product to be sold at a lower and lower price. Profit cannot be the goal. Profit must be a by-product. This is a state of mind and a philosophy. Actually an organization doing this job as it can be done will make large profits which must be properly divided between user, worker and stockholder. This takes ability and character.[1]

- If we were to isolate the one factor, above all others, that transformed the tiny company of 1902 into the industrial giant of 1952, while hundreds of competitors failed and are forgotten, I should say that it has been Texaco's settled policy of thinking first of quality of product and service to the customer, and only second to the size of its profit. To some of you, this may sound somewhat trite. But it is the starkest kind of business realism. In a highly competitive industry such as ours, the highest rewards are reserved for those who render the greatest service.[2]

- To make and sell quality products competitively and to perform those functions at the lowest attainable cost consistent with sound management policies, so as to return an adequate profit after taxes for services rendered. As a corollary objective, the corporation must be the

---

*Reprinted with permission from *Business Horizons.* Copyright 1956 by the Foundation for the School of Business, Indiana University.

[1] James F. Lincoln, *Intelligent Selfishness and Manufacturing* (Bulletin 434; New York: Lincoln Electric Co.).

[2] Harry T. Klein, *The Way Ahead* (New York: The Texas Co., 1952), p. 14.

low-cost producer of the product it offers for sale. (United States Steel Corporation statement of general company objectives.)

● The mission of the business organization is to acquire, produce and distribute certain values. The business objective, therefore, is the starting point for business thinking. The primary objectives of a business organization are always those economic values with which we serve the customer. The principal objective of a businessman, naturally, is a profit. And a profit is merely an academic consideration, nevertheless, until we get the customer's dollar.[3]

Numerous further examples of published and stated objectives of modern business management could be presented. However, all of them could be summarized with the conclusion that (1) *Profit* is the motivating force for managers. (2) *Service* to customers by the provision of desired economic values (goods and services) justifies the existence of the business. (3) *Social responsibilities* to exist for managers in accordance with ethical and moral codes established by the society in which the industry resides. The economic values with which customers are served include increased values at lower costs through innovation and creativity over a period of time.

In formulating and developing a modern management philosophy for successful practice, a combination of the above objectives in the correct proportion is required. Every decentralized organization unit and essential function must contribute to the realization of the general objectives by attaining the organizational, functional, and operational objectives. Unless predetermined objectives are set and accepted, little or no basis exists for measuring the success and effectiveness of those who perform the management functions.

The importance of predetermining the objectives desired has resulted in the formulation of the management principle of the objective. This principle may be stated as follows: Before initiating any course of action, the objectives in view must be clearly determined, understood, and stated.

[3] Ralph C. Davis, "What the Staff Function Actually Is," *Advanced Management*, vol. 19, p. 13, May 1954.

THE ENVIRONMENT MUST BE PRESERVED*

Chas. F. Jones

The environment must be preserved.

Our air, our water, our land, and the teeming terrestrial life forms which make up the irreplaceable ecology of our "spaceship Earth" must be preserved.

No longer can we afford to ask, "Should it be done?" Today our concerns must be operational in nature. How can it be done? How soon? What will it cost? What priorities should we set?

Every citizen bears partial responsibility for finding answers to these questions.

We in the petroleum industry have two imperative tasks. First, we must see that our own house is put in order. Second, we must help provide the leadership needed to put the total environmental problem in proper perspective so that proper actions can be effected.

Before we can presume to offer advice on what others should do, we must meet our own responsibilities — and meet them fully. In reviewing the situation in industry as it now stands, I find myself with mixed emotions. I feel compelled both to defend and to disapprove — to commend what we have done and in the same breath to criticize what we have not yet done.

In the past, industry and government have too often tended to oppose each other instead of opposing the problem. Only a few years ago, American industry seemed to be divided into two camps on the pollution issue. One faction believed that the pollution problem was real, and merited positive action; the other camp believed — or perhaps merely hoped — that public concern about the issue would simply fade away.

Anyone who still believes that the concern of the American public on this issue is merely a passing fancy has simply failed to measure the accelerated tempo of national feeling. Society is demanding action, and we as businessmen will be making a monumental miscalculation if we misinterpret either the seriousness or the urgency of this demand.

Fortunately, the greater part of the business community has responded. Many industries have firmly faced up to the necessity for action and have instituted adequate control measures at substantial expense. Since 1966, U. S. businesses have spent a grand total of about $4.5 billion on abatement equipment. During the three years ending in 1968, the petroleum

*Reprinted with permission from *Humble Way*, Second Quarter, 1970, pp. 17-19.

industry invested more than $1 billion on construction, operations and maintenance of air and water quality improvement projects. Our industry spent more for water conservation in 1968 than the federal government did under its construction grant program. And I feel sure our industry's expenditures will appreciably exceed this level in 1969 and for years to come.

We have every reason to be proud of this record, yet we recognize that a substantial body of public opinion still regards us as polluters. There are several reasons for this. First, in the general clamor over the negative aspects of pollution it is difficult to make positive actions generally known and appreciated. Second, there are still some in the ranks of American industry who are reluctant to face the problem. Perhaps they still hope that it will just go away. More likely, they are caught in the competitive economic situation engendered by the expense of pollution abatement. But whatever the reason, this minority is obscuring the positive attitudes and accomplishments of the majority of U. S. industry.

And we who are meeting our responsibilities do both ourselves and the public a disservice when, in speaking as a "united front," we shield unnecessarily those few among us whose persistent inaction brings censure upon us all. We are tarred with the same brush. The pollution issue is fast reaching a state wherein a clear distinction will be made between responsible business and irresponsible business. To those companies caught short, the public spotlight will be embarrassing indeed. And there will be no place to hide.

There is a third reason for the disfavor in which we are held. We have done much, but in the eyes of the public we have not yet done enough, nor have we done it fast enough. I know of nothing we are doing today that is not needed; in fact, most of it should have been done yesterday. But more must be done with all deliberate speed. The problem is whether we have the will to commit the money required.

And this pierces to the heart of the problem. Eliminating pollution takes money, either ours or someone else's. Perhaps this is why although our industry as a whole has ceased to oppose pollution regulation *per se,* we still tend to rate a regulation as a good one if it requires *others* to do something and as a bad regulation if it requires *us* to do something. I'm more inclined to feel that we should rate a regulation as good if it *properly balances* the demands of an expanding economy and the quality of the environment.

I am thoroughly convinced that until our operations are conducted in a manner that does not offend either the senses or the sensibilities of the public, we will remain open to criticism and possible regulatory reprisal. We must run our businesses in such a manner that our use of land, air, and water does not detract from their usefulness to other subsequent users.

What does this mean to the petroleum industry? To me, the proper and responsible use of these land, air, and water resources means the elimination of oilfield brines from surface streams and from dry creek beds or pits where someone else's use of water is materially curtailed.

It means the elimination of oil from the surface of the land and from surface waters where the esthetic sense of the public may be offended or its use of the resources restricted.

It means the cleanup of areas where past, less responsible practices have left their scars on the face of the land — or, alternatively, it means we share this responsibility with government.

It means the elimination of unpleasant odors from our operations anywhere the public can justifiably say the sense of smell is being offended.

It means the reduction of transfer losses in marketing operations and distribution systems to the lowest practicable level.

It means the responsible disposition of automotive crankcase drainings, and no oil in public sewers in any of our operations.

It means a pleasant appearance to our installations so that the landscape is not unjustifiably marred, and it means the elimination of offensive amounts of smoke from our facilities.

And in addition to correction of *overt* types of air and water pollution, it means more research and a better understanding of the *covert* ways in which our operations may be adversely affecting the environment. The subtleties of ecology are such that we could conceivably be upsetting the delicate balance of the environment in ways that we do not even realize.

And, finally, it means that we must be cognizant of problems created by the consumer use of our products — to the extent, for example, that we should consider a change in fuel composition if this is necessary to help bring about a pollution-free automobile. My company has publicly stated that it is prepared to make available to the American motorist a lead-free gasoline when cars designed for its use are on the market.

I am not saying that our industry must shut down tomorrow until all these things are done in their entirety. Such a viewpoint would be completely unfair and unrealistic.

But I *am* saying that if we have not done so already, we should adopt them as objectives and embark directionally upon them now. We have what seems to me to be an obvious choice. We can start on these jobs today with reasonable, scheduled outlays of capital — or we can delay and run the strong risk that government will soon tell us how, when, and at what speed we must accomplish these tasks.

I believe that we in industry must be our sternest critics. If we are not, others less knowledgeable about our operations and less sympathetic to our problems will assume the role of critic for us. And the end result will be waste of capital, waste of time, and waste of our air and water resources. In the public interest, then — and in our own — let us put our house in order.

But we have a second great challenge. The paradox of industry's role is that while the job of abatement cannot be done without us, we cannot do the whole job ourselves. Even if industry completely eliminated all pollution in its operations tomorrow, pollution would still be national in scope and disquieting in magnitude. In the hue and cry over industry's part in the lowering of air and water quality, the negative contributions of the American city and the American individual have been brushed aside as incidental. But in our urbanized, mechanized society we are all polluters.

The problem will never be solved merely by passing laws requiring industry to spend vast amounts of money. Although industry must do its share, so must America's thousands of municipalities. A report in 1969 by the Federal Water Pollution Control Administration pointed out that there are about 30 million people in this country who are living in areas with inadequate or no sewage installations. And the report estimated that about 2,400 communities in the United States need to install or improve treating facilities to avoid further destruction of the quality of water.

Likewise, our cities have monumental problems with the disposal of all manner of solid wastes. Yet American cities in recent years have experienced increasing difficulty in getting local bond issues passed to correct these situations.

But industries and cities need not absorb total blame for air and water pollution. No individual American can run away from at least partial responsibility for our current predicament. The homeowner who burns leaves and rubbish in his back yard; the farmer who plows his fields so that rainfall washes his topsoil into nearby streams; the vacationer who leaves behind unburied trash and who tosses bottles, cans, and paper from his car window; the boat owner who heaves garbage and flushes human wastes overboard – these and millions of other Americans contribute a proportionate share to our total environmental contamination.

These hard facts must be more widely recognized before we can delineate and implement solutions. And the solutions will be expensive. I don't believe that the American people are fully aware of the tremendous expense involved in cleaning up the national environment. Federal sources say that the national cost of cleaning up water pollution over the next five years – if it were done in that brief period – could range from $43 billion to $66 billion. The corresponding estimates on a five-year program of air cleanup range from a low of $19 billion to a high of $60 billion. Adding these up, we come to a minimum figure of $62 billion and a maximum of $126 billion. Averaging this out to 200 million Americans, the bill appears to range from a minimum of $300 to a maximum of over $600 per American, or from $1,200 to about $2,500 for a family of four.

Figures like this may change tomorrow, but one thing remains constant: the people will have to pay. Environmental pollution abatement will become a series of economic choices at many levels – national, state, local – on which the public will have to make a series of economic judgments on the basis of the cost versus the benefits.

For example, 1970 and 1971-model automobiles will carry devices to help control exhaust emissions which will add to the cost of the car and its maintenance.

On the state and city level, new bond issues will be required to upgrade public facilities such as sewage treatment plants; voters must decide whether they are willing to pay these costs.

Where industry is required to upgrade its pollution control, the cost of these facilities may be passed on to the consumer in the form of higher product prices.

Only if the economic facts are widely understood can the public make an informed decision in each case, based on willingness to pay for a stated degree of cleanliness in air and water.

As we set out into the 1970's we will need imagination and dedication in order to help create the new moral, intellectual, political, legal, social, and economic patterns that must soon be evolved to improve our environment. We must become social ecologists and alter our social balance in order to protect Nature's balance. The primary principle of ecology which Francis Bacon unknowingly stated in the 17th century still applies today: "We cannot command Nature except by obeying her."

WHERE DO CORPORATE RESPONSIBILITIES REALLY LIE?*

Arthur W. Lorig

To whom do top corporate executives feel most responsible? To society, as some claim? Or to a lesser group such as employees, stockholders, creditors, or customers? Some writers and university students — influenced, no doubt, by professors — insist that a corporation's chief responsibility is to society and that business decisions are made in accordance with that understanding. This is so contrary to my own belief and observations that I have undertaken to find the answer by going directly to those who administer corporations with a survey questioning where their chief loyalties do, indeed, lie.

The results of the survey were much as I expected: corporate executives do *not* feel their greatest responsibility is to society. Overwhelmingly, they reported that their chief responsibility was to stockholders as the owners of business. No other group was even a close second. Responsibility to society ranked at the very bottom, far below the closest group.

Furthermore, no real difference was found between the views of top executives (presidents and chairmen of boards of directors) and the controllers and financial executives. And, perhaps surprisingly, no discernible difference resulted from variation in size of corporations. The executives of corporations with annual sales of over $1 billion felt almost exactly as those of corporations with sales under $50 million. (Corporations with annual sales under $1 million were not included in the survey, for their executives are not likely to regard responsibility to society as an important consideration in their operations.)

THE SURVEY

Questionnaires were sent to 300 companies in the United States. (The companies selected were the odd-numbered ones in the list of 600 used by the American Institute of Certified Public Accountants in compiling its 1965 edition of *Accounting Trends and Techniques.*) The questionnaire listed groups interested in corporations (creditors, employees, society as a whole, stockholders, and others to be written in) and requested that responsibilities to them be ranked 1, 2, 3, and so forth. Groups of similar importance were to be given the same rank.

*Reprinted with permission from *Business Horizons,* Spring, 1967. Copyright 1967 by the Foundation for the School of Business, Indiana University.

One-half of the questionnaires were sent to the corporation presidents, who sometimes were also the chairmen of the boards of directors. In a few instances, answering the questionnaire was delegated by the president to another executive such as a vice-president or director of public relations. The remaining questionnaires were mailed to the controller or, if none was listed in *Poor's Register of Corporations,* to the treasurer or other chief financial officer. Two groups were used because it was thought that the officers dealing with finances might regard corporate responsibilities differently than do presidents. As mentioned previously, this was not the case.

To be certain that answers would be given freely and frankly, no identifying names or symbols were used on the questionnaires or return envelopes. Executives were invited to write out their views in letter form; some chose to do this, usually to explain their views at length or to state why they elected not to participate in the survey. The other respondents are unknown.

One hundred and fifty-two usable responses were received. An additional nine indicated the executives could not, or chose not to, rank their group responsibilities. Seven more ranked all groups equally and hence were omitted in the tabulation, and five came in after the tabulation was completed. It is significant that a total of 173 replies was received, constituting a 58 per cent response. Considering the work pressures, the response was gratifying.

RESULTS

The figures tell the story clearly. Table 1 presents the assignments of rank 1. The tally of rank 1 assignments in Table 1 is slightly greater than the number of responses used because some executives assigned rank 1 to more than one group. Some gave no ranking whatsoever to certain groups; hence, only one group, the stockholders, has a full 152 rankings. Customers as an important group were not included in the questionnaire list, but thirty-four executives added that group as a write-in. Other write-ins, such as suppliers and government, were very few and were ranked quite far down, none being ranked first.

With 84.2 per cent of the respondents ranking the stockholders as the group to which they owe greatest responsibility and only 2.4 per cent placing society as a whole in that rank, the evidence is conclusive that corporations are considered by the responding executives to be instruments of the stockholders, not society. However, several pointed out that providing a profitable operation for the stockholders served to benefit society as a whole. The reasoning usually was not given, but some hints appeared occasionally. For example, one executive stated that "no business can long expect to maximize profits [for the stockholders] unless it also consistently makes available to its customers products and services of competitive quality at competitive prices . . . and serves the basic interests of the society in which it is organized." Several mentioned

Table 1
Summary of rank 1 designations

	Times group was ranked	Times group was given rank 1	Percentage of responses given rank 1
Chief executives			
Stockholders	72	59	81.9
Employees	66	8	12.1
Customers	23	6	26.1
Creditors	51	6	11.8
Society	55	3	5.5
Controllers and finance executives			
Stockholders	80	69	86.2
Employees	76	8	10.5
Customers	11	0	0.0
Creditors	73	8	11.0
Society	70	0	0.0
Total			
Stockholders	152	128	84.2
Employees	142	16	11.3
Customers	34	6	17.6
Creditors	124	14	11.3
Society	125	3	2.4

that if the stockholders, employees, and customers were treated properly, society as a whole would be served. On the other hand, a couple of warnings were given that management does not have the right to utilize the assets and power of the corporation to carry out personal, political, or social viewpoints that are not demonstrably in the best interests of the shareholders.

Much the same information and conclusions are obtained by comparing the average ranks assigned to the various groups. Table 2 presents this comparison. The average group rankings for different sizes of corporations were also determined; sizes were measured by the annual sales reported on the questionnaires. Table 3 compares these rankings and discloses no appreciable difference in rank assignments because of corporate size.

REASONING BEHIND THE RANKINGS

The questionnaires invited the executives to give the reasons behind their selections for first rank; in most cases they complied. The reasons offered for ranking the stockholder group first were that (1) stockholders are the corporate owners; (2) stockholders, through their representatives the boards of directors, hire the executives to run the business; (3) stockholders created the corporations to make a profit for them and they take the greatest risk; and (4) the executives hold a trust or stewardship relationship toward the stockholders' properties and are accountable for those properties. Several replies were to the effect that if the stockholders' interests were safeguarded properly, those of the other groups would automatically be taken care of.

Table 2
Average ranks assigned to groups

	Times group was ranked	Average rank
Chief executives		
Stockholders	72	1.28
Employees	66	2.20
Customers	23	2.22
Creditors	51	2.92
Society	55	3.78
Controllers and finance executives		
Stockholders	80	1.20
Employees	76	2.16
Customers	11	2.55
Creditors	73	2.75
Society	70	3.91
Total		
Stockholders	152	1.24
Employees	142	2.18
Customers	34	2.32
Creditors	124	2.82
Society	125	3.86

Table 3
Average ranks by size of corporation
as determined by sales

Sales ($ millions)	Stock holders	Em- ployees	Cus- tomers	Cred- itors	Society
$5-50	1.25	2.05	2.00	2.85	3.79
50-500	1.23	2.18	2.56	2.80	3.95
500-1,000	1.33	2.29	2.60	2.68	3.70
Over 1,000	1.10	2.24	1.80	3.14	3.81
All corpo- rations	1.24	2.18	2.32	2.82	3.86

Some interesting single reasons were given also: the corporation is an economic, not a social, institution — a pooling of resources for profit; stockholders have a responsibility to society, but the corporation does not; stockholders are the primary source of new funds; and, first responsibility to the stockholders is necessary in building the company image. Several vigorous declarations were received — it is inconceivable to rank stockholders other than first; it is the American way of life.

The reasons given by those ranking other groups first (such as creditors, customers, and employees) dwelt upon the importance of the group to the operation of the corporation. The few executives insisting that all groups should be ranked equally also used this line of thought — the essential nature of each group to the corporation's existence and successful operation. As one executive stated, "Which of your children do you love the most? It is like riding a bicycle — you must keep your balance."

Probably no better summarization could be found of the prevailing attitude of top executives toward groups of principal concern to corporations than the letter received from a vice-president of a corporation with multibillion dollar annual sales. It accompanied the return of the questionnaire and is quoted with his permission.

In the . . . Company, the stockholder is regarded as the owner of the business. Dividends are viewed as distribution of profits. While acknowledging our considerable responsibilities to all other groups our prime responsibility is still to the owners as it is in all other forms of business organization. Although the interests of the various groups occasionally conflict and the short-term resolution may appear to be inconsistent with stockholder interest, each decision is made with the long-term interest of the stockholder in mind.

Every business enterprise is formed with one basic objective — to make a profit. The fundamental economics of capitalism is the formation of capital with the objective of producing a profit for the owners. This is undoubtedly more obvious in smaller corporations where owner and manager are the same. In our opinion, it becomes even more important that this fundamental be recognized as a company becomes larger.

Profits benefit all other groups through the creation of jobs, payment of taxes, etc., but the stockholder is the prime beneficiary and is most directly interested in increasing the wealth position of the company. Other groups have their own interests and responsibilities which are naturally oriented toward self-interest. Creditors are interested in company well-being primarily from the standpoint of solvency. Employees are vital to the success of a business and their loyalty is coveted by management, but the majority of them are primarily interested in the preservation and security of their own jobs rather than in the creation of new ones. Society as a whole is a little remote from the individual company and, of course, has many interests of which business is only one. Customers want high quality at the lowest possible cost and will go elsewhere, as they should, if the company cannot meet their requirements. Communities are interested in local purchases, job stability, and tax revenues and are fearful of volatile-type businesses. There is an interrelationship of all these interests and the corporation must be responsive and responsible to all of them within its own objectives and limitations. These responsibilities cannot be met without profits, and profits will not result unless corporate obligations are met.

The stewardship function of management has tended to become somewhat blurred in the emphasis on the income statement, earnings per share, and 'growth,' but the preservation of capital is still a basic responsibility to the stockholder and almost all spending proposals consider return on investment and risk as major criteria. Motivations vary among individual managers, but our officers and directors recognize there are limitations to the risks that can be taken with company assets.

A principal criterion of success of a company is its ability to raise substantial amounts of long-term capital at favorable cost. The stockholder is the basic source of this capital. Unless his long-term objectives are met, there will be no funds and, hence, no fulfillment of other responsibilities and obligations of the corporation. In this particular area, the management and stockholders are particularly well attuned. Both are interested in long-term growth. Individual manager motivation may be prestige, personal reward, sense of accomplishment, or other things, but the basic objective is the same for both groups.

Last, but far from least, is that the stockholder has a recourse other than selling his stock to register dissatisfaction — the vote. This is not legal fiction. Even in the largest corporation, the proxy fight is not impossible. It happens just enough to sober any manager who may tend to identify the company as something separate from the stockholders. Stockholder relations activities are increasing throughout the country. More and more information about company activities is disbursed to stockholders.

This is partly because the stockholder has a right to know as an owner and partly because he can be a source of capital, may be a customer, and can be an ambassador of the company in the community, all of which contributes to the mutual objectives of the company and its owners and also to the special interests of other groups.

HOW TO PREVENT ORGANIZATIONAL
DRY ROT*

John W. Gardner

Like people and plants, organizations have a life cycle. They have a green and supple youth, a time of flourishing strength, and a gnarled old age. We have all seen organizations that are still going through the diseases of childhood, and others so far gone in the rigidities of age that they ought to be pensioned off and sent to Florida to live out their days.

But organizations differ from people and plants in that their cycle isn't even approximately predictable. An organization may go from youth to old age in two or three decades, or it may last for centuries. More important, it may go through a period of stagnation and then revive. In short, decline is not inevitable. Organizations need not stagnate. They often do, to be sure, but that is because the arts of organizational renewal are not yet widely understood. Organizations can renew themselves continuously. That fact has far-reaching implications for our future.

We know at least some of the rules for organizational renewal. And those rules are relevant for all kinds of organizations — U. S. Steel, Yale University, the U. S. Navy, a government agency, or your local bank.

The first rule is that the organization must have an effective program for the recruitment and development of talent. People are the ultimate source of renewal. The shortage of able, highly trained, highly motivated men will be a permanent feature of our kind of society; and every organization that wants its share of the short supply is going to have to get out and fight for it. The organization must have the kind of recruitment policy that will bring in a steady flow of able and highly motivated individuals. And it cannot afford to let those men go to seed, or get sidetracked or boxed in. There must be positive, constructive programs of career development. In this respect, local, state, and federal government agencies are particularly deficient, and have been so for many years. Their provisions for the recruitment and development of talent are seriously behind the times.

The second rule for the organization capable of continuous renewal is that it must be a hospitable environment for the individual. Organizations that have killed the spark of individuality in their members will have greatly diminished their capacity for change. Individuals who have been made to feel like cogs in the machine will behave like cogs in the machine. They will not produce ideas for change. On the contrary, they will resist such ideas when produced by others.

The third rule is that the organization must have built-in provisions for self-criticism. It must have an atmosphere in which uncomfortable questions can be asked. I would lay it down as a basic principle of human organization that the individuals who hold the reins of power in any enterprise cannot trust themselves to be adequately self-critical. For those in power the danger of self-deception is very great, the danger of failing to see the problems or refusing to see them is ever-present. And the only protection is to create an atmosphere in which anyone can speak up. The most enlightened top executives are well aware of this. Of course, I don't need to tell those readers who are below the loftiest level of management that even with enlightened executives a certain amount of prudence is useful. The Turks have a proverb that says, "The man who tells the truth should have one foot in the stirrup."

But it depends on the individual executive. Some welcome criticism, others don't. Louis Armstrong once said, "There are some people that if they don't know, you can't tell 'em."

The fourth requirement for the organization that seeks continuous renewal is fluidity of internal structure. Obviously, no complex modern organization can exist without the structural arrangements of divisions, branches, departments, and so forth. I'm not one of those who imagine that the modern world can get away from specialization. Specialization and division of labor are at the heart of modern organization. In this connection I always recall a Marx Brothers movie in which Groucho played a shyster lawyer. When a client commented on the dozens of flies buzzing around his broken-down office, Groucho said, "We have a working agreement with them. They don't practice law and we don't climb the walls."

But jurisdictional boundaries tend to get set in concrete. Pretty soon, no solution to a problem is seriously considered if there is any danger that it will threaten jurisdictional lines. But those lines aren't sacred. They were established in some past time to achieve certain objectives. Perhaps the objectives are still valid, perhaps not. *Most organizations have a structure that was designed to solve problems that no longer exist.*

The fifth rule is that the organization must have an adequate system of internal communication. If I may make a rather reckless generalization, I'd say that renewal is a little like creativity in this respect — that it depends on the existence of a large number of diverse elements in a situation that permits an infinite variety of combinations and recombinations. The enormous potentialities of the human brain are in part explainable in terms of such possibilities for combination and recombination. And such recombination is facilitated by easy communication, impeded by poor communication.

The sixth rule: The organization must have some means of combating the process by which men become prisoners of their procedures. The rule book grows fatter as the ideas grow fewer. Thus almost every well-established organization is a coral reef of procedures that were laid down to achieve some long-forgotten objective.

It is in our nature to develop an affection for customary ways of doing things. Some years ago a wholesale firm noted that some of its small shopkeeper customers were losing money because of antiquated merchandising methods. The firm decided that it would be good business to assist the shopkeepers in bringing their methods up-to-date, but soon discovered that many had no desire to modernize. They loved the old, money-losing ways.

Sometimes the organization procedures men devise to advance their purposes serve in the long run to block those purposes. This was apparent in an experience a friend of mine had in Germany in the last days of World War II. He was in Aachen, which had only recently been occupied by the American forces, when he received a message instructing him to proceed to London immediately. He went directly to U. S. Army headquarters, and showed the message to a sergeant in the Adjutant's office.

The sergeant said that the only plane for London within the next few days was leaving from the nearest airfield in thirty minutes. He added that the airfield was twenty-five minutes away.

It was discouraging news. My friend knew that he could not proceed to London without written orders, and that was a process that took from an hour to a couple of days in a well-established and smoothly functioning headquarters. The present headquarters had been opened the day before, and was in a totally unorganized state.

My friend explained his dilemma to the sergeant and handed over his papers. The sergeant scratched his head and left the room. Four minutes later he returned and said, "Here are your orders, sir."

My friend said he had never been in such an efficient headquarters. The sergeant looked at him with a twinkle in his eye and said, "Sir, it's just lucky for you we weren't organized!"

The seventh rule: The organization capable of continuous renewal will have found some means of combating the vested interests that grow up in every human institution. We commonly associate the term "vested interests" with people of wealth and power, but in an organization vested interests exist at every level. The lowest employees have their vested interests, every foreman has his, and every department head has his. Every change threatens someone's privileges, someone's authority, someone's status. What wise managers try to do, of course, is to sell the idea that in the long run everyone's overriding vested interest is in the continuing vitality of the organization itself. If that fails, everyone loses. But it's a hard message to get across.

Nowhere can the operation of vested interests be more clearly seen than in the functioning of university departments. There are exceptions, of course: some departments rise above their vested interests. But the average department holds like grim death to its piece of intellectual terrain.

It teaches its neophytes a jealous devotion to the boundaries of the field. It assesses the significance of intellectual questions by the extent to which they can be answered without going outside the sacred territory. Such vested interests effectively block most efforts to reform undergraduate instruction.

The eighth rule is that the organization capable of continuous renewal is interested in what it is going to become and not what it has been. When I moved to New London, Connecticut, in 1938 I was astonished at the attitude of New Londoners toward their city's future. Having grown up in California, I was accustomed to cities and towns that looked ahead habitually (often with an almost absurd optimism). I was not prepared for a city that, so far as I could discover, had no view of its future, though it had a clear view of its past.

The need to look to the future is the reason so many corporations today have research and development programs. But an organization cannot guarantee its future by ritualistic spending on research. Its research-and-development program must be an outgrowth of a philosophy of innovation that guides the company in everything it does. The research program, which is a way of looking forward, cannot thrive if the rest of the organization has the habit of looking backward.

The ninth rule is obvious but difficult. An organization runs on motivation, on conviction, on morale. Men have to believe that it really makes a difference whether they do well or badly. They have to care. They have to believe that their efforts as individuals will mean something for the whole organization, and will be recognized by the whole organization.

Change is always risky, usually uncomfortable, often painful. It isn't accomplished by apathetic men and women. It requires high motivation to break through the rigidities of the aging organization.

So much for the rules.

One of the ominous facts about growth and decay is that the present success of an organization does not necessarily constitute grounds for optimism. In 1909 it would have been unwise to judge the future of the Central Leather Company by the fact that it ranked seventh in the nation in total assets. It would have been a disastrous long-term investment. A better bet would have been the relatively small Ford Motor Company which had been founded only six years earlier and was about to launch its Model T. As a company it wasn't huge or powerful, but to borrow a phrase from C. P. Snow, it had the future in its bones. (Not many of 1909's top twenty companies did — only four of them are in the top twenty today.)

Businessmen are fond of saying that, unlike other executives, they have a clear measure of present performance — the profit-and-loss statement. But the profits of today *may* be traceable to wise decisions made a good many years earlier. And current company officers may be making bad decisions that will spell disaster ten years from now.

I have collected many examples of organizations that experienced crises as a result of their failure to renew themselves. In the great majority, certainly nine out of ten, the trouble was not difficult to diagnose and there was ample warning of the coming catastrophe. In the case of a manufacturing concern that narrowly averted bankruptcy recently, the conditions that led to trouble were diagnosed by an outside consultant two years before the crisis came. In the case of another well-known organization, a published article outlined every essential difficulty that later led to disaster.

But if warning signals are plentiful, why doesn't the ailing organization take heed? The answer is clear: most ailing organizations have developed a functional blindness to their own defects. They are not suffering because they can't *solve* their problems but because they won't *see* their problems. They can look straight at their faults and rationalize them as virtues or necessities.

I was discussing these matters with a corporation president recently, and he said, "How do I know that *I* am not one of the blind ones? What do I do to find out? And if I am, what do I do about it?"

There are several ways to proceed. One way is to bring in an outside consultant who is not subject to the conditions that create functional blindness inside the organization.

A more direct approach, but one that is surrounded by subtle difficulties, is for the organization to encourage its internal critics. Every organization, no matter how far deteriorated, has a few stubbornly honest individuals who are not blinded by their own self-interests and have never quite accepted the rationalizations and self-deceptions shared by others in the organization. If they are encouraged to speak up they probably will. The head of a government agency said to me recently, "The shrewdest critics of this organization are right under this roof. But it would take a major change of atmosphere to get them to talk."

A somewhat more complicated solution is to bring new blood into at least a few of the key positions in the organization. If the top level of the organization is salted with vigorous individuals too new to be familiar with all the established ways of doing and thinking, they can be a source of fresh insights for the whole organization.

Still another means of getting fresh insights is rotation of personnel between parts of the organization. Not only is the individual broadened by the experience, but he brings a fresh point of view to his new post. After a few years of working together, men are likely to get so used to one another that the stimulus of intellectual conflict drops almost to zero. A fresh combination of individuals enlivens the atmosphere.

In the last analysis, however, everything depends on the wisdom of those who shape the organization's policy. Most policy makers today understand that they must sponsor creative research. But not many of them understand that the spirit of creativity and innovation so necessary in the research program is just as essential to the rest of the organization.

The future of this nation depends on its capacity for self-renewal. And that in turn depends on the vitality of the organizations and individuals that make it up. Americans have always been exceptionally gifted at organizational innovation. In fact, some observers say that this is the true

American inventiveness. Thanks to that inventiveness we now stand on the threshold of new solutions to some of the problems that have destroyed the vitality of human institutions since the beginning of time. We have already made progress in discovering how we may keep our institutions vital and creative. We could do even better if we put our minds to it.

II

HUMAN BEHAVIOR — THE BASIC RESOURCE
IN ORGANIZATIONS

Part II studies human behavior because it is the basic resource in organizations. Nothing is accomplished in organizations without well-directed human behavior.

In the first reading in Part II Jack H. Epstein and Robert H. Warren show how the behavioral sciences are becoming more important in improving organizational effectiveness. Howard Baumgartel then describes some problems of cooperation among specialists of different fields.

Several levels of human behavior, including individual, interpersonal, intraorganizational, and interorganizational, can be described. At the level of the individual, Harry Levinson explains the almost limitless problems of adjustment each person has. As his article makes clear, much of one's energy is devoted to trying to resolve his almost perpetual conflicts.

In the next article Elliot Carlson shows how persons influence the behavior of each other in regard to hair styles. Edgar H. Schein describes the process by which a person adjusts to the values, norms, and behavioral patterns of a group he joins. The next article dramatically illustrates the pressure to conform by describing the plight of union members who exceeded production quotas.

The interorganizational level of behavior is explored in an article dealing with the strike of a large labor union. The final article by Norman Pearlstine uniquely shows how this strike — a conflict of organizations — serves the internal needs of one of the conflicting organizations.

THE ROLE OF BEHAVIORAL SCIENCE
IN ORGANIZATIONS*

Jack H. Epstein and Robert H. Warren

This article concentrates on the role (functions, activities, direction) of behavioral science in organizations in which people earn a livelihood. Organizations per se are inanimate and meaningless unless we become concerned with the people in them. This concern, for our purposes, will take the route of individual and group motivation and its immediate periphery (e.g., needs, leadership, goals, communications, perception, expectations) with respect to organizational growth and effectiveness. The strong threads of behavioral science which will stand out in this pattern are psychology, social-psychology, intra and inter group dynamics, and, perhaps, some of the newer areas of managership and "organizationology."

The final portion of this article will include some prognoses about the future role of behavioral science in organizations. These observations are based upon subjective determinations which are, in turn, based on such objective facts as the increasing number of Want Ads for industrial psychologists and behavioral scientists, the increasing number of college students enrolled in behavioral science programs, and our perception of the signs of the future direction of behavioral science research. These predictions (in the sense of prior to knowledge rather than foretelling) will, hopefully, result in a myriad of questions, problems, and possibilities, the answers and solutions to which will be neither easy to come by nor obvious.

DEFINITIONS

It seems appropriate to begin with some definitions of terms. Webster defines behavior as: "A mode of conducting oneself. The way in which an organism, organ acts, especially in response to a stimulus."

Behavioral science is the study of human behavior in a "scientific" manner. It is interested in studying behavior, specifically human behavior in response to various stimuli — internal and mental, or external and physical. Behavioral science connotes all of the factors that go into man's fundamental personality: his needs, his emotions, his thinking, and his ability to relate his thoughts and feelings. It believes that man's actions are a result and a composite of all of these factors.

*Reprinted with permission from *Personnel Journal*, October, 1968.

Behavioral science studies human behavior to "establish generalizations that are supported by empirical evidence collected in an impersonal and objective way. The evidence must be capable of verification by other interested scholars and the procedures must be completely open to review and replication."[1]

Like any discipline, the behavioral sciences strive to conduct research that is systematic and cumulative and offers the how and why of its findings.

For the purposes of this paper we will discuss the role of the behavioral sciences within organizations. Organizations take many forms, but for the scope of this study we shall deal only with organizations in which people earn a living. Our concept of organization is:

The rational coordination of the activities of a number of people for the achievement of some common explicit purpose or goal, through the division of labor and function, and through a hierarchy of authority and responsibility.[2]

Role can be defined as the functions, activities, behavior of individuals with respect to a field, occupation, discipline, or profession in daily life.

We shall conclude our definitions of terms by defining the behavioral scientists. The behavioral scientist centers on three of the social sciences; anthropology, psychology, and sociology. He can also represent political science, psychiatry, geography, biology, physiology, economics, education, and business administration.

Whatever his profession, the behavioral scientist works within the framework of the scientific method. He applies tests of statistical and clinical validity to the evidence he collects. He does basic research by measuring and counting and by observing existing phenomena. He conducts experimental work based on a given hypothesis related to a theory, constructs, or concepts, and postulates generalizations or "laws" based on the evidence he gleans.

History rarely furnishes us with dates that mark the absolute beginning of cultural developments. To adopt a date as the beginning of the behavioral sciences is an impossibility. It suffices that the behavioral sciences are a distinct phenomenon of our times, in that some 90 to 95 per cent of all behavioral scientists are still living.

BACKGROUND

By the early 1950's, the behavioral sciences were a field in the full bloom of expansion. Business leaders had become vitally interested in the motivational factors behind consumer purchases. Labor and industry were

---

[1] Berelson, Bernard. *The Behavioral Sciences Today*, New York; Harper & Row, 1963.

[2] Schein, Edgar H. *Organizational Psychology*, Englewood Cliffs, New Jersey, Prentice-Hall, Inc., 1965.

fascinated with what made men work and how productivity could be increased. Due to a growing abundance of jobs, workers enjoyed a greater degree of choice as to how much they would produce and how well they would perform on the job. Therefore, industry began thinking in terms of providing an environment conducive to positive self-motivation.

Also underlining the rising prominence of the behavioral sciences in organizations in the fifties was the growing affluence of the American public. More income was remaining for the average American family after the purchase of the basic necessities. The consumption of option type commodities grew rapidly in this decade. Therefore, persuasion and resultant behavior became a matter of considerable business concern. Further, the source string of labor was shortening on both ends. Our population group in ages 25-34 was shrinking and the more elderly were retiring earlier.

These developments, among others, caused organizational leadership to look hopefully to the disciplines of human psychology, sociology, social-psychology and the semi-science of education for insights into human behavior. It was hoped that professionals in these fields would help to predict people's choices, satisfactions, attitudes, and behavior. It was also during this period that Rensis Likert began his research, the results of which now appear in its New Patterns of Management. Likert determined that work groups were most effective in meeting individual and organizational goals when supervisors/managers were perceived to be facilitative, supportive, and permissive in their style of managing. Further, he found that formal group leaders were "linking pins" correcting general organizational elements. For example, a leader/manager of one group was a member of the group leaders above him. Therefore, another aspect of effectiveness of organizations is the extent to which leaders are perceived by their subordinates as influential in dealing with problems which affect them and their well being.

Basic to the application of behavioral studies to organizations were the determinations made in regard to groups. Group studies indicated that individuals are not primarily rational beings but are basically social and purposive. Persons belong to all sorts of groups; families, work units, and communities. It is from these that individuals obtain many of their habits, values, ideas, and motivational stimuli.

A basic property of groups is that they tend to generate and enforce the shared feelings of their members. Also, the individuals within groups play a significant role in shaping the attitudes and goals of the group to which they belong. These characteristics make possible the identifying and transforming of group needs and aspirations to a position somewhat tandem to organizational needs and goals.

With the consolidation of organized labor, growing competition from abroad, increasing pressures of automation and increasing need for managerial talent, American organizational leadership began to realize that its primary advantage was in the optimum use of its human resources.

AN EMERGING FIELD

This growing realization helped to trigger the intensified inquiry into the how and why of human behavior as it manifested itself at work in specific situations under observable, measurable, and discriminating conditions. The prime effort was placed on manipulating the environment in which the rank and file individual worked. From here the field moved on to the supervisory, manager and executive levels as the core group which was responsible for effecting practices leading to organizational improvement. Supervisor and manager development was the vehicle for affecting change. It was during the mid and late fifties that the human relations era made a big impact. Recognizing the permanence of change, together with the need for a qualitative work force, organizational leaders selected human development and improvement programs as a way of making the organization more effective. Due to the factors of power, authority, responsibility, and complexity, the managerial hierarchy was prepared for growth opportunities which, hopefully, would lead to organizational change for "the better." In other words, individuals were sent to training and development programs from different parts of the total organization. It was expected that, upon return, these managers would, through changed behavior, influence subordinates, colleagues and bosses to change. Further, the behavior of the "trained" manager in working within his group would have a tremendous impact on that group's effectiveness. The emphasis was on changing individuals by increasing their knowledge and skill and providing opportunity for review of attitudes and values systems as both the lever and the fulcrum for organizational improvement.

Once again, we need to mention Likert's findings pertaining to managerial permissiveness, facilitativeness and support as keys to organizational effectiveness. McGregor's "Theory Y" is in the same democratic vein. Maslow's hierarchy of needs has been related to positive motivation efforts for improving organizations. Herzberg's theory of motivation as applied at Texas Instruments Co.[3] has established a kind of reverse causality scheme for organizational effectiveness. There, apparently, individual needs become primary and organizational needs secondary. Put another way, "what is good for the individual is good for the company."

Concurrently, with the emphasis on individual manager improvement we find a subtle shifting to considering groups as the core of change in organizations. Kurt Lewin's findings came to the fore, as did the role of the informal organization with respect to organizational well being. Intra and inter-group dynamics and effectiveness, along with studies of leadership patterns in these groups, cropped up. Alex Bavelas' communication networks experiments in work organizations is an example of the role of behavioral science during this period.

Another example is the conference leadership training that was and is

---

[3]M. Scott Meyers. *Who Are Your Motivated Workers*, Harvard Business Review, Jan-Feb 1964.

being conducted as a means of improving organizational effectiveness through increasing individual expertise about group dynamics. T-Group or Sensitivity Training goes into this area in greater depth and breadth, attempting to develop "intrinsic" insights into intra and inter-personal relationships and through this awareness, to proceed on to planned change. This sort of laboratory approach gets into both "basic" and "applied" research.

Blake's approach via the Managerial Grid departs further from individual development and treats organizational segments as entities. Through this approach, organizations proceed in a work-laboratory setting. This vertical training and development over a long-run seems to be aiming at the achievement of "Theory Y" in an organization.

The Gestalt Psychology approach has been translated into a way of viewing organizations as a total system made up of subsystems. Some authorities believe that organizations are open systems affecting and being affected by the environment. Others believe that organizations are social systems within themselves.

In summary, we find that the role of behavioral science in organizations has moved from research on the individual, to the group and group inter-relationships, to organizational studies on how to effect change affecting interaction, to the present concepts of organizations as systems with the behavioral sciences concentrating on systems effectiveness.*

Let us now consider more specifically some of the areas of emphasis of behavioral science in organizations.

BEHAVIORAL SCIENCE EMPHASIS IN ORGANIZATIONS

The following aspects of organizational life have received concentrated attention by behavioral scientists. These are presented to make the point that the field is both deep and wide. The following quote should provide a common frame of reference for reviewing these aspects:

In no area of social inquiry has a body of general law been established, comparable with outstanding theories in the natural sciences in scope of explanatory power or in capacity to yield precise and reliable predictions . . . . It is also generally acknowledged that in the social sciences there is nothing quite like the almost complete unanimity commonly found among competent workers in the natural sciences as to what are matters of established fact, what are the reasonably satisfactory explanations (if any) for the assumed facts, and what are some of the valid procedures in sound inquiry. . . . The social sciences are a battleground for interminably warring schools of thought, and that even subject matter which has been under intensive and prolonged study remains at the unsettled periphery of research. [4]

---

*W. F. Whyte's studies in restaurants resulted in keeping people apart by introducing mechanical things — the spindle or order keeper on which the waitresses placed orders for the chiefs to fill — to reduce conflict and friction.

[4] Berelson, Bernard & Steiner, Gary A. *Human Behavior: An Inventory of Scientific Findings,* Harcourt, Brace & World, Inc., New York, 1964.

This is not to imply that we have a pessimistic point of view. On the contrary, we are optimistic because of the strides already made in the behavioral sciences due in great measure to improved research methods.

Motivation. It is generally accepted that the key to performance is motivation. This elusive potential has been defined as a drive within the individual which, dependent upon his expectations of the level of satisfaction he can achieve, incites him to action. The relationship between motivation and group or individual productivity and effectiveness has produced a considerable number of assumptions, concepts, research, (mostly on nonadults) and theories. Maslow, Vroom, Herzberg and now McClelland have contributed in this area. Some factors that seem to affect motivation are the needs, perceptions and goals of an individual and group and how these needs and goals can be realized. The study of human motivation is a key factor for managerial consideration with respect to such things as providing a work climate conducive to individual self-generation and positive motivation for meeting with individual and organizational needs.

Decision making. This aspect of organizational life has had considerable treatment by behavioral scientists. This includes a realm of elements affecting the making of decisions by individuals and groups. Some of these considerations include power and authority, attitudes and value systems, and creativity, as an organization strives to make rational rather than intuitive decision at its various levels of operations. This rationality includes weighing of alternatives and both immediate and long range forces and after effects which can ensue from the implementation of a decision.

Conflict. This deals with the how and why of friction that exists or arises in an organization, its manifestation in interpersonal and intra and interdepartmental relationships, and its optimum resolution. The effect of conflict on motivation, goal establishment and achievement, a group's ability to function under stress, and the knowledge and skill necessary to face up to and cope with conflict are some of the insightful cognitions valuable to people at work.

Leadership. It is generally conceded that leadership is determined by the existential nature of the situation. The development of leadership is of prime importance to organizational growth, perpetuation and effectiveness. Leadership is something that is shared from time to time, situation to situation, by boss and subordinate. The relative effectiveness of democratic, laissez-faire, or autocratic leadership in different types of organizations of various sizes are some of the results of studies in this area.

Power and authority. This deals with the sources and limitations of power: the behavioral relationship between responsibility and authority roles played by peers, superiors, and subordinate relationships. Problems of ethics and delegation fall into this category.

Organizational theory. In addition to the study of individuals and groups, the behavioral sciences have contributed considerably to the study of organizations, the transformation of the United States from a rural to a technologically urban society and culture has changed our way of life from one of autonomy and independence to a life characterized by proximity and interdependence.

Traditionally, organizations have been viewed as a means of accomplishing (its) goals and objectives as determined and defined by management. Little thought has been given to the inner workings and internal purposes of the human organization and how these factors might offset and undermine human collaboration pulling and pushing together toward "organizational" goals. The behavioral sciences have helped to define and describe "theories" (some are yet untested, but nevertheless valuable) of organization. They have helped to develop new frameworks for structuring organizations which would have a better chance than previously, considering today's rapid changes, of stimulating and obtaining the optimum output of potential inherent in the humans who are the organization.

In addition, productivity, managerial style and control, status, job design, communications, appraisals, reward and punishment systems, and climate are among the myriad items relating to organizational theory and effectiveness.

To understand modern man, it has been said that it is necessary to know him in formal organizations. Behavioral science made a great contribution to the theory of organizations. Organizations have been defined by size, by form, by tolerance for internal variation, by number and kind of transactions with their environments. Organizations have been theorized as social, closed and open systems. Systems can vary as to whether they have one goal or more than one. They can vary as to whether their goals relate to internal relationships or with the relations of the system to its environment or both. Systems can vary as to their flexibility in modifying an existent goal or in acquiring new goals.

Organizational studies consist of many diverse approaches and methodologies. Two authorities define organizational theory as:

... both the end product and the starting point of scientific research. On the one hand, the objective of all scientific endeavor is to develop a body of substantive theory, that is, a set of interrelated verifiable generalizations that account for and predict the empirical phenomena that can be observed. On the other hand, scientific research must be guided by a theoretical framework, that is, a system of interrelated concepts that suggest theoretically fruitful lines of empirical investigations.[5]

Organizational theory began concentrating upon the anatomy of formal groups. Concepts of organizations have been built around, individually or in concert, these four concerns:

(a) The division of labor; (b) the scalar and functional processes which refer to the growth of the chain of command, the delegation of authority and responsibility, unity of command, and the obligations to report, (c) the structure and, (d) the span of control.

---

[5] Blau, Peter M. & Scott, W. R. *Formal Organizations,* San Francisco, Chandler Publishing Co., 1962.

The concentration on organizational theory has resulted in new concepts of management. Thus management has become less authoritarian, less preoccupied with administrative efficiency, and less concerned with hierarchal structures. The emphasis instead has shifted to a managerial concern with the many influences and environments within society that the organization has to deal with in its on-going life.

As indicated earlier, the study of organizational theory has resulted recently in a series of "systems" concepts as to how organizations function. The basic notion of a system is that it is a set of interrelated parts, the totality of which is greater than the sum of the parts. One significance of this is that organizations do not, therefore, exist in themselves. They are intimately connected with a wider variety of other units which cannot be ignored. A corporation, for example, can be a social system or a system of financial flowing. When an organization is defined from a systems point of view, no single group is dominant. The task of self definition and effectiveness is really a never ending one for most organizations because of the need for designing and coping with the entire realm of organizational theory and effectiveness.

Planned change.   This is perhaps the greatest challenge and role for behavioral sciences in organizations today. Here, efforts and studies deal with effecting technological, managerial, and organizational change within an organization through participation and/or nonparticipatory methods. The implementing of change, when indicated, and the consolidation of the effect of this change on organizational efficiency, morale and effectiveness, fall into this category.

Planned change is one of the more recent applications of the behavioral sciences to organizational life. Warren Bennis is one of the definitive authors of this concept. Planned change is thought of as the best possible alternative between a laissez-faire and a radical Marxist approach to the changing organization. Planned change has been defined as:

a conscious, deliberate and collaborative effort to improve the operations of a system whether it be a self-system, social system or a cultural system, through the utilization of scientific knowledge.[6]

The primary functions of the behavioral scientist in planning change according to Bennis, Benne and Chin, is to serve to bridge the communications gap between the findings of the research experts and their applied meaning for the organization.

Planned change does not come about within a vacuum. Some of the factors which indicate the necessity for determining the need for implementing planned change are:

Technological change, in which the human consequences are not always adequately anticipated, thus bringing about social disruptions.

[6]Bennis, W. G., Benne, K. D. & Chin, R. *The Planning of Change,* New York: Holt, Reinhart & Winston, 1961.

The collapse of automatic adjustment, in which changes occur too fast and their implications are too wide to be left to "nature."

The collapse of community, in which society has become more individualistic and mobile, so that the community is no longer the basis of joint decision and action.

The fragmentation of the service professions, each with separate training and different orientation, few with cross-professional communication, yet all trying to serve the same organization.

Schein[7] lists the following six stages as the process of planned change an organization can use. Schein calls this the adaptive-coping cycle:

–Sensing a change in the internal or external environment.

–Importing the relevant information about the change into those parts of the organization which can act upon it.

–Changing production or conversion processes inside the organizations according to the information obtained.

–Stabilizing internal changes which reduce the managing of undesired by-products (undesired changes in related systems which have resulted from the desired changes).

–Exporting new products, services, and so on, which are more in line with the originally perceived changes in the environment.

–Obtaining feedback on the success of the change through further sensing of the state of the external environment and the degree of integration of the internal environment.

Resistance to change or being in love with the "status quo" – the causes rather than the symptoms – appears to be the concern of behavioral scientists. It seems that this route will lead to findings which can be operationally applied by practitioners in moving toward more healthy organizations. It is generally agreed that a change agent is quite helpful in implementing a planned change process. Outside consultants and in-house managers of training and development have individually and in consonance performed this role.

QUO VADIS – BEHAVIORAL SCIENCES

We are assuming that the following conditions and circumstances, among others, will exist in the United States in the future – 1980:

–Our economy will continue to grow.

–The standard of living will rise.

–The work force will become more highly educated and skilled.

–The prime, sought-for people in the 25-34 year age group will increase in number at a rate double that for the labor force as a whole.

[7]Schein, Edgar H. *Op. cit.*

—Jobs for educated and skilled people will be plentiful.

—Automation will increase.

—People will retire earlier and live longer and many retirees will start second careers.

—Industry, business, government and educational institutions will become more democratic in their internal organization.

—Organizations will become larger and more complex.

Based on these assumptions, some predictions (in the sense of prior to actual knowledge rather than foretelling) for the role of behavioral science in organizations are:

—There will be increased emphasis on examining organizations as systems. This will include research with respect to determining the extent to which, if any, an organization has its own individuality. Warren Schmidt and Gordon Lippitt are exploring this from the angle of level of organizational development using a six step hierarchy of needs which range from the need to be born or infancy to the need to create and contribute to the larger society. This hierarchy is related to A. Maslow's hierarchy of individual needs which range from physical to self-actualization needs.

—Greater attempts will be made to classify and type organizations similar to classifications such as genus, specie, family, etc., that we have in the life sciences. If this could be done, it would be easier to understand, explain and predict behavior within these classified organizations.

—"Theories" of organization — and human behavior in them — will come closer to theories as we know them in the life and physical sciences. We emphasize "come closer," for we doubt that the level of exactness existing in the physical sciences will be reached by the behavioral sciences.

—Behavioral scientists as such will be increasingly employed in organizations. These people will function on a level above the Personnel Department. These departments, in order to survive as necessary and accepted subsystems, will have to upgrade and professionalize their staff members to the point where they can design, implement, interpret research and influence key officials to apply the findings resulting from the research in the specific organization. Improved research design and methodology will bring behavioral science closer to the level of empiricism enjoyed by the physical and life sciences. What happens in organizations will contribute to this maturation. The organization would then be its own laboratory and application system. The outside behavioral science consultant will probably play a lesser role than is now the case.

—Planned change processes will be further explored as a means of assuring that the organization is adaptive and flexible to confront and cope with the permanency of change, assuring thereby that the organization increases its chances of remaining viable and perpetuative. This will be a prime role of the organizational behavioral scientist performing as a change agent and using the consultative process and development program continuum as the methodology for planned change.

—Behavioral scientists will assist in finding ways to include human growth and development as an asset. This will provide an increased impetus to managers to plan, implement, and evaluate the training and development of their subordinates. It will also help encourage human development as part of the organization's ongoing life.

—We will probably see greater emphasis being placed on research pertaining to adults in a work setting. For example, with the trend toward interdisciplinary task groups as the mode of organizational functioning, there will be a need for more applied research on intra and inter-group relationships and effectiveness, as well as individual training and development on such matters as group warm-up, cohesiveness, processes and task orientation. Another example is the concern with adult careers. As an integral part of organizational effectiveness, we will learn more about the process of decision making as it pertains to adult career choice. Further, with the movement toward task groups rather than the individual as the core unit in organizations, we will see more movement in the direction of how the forming, disbanding, and reforming of groups will affect career development and the behavioral results therefrom.

—Organizations, recognizing their responsibilities to the national social system and the value and contributions of employees to the organization and larger national social system, will conduct applied research pertaining to preretirement behavior on the job and its predictive value to the productivity level of retirees. Guidance and counseling programs will be increased for people three to five years away from retirement as a means of bridging the gap between the psychic and economic income achieved from a lifetime of work, and the different kind and amount of that income to be realized in retirement or semi-retirement in a second career.

—Behavioral research in R&D organizations will increase. These organizations are mainly responsible for the scientific and technological advances behind the changes we are facing. Yet it appears, as a rule, that R&D organizations are slower in opening their doors to behavioral science research, and are slower in trying to understand and apply existing knowledge of human behavior within the organization. One underlying reason for this might be that scientists and engineers select these occupations because they need to live and work under conditions in which the application of a formula or equation always gives them a precise and constant answer to a problem. This, of course, is not the case in human relationships. The selected alternative which worked in one human relationship situation will, with a high degree of probability, not work in application to another situation even if it involves the same people. In addition, R&D organizations will be marked for behavioral science research, particularly with respect to productivity and creativity, because of the pernicious shortage of scientific and engineering personnel.

—The profession of education, particularly adult education, will be accepted as a behavioral science. Organization's training and development programs will be placed increasingly under the behavioral studies magnifying glass to determine such things as: What is the optimum tailor-made program for our individual organization? Under what conditions, climate and structure do adults in our organization learn best? How can this learning be translated into improved behavior on the job and be consistent with the goals and aspirations of the individual and the organization?

—Behavioral science will be concerned with the apparent dichotomy of the need for broad gauge executives who have perceptual skill to view the organization as a totality and the increasing number of specialists required in organizations. It is noted that the behavioral scientist is a generalist who transcends such specialties as psychology, anthropology, and sociology.

—Behavioral scientists will represent their ogranizations in helping educational institutions to shape their curricula. This will be especially so with respect to Business Administration schools. Here the behavioral scientist will act as the "linking pin" between corporations and academic assistance in meeting the needs and requirements of both.

—The role of behavioral science in organizations will include studying and helping to shape the basic philosophical attitudes supporting organizational value systems. This will be related to bringing out more of the individual's inherent potentiality and creativity in "marrying" individual and organizational goals.

—In this connection, there will be increased examination into and explanation of the attitudinal belief syndromes relating to behavior at work. This will include a hard look at the conditions and forces supporting or obstructing individuality — the pioneering, risk taking spirit as compared to conformity, group or organization norms — and how this contributes to democracy or totalitarianism.

In summary, we will probably see a reduction in the cultural gap existing between escalating technology and human ability to confront and cope with changes caused by advancing science. Managers, for example, will become more professional and have the increased capability not only to cope with change, but to help bring it about in the human area. We may well see organizations, rather than universities, leading the institutional parade with respect to providing the pragmatic wherewithal which individuals can apply for improved living in a complex, ever changing, pluralistic society composed of many subsystems/societies.

SOME HUMAN PROBLEMS IN
INTERPROFESSIONAL COMMUNICATION*

Howard Baumgartel

Keeping alive any meaningful interdepartmental and interdisciplinary communication and discussion on a university campus is a very difficult and time-consuming job. It takes, I am sure, some special devotion on the part of a few people to provide the vital opportunities. The fast pace of life in a modern university, the desires and pressures for individual achievement, the necessity of building internally cohesive departmental groups, all militate against fruitful collaboration. Old jealousies and, often, dead issues separate us. We all know of the violent antireligionist who hasn't been in a church since his days in a narrow Sunday School 25-35 years ago. And yet he still compulsively attacks the stupidity, unreason and reactionism of a reality that may no longer exist in progressive religious institutions. Similarly any of us may be reacting to erroneous or outdated images of psychologists, human relationists, speech people or businessmen — images formed long ago that may have no relevance for contemporary interaction. In fact certain kinds of contacts between different professional groups may, as sometimes works in race relations, act to increase as well as to reduce the autistic hostilities inherent in most intergroup relationships.

One of the biggest difficulties I have found in helping to encourage cross-discipline intellectual exploration has to do with the peculiar relationship that has developed between the producers and the users of behavioral science. We have people in speech, public administration, law, business administration and human relations who are anxious, in fact, excited about learning of new developments in behavioral theory and research. However, some of the active and creative producers of social science have no "need" to communicate to these "applied" people. They may personally abhor application as base and/or manipulative. They may feel that we don't know enough for anyone to act on the basis of their insights. But they are, on the other hand, most anxious to communicate their findings to high-level professional colleagues who can understand easily their theoretical and empirical manipulation. Furthermore, as we know from research on communication in hierarchies, these producers of scientific knowledge like other people want to tell about their work to higher status people whose comments and approval are so highly valued, in fact whose comments provide the great personal reward in academia.

*Reprinted with permission from *Journal of Communication*, September, 1964.

These tendencies on the part of the producers of science create great communication difficulties. The core values of the producing scientist actually depreciate application and emphasize solely the paramount importance of producing new knowledge. The net result is that the consumers are more motivated for interdisciplinary discussions than the producers. Of course many great creative behavioral scientists have never been able to rest until they have communicated their findings to a wider public, and further, as in the case of Kurt Lewin, some are not satisfied until the new concepts are applied to the solution of pressing human problems, until new knowledge is translated into new social practice.

Now what about the users of behavioral science? Sometimes the gulf in understanding of the scientific point of view *is* too great to bridge for even the interested researcher all by himself. In my own mind, unless a person has made a certain intellectual step he will always have difficulty in learning from research-oriented persons. This step is to differentiate *between* his own naive beliefs and opinions about the social world around him, no matter how well thought out or how insightful these beliefs may be, *and* the existence of a collective body of knowledge abstractly independent of any particular believer. This abstract knowledge based presumably, on sound logic and careful empirical investigation supercedes personal impression in the scientifically trained person. I have been in meetings where the whole discussion centered around the unconscious rebellion of one man to the whole idea of a rational and scientific understanding of human behavior. Having denied the existence of objective knowledge, he precluded the possibility of two-way communication with the scientist. No researcher enjoys such an experience unless he has made a contract to get paid for th job or unless he has a missionary zeal which, incidentally, may interfer with his being a good scientist in any event.

Communication between "scientists" and "practitioners" in closely related fields is even more complicated. Now it takes a great deal of humility to teach others, i.e., "applied people," particularly when you might learn something from their questions and observations; and it takes a great deal of humility to learn from an expert who may know more than you do about some aspects of your own work. I'll never forget the cold reception I got from a group of alert industrial training directors when I reported to them the results of a number of experimental studies which indicate that training programs have little effect on supervisory performance as compared with some other forms of social change. They had spent many years of effort in putting on good training programs; I had spent years studying and doing research on organizational problems. We each had commitments to our views. Likewise, it is hard to forget the pointed and brutal criticisms of a journal editor concerning a research paper on which I had put many hours of effort, if insufficient attention to study design.

The situation is further complicated by the fact that nowadays some of the "users" of behavioral science are often themselves producers of behavioral science at some level of proficiency and sophistication, although unfortunately it is my experience that applied research, no matter how "significant" the research problem often tends to be sloppily designed and executed. People's personal concern with the issues involved and the pressure for quick answers militate against sound scientific work in many cases.

The user, like other men, has his own pride in his own work, as well as in his personally developed conceptions. He is, hence, reluctant to take a learner role in relation to someone who may in fact be able to teach him something. The forces working against interrelatedness seem so great that many despair and turn to working more vigorously in their own gardens – often with the most remarkable results. And, for all our interest in cross-discipline stimulation, I do think that we should forget about cross-fertilization once in a while and just do some good work of our own. Such a comment, however, clearly indicates the value-conflict hidden in these interprofessional communications troubles. And, as we all know, it is the unspoken and hidden conflict that causes trouble.

Now, in my judgment, another aspect of the difficulties in obtaining productive communication between many users of behavioral science and many producers of social science lies in the differences in methodological assumptions each makes. The most beautiful example is, of course, the relationship between the psychoanalytic writer and the experimental psychologist or empirical sociologist. To the latter groups, schooled in logical empiricism, trained to suspect the value of any *ad hoc* theory, trained to think in operational, predictive and deductive terms, the theories of Freud and his followers, built as they were on the *ex post facto* analysis of cases, are clearly speculative and, what's worse, "philosophical" in nature – philosophical referring, of course, to any proposition which cannot be reduced to empirical referents. The fact is that careful research based on psychoanalytic conceptions has often come up with disappointing results, e.g., the work on accident proneness. Yet psychiatrists and clinical psychologists in their daily work with patients in hospitals and clinics find these theoretical conceptions of great help to them in understanding and treating patients. But all the while we know, too, that one of the greatest pastimes in human history has been that of trapping ourselves in self-confirming but untested and unreal sets of conceptions – not the least of which are some of our social and political belief structures of the present century of human progress. This basic difference in the *standards for establishing* the truth or falsity of propositions then constitutes another big barrier in the relationships between the users and producers of science.

WHAT KILLED BOB LYONS?*

Harry Levinson

Those who knew Bob Lyons thought extremely well of him. He was a highly successful executive who held an important position in a large company. As his superiors saw him, he was aggressive, with a knack for getting things done through other people. He worked hard and set a vigorous pace. He drove himself relentlessly. In less than ten years with his company, he had moved through several positions of responsibility,

Lyons had always been a good athlete. He was proud of his skill in swimming, hunting, golf, and tennis. In his college days he had lettered in football and baseball. On weekends he preferred to undertake rebuilding and repairing projects around the house, or to hunt, interspersing other sports for a change of pace. He was usually engaged, it seemed, in hard, physical work.

His life was not all work, however. He was active in his church and in the Boy Scouts. His wife delighted in entertaining and in being with other people, so their social life was a round of many parties and social activities. They shared much of their life with their three children.

Early in the spring of his ninth year with the company, Bob Lyons spoke with the vice president to whom he reported. "Things are a little quiet around here," he said. "Most of the big projects are over. The new building is finished, and we have a lot of things on the ball which four years ago were all fouled up. I don't like this idea of just riding a desk and looking out the window. I like action."

About a month later, Lyons was assigned additional responsibilities. He rushed into them with his usual vigor. Once again he seemed to be buoyant and cheerful. After six months on the assignment, Lyons had the project rolling smoothly. Again he spoke to his vice president, reporting that he was out of projects. The vice president, pleased with Lyons' performance, told him that he had earned the right to do a little dreaming and planning; and furthermore, dreaming and planning were a necessary part of the position he now held, toward which he had aspired for so long. Bob Lyons listened as his boss spoke, but it was plain to the vice president that the answer did not satisfy him.

About three months after this meeting, the vice president began to notice that replies to his memos and inquiries were not coming back from Lyons

---

with their usual rapidity. He noticed also that Lyons was developing a tendency to put things off, a most unusual behavior pattern for him. He observed that Lyons became easily angered and disturbed over minor difficulties which previously had not irritated him at all.

Bob Lyons then became involved in a conflict with two other executives over a policy issue. Such conflicts were not unusual in the organization since, inevitably, there were varying points of view on many issues. The conflict was not a personal one, but it did require intervention from higher management before a solution could be reached. In the process of resolving the conflict, Lyons' point of view prevailed on some questions, but not on others.

A few weeks after this conflict had been resolved, Lyons went to the vice president's office. He wanted to have a long private talk, he said. His first words were, "I'm losing my grip. The old steam is gone. I've had diarrhea for four weeks and several times in the past three weeks I've lost my breakfast. I'm worried and yet I don't know what about. I feel that some people have lost confidence in me."

He talked with his boss for an hour and a half. The vice president recounted his achievements in the company to reassure him. He then asked if Lyons thought he should see a doctor. Lyons agreed that he should and, in the presence of the vice president, called his family doctor for an appointment. By this time the vice president was very much concerned. He called Mrs. Lyons and arranged to meet her for lunch the next day. She reported that, in addition to his other symptoms, her husband had difficulty sleeping. She was relieved that the vice president had called her because she was beginning to become worried and had herself planned to call the vice president. Both were now alarmed. They decided that they should get Lyons into a hospital rather than wait for the doctor's appointment which was still a week off.

The next day Lyons was taken to the hospital. Meanwhile, with Mrs. Lyons' permission, the vice president reported to the family doctor Lyons' recent job behavior and the nature of their conversations. When the vice president had finished, the doctor concluded, "All he needs is a good rest. We don't want to tell him that it may be mental or nervous." The vice president replied that he didn't know what the cause was, but he knew Bob Lyons needed help quickly.

During five days in the hospital, Lyons was subjected to extensive laboratory tests. The vice president visited him daily. He seemed to welcome the rest and sedation at night. He said he was eating and sleeping much better. He talked about company problems, though he did not speak spontaneously without encouragement. While Lyons was out of the room, another executive who shared his hospital room confided to the vice president that he was worried about Lyons. "He seems to be so morose and depressed that I'm afraid he's losing his mind," the executive said.

By this time the president of the company, who had been kept informed, was also becoming concerned. He had talked to a psychiatrist and planned to talk to Lyons about psychiatric treatment if his doctor did not suggest it. Meanwhile, Lyons was discharged from the hospital as being without physical illness, and his doctor recommended a vacation. Lyons then remained at home for several days where he was again visited by the vice president. He and his wife took a trip to visit friends. He was then ready to come back to work, but the president suggested that he take another week off. The president also suggested that they visit together when Lyons returned.

A few days later, the president telephoned Lyons' home. Mrs. Lyons could not find him to answer the telephone. After 15 minutes she still had not found him and called the vice president about her concern. By the time the vice president arrived at the Lyons home, the police were already there. Bob Lyons had committed suicide.

WHY DID IT HAPPEN?

This tragic story is not an unusual one. Probably no other single emotional problem is as disturbing to those who must live with it as is suicide. No doubt Bob Lyons' colleagues and superiors suffered almost as much anguish as his family did. The president and vice president were concerned long afterward. They wondered if, despite their conscientious efforts, they had in some way been at fault or if they could have prevented it. Neither his family nor his colleagues could understand why it happened. It made no sense to them that a successful man in the prime of his life, like Lyons, should destroy himself.

Lyons' problem may have been extreme, but similar problems are not rare in business and industry. Executives, managers, supervisors, industrial physicians, and — to a lesser extent — all employees frequently must cope with emotional problems on the job. Many problems are of lesser proportion than Lyons' was, but all have four factors in common:

- They are painful both for the person who suffers from them and for those who must deal with him.
- They are usually destructive to both the sufferer and the organization.
- The origins of the problem are almost always more complex than either of the parties realizes; and only infrequently are even the precipitating events clear.
- Rarely does the person responsible for dealing with the on-the-job problem know what he should do about it.

As a result, few businesses have ways of dealing with these matters even reasonably well, and management actions tend to range from abrupt firing to hostile discipline to, in some instances, procrastination which goes on for years. Often there is a vacillating series of management efforts, accompanied by feelings of guilt, failure, and anger on the part of those who must make the managerial decisions. Emotional problems, then, are contagious. The disturbance suffered by one person has its effects on the emotions of others.

Was it hereditary?

How can we understand what happened to Bob Lyons and the ways his problem relates to problems with which all of us must deal? The customary commonsense reasons fail us. He had no serious illness. He did not fail in his business activity. There was no indication of difficulty in his family life. The course of the story told by the vice president is too consistent to attribute his death to an accident or to chance. Then, what was responsible?

Heredity? Can we say he inherited a tendency to suicide? Man inherits certain capacities and traits, but these are essentially physiological. He inherits the color of his eyes, the size of his nose, and other physical features. He inherits certain sensory and motor capacities. That is, he will be able to see, hear, or feel physical stimuli — color, sound, warmth — more or less keenly. Newborn infants in a hospital nursery will vary widely in their response to such stimuli. Some are calm and placid; an attendant could drop a metal tray with a clang, but these children would continue to sleep. Others, however, would be startled and awake crying.

The reasons for these differences in reaction are obscure. We have some clues from recent experiments with white rats. When pregnant rats are placed in crowded cages or in other situations where they experience stress, this stress apparently produces biochemical imbalances in the mothers which affect the rat fetuses. When the baby rats are born, they have greater anxiety and greater difficulty in adapting to the external world than rats whose mothers were not subjected to such stress. Among human beings, the mother's diet, the illnesses she has during pregnancy, and her general physical condition have their effects on the human fetus.

Something physical?

Apparently man also inherits the capacity to coordinate his muscles with greater or lesser efficiency. If a person inherits excellent coordination potential and develops it, he may ultimately become a good athlete or a good musician. If he inherits a better than usual capacity for abstracting sights and sounds, he may have the makings of an artist. Man does not inherit athletic or artistic skill, but some men and women inherit such a high level of sensitivity and physiological harmony that they seem to have a "natural bent" toward certain talents.

Some apparently are born with greater general intelligence; therefore, they have the potential for dealing with their environments with better reasoning power and more effective judgment. Others have more specialized capacities: the ability to abstract ideas readily, the ability to remember well, and so on. Such differences, which in some instances appear at birth, bring about different kinds of interactions with the environment. The irritable infant will have quite a different relationship with his mother than will the placid child. The child who walks and talks early comes into contact sooner with a wider range of experiences than does another child in the same general environment, in whom these skills develop later.

Heredity, then, to a large extent determines what a person will be, in the sense that all of us have to be two-armed, ten-fingered, two-legged men or women, short or tall, intelligent or unintelligent, and with different thresholds of our various senses. Each person is different in the combination of endowments that he has and in the degree to which they enable him to cope with life's stresses.

While hereditary factors predispose man to behave in gross, or general, ways, they have little direct effect on his specific behavior. Because of the high level of development of the frontal lobes of his brain, man is capable of both abstract and reflective thinking. He is also capable of a wide range of emotions, particularly feelings about himself in relation to other people. These capacities for thought and feeling make man extremely responsive to many nuances of environmental stimulation. They also make it possible for him to initiate a wide range of actions in keeping with his thoughts and feelings, as well as in response to his environment, particularly to the other people in it.

Family influence?

Another environmental factor which has an important influence on behavior is the extremely long period, particularly in Western cultures, during which the human child is dependent upon his parents. The intimacy of these relationships and the many social pressures which are transmitted through the parents to the children make family influences extremely important in guiding and controlling behavior. The extended period of dependency also presents a psychological problem because each person must then resolve the conflict between his wishes to retain the pleasures of dependency and his desire to become an independent adult. No one ever completely gives up the former or completely obtains the latter.

Each seeks some way of being interdependent with others that enables him to depend on others without losing his pride — because they in turn depend on him. Each person has dependency needs to varying degrees, the extent depending on how well each one has resolved this problem for himself. Some who have not resolved it well will always be more dependent than others. Some have resolved it reasonably well and can accept whatever dependency needs they have. Some have rejected or denied such needs and will have nothing to do with situations in which they might have to depend on others.

So, too, different companies will require different degrees of dependency in their employees. People who remain in a stable public utility company for a long time will be more dependent on their company for their security than will itinerant salesmen who sell magazines on commission. The fact that such a range of possibilities is available for fulfilling such needs at work is one of the health-giving aspects of work in business organizations.

SOMETHING INSIDE HIM

Thus, we cannot, after this, very well say that Bob Lyons committed suicide because of heredity. We might be able to say hereditary factors, interacting with environmental factors, led to his death, but in our present state of knowledge it would be extremely difficult to demonstrate a hereditary predisposition which contributed to his self-destruction. Of necessity, we must call on more purely psychological factors for an explanation. In a way, when people, in despair over accounting for why someone like Bob Lyons would kill himself, cry out, "There must have been something odd inside of him that drove him into doing it," they are partially right. Inside all of us are many emotional drives that seem odd when we do not understand them.

For an approach toward understanding, let us return for a moment to the first paragraph of his superiors' description of Lyons. There we find these phrases: "highly successful," "aggressive," "a knack for getting things done through other people," "worked hard," "set a vigorous pace," and "drove himself relentlessly." These phrases speak of drive or energy. The subsequent two paragraphs describe other ways in which he discharged his energy. Some of these ways were highly useful to himself, his company, his family, and his friends. Others had a destructive potential: "He drove himself relentlessly." In fact, his difficulties seemed to begin when he could no longer drive himself on his job.

Warring drives

The theories of Sigmund Freud help us understand the importance of such drives. According to Freud, there are two constantly operating psychological drives in the personality. One is a *constructive drive* and the other a *destructive drive.* Just as there are always processes of growth and destruction in all biological matter, anabolism and catabolism, so there are similar processes in the personality. These drives constitute the basic, primitive, energy sources for the personality.

The constructive drive (sometimes referred to as the *libido*) is the source of feelings of love, creativity, and psychological growth. The destructive drive gives rise to feelings of anger and hostility to others. The twin forces are variously referred to as Love and Hate, in terms of Greek mythology as Eros and Thanatos, or Sex and Aggression. (When used in this way, both the terms sex and aggression have a far broader meaning than they do in ordinary usage.)

A major psychological task for every human being is to so fuse these drives that the constructive drive tempers, guides, and controls the destructive drive and that the energy from both sources may thus be used in his own self-interest and that of society. If we speak of the destructive drive as the aggressive drive (recognizing that we are using the word aggressive according to its dictionary meaning and not as synonymous with assertion as in ordinary usage), we can say that it is far better for a person to use his aggressive drive, tempered by larger amounts of the constructive drive, in the pursuit of a career, the creation of a family, and in business competition than in destroying others as might be the case if the drives were not adequately fused.

Perhaps an analogy will help. Think of an automobile engine. A mixture of gasoline and air serves as the energy source. If there is too much gasoline, the engine will flood. If there is too much air, then it will sputter and die. With the right blend or fusion of fuel, and particularly with considerably more gasoline than air, which is then channeled through a mechanical structure, the automobile engine can serve a useful purpose.

Channeling the drives

In Bob Lyons' case we saw that much of his constructive and aggressive energy, and more of the former than the latter, was well fused and channeled into his work, his relationships with his family, and service to his community. In some ways his constructive drive was less dominant, for he drove himself, as the vice president put it, "relentlessly."

The two drives are included in a part of the personality (a set of functions, not a physical thing) to which Freud gave the name "id," the Latin neuter for "it." In addition to the two basic drives, the id also includes many memories and experiences which the person can no longer recall.

The brain acts like a vast tape recorder. Theoretically, a person should be able to recall all of the experiences and feelings about those experiences he has had. We know that under hypnosis, psychoanalysis, and under the influence of some drugs, a person can recall many of them. He could not do so before, no matter how hard he tried. Many of these memories, feelings, and impulses (impulses are derivatives of drives)are *repressed* or buried in the id, but they are still "alive," because they would be expressed, as we shall see later, if there were not adequate controls. For the id cares little about restraint; it operates on the pleasure principle: "I want what I want when I want it."

Repression, incidentally, is the process of "forgetting" or of making unconscious certain kinds of experiences and information which may be too troublesome or painful to handle on a conscious level. Here is how repression may have worked in Bob Lyons' case:

To judge from his behavior, he may have learned in his childhood that the only way to obtain love from his parents was by good performance. If high performance was the price of love, Lyons may well have resented his parents' attitude. But since such a conscious feeling of anger toward his parents would have been painful to live with, it was repressed. Lyons was no longer aware of his anger toward them, but it remained with him. The id, being unconscious, has no sense of time; it is inconsistent, contradictory, and not amenable to logic or persuasion. Thus, the early experiences that caused Bob Lyons' feelings of resentment were still "alive" and painful in his id.

Handling the Constructive Drive

In this article, because we are focusing on Bob Lyons' case, we are looking at ways in which the ego deals with the *aggressive* drive by calling into play certain defense mechanisms in order to maintain its equilibrium. But the ego also must deal with the *constructive* drive in order to maintain the proper balance. We see how it might handle sexual stimulation by control and refinement, or even denial, of the impulse. Other examples illustrate how the same mechanisms that are used to cope with the aggressive drive apply themselves to handling constructive drives and, in so doing, often cause us distress as well as relief:

1. *Fusion of drives.* Fused with the aggressive drive, and dominant over it, the constructive drive is directed toward appropriate targets in intimate relationships with one's family, the solution of work and family problems, citizenship activities, and so on. Idealistic love without an aggressive component might lead to merely fantasied images of a sweetheart rather than marriage, or a person might dream about job success rather than take action toward it.

2. *Displacement to less appropriate targets.* Like the aggressive drive, the constructive drive may be deflected from appropriate targets. Homosexuality is one such phenomenon whose dynamics are too complex for discussion here. In brief, the homosexual cannot establish adequate and satisfying relationships with those of the opposite sex. Instead, he uses the mechanism of substitution and builds up extended rationalizations to appease his superego.

Some people can invest themselves in causes, but not really in other people. Some lavish great affection on animals or houses or hobbies at the expense of personal relationships. Some adults can have affectionate relationships only with young children, but cannot tolerate other adults. These targets provide useful channels for love, but not the fully satisfying wide range of relationships enjoyed by most mature adults.

3. *Containment.* Some people, for complicated reasons, learned that it was psychologically safe not to express affection and have repressed their affectionate feelings. These people we know colloquially as "cold fish," people seemingly without emotion. They may be highly intellectual or great professional successes, but they have divorced compassion from judgment and feeling from reasoning. Others are known as ruthlessly efficient. They keep their emotions tightly controlled and their feelings of love deeply buried within themselves.

In speaking of the drives, we have said that psychological growth and survival require more of the constructive drive, implying that there are differences in the amount of drive energy. We assume that there are differences among people in how much drive energy they have. We don't know how these differences come about, nor do we have any satisfactory way of specifying amount other than grossly and comparatively. We do know, however, that warm, affectionate relationships, especially those between mother and child, give added strength to the constructive drive, while those in which the child experiences severe frustration and hostility from others stimulate more aggression in the child. In a general way, the same is true of adults: the relationships and experiences which provide affection and gratification bring out the good side of people, while those which precipitate frustration and anger bring out the bad side of people.

4. *Displacement onto the self.* Children rejected by their parents learn bitterly that it is too painful to try to love other people because they will not return love. In adult life, such people become highly self-centered. In conversation they are constantly talking about themselves. They give overmeticulous attention to their appearance, and revel in self-display. They tend to seek out activities which provide public adulation, and become extremely unhappy when they cannot get it. We find such people unpleasant to deal with because they are unable to give anything of themselves to someone else. Often they exploit others for their own gain. Because they cannot love others, they have almost no real friends and often are unable to sustain their marriages.

For these people much of the constructive drive is displaced onto themselves because environmental forces have made identification and introjection difficult, thereby impairing the possibility of relationships with other people. The early conflicts, now repressed, still exist unconsciously for the person. With its memories of early pain, the ego will not open itself again to the possibilities of rejection and narrowly constricts the constructive drive to a limited target to protect itself. Because of the limited range of attachments their egos permit, such people do not really enjoy life, despite what appears to others to be an extremely sparkling series of social adventures.

Each person must have a certain amount of self-love if he is to have self-respect. Overweening egocentricity, however, is ultimately destructive because of the absence of gratification, because of the pain caused other people, and because it diverts energy from social contributions the person could make.

An extreme form of egocentricity is hypochondriasis. Some people invest all of their energy in themselves in an extremely distorted way by being preoccupied with their own bodies. They are never free of aches and pains, often spend years and untold dollars "doctoring." They sacrifice most of life's pleasures to nurse their fancied ills, undeterred by repeated medical reports that show there is no need for surgery or that they do not have cancer, and the like. In some respects, such people commit slow suicide as they cut themselves off more and more from the outside world. In some cases, such persons will even allow one or more limbs to atrophy from disuse because they claim it is too painful to walk or to move.

SOMETHING OUTSIDE HIM

Not only did Bob Lyons (as do all of us) have the major psychological task of balancing or fusing his constructive and aggressive drives, but he also had to discharge these drives in socially acceptable ways only. It might have been permissible in more primitive times to hit a man on the head and take his wife, but it is no longer so. There are stringent cultural controls on how love and aggression may be expressed.

These controls on how we may express our basic drives vary from culture to culture, even from one social class to another; but they are transmitted through parents and other authority figures to children. Early in the child's development, the parents control and direct him. They permit some forms of behavior but prohibit others. As the child grows older, he incorporates into his own personality what his parents have taught him. He will incorporate these rules and values most effectively if he feels an affectionate bond with the parents and wants to be like them. This is one of the reasons the parent-child relationship is so important and why it should be one which enables the child to feel happy and secure.

Various values and rules can be "pounded into" the child, but these tend not to be genuinely his. He lives by them only as long as external pressures require him to, and abandons them when the external pressures diminish. Some parents who try to force piety and goodness into their children are dismayed to find them neither pious nor good when they grow up.

Still, small voice

When the child develops a conscience, he becomes self-governing. In Freudian terms, he has developed a *superego.* The superego is made up of four parts: (1) the values of the culture as transmitted through parents, teachers, friends, scoutmasters, ministers, and so on; (2) rules, prohibitions, and taboos; (3) an ego ideal—the image of ourselves at our future best which we never fully attain and as a result of which we are perennially discontended with ourselves; and (4) a police-judging or self-critical function.

Some theorists separate the superego and the conscience. They limit the superego to the values and the ego ideal (Parts 1 and 3 above), and refer to the rules (Part 2) and the self-critical function (Part 4) as the conscience. While that distinction is important scientifically, for our purposes we can ignore it. We will consider the conscience to be a part of the superego and include all four factors in the superego, as above.

The superego begins to develop in the child the first time the words "no" or "don't" enter his small world. Its general form tends to be established by the time the child enters elementary school, although it becomes further refined and expanded as a person grows up. Some features of the superego, developed early in life, are not conscious. The person is no longer aware of why he must live by certain rules and values; he knows only that if he does not do so, he feels uncomfortable or experiences anxiety. Some children, for example, feel that they must be the best in their class. They may not know why they feel they must, but if they are not always successful, they feel they are no good.

Conscience & culture

Because the superego is acquired from the culture in which a person lives (principally through the medium of his parents and later by incorporating the values, rules, and ideals of others he respects), it is reinforced by the culture. One's superego may keep him from stealing, for example, but there are also social penalties for stealing. Cultural changes may in turn, bring about some changes in the superego, particularly in those aspects of the superego which are conscious. Thus, every older generation contends that every younger generation is going to the dogs. While certain basic values and rules endure, others change with time. This is also why many parents are so concerned about where the family lives and about the beliefs and attitudes of their children's teachers and friends.

Among the directions that the superego provides are those which have to do with how the constructive and aggressive drives may be directed, how a person may love and how he may hate (and under what circumstances), and what kind of an adult person he should be. A man may love his parents but in a way different from the way he loves his wife. He may not, in Western cultures, love another woman as he loves his wife. In Italy and Spain he may express affection to other men by embracing them, but not in the United States. He may express his anger verbally, but not in physical attack. He may direct some of his aggressive drive in work, sports, and community activities, but not comfortably in those areas which are commonly regarded as feminine.

There are many variations among families and subcultures which become part of the superegos of people in those groups. Among middle-class American families there is a heavy emphasis on achievement, on cleanliness, on good manners, on hard work, and on the avoidance of open expressions of hostility. Lower class families, particularly those at the lowest socioeconomic levels, are not particularly concerned about these values. Some fundamentalist religious groups prohibit drinking and dancing. Some groups teach their children they are sinful by nature, others that almost anything they want to do is acceptable.

"Know Then Thyself"

How one looks upon himself, or his self-image, is related to the superego. One measure of self-evaluation is the disparity between the ego ideal and how one perceives himself at present. When one is depreciated by people who are important to him, this reinforces the critical aspects of the superego and lowers self-esteem. When self-esteem is enhanced, however, this counteracts the criticism of the superego and neutralizes some of the aggressive drive, thus stimulating the person to an expanded, more confident view of himself and his capacities.

It has been said that no wound is as painful as that inflicted by the superego. When a man behaves in ways not in keeping with the values and rules he has made a part of himself or when, in his judgment, he falls too short of his ego ideal, the superego induces a feeling of guilt. For most of us guilt feelings are so strong and so painful that we try to make up for violations of the superego by some form of atonement. The religious concept of penance is a recognition of this phenomenon. Restitution is another way to relieve guilt feelings. It is not unusual to see newspaper articles about people who have anonymously sent money to the government because they cheated on their taxes years before. Government officials speak of this as "conscience money."

Because the development of the superego begins early and the child is not in a position to judge rationally the relative importance of some of the rules he is taught, it is easy for the child to learn to judge himself more harshly than he should. With his limited capacity to reason, he may hold himself to blame for events he had nothing to do with. For example, suppose a two-year-old child is severely hurt in a fall. His four-year-old brother, who must inevitably have some feelings of hostility and rivalry toward the younger child, may come to feel he is responsible for the fall. As a matter of fact, he had nothing to do with the fall, but for a small child the wish is often tantamount to the act. To wish the younger child to be destroyed may be the same to a four-year-old as actually having pushed him. He may then harbor irrational guilt feelings for many years thereafter, completely unaware that he has such feelings or how they came about.

Since there is love and hate in every relationship, children have considerable hostility toward, as well as affection for, their parents. Usually young children do not understand that their hostile feelings are not "bad" and that parents will not be destroyed merely because their children have such feelings. As a result, most of us carry a considerable load of irrational guilt feelings. One of the major tasks in some forms of psychological treatment for people who are emotionally disturbed is to make such irrational unconscious feelings conscious so their irrationality may be recognized and they will no longer plague the person.

The balance wheel

The superego, then, becomes a built-in governor, as it were. It is the internalized civilizing agent. Without it, there would be no continuing self-guide to behavior. The superego is an automatic protective device. Because of it some issues are never raised; we never even ask: "Should I or should I not steal?" As a guide to behavior it makes for stability and consistency of performance.

If, however, the values and rules which the child is taught are inconsistent, then the superego will be inconsistent. If there are too many, too strict rules, then the superego becomes a harsh task master, either constricting too narrowly the way a person can behave or burdening him excessively with feelings of guilt and demanding constant atonement. But even without punishment or strict rules, a tyrannical superego can develop — if performance is the basis for obtaining love and there are unrealistic expectations of extremely high performance. In such a case, there tends to be a quality of drivenness to much of the person's behavior. He has a feeling that there is so much that he ought to do or must do as contrasted with so much he would enjoy doing. Unless he is constantly doing what he feels he ought to do, then he feels uncomfortable, not knowing either why he ought to be doing or why he feels uncomfortable if he is not doing. Lyons, for example, not only drove himself relentlessly, but also usually had to be working hard.

We have seen so far that the constructive and aggressive drives, which continuously seek discharge, are major motivating forces in the personality

The superego, with its capacity to induce guilt feelings, not only defines acceptable ways in which the drives may be discharged but also serves as a motivating force.

Home & Job

Not everything we do, of course, is completely influenced by our emotional drives. Our environment plays its part and should be considered in our attempt to understand Bob Lyons' suicide. For, in addition to the task of balancing or fusing our drives in keeping with the strictures of the superego, we do have to deal with our external environment. At times, this environment is a source of affection, support, and security. The infant in his mother's arms, a woman in a happy marriage, a man enjoying himself among his friends, a man building a business, a minister serving his congregation, all draw emotional nourishment from the environment. Such nourishment strengthens the constructive forces of the personality.

Looked at closely, *needs for status and esteem are essentially needs for love and affection.* Each person, no matter how old or jaded, wants to be held in esteem by some others. Few can survive long without giving and receiving love, though often these expressions are thoroughly disguised, even from the self. Status needs have to do with the constructive forces of the personality as we have described them here. When one seeks symbols of status, he simply searches for concrete indications that some others do or will hold him in esteem. One way to describe status needs is to say that the person needs infusions of love and of gratification to foster his own strength.

However, the environment may also stimulate aggression: anger and jealousy, exploitation, competition for various advantages, economic reverses, wars, and so on. Every person has to deal with the realities of his environment — whether with the necessities of earning a living, the frustration of an unsolved problem, the achievement of personal goals, the development of satisfying relationships with other people, or something else. We saw that Lyons was actively involved with all of these things in his environment.

EGO & REALITY

Now we have spoken of three sets of forces — id drives, the superego, and the environment — each interacting with the others, which must be kept in sufficient balance or equilibrium so that a person can function effectively. Some mechanism is required to do the balancing task, to serve as the executive part of the personality. Such a component of personality must fuse the drives, control their discharge in keeping with the conditions set by the superego, and act upon the environment. Freud gave the name *ego* to this set of functions. We tend to speak of the ego as a thing; actually, the term is merely a short way of describing *the organized executive functions of the personality, those functions that have to do with self-control and with testing reality.*

The ego includes such mental functions as recall, perception, judgment, attention, and conceptual or abstract thinking — those aspects of the personality which enable the individual to receive, organize, interpret, and act upon stimuli of psychological and physiological data. The ego develops (except in those who are mentally retarded) as the person grows. Like a computer, the ego acquires and stores information in the form of memory images, particularly information and experiences which previously have led to successful solution of problems. When an impulse arises from one of the drives, the ego contains the impulse until, in effect, it has checked with the superego and has determined what the consequences of acting on the impulse will be.

The impulse may have to be fully contained, or expressed in some modified fashion to meet both the conditions of the superego and the demands of the environment. The ego presumably checks its memory images to find acceptable ways of refining and discharging the impulse. When the ego can do this well, we speak of a strong ego or of psychological maturity. When it cannot do so adequately, we say a person does not have adequate strength or that he is immature. *The ego acts on the basis of what is called the reality principle:* "What are the long-run consequences of this behavior?"

The process of checking the memory images and organizing a response is what we know as thinking. Thinking is trial action or "dry run," as it were. Sometimes it goes on consciously, but much of the time it is an unconscious process. Thinking serves to delay impulses until they can be discharged in the most satisfactory way the person knows how. When a person acts impulsively in minor ways, for instance, in being inconsiderate of another person, we commonly speak of such behavior as "thoughtless."

The ego, operating on the reality principle and obeying the superego, must contain, refine, or redirect id impulses so that the integrity of the personality is preserved. The ego is constantly concerned with the cost and consequences of any action. In other words, the ego is concerned with psychological economy.

Beleaguered ego

This task puts the ego in a difficult position. This system of psychological functions is always a buffer between the other systems, the id and the superego, and also between them, and the forces of the environment. The ego, then, is always under psychological pressure. To carry on its integrating function well requires considerable strength. Strength comes from several sources: the basic inherited capacities, experiences of love and gratification which enhance the constructive forces, the development of skills and abilities which help it master the environment, and the physical health of the person. The ego may be weakened through physical injury or illness — a brain tumor, a debilitating sickness — or by having to devote too much of its energy to repressing or otherwise coping with severe multiple or chronic emotional pressures.

The ego cannot deal with all of the stimuli which impinge upon it. It is constantly being bombarded with all kinds of data. It would be swamped if it tried to deal with all of the information it had in the form of both past experiences and present ones. It must be selective in what it will deal with. Some data are therefore passed directly on to the id. The ego is never consciously aware of them. Furthermore, it has not been able to successfully resolve all of its psychological problems, some of which are extremely painful. With these it acts on the thesis, "If you can't lick it, forget it." These problems are repressed, or pushed down into the id. The little boy who erroneously thought he hurt his brother, then repressed his guilt feelings, is a case in point.

Perhaps some other examples will help us to understand these processes better:

Suppose someone walking along the street sees a new car parked at the curb. He has an impulse to take the car and, acting on the impulse, drives it off. We say he acted impulsively, by which we mean he was governed by an impulse from the id and not by rational considerations. To put it another way, we might say that the ego was weak, that it did not anticipate the consequences of the act and control the impulse. The price paid for acting on the impulse, perhaps a jail term, is a high one for what little momentary pleasure might have been gained. We say such a person is immature, meaning that his ego is not sufficiently developed to enable him to act in a wiser and less costly way.

A store manager might also be said not to have good judgment if he bought items without thinking through their marketing possibilities or merely because he liked the salesman who sold them. This is another form of impulsiveness or immaturity. Marketing men count on the irrational impulsiveness in all of us by creating in supermarkets such a vast array of stimuli to our desires for pleasure that the ego does not function quite as well as it might. Impulse buying results — unless the ego is bolstered by additional support in the form of a shopping list and a budget.

Here is a more personal example. If you observe young children, you see that they live extremely active lives. They have many pleasant moments and some painful ones. They remember experiences from day to day and recall exciting events like a trip to the zoo with great relish. Now try to remember your own early childhood experiences, especially those which occurred before you were four or five. Probably you will be able to recall few in any detail, if you can recall any at all. Many other experiences of childhood, adolescence, and even adulthood are beyond voluntary recall. Yet under hypnosis they could be recalled. This information, much of it not immediately necessary to solve today's problems, is stored in the id.

Memory traces of some of these experiences, which might help us solve problems, are stored in the ego, though even they are usually not conscious. A person may be surprised to find himself at home, having driven from work while preoccupied with a problem, without ever having noticed the turns, stop lights, or other cars. Obviously, he used many cues and did many specific things to get home safely, though he did so without being aware of what he was doing.

A final example illustrates the way the ego deals with impulses from the id. Suppose an attractive secretary comes to work in a new dress whose lines are calculated to stimulate the interest of men – in short, to stimulate the sexual impulse. When this impulse reaches the ego of one of the men in the office, the ego, acting within the limits set by the superego ("Look, but don't touch"), and its judgment of the consequences of giving vent to the impulse ("You'll destroy your reputation"), will control and refine the impulse. The man may then comment, "That's a pretty dress" – a highly attenuated derivative of the original impulse. Another man with a more rigid superego might never notice the dress. His superego would protect him by automatically prohibiting the ego from being sensitive to such a stimulus.

EGO'S ASSISTANTS

If the ego has the job of first balancing the forces from the id, the superego, and the environment, and then of mediating and synchronizing them into a system which operates relatively smoothly, it requires the assistance of two kinds of psychological devices to make its work possible. Thus:

1. It needs *anxiety* to serve as an alarm system to alert it to possible dangers to its equilibrium.
2. It must have *defense mechanisms* which can be called into play, triggered by the alarm system; these will help it either to fend off the possible threats or to counteract them.

Anxiety's purpose

The alarm-triggering system called anxiety is what we are conscious of whenever we are afraid of something. It is feeling of unease or tension. But there is a much more subtle and complex phenomenon of anxiety which operates spontaneously and unconsciously whenever the ego is threatened. Being unaware of its operation, we may not know consciously why we are restless, tense, or upset. Bob Lyons, we recall, was worried but he did not know why. We have all experienced his anxiety. A feeling of tension and restlessness that one person picks up from another is very common. Sensing that the other person is upset makes us feel uneasy for reasons which are not very clear to us. We do not consciously decide that we are threatened, but we feel we "can't relax," that we must be on guard.

Perhaps the work of unconscious anxiety may be likened to a gyroscope on a ship or an airplane. The gyroscope must sense the imbalance of the ship or plane as a result of waves, currents, or storms. It must then set into motion counteracting forces to regain the vehicle's balance. This analogy highlights something else for us: *There is no state of placid emotional stability, just as there is never a smooth ocean or an atmosphere devoid of air currents. There is no peace of mind short of the grave. Everyone is always engaged in maintaining his psychological equilibrium.* Even when a person is asleep, his dreaming is an effort to resolve psychological problems, to discharge tension, and to maintain sleep. The workings of unconscious anxiety may be seen in a number of different ways:

Suppose a three-year-old child, drinking milk from a glass, bites and shatters the edge of the glass. The glass cuts the child's lip, which bleeds profusely. Striving to remain calm, the mother places a compress under the lip and stops the bleeding. But she does not know whether the child has swallowed any of the glass and, therefore, what she should do next. She asks the child if he has swallowed glass. He says he has not. To be certain, she asks again, saying, "Please tell me if you have, because if you have, you might have a tummyache and we don't want you to have a tummyache." At this point the child says he has swallowed some glass. Now the mother does not know whether he has or has not.

Before the mother can decide that she had better take the child to the hospital, he begins to quiver as he might shake from the cold. This shaking is involuntary. Though the child has no conscious concept of the possible fatal danger of swallowing glass, and though the mother has tried to remain calm, unconsciously the child has sensed the inherent threat in the situation. Automatically, emergency physiological and biochemical processes are called into play to cope with the danger. It is the effects of these we see in the shaking. The manner and attitude of the hospital physician assure the child that there is no threat and gradually the shaking subsides.

Adults may have the same experience in many different ways. Suppose you are driving your car down the street and a youngster dashes out from between parked cars into the path of yours. You immediately slam on the brakes. For a moment you do not know whether you have hit the child. When you get out of the car, you see that you have not; but you find yourself shaking, your heart beating rapidly, your skin perspiring. You did not consciously cause any of these things to happen. The threat to your equilibrium, constituting a stress, aroused anxiety, which in turn mobilized your resources for dealing with the emergency. A similar experience is a commonplace among athletes. Some of them experience such psychological tension before competitive events that they cannot eat; if they do, they throw up.

Here we are speaking of conscious anxiety at one level. We are aware of certain threats and react to them. But at another, unconscious level, our reaction is disproportionate to the event. There is no objective reason for the driver to continue to be anxious when he discovers that he has not hit the child. The overt threat is past. Yet he may continue to shake for hours and may even dream about the event to the point of having nightmares. It is understandable that the athlete would want to win the game for conscious reasons. Why the competition should cause him such violent physical reaction is a more complex and obscure problem. He himself does not know why he must go to such extremes of defensive mobilization that his body cannot tolerate food. Unconscious anxiety is at work.

Ego defenses

If we are to penetrate deeply enough into Bob Lyons' reasons for suicide, we must go beyond admitting that he was undoubtedly anxious and under stress. We need to see why his ego was not sufficiently protected from such a completely destructive attack — why the defense mechanisms mentioned earlier as one of the ego's assistants did not enable him to overcome his anxiety.

There are a number of personality mechanisms which operate automatically to help the ego maintain or regain its equilibrium. These mechanisms may be viewed as falling into three broad classes:

(1) One group has to do with shaping or forming the personality. Included in this category is *identification,* the process of behaving like someone else. A man identifies himself with his boss when he dresses or speaks as his boss does. Women identify themselves with a leading movie star when they adopt her hair style. Another device, *introjection,* is a stronger form of identification, although the line between them is hazy. When one introjects the mannerisms or attitudes of another, he makes these firmly a part of himself. We speak of introjecting the values of the parents and thereby of becoming a "chip off the old block."

(2) Another group of mechanisms are universally used devices which are required to control, guide, refine, and channel the basic drives or impulses from the id. We have already talked about *repression.* Another mechanism, *sublimation,* is the process by which basic drives are refined and directed into acceptable channels. Lyons, for example, *sublimated* much of his aggressive drive in his work

(3) A third group of mechanisms is made up of temporary devices which are called into play automatically when there is some threat to the personality.

Denial a form of repression, is one of these devices, and can be clarified by an example.

Suppose a plant superintendent has five years to go to retirement and his boss suggests that he pick a successor and train him. But our plant superintendent does not select a successor, despite repeated requests from the boss. He cannot "hear" what the boss is saying. He may be forced to select such a man. When the time for retirement arrives, he may then say to his boss that the boss really did not intend to retire him. He cannot believe the boss will compel him to leave. This behavior reflects a denial of the reality of the situation because the ego has difficulty accepting what it regards to be a loss of love (status, esteem, etc.).

Rationalization is another temporary mechanism that all of us use from time to time. In fact, as the following example shows, it provides the subject matter for comedy!

A man's wife suggests that it is time to get a new car because theirs is already eight years old and getting shabby. At first, acting under the influence of the superego, the man doubts if he needs a new car. He cannot justify it to himself. To buy one without an adequate reason would be a waste of money for him. "You're too mature to be so extravagant and to fall for style," his superego says. The guilt aroused by the thought of buying a new car gives rise to anxiety, and the idea is rejected to appease the superego. The old car still runs well, he says; it gives no trouble, and a new one would be expensive. Soon we see him in an automobile showroom. "Just looking," he tells the salesman. "He thinks he's found a sucker," he chuckles to himself to avoid the condemnation of the superego. Next, however, he begins to complain to his wife and his friends that the old car will soon need repairs, that it will never be worth more on a trade-in. Before long he has developed a complete rationale for buying the new car, and has convinced himself to do so.

Projection, another temporary mechanism, is the process of attributing one's own feelings to someone else. If, for example, one can project hostility onto someone else ("He's mad at me; he's out to get me"), then one can justify to his superego his hostility toward the other person ("It's all right for me to get him first").

Idealization is the process of putting a halo around someone else and thereby being unable to see his faults. This process is seen most vividly in people who are in love or who have identified strongly with political leaders. It enhances the image of the idealized person as a source of strength and gratification.

Reaction formation is a formidable term for the process of doing the opposite of what one wants to do to avoid the threat of giving rein to impulses. Some people become so frightened of their own aggressive impulses that they act in an extremely meek and mild manner, avoiding all suggestion of aggression.

Another important mechanism is *substitution,* or displacement. This is the process in which the ego, unable to direct impulses to the appropriate target, directs them to a substitute target. In a benign way, this is what happens when a person devotes much of his affection to pets or to his work if, for whatever reasons, he does not have satisfactory ways of giving his affection to other people. More destructive displacement occurs when a person seeks substitute targets for his aggression. Unable to express his anger at his boss to the boss, a man may displace it onto the working conditions or wages. He may even unwittingly carry it home and criticize his wife or his children. This is the mechanism which is behind scapegoating and prejudice. Not only does displacement of this kind hurt others; worse yet, it doesn't contribute to the solution of the real problem.

Compensation is still another mechanism, and often a highly constructive one. This is the process of developing talents and skills to make up for one's deficiencies, or of undertaking activities and relationships to regain lost gratification. In certain respects, compensation and substitution are, of course, closely related.

THE DEFENSIVE PROCESS

These mechanisms need not be elaborated further here. Our answer to why Bob Lyons killed himself has necessarily been delayed long enough. Now we see the point, however. When the ego is threatened in some fashion, anxiety spontaneously and unconsciously triggers off mechanisms to counteract the threat. If there are too many emergencies for the personality, it may then overuse these mechanisms, and this in turn will seriously distort the person's view of reality, or cripple him psychologically. To identify with those one respects is fine; to imitate them slavishly is to lose one's individuality. It is one thing to rationalize occasionally, as we all do, but another to base judgments consistently on rationalizations. At times all of us project our own feelings, but we would be sick indeed if we felt most of the time that everyone else had it in for us.

By and large, self-fulfillment has to do with the ego's capacity to function as effectively as it can. When emotional conflicts can be diminished, when the need for defensiveness can be decreased, the energy which ordinarily maintained the defenses is freed for more useful activity. In a sense, the effect is to remove some of the brakes from the psychological wheels. Furthermore, when, as threats are removed, the defenses need no longer be used, one perceives reality more accurately. He then can relate to other people more reasonably and can communicate more clearly. A psychological blossoming-out can occur. When such balancing fails to take place, the ego is overwhelmed for the time being. In Bob Lyons' case, he acted to relieve his emotional pain and killed himself before equilibrium could be restored in a less destructive way. Since this balancing process is the ultimate key to an understanding of Lyons' act, let us make sure we understand how it works and then apply our knowledge directly to Bob Lyons' case:

Fusion of drives toward appropriate target. Suppose a man is called into his boss's office and his boss criticizes him harshly for something he did not do. The ideally healthy man, if he exists, will listen calmly to what his boss has to say and, in good control of his rising aggressive impulse, might well reply, "Boss, I'm sorry that such a mistake has happened. I had nothing to do with that particular activity, but perhaps I can help you figure out a way to keep the same mistake from happening again." His boss, also brimming with good mental health, might then respond, "I'm sorry that I criticized you unfairly. I would appreciate your giving me a hand on this." Together they direct their energies toward the solution of the problem.

Displacement to less appropriate target. But take a similar situation where, however, the man knows his boss will brook no contradiction or is so emotionally overwrought that there is little point in trying to be reasonable with him. This man may fume with anger at the unjust attack, but control his impulse to strike back at the boss. His reality-testing ego tells him that such action won't help the situation at all. He takes the criticism, anticipating a better solution when the boss cools off. Nevertheless, he is angry for being unjustly criticized, and there has been no opportunity to discharge his aroused aggressive impulse in an appropriate way toward the solution of the problem.

Because in this situation it seems so rational to control one's impulse (i.e., the boss is upset and there's no point in discussing it with him now), the ego finds this secondary anger an inappropriate feeling to allow into consciousness. The more primitive secondary anger is then repressed. When the employee goes bowling that night, he gets particular pleasure from knocking the pins down, without knowing why. Unconsciously he is using bowling to drain off his excess aggression. Such a displacement is a partially constructive way of discharging aggression: it hurts no one, it provides gratification. However, it does not contribute directly to resolving the problem itself, presuming that some further action toward solution might be required.

Containment of drives. Suppose that another man finds himself in the same situation. This man has learned in the course of growing up that it is not permissible to express one's aggression directly to authority figures. Being human, he has aggressive impulses, but also, having a severe superego, he feels guilty about them and goes to great lengths to repress them. When the boss criticizes him and his aggressive impulse is stimulated, repression automatically sets in and the impulse is controlled without his being aware of it. However, it is so controlled that he can't speak up to contribute to the solution of the problem.

Because this man constantly maintains a high degree of control to meet the demands of his superego, he is already in a potentially more explosive situation, ready to defend himself from the slightest possible threat. If he has to contain more of his anger within himself, we have a situation which is much like rising steam pressure in a boiler. If this situation is repetitive or chronic, the mobilization and remobilization of defenses almost requires of the ego that it be in a steady emergency state. The alarm bells are ringing most of the time. This kind of reaction strains the ego's resources and is particularly wearing physiologically because each psychological response to stress is accompanied by physiological mobilization, too.

The result is psychosomatic symptoms. The body is literally damaged by its own fluids, leading to ulcers, hypertension, and similar phenomena. This experience is commonly recognized in the phrase, "stewing in one's own juice," Clinical data seem to show that there are reasons why one particular organ is the site for a psychosomatic symptom, but often these reasons are obscure.

Displacement onto the self.   Take still another man. This one also has learned that aggression should not be expressed to others, and he cannot do so without feelings of guilt. In fact, his superego won't tolerate much hostility on his part, so he lives constantly with feelings of guilt. The guilt, in turn, makes him feel inadequate as his superego repeatedly berates him for his hostility. No matter how nice, by means of reaction formation, he may try to be, he can't satisfy his superego. Somehow, he himself always seems to be at fault. With such a rigid, punitive superego, this man under the same kind of attack may then respond by saying, "I guess you're right. I'm always wrong; it's my fault. I never seem to do things right." He may also then have a mild depression. Depression is always an indication of anger with one's self, originating from anger toward another, and reflects the attack of the superego on the ego. The aggression is displaced from the appropriate target back onto the self and results in a form of self-blame and self-punishment.

Another form of self-attack or self-punishment is seen in many accidents. Most accidents are not actually accidents in the sense that they occur by chance, but are unconscious modes of self-punishment. The "forgetting" to turn the motor switch off before repairing the machine or not seeing or hearing possible threats frequently are indications that denial or repression has been operating in order to permit the person to hurt himself to appease his own superego. In extreme form, this self-directed aggression is the mechanism behind suicide, and now we are prepared to see what happened to Bob Lyons.

THE REASON WHY

Driven by an extremely severe superego, Bob Lyons sublimated his drives successfully in his work as long as he could work hard. There was an ego-superego-id environment equilibrium, although only a tenuous one. By driving himself, he could appease the relentless pressure of his superego.

Such a superego, however, is never satisfied. Its demands arise from unconscious sources, which, because they are unconscious, probably have existed from early childhood and are to a large extent irrational. If they were not irrational, their terms could be met.

Whenever he reached a goal toward which he had aspired, Lyons got no satisfaction from it, for his superego still drove him. And when he could no longer work as hard as he had, this for him was an environmental deprivation. He could no longer earn love by performing well. His superego became more relentless. The vacation, with no demands on him at all, simply added to his guilt, his feelings of unworthiness and inadequacy. With sublimations and displacements reduced, given the kind of superego he had, his aggressive drive had only his ego as a major target.

And at that moment, the only way that Bob Lyons knew to appease his superego was to kill himself.

Had his superego been developed differently, Lyons might have achieved as he did because of ego reasons (the pleasure and gratification he got from his work); with a mild assist from the superego to do well. When his superego developed so strongly, probably because of a heavy burden of hostility in childhood for which he felt irrationally guilty for a lifetime, there was no real pleasure in what he did and nothing more than temporary gratification. The relentless driving of himself was a form of self-sacrifice, just as are alcoholism, most accidents, repeated failures on the job, presenting the worst side of one's self to others, and some forms of crime.

We should recognize that there is a bit of this phenomenon in all of us, just as we can see something of ourselves at times in each of the preceding three examples. The ancient observation that "man is his own worst enemy" is testimony to the self-destructive potential in each person. Bob Lyons differed from the rest of us only in degree, and only because of a combination of forces at a given point which precipitated his death. A change in any single force might conceivably have prevented it: more and harder work, psychiatric treatment, no vacation to add to the feelings of guilt and uselessness or open recognition by his physician of the seriousness of mental illness.

Groping for shadows

But how would his physician or his friends have recognized early symptions of Bob Lyons' illness? It would not have been easy. We cannot put an ego under a microscope or locate the id in any part of the body. These are simply names given to what seem to be systems of forces operating in the personality. We cannot see repression — it is only a name for the observation that some things are forgotten and can be recalled only under certain circumstances. The same is true when we speak of something being unconscious. It is not relegated to a given physical organ or place. One is merely not able to call it into consciousness.

If the ego has a constant balancing task and calls certain mechanisms into play to carry it out, being concerned with psychological economy, the ego will develop preferred mechanisms, preferred because they work best consistently. These become the established personality traits. As individuals we make our preferred modes of adjustment those ways of behaving which are most comfortable (least anxiety-arousing) to us.

The consistent modes of adjustment, the personality traits, become the hallmarks by which we are known to others. Even physical styles of behavior become part of this system. If we hear on the telephone a voice that we recognize, we can place it with a name. If we meet a friend we have not seen in ten years, we will observe that he seems to be the same as he always was — he talks, reacts, thinks in much the same way. Some are hail-fellow-well-met gregarious types, others more diffident and conservative. Each has his own preferred modes of adjustment, his preferred way of consistently maintaining equilibrium.

Given these entrenched modes of adaptation, even clinical psychologists and psychiatrists are unlikely to make radical changes in people, although they can often help alter certain forces so that people can behave more healthily than they did previously. The alteration of internal forces (ego-superego-id) is the job of the clinician. The layman often can make a contribution to the alteration of external forces (ego-environment). Even minor changes of the balance of forces can make significant differences in how people feel, think, and behave.

The very fact that people do not radically change their styles of behavior makes it possible to detect signs of emotional stress. Given certain characteristic modes of adaptation in the form of personality traits, once a person experiences some kind of emotional stress, he is likely first to make greater use of those mechanisms which worked best for him before. The first sign of stress is that a person seems to be conspicuously more like he always was. If he ordinarily is a quiet man, under stress he may become withdrawn. If he is like Lyons, his first reaction may well be to try to work harder.

Secondly, if this first line of defense does not work too well (or if the stress is too severe or chronic for that method alone), we will begin to see the appearance of inefficient functioning — vague fears, inability to concentrate, compulsions to do certain things, increasing irritability, and declining work performance. We will also see the results of physiological defensive efforts. We saw in Lyons' case that tension, jitteriness, and inability to hold food or to sleep all accompanied his psychological stress. The whole organism — physiological and psychological — was involved in the struggle.

Psychological and physiological symptoms are ways of "binding" or attempting to control the anxiety. They are ways of trying to do something about a problem, however ineffective they may be. And they are the best ways of dealing with that problem that the person has available to him at the moment, though better ways of coping may be apparent to others who do not have his psychological makeup. That's why it is dangerous to try to remove symptoms. Instead, it is wiser to resolve the underlying problem.

Thirdly, if neither of these types of defenses can contain the anxiety, we may see sharp changes in personality. The person no longer behaves as he did before. Lyons felt himself to be falling apart, unable to work as he did previously. A neat person may become slovenly, an efficient one alcoholic. Radical changes in personality indicate severe illness which usually requires hospitalization.

Conspicuous change in behavior indicates that the ego is no longer able to maintain effective control. If a person is so upset that he hears voices or sees things which do not exist, previously unconscious thoughts and feelings are breaking through. Obviously irrational behavior indicates the same thing. There is a loss of contact with reality, seriously impaired judgment, and an inability to be responsible for oneself. In such a state, Bob Lyons committed suicide.

CONCLUSION

Now that we *think* we understand why Bob Lyons killed himself, it is important that two cautions be raised.

About ourselves

First, the reader newly exposed to psychoanalytic theory invariably falls victim to what may be called the freshman medical student's syndrome: he gets every symptom in the book. Everything to which this article refers, the average reader will be able to see in himself. As we were discussing Lyons, we were talking about human beings and human motivation; so it was inevitable that we ended up talking about ourselves. We must recognize this tendency to read ourselves into these pages, and compensate for this by consciously trying to maintain an objective distance from the materials.

At the same time, does this very experience not make it clear to us that everyone has the continuing task of maintaining an equilibrium? At any given time any one of us may be listing to starboard a little, or trying to keep from being buffeted about by a sudden storm. Despite these pressures, we must nevertheless move forward, correcting for the list as best we can, or conserving our strength to ride out the storm. Each will defend himself the best way he knows how. As he does so, the more energy he must devote to defense, the less he will have available for forward movement.

Each of us at one time or another, therefore, will be emotionally disturbed or upset. For a few hours, a few days, a few weeks, we may be irritable or angry ("I got up on the wrong side of the bed"), or blue ("I'm feeling low today"), or hypersensitive. When we feel these ways, when we are having difficulty maintaining an equilibrium, for that brief period of time we are emotionally disturbed. We cannot work as well as we usually do. It is more difficult for us to sustain our relationships with other people. We may feel hopeless or helpless. We're just not ourselves.

But just because we are mildly emotionally disturbed does not mean we need professional help or hospitalization. A cold is a minor form of upper respiratory infection, the extreme of which is pneumonia. If one has a cold, that does not mean he will have pneumonia. Even if he does get pneumonia, with present treatment methods most people recover, and the same is true of mental illness. The difference between the mild and the severe is one of degree, not of kind. It is just more of the same thing.

Because each of us is human and no one of us has had either perfect heredity or perfect environment, each of us has his weak spots. When the balance of forces is such that there is stress where we are weak, we will have difficulty. The incidence of mental illness, then, is not one out of twenty or some other proportionate statistic. Rather it is one out of one!

What we can do

The second caution has to do with the limitations of this exposition and the reader's preparation for understanding it. This necessarily has been a highly condensed version of some aspects of psychoanalytic theory. Many important aspects of the theory have been omitted and others have been presented without the many qualifications a serious scientific presentation would require. The reader should therefore look upon what is presented only as an introduction to better understanding of problems. He should be careful about overgeneralization and should studiously avoid using jargon or interpreting people's behavior to them.

Unless he observes these limitations, the layman will be unable to help anyone. Within these limitations, however, a businessman can render extremely important help to others in his company – and to himself. Specifically, he can recognize that:

- *All* behavior is motivated, much of it by thoughts and feelings of which the person himself is not aware. Behavior does not occur by chance.
- At any one time each person is doing the best he can, as a result of the multiple forces which bring about any given behavior. A change in the forces is required to bring about a change in behavior.
- Love neutralizes aggression and diminishes hostility. "A soft word turneth away wrath," says the old aphorism. This does not mean maudlin expressions, but actions which reflect esteem and regard for the other person as a human being. The most useful demonstration of affection is support which takes the form of:

– *Understanding* that the pain of emotional distress is real. It will not go away by wishing it away, by dismissing it as "all in your head," or by urging the person to "forget it," "snap out of it," or to "take a vacation."

– *Listening* if the person brings his problem to you, or if it so impairs his work that you must call his work performance to his attention. Listening permits him to define his problem more clearly and thereby to examine courses of action. Acting constructively to solve a problem is the best way the ego has to maintain the fusion of drives in dealing with reality. Listening, by providing some relief for the distressed person, already brings about some alteration in the balance of forces.

If you listen, however, you must clearly recognize your limitations: (1) you can offer only emergency help; (2) you cannot hold yourself *responsible* for other people's personal problems, some of which would defy the most competent specialist.

– *Referring* the troubled person to professional sources of help if the problem is more than a temporary one, or if the person is severely upset. Every organization should have channels for referral. If a person who has responsibility for other people has no formal organizational channels for referral, he would do well to establish contact with a psychiatrist, a clinical psychologist, or a community mental health agency. He will then have professional sources of guidance available when problems arise.

Finally, we can maintain a watchful, but nor morbid, eye on ourselves. If we find that we are having difficulties which interfere with our work or with gratifying relationships with other people, then we should be wise enough to seek professional help.

STRIFE OVER HAIR: THE HISTORICAL ROOTS*

Elliot Carlson

A list of the wedges that have steadily widened the generation gap might run like this: The Vietnam war, racial violence, environmental pollution, the drug problem and — often the most acrimonious of all — the length of hair.

Long hair — whether flowing, gnarled or matted — has obviously somehow performed a vital function in the New Left and Hippie movements. To dissidents an abundant shag and/or beards and sideburns apparently express both a commitment to a more freewheeling life style and an alienation from their closely-cropped elders. It is even celebrated in the younger generation's songs: In "Hair," from the rock musical of the same name, a tribe of pop revolutionaries intone, "Flow it, show it, long as God can grow it, my hair."

Oldsters, on the other hand, have clearly been repelled by the spectacle, often viewing in luxuriant locks the breakdown of the moral order. The other day, in fact, the Cook County jailer ordered shears taken to the turbulent thatches of the Chicago Seven (minus balding David Dellinger). The move stirred a frightful anguish in Messrs. Abbie Hoffman, Jerry Rubin, Tom Hayden and all, but it seems that members of the "silent majority" applauded.

Frivolous as a logical mind will find it, this preoccupation with hair is no modern development, but has deep historical roots. In all ages men have worried about their hair, and most of all during revolutions and times of political turmoil. Historically, political outs have displayed unhappiness with ruling orders by departing from approved hair styles.

To take a leading example: Perhaps in no struggle were the forces of long and short hair so violently joined as during the 17th Century civil war in England that pitted Cavaliers against Roundheads. Quite literally, contending parties were identified in terms of their haircuts.

The Cavaliers — royalist supporters of King Charles I — wore ringlets that cascaded down the back. One ringlet, known as a lovelock, was worn carelessly over one shoulder and tied with a ribbon bow. They referred derisively to their adversaries—the parliamentary forces of Oliver Cromwell—as Roundheads, so named because of the pudding-basin cut they affected.

Composed largely of Puritans, Roundhead forces tended to see long hair as a source of vice. Meantime, Cavaliers imagined their opponents as

*Reprinted with permission from *The Wall Street Journal*, April 23, 1970, p. 18.

destitute of wit as they were of hair. "A man's locks were the symbol of his creed, both in politics and religion." wrote Charles MacKay in his 1841 book, "Extraordinary Popular Delusions and the Madness of Crowds." He observed, "The more abundant the hair, the more scant the faith; and the balder the head, the more sincere the piety."

Another example comes from even earlier in English history. The 11th Century Norman conquerors of England wore their hair very short. Humiliated by their defeat, the conquered Saxons encouraged the growth of long hair so that they might resemble as little as possible their cropped masters.

Sometimes revolutionaries seem motivated in hair design less by idealism than by a desire to win the adulation of faddish crowds. A case in point would seem to be provided by Jean-Paul Marat, the French revolutionist who edited the rambunctious newspaper, "The People's Friend."

Once a respectable gentleman, Marat early in the revolution gave up his luxurious tastes to become an early-day variant of the Hippie. He dressed in beggar's rags and shunned soap. From then on, wherever he went he brought with him a shaggy thatch, a week's growth of beard and the smell of sweat. Suddenly he found himself a kind of culture hero. In his biography of Danton, Robert Christophe writes: "Marat became all the rage, a nine days' wonder, so that when the storm broke he found himself a leader of the new revolutionary fashion."

On occasion this foppery yielded practical benefits. Once Marat escaped a police cordon set up outside his apartment building by shaving, washing and outfitting himself in a clean frock coat and hat. Thus disguised, he was able to pass unnoticed through the barricade.

Jean-Paul Marat and Abbie Hoffman to the contrary, long hair has not always marked the political outs. Indeed, long hair was the symbol of sovereignty in ancient Rome and medieval Europe. The Caesars took their name from their long hair (Caesaries). And French kings from the Sixth to Ninth Centuries wore their hair long and curled.

THE OPPOSING FASHION

So the sign of protest — long hair or short — has been the opposite of whichever was prevailing fashion of the time. Marat's unkempt bush contrasted with both the Bourbons' well-trained tresses and the bourgeoisie's prim style. But during the Cromwell-led insurgency in England, and with Savonarola's reform movement in Renaissance Florence, rebels clipped their hair short.

It does seem to be true, though, that bushy heads have mostly been favored by voluptuaries or forces considered worldly-minded, while cropped hair has been fancied by groups tending to be puritanical or morally censorious. Priests have regularly declaimed against the evils of long hair: toward the end of the 11th Century, the Pope decreed that persons wearing long hair should be excommunicated, and not prayed for when dead.

The famous St. Wulstan, the Bishop of Worcester, was particularly incensed whenever he saw a man in long hair. In fact, he often carried in his pocket a small knife that he used on long-haired persons kneeling before him to receive the blessing. The good Bishop would whip the knife out slyly, cut off a handful of hair and then bid the startled fellow to finish the job or go to hell.

Such antics have never been a peculiarity limited solely to Western civilization. Orientals have surrendered to a similar weakness. Thus, the unsuccessful Taiping revolt against the Manchu Dynasty in China was known as the Long-Haired Rebellion. The revolt was so named because rebels, among other things, refused to shave the front of their heads as prescribed by the hated Manchus. (The Manchus really had few complaints on these grounds, since it was they who imposed the pigtail on the Chinese after conquering the country in 1644.)

Why hair should have such powerful significance has long bemused pedants. Freudian analysts, for example, insist hair is fraught with symbolic and obscure emotional meanings. One, Charles Berg, has written a whole book, "The Unconscious Significance of Hair." He suggests, among other things, that in pruning their locks Cromwell's men were guilty of symbolic self-castration. Freudians generally aver that hair styles change when issues of sexual morality get wrapped up with political events.

Sociologist Lewis Feuer, on the other hand, thinks historical hair styles relate to discipline and the Protestant ethic of efficiency and cleanliness. He says the Roundheads represented the rising middle class, and their short hair expressed contempt for the luxurious ways of the upper classes. Similarly, Lenin was nearly bald at 21 and so severe in his life-style that colleagues referred to him as "the old man" when he was 24. Mr. Feuer comments, "He fretted that Russian intellectuals had always been sloppy and flabby and perpetual failures at whatever they tried. He decided discipline was needed, so he turned to the virtues of the Protestant ethic."

"Protesters today are against the virtues associated with the Protestant ethic," continues Mr. Feuer, once a target of "free-speech" rebels at Berkeley and author of the 1969 book, "The Conflict of Generations." He notes that today the outs try to look "as uncouth as possible," and adds, "This way rebels believe they're striking at the very roots of our industrial society — and undermining the virtues on which it depends."

FRIGHTENING THE ENEMY

Other explanations abound in history. The Chetniks, a 19th Century band of Serbian rebels, grew ferocious beards on the quaint grounds that such displays, as one Yugoslav writer put it, "Strike terror into the heart of the enemy." And Alexander the Great, worried that beards would provide the enemy with convenient handles, ordered his army to be closely shaven.

Ultimately the length of hair has mattered little, since polarization over hair has seldom outlived any given rebellion. A few years after the French revolution had run its course Marat's bushy head was forgotten and Parisian pleasure-seekers were again wearing their hair cut short. Even today, the newest rebels are the Skinheads, a gang of closely cropped toughs in England who pick fights with Hippies and motorcycle gangs and disdain bellbottom trousers and other trappings of youthful affluence. And the other day the Beatles' John Lennon inexplicably sheared his once-prodigious mop in a manner that would have pleased the most neatly-trimmed youth of the 1950's.

It's quite unlikely, of course, that recent clippings given Mr. Lennon, or Mr. Hoffman and the rest, will have much effect on their behavior. But that probably won't stop either the revolutionaries or the multitudes from worrying about the length of other people's locks. History seems to teach that, frivolous or not, preoccupation with hair is an enduring human foible.

ORGANIZATIONAL SOCIALIZATION AND THE PROFESSION OF MANAGEMENT*

Edgar H. Schein

Some basic elements of organizational socialization. The term socialization has a fairly clear meaning in sociology, but it has been a difficult one to assimilate in the behavioral sciences and in management. To many of my colleagues it implies unnecessary jargon, and to many of my business acquaintances it implies the teaching of socialism — a kiss of death for the concept right there. Yet the concept is most useful because it focuses clearly on the interaction between a stable social system and the new members who enter it. The concept refers to the process by which a new member learns the value system, the norms, and the required behavior patterns of the society, organization, or group which he is entering. It does not include all learning. It includes only the learning of those values, norms, and behavior patterns which, from the organization's point of view or group's point of view, it is necessary for any new member to learn. This learning is defined as the price of membership.

What are such values, norms, and behavior patterns all about? Usually they involve:

1. The basic *goals* of the organization.
2. The preferred *means* by which these goals should be attained.
3. The basic *responsibilities* of the member in the role which is being granted to him by the organization.
4. The *behavior patterns* which are required for effective performance in the role.
5. A set of rules or principles which pertain to the *maintenance of the identity and integrity* of the organization.

The new member must learn not to drive Chevrolets if he is working for Ford, not to criticize the organization in public, not to wear the wrong kind of clothes or be seen in the wrong kinds of places. If the organization is a school, beyond learning the content of what is taught, the student must accept the value of education, he must try to learn without cheating, he must accept the authority of the faculty and behave appropriately to the student role. He must not be rude in the classroom or openly disrespectful to the professor.

*Reprinted with permission from *Industrial Management Review*, Winter, 1968.

By what processes does the novice learn the required values and norms? The answer to this question depends in part upon the degree of prior socialization. If the novice has correctly anticipated the norms of the organization he is joining, the socialization process merely involves a reaffirmation of these norms through various communication channels, the personal example of key people in the organization, and direct instructions from supervisors, trainers, and informal coaches.

If, however, the novice comes to the organization with values and behavior patterns which are in varying degrees out of line with those expected by the organization, then the socialization process first involves a destructive or unfreezing phase. This phase serves the function of detaching the person from his former values, of proving to him that his present self is worthless from the point of view of the organization and that he must redefine himself in terms of the new roles which he is to be granted.

The extremes of this process can be seen in initiation rites or novitiates for religious orders. When the novice enters his training period, his old self is symbolically destroyed by loss of clothing, name, often his hair, titles and other self-defining equipment. These are replaced with uniforms, new names and titles, and other self-defining equipment consonant with the role he is being trained for.

It may be comforting to think of activities like this as being characteristic only of primitive tribes or total institutions like military basic training camps, academies, and religious orders. But even a little examination of areas closer to home will reveal the same processes both in our graduate schools and in the business organizations to which our graduates go.

Perhaps the commonest version of the process in school is the imposition of a tight schedule, of an impossibly heavy reading program, and of the assignment of problems which are likely to be too difficult for the student to solve. Whether these techniques are deliberate or not they serve effectively to remind the student that he is not as smart or capable as he may have thought he was, and therefore, that there are still things to be learned. As our Sloan Fellows tell us every year, the first summer in the program pretty well destroys many aspects of their self-image. Homework in statistics appears to enjoy a unique status comparable to having one's head shaved and clothes burned.

Studies of medical schools and our own observations of the Sloan program suggest that the work overload on students leads to the development of a peer culture, a kind of banding together of the students as a defense against the threatening faculty and as a problem-solving device to develop norms of what and how to study. If the group solutions which are developed support the organizational norms, the peer group becomes an effective instrument of socialization. However, from the school's point of view, there is the risk that peer group norms will set up counter-socializing forces and sow the seeds of sabotage, rebellion, or revolution. The positive gains of a supportive peer group generally make it worth while to run the risks of rebellion, however, which usually motivates the organization to encourage or actually to facilitate peer group formation.

Many of our Sloan Fellow alumni tell us that one of the most powerful features of the Sloan program is the fact that a group of some 40 men share the same fate of being put through a very tough educational regimen. The peer group ties formed during the year have proven to be one of the most durable end-results of the educational program and, of course, are one of the key supports to the maintaining of some of the values and attitudes learned in school. The power of this kind of socializing force can be appreciated best by pondering a further statement which many alumni have made. They stated that prior to the program they identified themselves primarily with their company. Following the program they identified themselves primarily with the other Sloan Fellows, and such identification has lasted, as far as we can tell, for the rest of their career.

Let me next illustrate the industrial counterpart of these processes. Many of my panel members, when interviewed about the first six months in their new jobs, told stories of what we finally labeled as "upending experiences." Upending experiences are deliberately planned or accidentally created circumstances which dramatically and unequivocally upset or disconfirm some of the major assumptions which the new man holds about himself, his company, or his job.

One class of such experiences is to receive assignments which are so easy or so trivial that they carry the clear message that the new man is not worthy of being given anything important to do. Another class of such experiences is at the other extreme — assignments which are so difficult that failure is a certainty, thus proving unequivocally to the new man that he may not be as smart as he thought he was. Giving work which is clearly for practice only, asking for reports which are then unread or not acted upon, protracted periods of training during which the person observes others work, all have the same upending effect.

The most vivid example came from an engineering company where a supervisor had a conscious and deliberate strategy for dealing with what he considered to be unwarranted arrogance on the part of engineers whom they hired. He asked each new man to examine and diagnose a particular complex circuit, which happened to violate a number of textbook principles but actually worked very well. The new man would usually announce with confidence, even after an invitation to double-check, that the circuit could not possibly work. At this point the manager would demonstrate the circuit, tell the new man that they had been selling it for several years without customer complaint, and demand that the new man figure out why it did work. None of the men so far tested were able to do it, but all of them were thoroughly chastened and came to the manager anxious to learn where their knowledge was inadequate and needed supplementing. According to this manager, it was much easier from this point on to establish a good give-and-take relationship with his new man.

It should be noted that the success of such socializing techniques depends upon two factors which are not always under the control of the organization. The first factor is the initial motivation of the entrant to join the organization. If his motivation is high, as in the case of a fraternity pledge, he will tolerate all kinds of uncomfortable socialization experiences, even to extremes of hell week. If his motivation for membership is low, he may well decide to leave the organization rather than tolerate uncomfortable initiation rites. If he leaves, the socialization process has obviously failed.

The second factor is the degree to which the organization can hold the new member captive during the period of socialization. His motivation is obviously one element here, but one finds organizations using other forces as well. In the case of basic training there are legal forces to remain. In the case of many schools one must pay one's tuition in advance, in other words, invest one's self materially so that leaving the system becomes expensive. In the case of religious orders one must make strong initial psychological commitments in the form of vows and the severing of relationships outside the religious order. The situation is defined as one in which one will lose face or be humiliated if one leaves the organization.

In the case of business organizations the pressures are more subtle but nevertheless identifiable. New members are encouraged to get financially committed by joining pension plans, stock option plans, and/or house purchasing plans which would mean material loss if the person decided to leave. Even more subtle is the reminder by the boss that it takes a year or so to learn any new business; therefore, if you leave, you will have to start all over again. Why not suffer it out with the hope that things will look more rosy once the initiation period is over.

Several of my panel members told me at the end of one year at work that they were quite dissatisfied, but were not sure they should leave because they had invested a year of learning in that company. Usually their boss encouraged them to think about staying. Whether or not such pressures will work depends, of course, on the labor market and other factors not under the control of the organization.

Let me summarize thus far. Organizations socialize their new members by creating a series of events which serve the function of undoing old values so that the person will be prepared to learn the new values. This process of undoing or unfreezing is often unpleasant and therefore requires either strong motivation to endure it or strong organizational forces to make the person endure it. The formation of a peer group of novices is often a solution to the problem of defense against the powerful organization, and, at the same time, can strongly enhance the socialization process if peer group norms support organizational norms.

Let us look next at the positive side of the socialization process. Given some readiness to learn, how does the novice acquire his new learning? The answer is that he acquires it from multiple sources — the official literature of the organization; the example set by key models in the organization; the instructions given to him directly by his trainer, coach, or boss; the example of peers who have been in the organization longer and thus serve as big brothers; the rewards and punishments which result from his own efforts at problem solving and experimenting with new values and new behavior.

The instructions and guidelines given by senior members of the organization are probably one of the most potent sources. I can illustrate this point best by recalling several incidents from my own socialization into the Sloan School back in 1956. I came here at the invitation of Doug McGregor from a research job. I had no prior teaching experience or knowledge of organizational or managerial matters. Contrary to my expectations, I was told by Doug that knowledge of organizational psychology and management was not important, but that some interest in learning about these matters was.

The first socializing incident occurred in an initial interview with Elting Morison, who was then on our faculty. He said in a completely blunt manner that if I knew what I wanted to do and could go ahead on my own, the Sloan School would be a great place to be. If I wasn't sure and would look to others for guidance, not to bother to come.

The second incident occurred in a conversation with our then Dean, Penn Brooks, a few weeks before the opening of the semester. We were discussing what and how I might teach. Penn said to me that he basically wanted each of his faculty members to find his own approach to management education. I could do whatever I wanted — so long as I did not imitate our sister school up the river. Case discussion leaders need not apply, was the clear message.

The third incident (you see I was a slow learner) occurred a few days later when I was planning my subject in social psychology for our Master's students. I was quite nervous about it and unsure of how to decide what to include in the subject. I went to Doug and innocently asked him to lend me outlines of previous versions of the subject, which had been taught by Alex Bavelas, or at least to give me some advice on what to include and exclude. Doug was very nice and very patient, but also quite firm in his refusal to give me either outlines or advice. He thought there was really no need to rely on history, and expressed confidence that I could probably make up my own mind. I suffered that term but learned a good deal about the value system of the Sloan School, as well as how to organize a subject. I was, in fact, so well socialized by these early experiences that nowadays no one can get me to coordinate anything with anybody else.

Similar kinds of lessons can be learned during the course of training programs, in orientation sessions, and through company literature. But the more subtle kinds of values which the organization holds, which indeed may not even be well understood by the senior people, are often communicated through peers operating as helpful big brothers. They can communicate the subtleties of how the boss wants things done, how higher management feels about things, the kinds of things which are considered heroic in the organization, the kinds of things which are taboo.

Of course, sometimes the values of the immediate group into which a new person is hired are partially out of line with the value system of the organization as a whole. If this is the case, the person will learn the immediate group's values much more quickly than those of the total organization, often to the chagrin of the higher levels of management

This is best exemplified at the level of hourly workers where fellow employees will have much more socializing power than the boss.

An interesting managerial example of this conflict was provided by one recent graduate who was hired into a group whose purpose was to develop cost reduction systems for a large manufacturing operation. His colleagues on the job, however, showed him how to pad his expense account whenever they traveled together. The end result of this kind of conflict was to accept neither the cost reduction values of the company nor the cost inflation values of the peer group. The man left the company in disgust to start up some businesses of his own.

One of the important functions of organizational socialization is to build commitment and loyalty to the organization. How is this accomplished? One mechanism is to invest much effort and time in the new member and thereby build up expectations of being repaid by loyalty, hard work, and rapid learning. Another mechanism is to get the new member to make a series of small behavioral commitments which can only be justified by him through the acceptance and incorporation of company values. He then becomes his own agent of socialization. Both mechanisms involve the subtle manipulation of guilt.

To illustrate the first mechanism, one of our graduates went to a public relations firm which made it clear to him that he had sufficient knowledge and skill to advance, but that his values and attitudes would have to be evaluated for a couple of years before he would be fully accepted. During the first several months he was frequently invited to join high ranking members of the organization at their luncheon meetings in order to learn more about how they thought about things. He was so flattered by the amount of time they spent on him, that he worked extra hard to learn their values and became highly committed to the organization. He said that he would have felt guilty at the thought of not learning or of leaving the company. Sending people to expensive training programs, giving them extra perquisites, indeed the whole philosophy of paternalism, is built on the assumption that if you invest in the employee he will repay the company with loyalty and hard work. He would feel guilty if he did not.

The second mechanism, that of getting behavioral commitments, was beautifully illustrated in Communist techniques of coercive persuasion. The Communists made tremendous efforts to elicit a public confession from a prisoner. One of the key functions of such a public confession, even if the prisoner knew he was making a false confession, was that it committed him publicly. Once he made this commitment, he found himself under strong internal and external pressure to justify why he had confessed. For many people it proved easier to justify the confession by coming to believe in their own crimes than to have to face the fact that they were too weak to withstand the captor's pressure.

In organizations, a similar effect can be achieved by promoting a rebellious person into a position of responsibility. The same values which the new member may have criticized and jeered at from his position at the bottom of the hierarchy suddenly look different when he has subordinates of his own whose commitment he must obtain.

Many of my panel members had very strong moral and ethical standards when they first went to work, and these stood up quite well during their first year at work even in the face of less ethical practices by their peers and superiors. But they reported with considerable shock that some of the practices they had condemned in their bosses were quickly adopted by them once they had themselves been promoted and faced the pressures of the new position. As one man put it very poignantly — "my ethical standards changed so gradually over the first five years of work that I hardly noticed it, but it was a great shock to suddenly realize what my feelings had been five years ago and how much they had changed."

Another version of obtaining commitment is to gain the new member's acceptance of very general ideals like "one must work for the good of the company," or "one must meet the competition." Whenever any counter-organizational behavior occurs one can then point out that the ideal is being violated. The engineer who does not come to work on time is reminded that his behavior indicates lack of concern for the good of the company. The employee who wears the wrong kind of clothes, lives in the wrong neighborhood, or associates with the wrong people can be reminded that he is hurting the company image.

One of my panel members on a product research assignment discovered that an additive which was approved by the Food and Drug Administration might in fact be harmful to consumers. He was strongly encouraged to forget about it. His boss told him that it was the F.D.A.'s problem. If the company worried about things like that it might force prices up and thus make it tough to meet the competition.

Many of the upending experiences which new members of organizations endure are justified to them by the unarguable ideal that they should learn how the company really works before expecting a position of real responsibility. Once the new man accepts this ideal it serves to justify all kinds of training and quantities of menial work which others who have been around longer are unwilling to do themselves. This practice is known as "learning the business from the ground up," or "I had to do it when I first joined the company, now it's someone else's turn." There are clear elements of hazing involved not too different from those associated with fraternity initiations and other rites of passage.

The final mechanism to be noted in a socialization process is the transition to full fledged member. The purpose of such transitional events is to help the new member incorporate his new values, attitudes, and norms into his identity so that they become part of him, not merely something to which he pays lip-service. Initiation rites which involve severe tests of the novice serve to prove to him that he is capable of fulfilling the new role — that he now is a man, no longer merely a boy.

Organizations usually signal this transition by giving the new man some important responsibility or a position of power which, if mishandled or misused, could genuinely hurt the organization. With this transition often come titles, symbols of status, extra rights or prerogatives, sharing of confidential information or other things which in one way or another indicate that the new member has earned the trust of the organization. Although such events may not always be visible to the outside observer, they are felt strongly by the new member. He knows when he has finally "been accepted," and feels it when he becomes "identified with the company."

So much for examples of the process of socialization. Let us now look at some of the dilemmas and conflicts which arise within it.

Failures of socialization — non-conformity and over-conformity. Most organizations attach differing amounts of importance to different norms and values. Some are *pivotal.* Any member of a business organization who does not believe in the value of getting a job done will not survive long. Other pivotal values in most business organizations might be belief in a reasonable profit, belief in the free enterprise system and competition, belief in a hierarchy of authority as a good way to get things done, and so on.

Other values or norms are what may be called *relevant.* These are norms which it is not absolutely necessary to accept as the price of membership, but which are considered desirable and good to accept. Many of these norms pertain to standards of dress and decorum, not being publicly disloyal to the company, living in the right neighborhood and belonging to the right political party and clubs. In some organizations some of these norms may be pivotal. Organizations vary in this regard. You all know the stereotype of IBM as a company that requires the wearing of white shirts and hats. In some parts of IBM such values are indeed pivotal; in other parts they are only relevant, and in some parts they are quite peripheral. The point is that not all norms to which the new member is exposed are equally important for the organization.

The socialization process operates across the whole range of norms, but the amount of reward and punishment for compliance or non-compliance will vary with the importance of the norm. This variation allows the new member some degrees of freedom in terms of how far to conform and allows the organization some degrees of freedom in how much conformity to demand. The new man can accept none of the values, he can accept only the pivotal values, but carefully remain independent on all those areas not seen as pivotal, or he can accept the whole range of values and norms. He can tune in so completely on what he sees to be the way others are handling themselves that he becomes a carbon-copy and sometimes a caricature of them.

These basic responses to socialization can be labeled as follows:

Type 1 Rebellion
    Rejection of all values and norms
Type 2 Creative individualism
    Acceptance only of pivotal values and norms; rejection of all others

Type 3   Conformity
Acceptance of all values and norms

Most analyses of conformity deal only with the type 1 and 3 cases, failing to note that both can be viewed as socialization failures. The rebellious individual either is expelled from the organization or turns his energies toward defeating its goals. The conforming individual curbs his creativity and thereby moves the organization toward a sterile form of bureaucracy. The trick for most organizations is to create the type 2 response — acceptance of pivotal values and norms, but rejection of all others, a response which I would like to call "creative individualism."

To remain creatively individualistic in an organization is particularly difficult because of the constant resocialization pressures which come with promotion or lateral transfer. Every time the employee learns part of the value system of the particular group to which he is assigned, he may be laying the groundwork for conflict when he is transferred. The engineer has difficulty accepting the values of the sales department, the staff man has difficulty accepting the high pressure ways of the production department, and the line manager has difficulties accepting the service and helping ethic of a staff group. With each transfer, the forces are great toward either conforming or rebelling. It is difficult to keep focused on what is pivotal and retain one's basic individualism.

HIGH COURT DECIDES UNIONS MAY PENALIZE
MEMBERS WHO EXCEED PRODUCTION QUOTAS*

Anonymous

The Supreme Court decided that labor unions may fine members who exceed daily production ceilings fixed in union rules.

The decision was the latest of several in union rules governing member's job conduct and thus narrowed the meaning of the law forbidding unions to "restrain or coerce" their members.

The broadening scope of such regulations, unilaterally adopted by a union, and their affirmation by the Justices may well heighten criticism by employers who assert that unions are using such rules to accomplish what normally is a collective bargaining matter.

The labor controversy centers on two provisions of the National Labor Relations Act. One guarantees to workers the right to both join a union and engage in its activities. It also guarantees the right to refrain from such activities. The other provision says unions can't "restrain or coerce" employes who want to refrain. But it also says the National Labor Relations Board, in enforcing the ban on union coercion of employes, can't interfere with a union's right "to prescribe its own rules with respect to . . . membership."

Justice White said the UAW rule reflected a legitimate union interest. Unions, he asserted, rightly are suspicious of piecework pay systems that can generate competitive pressures among workers. Such pressures, he said, can "endanger workers' health, foment jealousies" and ultimately reduce the number of employes a company requires. If ambitious workers are frustrated by union ceilings on production, they are free to "leave the union," he declared. He didn't touch on the consequences of leaving, however. At many plants, union membership is a requirement for continued employment.

*Reprinted with permission from *The Wall Street Journal*, April, 1, 1969, p.4.

READING 18

AUTO WORKERS HEAR THE DRUMS AGAIN*

Anonymous

Standing in the rain to collect their strike pay — $30 a week for a single man, $40 for a family — the strikers in their baggy cotton pants and frayed shirts evoked an image of the 1930s. The line stretched around the grimy headquarters of United Auto Workers Local 235 in Hamtramck, Mich. Occasionally, one of the men raised a clenched fist in salute, or another flashed a smile for photographers or a V-for-victory gesture, but mostly they were strangely silent. Across the street, pickets patrolled Chevrolet's gear and axle plant, carrying signs that proclaimed: UAM ON STRIKE FOR JUSTICE, or INCREASED PENSIONS or, simply EQUITY. Said one of the pickets, Robert Jackson: "They told us the strike would last till next year. We're going to see Christmas on these picket lines, but we're fighting for a purpose."

In that atmosphere, a strike that could turn out to be the most significant one since the 116-day walkout of the steelworkers in 1959 began last week in Detroit. The nation's largest industrial union, the 1,600,000-member United Auto Workers, invoked labor's ultimate weapon against General Motors, the world's largest manufacturer. In a classic test of raw power, the strike pulled 344,000 workers off their jobs in 145 U.S. and Canadian plants. Every day that it lasts, G.M. says, the company will lose $90 million in sales, the men will be deprived of $12 million in wages, and federal, state and local governments will be denied $20 million in taxes.

Crusades in conflict. For both sides, the costly contest was almost a *jihad*, or holy war. To Leonard Woodcock, the quiet, scholarly leader who took over as president of the U.A.W. last May after Walter Reuther died in an airplane crash, the strike was a call to arms for a younger generation or workers who know nothing of the union battles of the '30s. In meeting after meeting, he has told the men to dig in for a long, bitter siege, warning that they will have to go without strike pay after the union's $120 million war chest runs out in about seven weeks' time. "We have to be prepared to fight, as we used to do, in an old-fashioned way," he told workers. "A union with money is a bureaucracy. A union without money is a crusade."

*Reprinted by permission from *Time*, The Weekly Newsmagazine; Copyright Time, Inc., 1970.

G.M.'s management is holding out in what it sees as a higher cause: halting runaway wage increases. Chairman James Roche declared: "We must restore the balance that has been lost between wages and productivity, for upon this balance rests our national ability to cope with inflation, to resolve the crisis of cost. This in turn determines our capacity to achieve the lofty national goals we have set for ourselves."

In management's view, the strike will decide whether the U.S. auto industry is destined to join the long list of others—textiles, radios, shoes, barber chairs − that can no longer freely and vigorously compete against lower wage foreign manufacturers. In July, imported cars captured an all-time high 15.6% of the nation's auto market. Last week Chevrolet Chief John Z. DeLorean observed that U.S. wage rates are 2.1 times as high as Germany's, 2.8 times Britain's and four times Japan's. Though wages abroad are leaping ahead faster in percentage terms than those in the U.S., American wages are so much higher to begin with that the dollars-and-cents gap has actually widened.

How long? The current collision between auto labor and management in Detroit hurts much of the rest of the U.S. and Canada. G.M. uses 10% of the U.S.'s steel, 5% of its aluminum and large portions of its glass, rubber and textiles. Last week in Lexington, Ky., Irvin Industries laid off 375 workers who make seat belts. In Stratford, Ont., the auto strike put 100 workers out of their jobs at Standard Products, which manufactures rubber parts. The beleaguered Penn Central railroad began laying off workers who normally handle shipments of G.M. cars and trucks. In a month, a million more men could be out of work across the U.S.

Moreover, the strike is likely to trim down any third-quarter economic upturn (see data, page 115). One consequence is that the industrial-production index, which declined in August for the first time in five months, will fall further. If the strike lasts more than six weeks, it will depress many businesses indirectly connected with the auto industry. In that case, lower corporate profits and more unemployment will sink the federal budget deeper in the red, increasing the prospects for a tax increase. The Nixon Administration expects that the strike will be over in six to eight weeks, but the consensus in Detroit is that it quite possibly could stretch out to twelve or 15 weeks, or even more. (G.M. dealers' supply of cars will last for six to seven weeks, including 1970 models.) Even after the auto strike is settled, the economy will be further distorted as General Motors and its suppliers work overtime to make up for lost production.

The walkout is one more sign that union members everywhere are marching to a martial drum. This year the pace of American life has been snarled by an unusual number of strikes, and the appetites of union members have been whetted by some outrageously high settlements. Construction workers in this year's first quarter squeezed out wage increases averaging 18%. Last June, the Teamsters won hourly raises of $1.85 over 39 months.

Now the railroad workers demand a 40% wage increase. Last week 45,000 workers halted trains for about twelve hours on Southern Pacific, Chesapeake & Ohio and Baltimore & Ohio railroads. The men returned to work under a court injunction, and late in the week President Nixon signed an executive order delaying any national rail strike for 60 days.

Younger and impatient. The auto workers' union has become noticeably more militant this year, largely because its membership is becoming younger — and impatient. Over the past decade, the median age of men in the auto plants has declined from 41 to 37; more than one-third of the strikers are under 25. The youngsters insist on big gains — now. A common refrain among union leaders is voiced by Leonard Paula, who represents 4,700 white-collar workers in U.A.W. Local 112 at Chrysler: "I try to tell the young guys that they have to wait for some things but they come up with their beards and mop heads and say, 'Hey, mother, you're ancient.' They do not even listen."

The 26¢ battle. Because of inflation, many workers cannot make ends meet. The average hourly pay of G.M. workers is $4.05, but by Leonard Woodcock's reckoning, they have a great deal of catching up to do. As a result of reductions in overtime work, the auto worker earns 1.7% less than he did a year ago; in addition, inflation has taken a 7.4% cut out of the purchasing power of what he earns. Just to get back to where he was in the spring of 1969, by the U.A.W.'s calculation, the auto worker would have to have a raise of at least 8% an hour. The union asks for a 61.5¢ increase in the first year of a new contract and further raises in the second and third years; the amounts will depend on whatever cost-of-living settlement is agreed on. G.M. is offering 38¢ in the first year, and second- and third-year increases of 12¢ each. The company says that that would give the typical assembly-line worker an annual income, including the value of fringe benefits, of more than $12,000 by the fall of 1973.

The two sides are farther apart than the figures indicate, because of a highly ambiguous clause in an agreement that Reuther negotiated to end the 66-day strike against Ford in 1967. The resulting conflict is an object lesson of the perils of postponing trouble. In the 1967 contract, the union accepted a ceiling on cost-of-living increases in return for an agreement that compensation for inflation above that ceiling "shall be available" in 1970. The difference now amounts to 26¢ an hour, which the union considers to be money already owed its members above and beyond any new settlement; the company includes the 26¢ as part of its 38¢ offer. In the next contract, the union is insisting that there be no ceiling on cost-of-living increases.

For many of the pickets, a more crucial issue is the union's demand for "30 and out" — voluntary retirement at any age after 30 years of service on a minimum pension of $500 a month. G.M. has 41,000 employees with 25 years or more of service, and, says the company's chief negotiator, Vice President Earl Bramblett, "the possibility of losing such a large number of highly skilled and experienced personnel could be a crippling blow." The company offers instead what might be called "58 and out" — retirement on a $500-a-month pension at 58, with $40 a month deducted for every year a worker is below that age when he leaves.

How can the impasse be settled? One way might be for G.M. to offer a more liberal cost-of-living allowance in return for a lower wage settlement, figuring that inflation will slow during the next two years. Woodcock has hinted at the possibility of such a deal. In a remarkable statement, he expressed his preference for cost-of-living escalators in place of huge wage increases in the later years of a contract. "I believe that if you bargain wages to anticipate an inflation, then you are guaranteeing that inflation," he said. "I am concerned about constantly escalating future wage increases further distorting the economy and possibly leading to a major recession, if not worse."

Prices and politics.   The eventual settlement of the U.A.W. strike will be a bench mark. A settlement in line with G.M.'s offer would provide other companies with an example of successful resistance, discouraging future strikes. On the other hand, a large wage gain would give other unions a new goal to shoot at, and would doubtless be followed by another increase in the price of cars and trucks. Last week Ford, which is still producing cars, as are Chrysler and American Motors, raised prices on its 1971 autos by 4.8%, the biggest increase in 14 years. Ford executives hinted that there might be even higher raises after a new labor contract is signed. Yet the auto industry cannot pass all of its increasing labor costs on to consumers. Detroit is dreadfully frightened that Americans will continue to shift to lower-priced imported autos. U.S. car sales are down this year partly because the U.S. public, hurt by both inflation and unemployment, is hesitant to invest in big-ticket purchases. To fight the price rise, Detroit is automating to the extent of using robot welders on G.M.'s Vega 2300 assembly line. Still, prices continue to climb.

The Administration is resigned to the likelihood that almost any settlement that will bring the men back to work is bound to be inflationary. Government economists have privately voiced hopes that the wage deal would be in the range of 8% to 10%. G.M.'s final offer before the workers went out amounted to 9.8%. At least for now, the Administration has no plans to use its power to try to force a settlement. But if the strike drags on until snow falls, the pickets will be faced with the prospect of doing without strike pay, and part of their anger is bound to be directed at the Government. The public will blame the Administration if widespread layoffs brought about by a long stoppage send unemployment over 6%. Unless there is an unexpected break in the strike before the November elections, Republican votes will be hard to come by in areas where the U.A.W.'s picket lines have disrupted the local economy.

In a free economy, conflicts between powerful competing forces are inevitable. U.S. labor has won many of its greatest advances only after striking. Yet the auto walkout comes at a particularly bad time, when the nation is troubled and its economy is sluggish. If the pessimists are proved correct and the strike drags on, it may well become a *cause celebre* for organized labor, drawing to the workers' side protest movements of all sorts. The real tragedy of the bitter battle is that it hits the U.S. when the country can ill afford any further social tension.

HOW THE STRIKE WILL HURT

What damage will the auto strike do to U.S. business? If the workers return to their jobs within a month or so, the impact will be minimal — except for the losses and layoffs suffered by G.M.'s suppliers. But if, as most authorities expect, the walkout lasts for six weeks or more, the effects could be unsettling. Last week Data Resources Inc., an economic consulting firm headed by Harvard's Otto Eckstein, a former member of the President's Council of Economic Advisers and a member of TIME's Board of Economists, made some projections for TIME. By analyzing 320 economic equations in a computer, Data Resources projected what the economy would have looked like in this year's fourth quarter had there been no strike, and compared these results with what is likely to happen if the work stoppage lasts six weeks or twelve weeks. The figures listed below are in billions of dollars at an annual rate, except where otherwise stated.

	Without strike	*Six weeks*	*Twelve weeks*
G.N.P.	$1,003.3	996.5	987.2
Corporate profits after taxes	45.9	43.4	41.1
Unemployment rate	5.1%	5.4%	5.6%
Total federal deficit	10.7	13.6	16.9
Consumer purchases of autos and parts	40.6	35.8	29.5
Auto industry profits	2.8	1.9	.434

In addition, Eckstein's group also examined the effects of the hypothetical six- or twelve-week strikes on industries that are major suppliers to the auto companies. The figures listed below indicate the declines that those industries would be expected to sustain in fourth-quarter profits and production.

	Six Weeks		*Twelve Weeks*	
	Profits	*Production*	*Profits*	*Production*
Textiles	8%	2%	18%	5%
Rubber	9%	2%	22%	6%
Steel	11%	3%	26%	8%
Nonferrous metals	4%	2%	9%	5%
Fabricated metals	3%	2%	7%	5%
Nonelectrical machinery	4%	3%	6%	5%
Electrical machinery	4%	3%	9%	7%

RALLYING THE RANKS: UAW USES GM STRIKE TO "EDUCATE" WORKERS, PULL TOGETHER FACTIONS*

Norman Pearlstine

It's a scene straight out of the 1930s. Some 5,000 workers assembled in the Civic Center here rise to their feet and, to the tune of the "Battle Hymn of the Republic," sing the emotional words of "Solidarity Forever," the trade union anthem:

When the union's inspiration through the
  workers' blood shall run,
There can be no power greater any-
  where beneath the sun.
Yet what force on earth is weaker than
  the feeble strength of one.
But the union makes us strong.
Solidarity forever, solidarity forever,
Solidarity forever, for the union makes
  us strong.

But it is not the 1930s, of course. It is 1970 and the UAW is on strike against General Motors. The singing of the labor anthem signals the opening of yet another weekly session of a "strike school" that the UAW has been running for members since they walked off the assembly line six weeks ago. As the final chorus dies, Emil Mazey, the doughty 57-year-old secretary-treasurer of the UAW, and another union official lead some new members in a recitation of the UAW's oath, which includes promises to divulge no union secrets and to support the union constitution.

A HISTORY LESSON

Then Mr. Mazey waxes loquacious — for an hour. He touches briefly on the status of the current bargaining, but mostly he reminisces about the history of the union and the gains it has won in years gone by and emphasizes the need for "solidarity" and the importance of voting for pro-labor candidates in the coming elections. Finally the "class" breaks up and the strikers go home, richer by $30 to $40. That is the "wage" they get for attending the session.

*Reprinted with permission from *The Wall Street Journal*, October 29, 1970, p.1.

The strike school here, billed by the UAW as an educational venture, underscores an aspect of this strike and many others that is often ignored: To a union leader a strike can be fully as important as a technique to build loyalty and improve relations with the rank and file as it is a tactic to force management to loosen the pursestrings.

No one disputes, of course, that the main reason most strikes are called is to force companies to cough up more money or fatten fringe benefits. Few unions ever end a strike without winning gains greater than those offered before the strike. But, labor observers say, there are some equally compelling internal reasons union leaders call major strikes. And to many a union official those reasons take on new appeal as their unions grow bigger and they find themselves more distant from workers at a time when restlessness and discontent among young members is on the rise. A long strike, they say, can:

— Teach young members who have never experienced hard times that all gains are not easily won and that struggle and unity are necessary.

— Help to wear down the expectations of members, expectations that in the current situation have been whetted by memories of recent good times and by the bite of inflation. This trimming of hopes eases the difficult task of getting members to ratify settlements leaders have negotiated. (More than one of every 10 agreements hammered out by union officials is rejected by union members.)

— Foster union loyalty and pull together various rank-and-file factions by uniting them against a common enemy.

— Strengthen the position of union leaders, who must stand for re-election regularly by a membership that is constantly turning over and that is wary of leaders in general, union leaders included.

— Create an escape valve for the frustrations of workers bitter about what they consider intolerable working conditions imposed by companies' single-minded drive for greater production and profits.

CRITICAL OF MEANY

Because union leaders believe strikes can serve these functions, they are sharply critical of the view that the strike is an anachronism, a vestige of another age that is not suited to solve modern labor-management conflicts. This view, held by some Government officials and academicians and even by AFL-CIO president George Meany, holds that in many cases strikes should be replaced by voluntary arbitration or by national product boycotts.

Such thinking shows little understanding of either the political nature of unions or of the "temper of the times," says Joseph P. Molony, vice president of the United Steelworkers. Declares a UAW official: "George Meany has never done any real bargaining. Anyone who talks about strikes being obsolete doesn't really understand the problems we have."

Surprisingly, among those who do understand the need for strikes to ease intraunion pressures are many company bargainers. Though they hardly approve of strikes called to reduce such pressures, they are aware that union leaders may need such strikes to get contracts ratified and to get reelected. In fact, some company bargainers figure strikes actually help stabilize fragmented unions and, by allowing workers to vent their "strike need," actually buy peace in future years

FUNCTIONS OF MANAGEMENT

Part III studies the functions of management, which in this book are considered to be creating, planning, organizing, motivating, communicating, and controlling. Other authors may have different lists of functions, but the difference usually is not substantial.

In the first article, Maneck S. Wadia gives an overview of managerial functions, listing them as planning, organizing, motivating, innovating, and controlling. John F. Mee then defines the creative process and lists the steps that are ordinarily involved in creating something. In the next article, M.R. Feinberg offers fourteen suggestions for increasing creativity in organizations. Robert Albanese then explains that both creativity and stability are needed for an organization to continue to prosper.

The planning function is represented in the article by Bruce D. Henderson, who suggests that company strategy must be methodical, analytical, and deliberate.

For the organizing function, S. Avery Raube explains eleven principles of effective organization. Keith Davis then points out that informal group behavior in organizations often does not conform to the lines of the formal organization.

Charles D. McDermid, in the first reading on motivating, points out that money helps to satisfy man's needs at all levels. Frederick Herzberg next suggests that achievement, recognition, responsibility, advancement, and the work itself may be more the powerful motivators than the tangible rewards of the work. Next, James MacGregor reports on a company in which some workers became more productive when given more freedom.

In the next article on motivating, Keith Davis explains that managerial practices have evolved and are continuing to evolve from an autocratic, to a custodial, to a supportive, and then to a collegial model. Each in turn serves higher-order needs and is more democratic. Norman R.F. Maier describes in his article the effective ways of achieving discipline in organizations. Procedures for management by objectives are explained by Edward C. Schleh.

Stuart Chase presents the first article on communicating, explaining how semantics causes many communication problems for executives. Earl G. Planty and William Machaver then suggest ways of improving upward communication in organizations.

The article on controlling was written by Earnest I. Hanson. It shows how one of the most popular devices for controlling—a budget—works.

THE FUNCTIONS OF MANAGEMENT*

Maneck S. Wadia

The concept of management functions was first identified by the French industrialist Henri Fayol in 1916. He referred to five functions: planning, organizing, commanding, coordinating, and controlling. In 1925, when Fayol's ideas were translated into English, the concept of management functions was transplanted to the United States, where it flourished and led to a variety of classifications. Mee has cited a list of examples that show how different authorities identify the various functions of management.[1]

Though there is disagreement over the grouping and classification of management functions, there is general agreement that certain management functions exist. As Simon has stated, scholars interested in managerial behavior are interested in management functions.[2] These functions, no matter what their variety and definitions, are concerned with the achievement of organizational purposes through human effort within the internal and external environment of the organization.

The various functions of management, considered as a whole, make up the management process. Hence, planning, organizing, motivating, innovating, and controlling, considered separately, are management functions; when looked upon in their total approach to achieving objectives, they form a management process. The management process is determined by the functions, and though "there are some slight differences of opinion among the authorities, the instructors, and the practitioners on the breakdown of the subfunctions and their identifying terms, the nature of the process seems to have general agreement."[3]

The management process has often been misinterpreted by its advocates and its critics alike either as a sequence of functions that follow one another in a particular order or as a group of separate and unrelated functions. Some of the literature implies that the management process, whatever its functions, is concerned primarily with each function as a

---

*From *The Nature and Scope of Management* by Maneck S. Wadia. Copyright © 1966 by Scott, Foresman and Company.

[1] John F. Mee, *Management Thought in a Dynamic Economy* (New York: New York University Press, 1963), pp. 56-57.

[2] Herbert A. Simon, "Approaching the Theory of Management," in Harold Koontz, ed., *Toward A Unified Theory of Management* (New York: McGraw-Hill Book Co., 1964), p. 77.

[3] Mee, *Management Thought in a Dynamic Economy*, p. 56.

separate entity and concerned very little with its relationship to other functions or to the internal and external environment of the organization. These misinterpretations are due to the fact that the concept of functions has been borrowed from the social sciences without due regard for the theoretical complexities involved. Some scholars either fail to discuss what the concept involves or give an oversimplified definition such as "function is any distinct phase of work."[4]

Radcliffe-Brown, an eminent anthropologist, has taken a complicated but more realistic view of this concept. To him, the concept of function

involves the notion of a structure consisting of a set of relations among unit entities, the continuity of the structure being maintained by a life-process made up of the activities of the constituent units. . . . By the definition here offered "function" is the contribution which a partial activity makes to the total activity of which it is a part. The function of a particular social usage is the contribution it makes to the total social life as the functioning of the total social system. Such a view implies that a social system (the total social structure of a society together with the totality of social usages, in which that structure appears and on which it depends for its continued existence) has a certain kind of unity, which we may speak of as a functional unity.[5]

A management function is thus not a separate entity but an integral part of a larger entity made up of various functions that are related to one another as well as to the larger entity. Hence, as Gestalt psychologists have pointed out, the total is different from the sum of its parts. Only when the concept of function is viewed in this light does the management process emerge as truly dynamic.

In this book, we consider the functions of management to be planning and decision-making, organizing, motivating, innovating, and controlling. Figure 1 shows one image of the management process created by an improper understanding of the concept of functions.

FIGURE 1

planning
↓
organizing
↓
motivating
↓
innovating
↓
controlling

[4]Ralph Currier Davis, *Industrial Organization and Management* (New York: Harper & Brothers, 1957), p. 23.

[5]A.R. Radcliffe-Brown, "Concept of Function in Social Science," *American Anthropologist*, XXXVII (July-September 1935).

Figure 2, on the other hand, shows the more realistic image of the management process created by the more dynamic approach to the concept of functions as expounded by Radcliffe-Brown and further elaborated by Leighton.[6] The history of social sciences teaches us not to look upon the sequence of activities as either completely random or rigidly predetermined. The process of management is a complex one, with varying degrees of interaction among the functions.

FIGURE 2

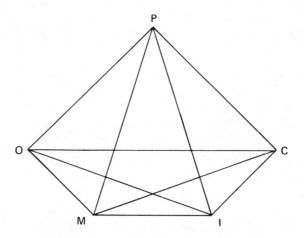

Mee has suggested that the concept of management process has lately come under strong criticism.[7] The management process, through its functions, is but the framework within which one may study the various aspects of management, however. What has come under stronger criticism is not the framework but the structure that has been built onto it and the principles that have been derived from it. One can criticize a rigorous step-by-step approach to planning without rejecting the function of planning; one can reject a nonempirical approach to organizing without rejecting the function of organizing; one can criticize close control of human effort without rejecting the function of control; and one can criticize different approaches to motivating and innovating without suggesting that these functions are unimportant in the management process.

The concepts of management function and management process have been most useful in developing an identifiable discipline for study and

[6]Alexander H. Leighton, *Human Relations in a Changing World* (New York: E.P. Dutton & Co., Inc. 1949), pp. 156-161.

[7]Mee, *Management Thought in a Dynamic Economy*, pp. 87-92.

research. No scholar or practitioner has questioned that managers perform certain functions and that these functions are performed in a variety of organizations and at different managerial levels. The controversy arises when various approaches are used to explore, understand, and teach the art and science of management.

THE CREATIVE THINKING PROCESS*

John F. Mee

The creative thinking process is in wide use today for purposes of stimulating scientific research in both the physical sciences and the social sciences. It is used also to help executives and employees discover better ways to achieve desired results. Individuals can use it to solve personal problems. There is strong evidence that anyone can increase his creativity if he has the desire and patience to master the creative process. The success of numerous creative thinking training programs for executives supplies the evidence.

OPERATIVE DEFINITION

Creative thinking is the process of bringing a problem before one's mind clearly as by imagining, visualizing, supposing, musing, contemplating, or the like, and then originating or inventing an idea, concept, realization, or picture along new or unconventional lines. It involves study and reflection rather than action.

SUBJECT AREAS FOR CREATIVE THINKING

Some of the most fruitful areas for applying the process of creative thinking are:

Good. The creation and introduction of a new good or service which is unfamiliar to consumers.

Method. The invention and introduction of a new method of production, one not yet tested in the branch of manufacture concerned. A new method also may be a new way to market a product commercially or a new method for financing.

Market. The creation and opening of a new market into which the particular branch of manufacture or product has not previously entered.

Supply. The creation and conquest of a new source of supply of raw material or manufactured goods.

*Reprinted with permission from *Indiana Business Review*, February, 1956.

Organization.   The establishment or formulation of a new way of organizing, such as the trend toward organizational decentralization into many individual profit centers with central policy and decentralized authority for decision-making by individual managers, indicating that creative thinking has been done in this area.

Management or administration.   The creation and development of a new philosophy for more effectively achieving objectives through human effort is a possible area for consideration. For example, attention given to the administrative point of view or the management process may result in creative thinking in this area.[1]

EXAMPLES OF CREATIVE THINKING

Creation of a new good.   In Hamilton, Ohio, a young man who had inherited a strongbox factory looked at a minnow bucket. He got a new idea. He brought into his mind clearly the visualization of insulation between the two cans, a cover, and ice cubes. He imagined a picnic container that would keep drinks or food cold for a long period of time. He brought into his mind the concept of the now well-known Skotch Kooler. His factory now has a gross volume of over $5 million a year.

Creation of a new method.   A former second baseman of the Washington Senators at the end of his playing career got a job with the Consolidated Vultee aircraft plant in Nashville, Tennessee. He had only a high school education and worked on the assembly line. The plant was not meeting its quota of engines, and the obvious waste of manpower irritated him. In his spare time, he designed a new assembly line procedural method which gave each worker a simple, timed assignment. When the general foreman was on vacation, he obtained consent to try his procedure. The result was the meeting of the plant's quota with less manpower. This man had no formal engineering education; but he did have the ability to use the creative process of thinking.

Creation of a new market.   A salesman some time ago was forced to spend the night in Harrisburg, Pennsylvania. He looked in vain for a television set to see a special program. There was none. Although Harrisburg was within normal reach of several television stations, the mountains cut off the signals. This salesman brought into his mind the idea of a community antenna on a nearby mountain top which could serve those homes desiring television. He formed a new business which has

---

[1]The areas presented were adapted from Schumpeter's *The Theory of Economic Development* (Cambridge: Harvard University Press, 1934).

erected over 290 community antennas and is a million-dollar business. He created a new market for television as well as a new product.[2]

Many examples could be given of products, methods, and markets with which we are now familiar but which first had to be created in someone's imagination. Without composers, musicians would have to make up their own music to play on instruments. Without architects, builders would be very limited. Without engineers, we could not shift so well from physical to mechanical energy. However, creativity is not limited to mechanical or artistic inventiveness. Creativity is being sought and used in marketing, advertising, production, transportation, financing, real estate, and personnel relations. A. C. Monteith, Vice President of Westinghouse, has stated, "Creative thinking has become the spark plug of American business. If we don't find enough imaginative men to supply that spark plug, the machine will run down."[3]

MAIN LEVELS OF THINKING

Three main levels of thinking have been advanced by Professor B. H. Jarman of George Washington University. They are the habit level, the problem-solving level, and the creative or insight level.[4]

The habit level of thinking results from either the conditioned response or trial and error methods. It is routine and unimaginative. Those who work at the habit level are following "beaten paths for beaten men." They work from plans of other men's minds by performing standard operating procedures or methods. They depend upon memory of techniques and formulae. The well-known poem by Sam W. Foss, "The Calf-Path," describes the thinking of such individuals.

Thinking on the problem-solving level is logical because it proceeds from facts which are either given or obtained. The scientific method of attack may be used at this level. The well-known "case study" approach to education, in which certain business situations are simulated, is used to provoke problem-solving thinking. A problem is discovered. Analysis and evaluation of the facts are made. Then a decision is made to resolve the problem.

Thinking on the creative or insight level may not be logical because it is done when only some facts are known and others are missing. Creative thinking occurs when sound conclusions or judgments are reached when some important facts or data are either unknown or withheld. Creative thinking results from a partial knowledge of a situation. Combinations and eliminations of associated facts begin to clarify the

[2]The preceding three examples were adapted from Bill Davidson, "How to Think Your Way to the Top," *Collier's* CXXXV, No. 3 (February 4, 1955), pp. 26, 27.
[3]*Ibid.*, p. 26.
[4]B. H. Jarman, "Can Executives Be Taught to Think," *Advanced Management* (January, 1954), p. 6.

imagery or idea that will lead to a solution. Insight then provides the imagination with the searched-for concept or idea. The imagination is required to set up a number of hypotheses that can be checked, compared, and evaluated, so that a superior solution can be developed from the best elements of the competing hypotheses. Examples of such insight were Trudeau's flash of inspiration that tuberculosis could be cured if a victim's environment could be controlled; and Reed's insight that yellow fever was associated with mosquitos.

There is a close relationship between these levels of thinking and the levels of management practice as described by Barnard.[5]

Levels of management practice

1. Job know-how
2. Specific organization practice
3. Principles and fundamentals

Levels of thinking

1. Routine or habit
2. Problem-solving
3. Creative

STEPS IN THE CREATIVE THINKING PROCESS

The creative thinking process has been described in the literature of the field by numerous authorities and practitioners. The presentation here represents a selection and combination of the best elements of all these methods for creative thinking.

When 'Omer smote 'is bloomin' lyre,
He'd 'eard men sing by land an' sea;
An' what 'e thought 'e might require,
'E went an' took — the same as me!
 —Kipling, "When 'Omer Smote 'is Bloomin' Lyre"

Attitude and concentration. There should be established in one's mind a positive attitude toward complete freedom of ideas even though they may seem impractical or unorthodox at first. Attempts to criticize or evaluate should be held in abeyance. Concentration for periods of about 30 minutes' duration should be practiced each day. To become proficient in the creative thinking process, it is essential that one develop the desire and the will to concentrate on a problem for a period of time without

---

[5]Herbert A. Simon, *Administrative Behavior,* Foreword by Chester I. Bernard (New York: The Macmillan Co., 1948), pp. x-xii.

interrupting by getting a drink, turning on the radio or television, making a phone call, or looking out the window. A positive attitude and the ability to concentrate are basic essentials for a climate friendly to creative thinking.

Selecting or defining a problem. First, determine your purpose. Ignore ideas until you have determined why you want or need ideas. Find out what needs to be done or what you want to accomplish. You will not get started on the creative process by looking around for ideas that are new. To try to be creative by random search for original ideas will result only in futile frustration. C. F. Kettering, a very creative person, once stated that "All research is simply finding out what is wrong with something, and then fixing it." Therefore, start by selecting a problem in your area, and make sure that you know what the problem is. Define the problem clearly; then write it down as a "fix point" for the start of the creative process. It is suggested that "limiting factors" be listed and a "difficulty inventory" and a "difficulty analysis" be used in getting a "fix point" on the problem at the start of the creative process.

C. F. Kettering set out to develop the electric self-starter for motors, and he did it. In a demonstration, objection was made to his invention because he used more current through the wires than established formulae allowed. Kettering stated that his problem was to start an automobile. He was not interested in formulae. He had defined and picked his problem; then he stayed with it until a solution was reached. Previous failures of others to develop the electric starter did not bother him. He considered other failures an opportunity for him.

In selecting a problem, remember that the positive attitude and concentration climate are important. Regardless of the difficulty or the apparent impracticability of the problem, a solution can be reached through the creative process. Have the courage to depart from traditional formulae or thinking. Remember the plight of the bumblebee: "According to theory of aerodynamics and as may be readily demonstrated through laboratory tests and wind tunnel experiments, the bumblebee is unable to fly. This is because the size, weight, and shape of his body, in relation to the total wing spread, makes flying impossible. But — the bumblebee, being ignorant of these profound scientific truths, goes ahead and flies anyway — and manages to make a little honey every day!" The world of business is filled with opportunity for those who will and can select problems that impede economic or technological progress and solve them through the process of creative thinking.

Exploration and preparation. New or unconventional ideas are not created by wishing. They must be laboriously and carefully created from raw materials. The raw materials may be called knowledge. In the creative thinking process, ideas are originated by associations of existing ideas and factual information. New combinations and eliminations are brought about. Facts are matched against facts.

The exploration and preparation step in the creative process involves gathering, refining, and organizing all of the obtainable raw materials and knowledge that bear upon the problem selected. The purpose is to enable one to soak up information that will be grist for the mind later. One is not concerned with new ideas in this step — they come later. Raw materials and knowledge may be obtained from journals, books, magazines, research reports, associations with informed people, personal observations, lectures, and experience. In the exploration and preparation step, one should search for knowledge over as broad a field as possible. Every effort should be made to determine what underlies the facts and whether or not fundamentals or principles are apparent. For best results the raw materials or knowledge gathered should be written down for proper organization and refinement.

The exploration and preparation work is probably the most difficult of all of the steps in the creative thinking process because it involves a great amount of painstaking mental and physical effort. There are no short cuts. One must force oneself to gather, refine, and organize raw material and knowledge pertaining to the problem until every source is exhausted. This requires great self-discipline and tenacity of purpose. The lazy or the indolent will fail in this step. One must continue the exploration and preparation step until no new or additional raw materials and knowledge are obtainable. Remember, in creative thinking some facts are known and some are missing. Therefore, all possible facts and information must be obtained. Furthermore, the facts should be classified on some logical basis for later analysis and evaluation. Otherwise, the gaps in the later mental configuration may be too great for insight to bridge.

Hypotheses, brainstorming, or wild thinking. This step involves the application of all existing ideas or knowledge to the solution of the problem in all possible combinations. Pareto's concept of "instinct of combinations" in *Mind and Society* describes the method for this step.[6] It is during this step of the creative thinking process that one gives his mind full freedom to range for a new idea to resolve the problem.

All possible relationships of existing raw materials and knowledge are combined. Some will be very wild and impractical; but the more the better, because of the increased probability that one will hit on the solution. All should be written down and preserved for later reference. Charles S. Whiting of McCann-Erickson, Inc., has described some operational techniques for this step: the analytical technique, the forced relationship technique, and the free association technique.[7]

The analytical technique involves the use of a pattern for establishing all possible relationships of knowledge to a problem. Alex F. Osborn's

---

[6] Vilfredo Pareto, *Mind and Society* (New York: Harcourt, Brace, 1935).

[7] Whiting, "Operational Techniques of Creative Thinking," *Advanced Management,* XX, No. 10 (October, 1955), p. 25.

check list illustrates this technique by asking the following questions. Let's take an existing product or service as an example. (1) Can it be put to other uses? (2) Can it be adapted? (3) Can it be modified? (4) Can it be magnified? (5) Can it be minified? (6) Can it be substituted for others? (7) Can it be rearranged? (8) Can it be reversed? (9) Can it be combined with something?[8] This technique is well known for methods work and work simplification.

The forced relationship technique involves making a list of objects or ideas which may have some possible relationship, and then considering each object or idea in relation to every other one on the list. An example of this technique in action would be forcing the combination of all chemical elements in all possible relationships in an attempt to find a cure for cancer or the common cold. Obviously this is a laborious and time-consuming effort, although the use of electronic machines can be helpful.

The free association technique involves wild thinking or brainstorming. This technique is based on values which come from allowing any idea which comes to mind on a problem to be recorded. No attempt is made to evaluate ideas until all possible ideas have been expressed. A positive attitude and a receptive climate are essential for this technique because the purpose is to write down all possible ideas generated on a problem regardless of how silly or impractical they at first seem to be.

If a brainstorming session is to be held, the exploration or preparation step is minimized because the raw materials or knowledge obtainable exist in the experience and minds of the members of the group that participates. The group is presented with a problem, and everyone is encouraged to contribute ideas. For example, in the General Motors A C Spark Plug Division, one brainstorming session produced over 100 ideas on how to finish off a casting. The Ethyl Corporation got 71 ideas in less than an hour on a new booklet for employee benefit plans.

The digestion of the raw materials and knowledge obtained in exploration and preparation should continue by wild thinking on relationships, the establishment of possible hypotheses, brainstorming, and the like until a feeling of frustration appears. When all possible relationships have been combined and mental fatigue occurs, it is time for diversion — the next step. When Sherlock Holmes seemingly ceased work on a case and dragged his friend, Dr. Watson, to a concert or played his violin, he was actually moving up a step in his brilliant creative thinking.

Incubation or gestation.   This step involves unconscious cerebration. One can contribute little to this step directly. One must either arrange to think about other subjects or problems, or even rest from any form of conscious thought by seeking recreation or entertainment. When those responsible for assignments requiring creative thinking indulge in reading wild West or detective stories, or listen to jazz music, don't malign or

[8]Adapted from Alex F. Osborn, *Applied Imagination* (New York: Charles Scribner's, 1953), p. 284.

belittle them. They are probably engaging in this step of the creative process. Likewise, a hobby is a valuable asset to a creative thinker. During this step of incubation or gestation, one's mind will continue to operate on the problem unconsciously. However, it is important to prevent emotional or mental blocks by some form of diversion which will result in one's not thinking about the problem or associated ideas. This is important because the next step should result in illumination or insight which brings to mind the idea sought to solve the problem.

Illumination. This step often occurs when least expected. The idea will appear when one is eating, bathing, relaxing, driving, or engaging in some similar activity. If the previous steps of exploration and preparation, digestion of relationships, and incubation or gestation have been accomplished properly, the new idea will be brought to mind. However, other ideas will follow in quick order. Many fail in the creative thinking process on this step because ideas come to mind faster than one's memory can absorb or retain them. Therefore, it is important that some means of writing down the ideas as they occur be devised. Otherwise, they will be lost and the previous work in the creative process nullified.

Verification and application. The final step in the creative process of thinking is that of verifying, modifying, or applying the idea toward the solution of the problem selected and defined. However, the same freedom of thinking and imagination should be used in verifying or applying the new idea brought to mind as in the other steps of the creative process. This step is essential if one is to get his ideas accepted and used.

The creative thinking process is based upon three essential elements: knowledge, proficiency, and attitude. Knowledge supplies the grist for the mental process. Proficiency in all steps of the creative thinking process is vital for success in using it. There must be a positive attitude and a receptive climate for using the process.

They copied all they could follow,
but they couldn't copy my mind,
And I left 'em sweating and stealing
a year and a half behind.
　　—Kipling, "The Mary Gloster"

One may be able to follow a career and earn a living by operating on the routine or problem-solving levels of thinking. However, the highest rewards in recognition and income will be offered to those who will contribute to economic, business, and technological progress through creative thinking about the world's problems. Fortunately, the process of creative thinking is not patented or withheld from anyone. It is available and free for all to use.

14 SUGGESTIONS FOR MANAGING SCIENTIFIC CREATIVITY*

M. R. Feinberg

The major challenge of the industrial research director is to manage truly creative efforts that meet the test of profitability. Because of today's more sophisticated competition and increased financial pressures, this management assignment has never been more difficult.

The problem is compounded by the fact that most research directors do not find their dual role as scientist-administrator easily resolved. Usually, the scientist or any other professional functioning in a creative capacity is responsible for development of a single project and has considerable personal latitude. However, as a manager, the scientist must involve himself in a series of personal relationships that affect both group performance and individual creativity of group members.

As a scientist, he motivates himself. As a manager, he must motivate others to meet company objectives. This can be somewhat difficult in certain research environments where highly educated and intelligent scientists frequently generate more loyalty to their professions than to their employers. In other words, the scientist often holds approbation from his professional colleagues in higher regard than that from company associates.

RECOGNIZING CREATIVE SCIENTISTS

All professional scientists have certain elements in common: their discipline and their total commitment to data. Some scientists, obviously, are more creative than others, and their early recognition is desirable. The first opportunity, of course, for evaluating individual creativity is when reviewing job candidates. The following points are generally reliable guidelines for determining creativity:

1. More and less creative scientists do not differ significantly from each other in a test of verbal intelligence.
2. More creative men are less anxious than less creative men.

---

*Reprinted with permission of *Research Management*, vol. XI, no. 2 (1968). As condensed in *Management Review*, December 1968, published by the American Management Association, Inc. It is the editor's opinion that the ideas expressed in this article apply to all members of organizations, not just to scientists.

3. More creative scientists are more autonomous, dynamic and integrative than their colleagues.

4. More creative men see their attitudes as being more different from those of others.

5. More creative men have comparatively fewer authoritarian attitudes than do colleagues.

6. More creative scientists place higher values on practical matters and utility, more emphasis on harmony and form and less emphasis on mystical values.

7. More creative men are oriented more toward achievement and acceptance of their inner impulses, while less creative colleagues are oriented more toward avoiding situations in which they might feel inferior or might be blamed for their activities.

8. More creative men give greater evidence of psychological well-being.

9. More creative men appear to take fewer unwarranted risks than do their colleagues.

10. The more creative scientist works slowly and cautiously while analyzing problems and gathering data, but rapidly after obtaining basic data and approaching the point of synthesis. The less creative man spends less time in analyzing the problem but more time in synthesizing his material.

STIMULATING CREATIVE SCIENTISTS

What can an industrial research director do to stimulate scientific creativity? Research directors are widely agreed that, as discipline to the task, some pressure on any laboratory work group is necessary for creative productivity. How much depends on the circumstances.

In the case of a research group with a short-term goal, it makes sense to apply moderate pressure to emphasize the need for result-oriented action. Yet, the same amount of pressure applied for a longer period may serve to frustrate rather than motivate. Pressure under such circumstances should be used sparingly and with caution even though there is also pressure on *you* as director. Also, there is a need to provide a creative climate —one conducive to development and validation of ideas. Assuming that the scientist has adequate professional background, he must also be thoroughly familiar with the policy framework within which he is to operate.

The creative scientist also must be self-motivated. He is rarely complacent, self-satisfied or happy with his current situation. However, psychological research has shown that his personal motivation cannot be intermixed with frustration, anxiety or fear. The compelling force in the creative professional person must be a positive attitude, in contrast to the defensive attitude of the fearful or frustrated person. A man dominated by fear motivation is more likely to play it safe than to create. Therefore, if you are trying to make your subordinates more creative, be sure they don't feel threatened by product demands. Threats generate resistance, not results.

SPECIFIC GUIDELINES

Most experts agree on one general point: In managing talented, creative personnel, good supervision is the critical factor. The creative man's relationship with his immediate superior overshadows every other influence. Successful managers suggest these 14 rules as guidelines for supervising creative people:

1. *Gear the pressure to goals.* Many creative people need the reassurance of just enough gentle pressure on the reins to keep them aware of their objectives. Setting some definite goals and an approximate time limit will help provide the needed sense of urgency.

2. *Maintain contact.* Contact must never be lost between the individual and his superior. Frequent communication, coupled with freedom to make certain decisions alone, appears to be the ideal compromise. It is apparent to any good research executive that a creative person needs a sympathetic ear — a sounding board for his ideas.

3. *Let him know where he stands.* The creative man is eager for evaluation of his efforts. The problem is that appraisal of creative efforts is often difficult because any real results may be long postponed. Therefore, be especially alert for signs of resentment, talk informally with him and demonstrate your interest, indicate your understanding of his goals, and let him know the importance of his results and the positive reactions of others in management as soon as possible.

4. *Defend him.* There is a limit to how much of a guardian angel a scientist deserves, but the nature of his job may make it wise to tolerate his idiosyncrasies and impatience.

In defending him, make the most of his accomplishments. Make these two points: First, the inconsistency of his habits may be necessary to creativity. Second, his impatience may come from deep absorption in a task — not personal animosity.

5. *Give him ample time alone.* Many of the creative man's oest ideas come during an idle period immediately following intense concentration. That's when his unconscious presents his conscious mind with new insight. Sometimes ideas need time to ripen.

The individual whose creative effort is part of a group project often develops ideas when he is alone, but the reverse is also true. Several scientists coming together after individual study stimulate each other's thinking and accomplish more together than they could alone. However, creativity on a solely group basis doesn't work — with the possible exception of an occasional brainstorming session.

6.   *Bolster his confidence.* Any person whose contribution is principally in the realm of ideas rather than action is normally at his best when only his mind — not his security or ego — is challenged. You must encourage him in order to build his self-confidence to the maximum.

The problem to be solved involves considerable tension. It is important to offset this by paying your creative personnel well, supplying security and satisfaction in their jobs, and granting any reasonable requests they make.

7.   *Show tolerance for failure.* A creative atmosphere requires that a man be able to present radical, even unworkable ideas without being harshly judged. The best product your company ever produced may have sounded silly when first proposed.

When you ask a man to experiment with ideas and innovate and create, you must give him a wide margin for error. If you do not provide this, his fear of failure will prevent true initiative.

8.   *Need for outside stimuli.* The creative thinker must be free to communicate with others having useful knowledge and ideas of their own. He needs the professional status acquired through identification with an elite transcending business interests. Thus the scientist tends to spend considerable time in non-company activities — professional societies, community events, attendance at conventions and so on. Many firms mistakenly discourage these activities not realizing that a creative man's professional needs cannot be wholly satisfied within any company.

9.   *Provide appropriate direction.* Although you should be tolerant; you cannot pamper the creative person. You must distinguish between an inventive man's legitimate impatience with unrealized possibilities and petulance over failure.

10.   *Provide a creative atmosphere.* Few men can produce new ideas and creative solutions working in an uncomfortable environment. Management should provide conditions conducive to creative thought. When possible, creative people should be relieved of routine chores and supplied an office and secretarial assistance.

11.   *Recognize creativity.* Creative people regard themselves as a different breed worthy of special consideration by management. Within reason, management should recognize and respond to this feeling.

12.   *Don't demand total creativity.* When hiring creative people, don't seek those who are only creative. A man with additional talent is to be preferred, even if his creativity is slightly less than that of another candidate.

13. *Evaluate ideas quickly.* Creative people are impatient. They like to have their ideas evaluated quickly. Even though premature decisions are to be avoided, give the creative man a quick reading on his progress, even if you only indicate that his ideas are under study.

14. *Overlook individual quirks.* Don't deny scientists a few harmless quirks. Such extras as special furniture or decor and window views may be crucial to the creative function

OVERCOMING RESISTANCE TO STABILITY:
A TIME TO MOVE; A TIME TO PAUSE*

Robert Albanese

One of my children recently brought home a paper on which she had written the figure three backwards. I asked her why the three was that way, and she replied, "Just for a change." A good answer, I thought to myself. The world needs people willing to try new things; we should not be boxed in by accustomed ways of behaving and thinking; we need to be open to new experiences and willing to take the risks involved — even when the risks cannot be calculated. The "old ways" no longer seem to work. Change for the sake of change *is* desirable and even necessary sometimes, although the result is from bad to worse.

Increasingly, our stance must be to take the risk of experimenting with new ways of being and doing. Individuals are finding that their most prized possession is the capacity to cope with and adapt to changes while still maintaining a unique identity and personality. Groups need to acquire new skills and attitudes that will make them effective vehicles of growth and performance, and provide satisfaction to individual members. Organizations of all kinds not only have to experiment with applying new knowledge to problems of internal operations, but they must also learn to know their external environment and utilize decision processes that recognize environment as an integral part of the organization. Communities, cities, and nations face new and enormous problems that, if solvable at all, require imaginative and untried approaches.

This general notion of being receptive to change and willing to experience new behaviors and attitudes is a common theme in today's business literature; it became popular after the appearance of two well-known articles on the subject.[1] The idea has assumed an identity of its own, separate from the reality it describes — one can be for or against change without reference to any particular subject. The main thrust of the writing is toward the idea of accepting and coping with changes, and becoming more open (less resistant) to those proposed and desired. Managers are called on to be "change seekers" and to recognize the management of

---

*Reprinted by permission from *Business Horizons.* Copyright 1970 by the Foundation for the School of Business, Indiana University.

[1]Lester Coch and John R.P. French, "Overcoming Resistance to Change," *Human Relations,* I (1948); Paul R. Lawrence, "How to Deal With Resistance to Change," *Harvard Business Review,* XLVII (January-February, 1969).

change as their main function: "The future belongs to those leaders of organizations who can demonstrate the necessary managerial skill and imagination to cope with the enormous changes around them"; "Existing organizations will have to learn to reach out for change as an opportunity, will have to learn to resist continuity."[2] Change is necessary! Resistance is dysfunctional!

There is a tendency to want to be on the side of change and to participate in a continuous process directed toward progress and growth. However, continuity and stability are also necessary ingredients of progress and growth, and they require analysis. They are necessary because progressive change is almost always a process of blending innovations with prevailing behaviors, attitudes, and values. They require analysis if we are to better understand that mysterious process by which human systems grow and develop. What exists today is the origin of what will exist tomorrow.

The idea of resisting change does not receive adequate attention. Over fifteen years ago, and again in the article cited previously, Lawrence cautioned against viewing such resistance as either good or bad or as something to be overcome: "Resistance may be soundly based or not. It is always, however, an important signal calling for further inquiry by management." But the *absence* of resistance may also be an important signal calling for further inquiry. Even resistance considered natural and understandable is frequently considered as a problem to be dealt with and overcome. The implicit assumption in most discussions of change is that the proposals are desirable and worthy of adoption. Calling into question the efficacy of a change is interpreted as resistance:

To some will come a time when change
Itself is beauty, if not heaven.[3]

This article explores some reasons for the present emphasis on change, argues for a need for more intelligent resistance, and suggests some ways to balance the needs for change, stability, and continuity. First, it is worth noting that words used in discussions of this topic do not have precise meanings. For example, what does it mean to speak of change? Most changes in organizations probably are not resisted. Even if two individuals could agree on the substance of a change they would differ in their interpretation of its meaning and significance. Similarly, what precisely does continuity mean? What actually happens when continuity and change are balanced? What is stability? The absence of precise definitions for such terms makes communication more difficult.

---

[2]First quotation from Alfred J. Marrow and others, *Management by Participation: Creating a Climate for Personal and Organizational Development* (New York: Harper & Row, Publishers, 1967), p. 247. Second from Peter F. Drucker, "Managements' New Role," *Harvard Business Review*, XLVII (November-December, 1969), p. 52.

[3]E.A. Robinson, "Llewellyn and the Tree."

THE EMPHASIS ON CHANGE

Why is change emphasized so heavily today? Five explanations are suggested: change is needed; businesses with organizational slack are more receptive and willing to experiment; the notion of novelty is appealing; basic theories of operations help business measure proposed changes; and changes are being called for by social scientists, who have often been involved in a program as consultants.

The need for change

The explanation that requires the least discussion is the most important: the great and urgent need for change. It is only a mild exaggeration to say that wherever one looks one can see an overdue need to reshape the priorities, values, structures, and behavior that characterize social systems. Indeed, we should be genuinely concerned if the literature dealing with change did not reflect this need and urgency.

Today this need is recognized on a broad scale and is felt in a personal way. In addition, change is viewed more as an ongoing process than as a discrete event, and the knowledge and understanding required for implementation have increased. All of these factors have helped the idea catch on that things can be changed and that they will be changed. Now!

Effect of organizational slack

The concept of organizational slack is useful in understanding some organizational innovations and change efforts. This condition is defined as "the difference between the payments required to maintain an organization and the resources obtained from the environment. . . ."[4] Not all business organizations are experiencing affluent times but most are experiencing slack, as defined.

The following linkage exists between slack and innovation: organizational effectiveness and success tend to cause slack; slack tends to deemphasize the priority of problems of scarcity; this deemphasis results in a loosening of the review of budget requests by organizational subunits; as a result, more requests motivated primarily by concerns of status and subunit prestige are approved (as opposed to requests motivated primarily by concern for performance goals and problem solving). The innovations and changes that result from such requests may or may not be organizationally worthwhile. Slack is their source of funds, and such innovations are often organizationally nonrational, that is, the

[4]Richard M. Cyert and James G. March, *A Behavioral Theory of the Firm* (Englewood Cliffs, N.J.: Prentice-Hall, Inc., 1963), p. 278.

relationship between the innovation and some measure of total organizational effectiveness is problematical.

It is difficult, in practice, to distinguish innovations motivated primarily by performance goals from those motivated primarily by status and prestige goals of organizational subunits, but the distinction is real. Many business organizations are more open to change and willing to experiment with change today because they have "organizational slack." They are less concerned with evidence that a proposed change or innovation is going to solve an immediate problem and contribute to the fulfillment of organizational goals. There is less insistence on organizationally rational behavior.

The appeal of novelty

Change may be admired more for its novelty than for its utility. There is evidence that "striving for stimulation, information, knowledge, or understanding is a universal motive among the primates, and especially man." Berlyne suggests that "prolonged subjection to an inordinately monotonous or unstimulating environment is detrimental to a variety of psychological functions. How much excitement or challenge is optimal will fluctuate widely with personality, culture, psychophysiological state, and recent or remote experience."[5]

Was the seemingly unending search for novelty, excitement, and new experience that characterized the late 1960's in the United States a collective reaction to the "inordinately monotonous or unstimulating environment" of the 1950's? The label Fabulous Fifties notwithstanding, there is some agreement that the fifties were unexciting. Perhaps it is possible to add up all the dullness of the fifties and imagine some total social capacity for dullness that was exceeded. Was there a social cost to this decade of inadequate stimulation that had to be offset by a decade of excessive stimulation? Such stimulation may be required, even when there is no apparent extrinsic reward involved, simply to keep the social nervous system balanced.

The notion of novelty helps explain many organizational changes that are now taking place in business organizations. Although not without substantive merit, the extensive use of current practices such as management by objectives, PERT, sensitivity training, and PPBS cannot be explained fully without recognizing the need in organizations for stimulation and for keeping up with the organizational Joneses. There is some novelty component in the current interest in participative management. Participative approaches to decision making, if adequately informed by an understanding of the assumptions and requirements

[5]First quotation from Bernard Berelson and Gary Steiner, *Human Behavior: An Inventory of Scientific Findings* (New York: Harcourt, Brace & World, Inc., 1964), p. 245. Second from D.E. Berlyne, "Curiosity and Exploration." *Science,* CXLIII (July, 1966), pp. 25-33.

involved, are frequently superior to unilateral approaches. Sometimes participative approaches are useful and sometimes they are not, but, when used, they are almost always different from previous practices. The novelty of this difference, rather than the substantive aspects of participation, may be the attraction to organizations.

Theory as a measure

Despite the fact that many theories can find no reality to explain or predict, it is still true that nothing is more practical than a good theory. Among other benefits, an operational theory helps an organization respond to change in a rational manner. If an organization knows why it is doing what it is doing, it is in a better position to evaluate proposed changes. If there is no good reason for an organizational practice ("It's just policy"), it is no wonder that resistance frustrates those who seek to change the practice.

Barzun has noted that American universities until recently were governed by principles of influence, deference, rationality, civility, and reciprocity. Study was the sole aim and test of the university. He further observes that these principles were not broadly understood:

Most people, including some academic men, had, of course, no idea how American or any other universities were run and could discern no principles whatever in the day-to-day operations. So when the cry of tyranny and revolt was raised, they rushed to pull down the fabric, on the assumption that where there's a complaint there must be an evil. The questions of what evil and where it lay precisely were never thought of. Indignation in some, passivity in others conspired to establish as a universal truth that the American university was an engine of oppression, rotten to the core, a stinking anachronism. So down it came.[6]

If American universities had an adequate, broadly understood and supported theory of operations they would be in a better (although always imperfect) position to assimilate crucial changes required by contemporary needs. As it is, many changes are made on the basis of short-run expediency with almost no consideration of the trade-offs involved. Such changes, sometimes harmful in themselves, bear the additional burden of making it more difficult to detect the principles that guide day-to-day operations.

American business organizations have a reasonably adequate and broadly understood basic theory of operations. Although the theory is incomplete as a theory of total organizational effectiveness, its emphasis on performance and productivity provides a focus for behavior and a criterion

[6]Jacques Barzun, "Tomorrow's University — Back to the Middle Ages," *Saturday Review* (Nov. 15, 1969), p. 25.

against which to measure proposed changes. Sometimes the very clarity of performance measurements and the insistence on short-run pay-offs in business organizations relative to other types of organizations present a barrier to change that hinders organizational growth and development. Nevertheless, the theory provides some modicum of assurance that proposed changes will be consistent with the focus. Its incompleteness, however, assures business organizations of their share of organizationally irrational changes.

Change and the social scientist

Social scientists are in the forefront of those calling for change in individuals, groups, organizations, and communities; their writings are frequently supported by empirical studies of change efforts. Often the writers have been involved in a program as consultants. Since they are not called in by a firm to facilitate the continuance of a stable situation, it is understandable that their writings focus on system features that need to be altered. They are in the change business; they are change agents.

Such agents enter organizations for the purpose of facilitating a process of change, and descriptions of their efforts appear in the literature as contributions to a greater understanding of organizational change. In addition, most social scientists are concerned about the world and the opportunities for growth and development open to individuals and organizations if certain basic attitude and behavior shifts were to occur. Thus, their emphasis on the need for change is understandable, even if not tempered by the obligation of implementing and being responsible for such efforts

THE NEED TO RESIST CHANGE

The preceding factors help to explain some of today's emphasis on change. Nevertheless, in particular situations, the need may be to resist and to emphasize the need for stability and continuity.

Maintenance and growth

Human systems, including individuals, groups, organizations, communities, nations, and so on, tend to maintain themselves and to grow.[7] The maintenance tendency refers to behavior aimed at keeping the

---

[7]For two brief but useful discussions, see Gene W. Dalton, "Criteria for Planning Organizational Change" in Paul R. Lawrence and John A. Seiler, *Organizational Behavior and Administration* (Homewood, III: Richard D. Irwin, Inc., 1965), pp. 914-15; and Robert F. Bales, "Adaptive and Integrative Changes as Sources of Strain in Social Systems," in A. Paul Hare and others, eds., *Small Groups: Studies in Social Interaction* (New York: Alfred A. Knopf, 1962), pp. 127-31.

human system in a steady state, and produces conditions that include predictability, stability, control, conformity, and programmed behavior. This tendency requires change and adaptation in order to remain useful in the human system. The growth tendency refers to behavior aimed at development of the human system in terms of its increased capacity to cope with its environment, and produces conditions that include unpredictability, dynamism, change, freedom, ambiguity, uncertainty, divergence, and unprogrammed behavior.

The growth and maintenance tendencies are widely recognized, but the major emphasis in the literature is on the former. It is important to remember that both are part of all human systems. An individual needs to grow and develop, but he also needs to maintain a steady state that is suitable for him — some minimum level of imbalance between himself and his environment. Therefore, resistance to proposals that human systems change their present state can indicate a fully functioning system. The absence of resistance can be a danger signal for an organization just as the presence of resistance can be. If a human system can be overly defensive, it can also fail to accept its necessary and natural tendencies to maintain its present system capacities.

At the individual level, there is a need for emphasis on owning and accepting our own experience. Although an individual may not be able to articulate to the satisfaction of others why he holds to a particular position or behavior, it is not accurate to conclude that the position or behavior is wrong and should be changed. Perhaps change is eventually called for, but perhaps the first need is for a clearer understanding of the behavior and an acceptance of it as appropriate for that person. The same general idea applies to groups and other social systems.

We need to accept both maintenance and growth tendencies in human systems as part of the system. To the extent that either tendency is prevented from operating, the system is less capable of choosing its own direction. An interest in maximizing opportunities for individuals and other human systems to make their own choices requires also an interest in developing the capacities of the systems to respond to both maintenance and growth tendencies. Resistance to change *is* natural and understandable; care should be taken in dealing with and overcoming it.

Diagnosis and prescription

Another reason for resisting change is the low state of the art of diagnosis and prescription of human system problems. Organizations, in particular, have difficulty in getting agreement on what the problem is and what causes it. The total systemic impact of the problem may not be seen or understood, and opinions will differ regarding the proper solution. Nevertheless, one solution must be selected. It is important that the changes benefit from intelligent resistance in order to ensure that the solution chosen is the best one.

Often a particular solution is known to be favored by management and consequently does not benefit from a thorough discussion. Under such conditions, acceptance is built in, and the organization's growth and change is limited to the diagnostic and prescriptive capacities of those who proposed the change. The absence of intelligent resistance may be attractive in the short run, but the long-run price paid for such built-in acceptance is the loss of the unique contributions of a larger cross section of the organization's members.

Even when an organizational problem has been correctly diagnosed and an adequate solution prescribed, resistance may be needed to the pace and manner of introducing the change. A general guide for introducing major organizational changes is that they must be introduced gradually in order to avoid anxiety and hostility. When this guide is violated, as it often is today, the organization should anticipate dysfunctional consequences. Such consequences may have a detrimental effect on the over-all long-range effectiveness of the organization.

Manipulation

It is often difficult to distinguish acceptance of change from manipulation. This seems particularly true today when so much of the discussion of change is in humanitarian terms. Manipulation and control are shunned; collaboration, consensus, and influence are valued.

Nevertheless, unless precautions are taken to ensure that the right and skill to resist change is an accepted organizational value, collaboration and consensus may be merely new labels for the manipulation and control of behavior. There may be, for example, more actual manipulation of employee behavior through a managerial style described as participative than through a style that is clearly autocratic. The conditions for genuine collaborative decision making are seldom realized in practice. However, the vocabulary of collaboration is enough in some cases to mesmerize participants into accepting predetermined behavioral changes.

Leavitt has commented on the presence of manipulation in the classic studies by Lewin and Coch and French dealing with resistance to change. More recently, Marrow's study of organizational change in the Weldon Manufacturing Company is an example of the potential danger hiding behind such words as collaboration and participation.[8] This unique study reports what happens when a group of consultants, applying general principles of social science research, diagnose, prescribe, and implement a change program in the Weldon Manufacturing Company. The study is

---

[8]Harold J. Leavitt, "Applied Organizational Change in Industry," in James G. March, ed., *Handbook of Organizations* (Chicago: Rand McNally & Co., 1965), pp. 1152-53. Also see *Management by Participation: Creating a Climate for Personal and Organizational Development.*

essentially a report of the two contrasting managerial approaches of Weldon and Harwood Manufacturing Corporation and how the Harwood approach was used as a model for revising the Weldon approach.

Elements of manipulation and coercion were clearly present in the change program; required attendance at sensitivity training programs is only one example. As one reads this study, the question of the freedom of Weldon employees to resist change frequently arises. It is only conjecture to suggest that the total organizational change described in this study might have been more effective had there existed a climate in which the employees felt free to resist the specific changes imposed on them. This observation is all the more significant because the study "makes clear the contribution which quantitative social science research can make to an enterprise: General principles and new specific insights emerging from such research were used to plan and guide all changes made in the Weldon plant."

Do such principles and insights include an adequate appreciation for the legitimacy of resistance to change? It is a serious undertaking to ask people to alter their behavior and attitudes. Such changes strike at the core of a person's identity and self-esteem. They simply may not be able to assimilate these changes into their present mode of behavior; they may not be able to articulate their opposition; and they may not feel free to express their opposing views. The presence of such conditions in an organizational setting can only be detrimental to the long-run effectiveness of the organization.

BALANCE CHANGE AND STABILITY

Are there any special tools that the manager can use in overcoming resistance to stability? Many defensive mechanisms and tactics of obstruction can be used by managers, groups, and organizations to stifle innovation.[9] Such devices are obstacles to essential renewal and create an atmosphere unsympathetic to change. There is an adequate amount of that kind of behavior and it is performed skillfully and effectively.

The question here concerns intelligent resistance. In particular situations, the most progressive, rational, modern, future-oriented stance may be to resist change. However, the organizational climate may be totally unfriendly to the idea of resistance. One who resists is considered defensive, old-fashioned, nonadaptable, over-the-hill, and not part of the managerial Mod Squad. It could be career suicide for a manager to resist the latest program that has attracted the fancy of the company president.

[9]John W. Gardner, *Self-Renewal, the Individual and the Innovative Society* (New York: Harper & Row, Publishers, 1963), pp. 43-53.

There are no special tools for intelligent resistance of change. What is needed is a way of looking at individual, group, and organizational proposals that is complete enough to recognize that, in some situations, a change should be resisted and even rejected. Lewin's force-field model for thinking about change and the expansion of this model by Lippitt, Watson, and Westley into several phases of planned alteration is at present the most complete way of looking at the problem.[10] This model is usually discussed as a strategy for achieving change — not as a strategy for resisting, a fault of discussions of the model and not of the model itself.

For example, in the Lewin model, the present level of behavior is seen as a dynamic balance of driving and restraining forces working in opposite directions. The balance between the two sets of forces represents behavior at a quasi-stationary equilibrium. In order to achieve a behavioral change, an imbalance has to occur between the sum of the driving forces and the sum of the restraining forces. Therefore, using this model, intelligent resistance requires that the magnitude of the driving forces be decreased, that the magnitude of the restraining forces be increased, or that some combination of these occur in order to maintain behavior at its present level of balance or equilibrium.[11] Stability or continuity will prevail when no imbalance occurs between the sum of the restraining forces and the sum of the driving forces.

The phases of planned change as described by Lippitt are an expansion of Lewin's three-phase process of change. Lewin noted that a successful behavioral change had three aspects: an unfreezing or disruption of the initial steady behavioral state, a period of adapting and moving toward a new behavioral level, and finally a period of refreezing in a new steady state. One of the crucial elements in the unfreezing phase is nonsupport; the potential changee must receive some signals that present behavior patterns are inadequate. Such signals are unsupporting information; they tell the changee that something is wrong with present behavior or attitudes.

How does an organization know when it is receiving nonsupport? What precise behavior or attitude is the target? Intelligent resistance to change requires validation of such alleged information. The capacity to discern a temporary inability to cope with a situation arising from nonsupport requires skill and an accepting of one's own (individual, group, or organization) behavior.

The second phase of the change process involves moving to a new level of behavior. This phase suggests the need for a model representing the new behavior. Does such a model exist? If so, can it be understood and is it operational? Intelligent resistance to change insists on an understood

---

[10]Kurt Lewin, "Frontiers in Group Dynamics." *Human Relations* (1947), pp. 5-41; Ronald Lippitt and others. *The Dynamics of Planned Change* (New York: Harcourt, Brace & World, Inc., 1958).

[11]For another view, see "Adaptive and Integrative Changes as Sources of Strain in Social Systems."

and operative model of new behavior before discarding older behavior patterns. What is the objective function and the constraints of the new model versus the old?

Although the above factors are worth noting, they are secondary to the more general factor of climate. Precautions must be taken to assure that the right and skill to resist change is a valued part of the organizational climate. Such a right should be valued as much as the right and skill to innovate and to propose change. Given the tendencies of organizations to rigidify and to discourage innovation, it is understandable why so much attention in recent years has focused on organizational change. Nevertheless, the right to resist change is an organizational liberty.

If there is agreement on anything these days it is that we live in a period of radical and rapid change. Business managers live and work in the reality of reshaping markets, technology, environment, attitudes, and values. Adaptation is necessary just to stand still. Often the choice open to the manager is not whether or what change, but how and when. Strong resistance, however, still prevents many essential changes from taking place in business organizations. Perhaps there is such a need for change that it is a disservice to caution against it, even when excesses can be seen.

However, there is no need to become "change happy." An individual will not perform well when there is an excessive imbalance between himself and his environment; he will not grow, or develop, or self-actualize. Individuals, groups, and organizations cannot enhance their sense of competence in a continuous state of flux. It is essential to recognize that stability and continuity are needed and that they are two parts of the growth process.

During the past decade, the business literature has served the manager well, not only because it has recognized the need for change, but also because it has communicated new knowledge and techniques for overcoming resistance to necessary change. However, it is also desirable to apply such knowledge and techniques to overcoming resistance to necessary stability and continuity. A healthy organizational climate recognizes such resistance as a legitimate tendency of human systems.

STRATEGY PLANNING*

Bruce D. Henderson

For too many companies life consists of working very hard to make small differences in performance produce small differences in profitability. The really significant alterations in corporate fortunes, however, depend upon those relatively few major and basic decisions that determine the chances of success — decisions that enable the company to fight corporate wars with its best weapons, not those of competitors, and that enable it to choose the time and place where competitive strength really counts. The final choice of strategy rests on intuition, philosophy, and genius, but the development of strategy alternatives for examination must be methodical, analytical, and deliberate.

We know little about how most companies actually reach their strategy decisions, since strategy is usually a carefully guarded secret. (Consultants probably see the process more often than anyone else.) However, business history offers many examples of the effect of a superior choice made in the field of strategy.

Georgia Pacific Corporation reversed a declining trend in 1952, and increased sales by five times and earnings by ten times during the next ten years. Its largest competitor, Weyerhauser, had lower earnings at the end of ten years even though sales volume doubled.

Scott Paper Company doubled its profits between 1952 and 1962, increasing earnings every year except one. Profit margins actually increased. Of the five paper companies that were larger than Scott in 1963, not one maintained its profit margin. The average margin for these five companies was two-thirds the 1952 level.

Air Products and Chemical Company had sales of $8 million in 1952, $100 million in 1962; profits per share of 30 cents increased to $2.84. Its major competitor, Air Reduction, did little better than double sales, and increased earnings less than 50 cent.

Minnesota Mining has earned fame for growth and profitability. In ten years, sales more than tripled and earnings per share increased five times. In no year in the last ten did earnings per share fail to grow. The product line at 3M defies comparison; it ranges from sandpaper to movie cameras.

*Reprinted by permission from *Business Horizons*. Copyright 1964 by the Foundation for the School of Business, Indiana University.

Each of these companies had good management and good performance to start with, but, for the most part, so did their competitors. The differences in performance appear to result not from better operating management, but from superior strategy.

Where the right strategy and good management have been applied to sick companies, the results have been even more spectacular. American Motors' success story with the compact car is well known. Indian Head Mills was a weak company ten years ago, burdened with debt and an obsolete plant. The textile business is traditionally one of the most competitive of all, yet Indian Head sales today are more than ten times those of ten years ago, and net profits per share are several times the book value.

Of course, spectacular failures occur too. A few years ago, J. I. Case looked like a champion, then proved to be nearly bankrupt. General Dynamics' strategy with Convair jetliners produced perhaps the largest single corporate loss in a single year that any company has ever survived. The loss is estimated to be nearly a half a billion dollars.

Unfortunately, the results of bad strategy are not often as conspicuous as success stories. Typically, inferior strategy results from long and diligent pursuit of an obsolete concept, and the fate of companies who pursue obsolete strategies is rarely spectacular. More often it is a slow and grinding erosion of profits, markets, and vitality until the company dies of old age or is absorbed by a more imaginative competitor.

To the public at large, the reason for mediocrity and failure is almost always "poor management." And yet every chief executive in the land carries in his mind's eye a picture of the way he hopes and expects his company to be some day. Each of these executives has a strong conviction that certain ideas and certain policies are the best way to achieve his corporate ideal. As he goes about his daily business, he makes his decisions and judges his subordinates by these standards. For some companies, that is all the strategy there is.

STRATEGY AND CHANGE

Some businessmen have an uncanny ability to integrate all they see, hear, or know and lead their companies to success after success. Without at least a touch of this kind of idealism, imagination, and leadership, it is hard to imagine any real and continuing competitive success. But my personal conviction is that self-confidence and intuition — even when combined with inspired leadership and hard work — are just not enough. If a company's strategy is sound, ordinary men with ordinary resources can frequently win over superior competition. If its strategy is wrong, even inspired leadership, dedicated men, and superior resources may be doomed to failure.

If we agree that strategy is critical, then we must decide whether intuitive judgments are adequate, or whether we must include methodical and analytical planning in our strategy. I believe that intuition and analytical planning are equally necessary, but that analytical strategy planning is often neglected. The intuitive approach to strategy planning was geared to a slower-paced era. When change was slower, trial and error was the useful guide, and experience was far more reliable as a forecaster of the future. When change is accelerated, experience alone is no longer adequate.

Changes in military hardware perhaps best illustrate the effect of faster change. In the twenty years after World War I, changes were mostly refinements in existing equipment. Airplanes and aircraft carriers commanded significant positions in military budgets. Contrast this situation with the situation twenty years after World War II. The atomic weapon has become the dominant military fact of life; jet engines have virtually replaced reciprocating engines in military aircraft; atomic propulsion has revolutionized submarine capabilities; space vehicles are emerging as a major weapons delivery system; and communication and data processing builders of a different order of magnitude have become essential for weapons control. Today, a military contractor's whole future may depend heavily upon his decisions of several years ago and on how well he forecast future weapons systems.

Change is also accelerated in the civilian sector. It may be less dramatic, but it is equally pervasive. Television, transoceanic air transport, discount retailing, synthetic fabrics, leisure time industries, natural gas home heating, and many other amenities we take for granted are actually postwar industries.

If there is any payout in research, then accelerated change is inevitable and should not surprise us. Twice as much is being spent for research this year in the United States as the sum total spent between the landing of the Pilgrims and the end of World War II. Research expenditures have been doubling about every six years for some time now.

As a rule of thumb, the time lag between research results and commerical production is estimated at seven to eight years. If this is so and if payout increases as research increases, we are faced with a startling conclusion. *Change is already in the works for the next five to eight years many times over what has occurred in our nation's whole history.* We can promise that business will have its share of this change, and strategy planning will become even more important than it is today.

STRATEGY FORMULATION

But just what is strategy planning, and, more important, how do we go about it? Strategy, for our purposes, is the corporate goal and plan for achievements that will be maintained essentially without regard for competitors' tactics. For most companies, we mean goals for the period five to ten years in the future. Less than five years is usually insufficient time to make a major change in corporate character or direction effective, and more than ten years is too far in the future to allow meaningful predictions of corporate environment. This, then, is our definition of strategy: our goals in terms of corporate character and direction in the period five to ten years ahead and the methods to be used in achieving these goals.

In strategy formulation, we have the following major objectives:

Appraisal of corporate resources relative to competition

Forecasting the changes in the significant factors in the corporate environment

Assessing the values of possible corporate goals to each significant corporate group — stockholders, top management, employees, and others

Developing a best-fit concept of the corporate goals that are reasonably attainable

Constructing an optimum strategy to achieve the chosen goals

Obtaining acceptance of goals and strategy by every significant corporate participant

Translating strategy into operating plans, assignments, and controls

Obviously, this is not just an analytical process. All phases of strategy formulation are interwoven into a pattern too complex to be developed by analytical techniques alone, and many of the key factors are intangible values, personal perspectives, and other subjective criteria. We must recognize that strategy formulation is an art, an art of conceptual creativity. But to be at our best we must also use wisely the facts, techniques, and analytical processes that are available.

How practical is it to apply analysis to the objectives we listed earlier?

First, can we appraise corporate resources? Of course we can, but it is extremely difficult to be realistic and objective in this appraisal. The needs of morale and self-confidence often conflict with the need for perspective. The problem of being unable to see the forest for the trees can easily arise here.

Second, can we forecast the changes in the corporate environment? This is even harder to do with objectivity. In the midst of day-to-day operation, it is difficult to visualize future changes in our competitive world. But the facts *are* around us; we *can* make observations if we try. Most companies can make a surprisingly useful forecast of things to come, if (and it is a big if) they go about it methodically and analyze what they do know.

Third, can we assess corporate values attached to corporate goals? Now we are beginning to deal with intangibles. Individuals within an organization have differing values and goals. Moreover, the less factual data available, the more intuition — that is to say, preconceived notions— will be substituted. This makes the resolution of differences of opinion quite difficult because their basis is emotional rather than logical. The corporate goals and values must be compromises; to develop them requires time and close talk. This phase of corporate thinking can rarely be cut short except where special conditions exist — for example, if the corporation is suddenly faced with an emergency or major threat.

Fourth, can we develop a best-fit concept of appropriate corporate goals? Here, insights must combine with hard reality. Not all things are possible, but even some that are possible are hardly worth the risk. The choice of a best fit of corporate goals is the job of a chief executive, but only after his homework has been well done.

Fifth, how can we develop an optimum strategy to achieve the chosen goals? This begins with hard-headed analysis — putting together the facts and the forecast to develop the strategic alternatives. It requires general staff work at its highest order of performance. The chief's intuition may correctly indicate the final choice, but the caliber of the preliminary staff work determines his chances of finding the right choice.

Strategy has been defined as a plan that takes into account all factors—people's feelings, the future, and what competitors might do. That definition appeals because it explains why there is no single provable best strategy. Most important, it makes it obvious that the intangible always makes strategy an art just as the need for facts makes it depend on analysis.

All chief executives know the choice of the right strategy is only the beginning and that the role of the chief executive must always be difficult. A change in strategy usually challenges cherished corporate traditions and means eventual change in corporate character. The heart says stay, but the head says go. Only the orderly, methodical. analytical process permits the deliberate and considered challenge of past beliefs. Only an extended, objective examination of the rationale of corporate strategy permits the heart and the head together to produce wisdom. The beginning of wisdom is a deliberate decision to plan the strategy.

THE MISSING INGREDIENT

The environment of change makes strategy planning necessary. But what makes it effective? The first and most important ingredient, one too frequently missing in the approach of many companies, is a genuine emotional consensus among top management as to what it wants to do and how it wants to go about getting there. This consensus is not a prerequisite to strategy planning; its achievement is an essential result or major step in the planning process. It can only be accomplished by conscious, deliberate, continued, *verbal* examination of goals, alternatives, and possible consequences. These must be talked out until they are mutually understood and accepted by the key members of management. This consensus must be transmitted to the organization consistently and clearly so that day-to-day operating decisions can be made with reference to corporate goals. Effective strategy planning and implementation cannot take place without this consensus, which must be based on a desire to deal with change.

ORGANIZATION PRINCIPLES*

S. Avery Raube

Like the engineer who designs his bridge to meet special needs, the organization planner, in designing a company structure, applies principles. For through years of experience it has been learned that if certain principles are followed, regardless of the size of the enterprise, the result will be good organization. Some of these basic laws follow:

1. *There must be clear lines of authority running from the top to the bottom of the organization.* Lt. Col. Lyndall Urwick[1] defines authority as "the formal right to require action of others." Mr. R. E. Gillmore[2] says it is "the right to direct, coordinate and decide."

Clarity is achieved through delegation by steps or levels from the leader to the working level, from the highest executive ot the employee who has least responsibility in the organization and no authority over others. From the president, a line of authority may proceed to a vice president, to a general manager, to a foreman, to a leadman, and finally to a worker on an assembly line. It should be possible to trace such a line from the president, or whoever is top coordinating executive, to every employee in the company.

Following military parlance, this line is sometimes referred to as "the chain of command." The principle is known as the "scalar principle." It is the vertical division of authority.

2. *No one in the organization should report to more than one line supervisor. Everyone in the organization should know to whom he reports, and who reports to him.* This is known as the "unity of command" principle. Stated simply, everyone should have only one boss.

This principle is one of those most frequently violated and the cause of many internal difficulties. It may be a matter of several stenographers working for a group of executives, any one of whom can require directly the services of any of the individual girls. The best of the stenographers is overloaded with work, the least efficient has nothing to do.[3] It may be a

---

*Reprinted with permission from *Company Organization Charts*, National Industrial Conference Board, New York, 1954.

[1] Eminent British specialist in the field of organization.

[2] Vice-President, the Sperry Corporation, and author of many articles on organization subjects.

[3] In secretarial "pools," this situation is avoided and the principle adhered to by having all of the stenographers report to a single supervisor who receives all requests for stenographic assistance and assigns work to the individuals.

matter of partners running a business, with each giving orders independently to the executive vice president.

The harassed individual who receives orders from several bosses is faced with problems such as whose orders to follow first, how to allocate his time so as to displease none and satisfy all, what to do if he receives conflicting orders from different sources. The lazy employee is afforded an excellent opportunity to avoid work by explaining to one boss that he cannot accept more tasks because he is busy carrying out (imaginary) assignments given by another.

3. *The responsibility and authority of each supervisor should be clearly defined in writing.* Putting his responsibilities into writing enables the supervisor, himself, to know what is expected of him and the limits of his authority. It prevents overlapping of authority, with resultant confusion. It avoids gaps between responsibilities. And it enables quick determination of the proper point for decision.

Many executives say complacently, "We all know what we are supposed to do. There is no need to put our duties in writing." But in many companies, management has been startled when top executives have been asked, independently, to list their duties. It is an eye-opener to discover that three and four individuals believe themselves responsible for an identical function, and that time and money are being wasted in duplicated effort. Therein, too, lie the seeds of jurisdictional dispute.

When an executive is lost suddenly, through death or lure of a competitor, it is not uncommon to find that no one knows exactly what the executive did, and therefore what to require of his successor. Even when a vacancy is expected, it is difficult to train a replacement without an accurate knowledge of the content of the position.

4. *Responsibility should always be coupled with corresponding authority.* This principle suggests that if a plant manager in multi-unit organization is held responsible for all activities in his plant, he should not be subject to *orders* from company headquarters specifying the quantity of raw materials he should buy or from whom he should purchase them.[4] If a supervisor is responsible for the quality of work put out in his department, he should not have to accept as a member of his working force an employee who has been hired without consulting him.

There are many executives who delegate authority and then undermine it by making decisions that belong to the individual who is being held responsible. Over a luncheon table a company president makes a promise of delivery to a favored customer, which upsets the carefully planned schedules of the sales manager. A plant superintendent makes

---

[4]He may, however, welcome advice or suggestions from a purchasing specialist on the company's central staff.

a casual statement to the press which strews rocks in the path of the director of public relations.

This principle can be stated conversely: "Authority should always be coupled with corresponding responsibility." Those given authority, unless they are held accountable, may easily become dictators.

5. *The responsibility of higher authority for the acts of its subordinates is absolute.* Lt. Col. Urwick has expressed the principle in these words. Another way of saying it is that although a supervisor delegates authority, he still remains responsible for what is done by those to whom he has delegated it.

The head of maintenance is responsible for keeping the plant lighting system in order. He does not screw a new electric light bulb in place when an old one burns out. That responsibility has been delegated to the plant electrician. But if the electrician fails to replace a bulb when one is needed, the head of maintenance is as accountable as the electrician. He is responsible for the electrician's inefficiency.

In accord with this principle, an executive cannot disassociate himself from the acts of his subordinates. He is as responsible as they, for what they do and neglect to do.

6. *Authority should be delegated as far down the line as possible.* Permitting decisions to be made on as low a level as possible releases the energies of those on higher levels for matters which only they can attend to. The head of a pottery factory does not concern himself with whether the rose on the breakfast plate is to be red or yellow. The head of a large company does not personally sign every paycheck or personally approve the salary increase of every typist. For those are duties that may easily and efficiently be delegated farther down the line.

Application of this principle can be observed in the current trend toward decentralization of large companies. Decision-making power is being placed nearer the scene of action. The plant or division manager is allowed to make all decisions in his unit, within the confines of company-wide policy. This enables members of top corporate management to devote more time to over-all thinking and planning.

7. *The number of levels of authority should be kept at a minimum.* The greater the number of levels, the longer is the chain of command, and the longer it takes for instructions to travel down and for information to travel up and down within the organization.

Too many levels encourage "run-arounds." To obtain a quicker decision, a worker fails to consult his immediate supervisor, but appeals to an executive higher up the line.

Mr. Gillmore has figured out mathematically that most organizations would never need more than six levels of supervision, including that of the top executive. With six such levels, he says, with a span of control of five at the top levels, and twenty workers reporting to each supervisor at the lowest level of supervision, there is room in an organization for 62,500 workers and 3,905 executives.[5]

8. *The work of every person in the organization should be confined as far as possible to the performance of a single leading function.* This is the principle of specialization. It applies to departments and divisions as well as to individuals. It concerns delegation of authority *horizontally*, rather than vertically, as in the case of the scalar principle.

The total duties in the organization are divided according to functions, and a department or division is made responsible for each.[6]

There may be functional division according to the *kind* of work to be done — manufacturing, sales, finance, or engineering. Or, within a department, for example the financial department, a company may have subdivisions for billing, receiving, payroll, etc.

There may also be functional division according to the *way* in which the work is done. For example, divisions may be set up for typists, comptometer operators, etc.

This principle requires that if a person is held responsible for more than one duty, and this is often the case in small companies, the duties should be similar. Public relations is grouped with industrial relations, rather than with engineering. The specialist specializes. In the interests of efficiency, he concentrates on the things he can do best.

In organizations which have been allowed to grow without design, individuals are frequently found who are performing two or more unrelated duties. Sometimes this comes about because a certain individual happens to have a little free time when an activity is added. Sometimes it is because a man happens to have some experience in his background which qualifies him to handle the new assignment, even though it has nothing to do with his major duties. Sometimes it is because he has a particular interest in the activity. Sometimes an individual seizes a floating activity simply because he is a power-grabber.

A combination of ill-related assignments often seems to work satisfactorily, so long as a particular person holds a post. But it is not considered good organization. Should he leave, the prospects of finding another person who has the identical abilities to handle the widely different duties are usually slim. The organization structure which has to be changed to fit persons cannot adhere to a design which it is believed will best achieve the company's objectives.

---

[5]"A Practical Manual of Organization," by R. E. Gillmor, Funk & Wagnals Company, New York, 1948.

[6]There is no uniformity in the use of the terms "department" and "division." They mean whatever a company wants them to mean. Some companies have departments within divisions; some have divisions within departments. Some use "department" for their staff units, and "division" for the operating units.

9. *Whenever possible, line functions should be separated from staff functions, and adequate emphasis should be placed on important staff activities.* Line functions are those which accomplish the main objectives of the company. In many manufacturing companies, the manufacturing and distribution functions are considered line. The manufacturing and sales departments are considered the departments that are accomplishing the main objectives of the business.

In companies that are not attempting to reach the ultimate consumer with their products, for example those that sell their products to outside distributors or to the government, the sales function may not be considered a line function.

In some companies in which engineering is practically a part of production, it is considered a line function. In certain chemical companies, research is so closely integrated with production that it is thought of as a line activity. Procurement of raw materials may be considered line by a metal manufacturing company that does its own mining and quarrying.

Line departments are often called "operating" departments.

Staff functions are those which aid in, or are auxiliary to, the line functions. Some companies call their staff departments "auxiliary departments."

Members of staff departments provide service, advice, coordination and control for the line or operating departments. (They may perform one or more of these functions.) Purchasing and advertising departments, for instance, provide service. Legal and public relations departments provide advice. Production planning serves as an example of a coordinating agency. Industrial engineering and accounting departments are examples of departments that provide control. Many of these departments serve more than one of the purposes. The department which provides service may also provide advice; the department that coordinates may also help with control.

Committees are usually considered staff agencies. Their members advise, coordinate, and control.

There are also individuals, who are not members of a department or committee, who perform staff functions. These are called staff assistants. The specialist retained from an outside firm, such as a legal consultant or public relations consultant, is an example. Or, within an organization, there may be an assistant to the president who has no supervisory duties but who investigates problems that are referred to him by the president, putting before the president data upon the basis of which the chief executive can make decisions. The staff assistant's duties are chiefly the detailed work of command, so that the energies of the line executive can be released for larger activities.

10. *There is a limit to the number of positions that can be coordinated by a single executive.* This is known as the "span of control" principle.

The number of positions (groups of activities) which an executive is able to coordinate, depends on:

a. The similarity or dissimilarity of the subordinate positions and how interdependent they are. The more positions interlock, the greater is the work of coordination.

b. How far the people and activities are apart geographically. The manager who is coordinating activities within a single plant can coordinate more than if these activities are carried on at widely scattered locations.

c. The complexity of the duties of each of the positions to be coordinated.

d. The stability of the business.

e. The frequency with which new types of problems arise. If a company has been in business for many years, the problems which come up from day to day have probably been encountered before, and the work of coordination is therefore less than if the problems were brand new.

The span of control is seldom uniform throughout an organization. At the upper levels, where positions are interdependent and dissimilar, many organization specialists urge that the span of control embrace not more than five or six subordinates. In some decentralized companies, however, in which the operating units are practically autonomous, the top executive is successfully coordinating as many as twelve or fifteen positions.

At the lowest supervisory level — the level of the last executives who have any supervisory responsibilities — organization specialists say that a supervisor may supervise as many as twenty workers. This might be a foreman or leadman supervising men on an assembly line.

As attention has been given to the human relations aspects of the supervisor's responsibilities, there has been a tendency to shorten the span of control even at the lowest level. While a foreman might be able to supervise the work of twenty men, all of whom are performing an identical, simple operation, he might not have time to give them individual attention as persons. He might not have time to communicate information on company policies, listen to their suggestions or grievances, learn the causes of poor performance. For these reasons a large paper company announced that it had decided to limit the number of workers supervised by each of its foremen to ten. A manufacturer of metal products, because of such reasons, has adopted a maximum ratio of twelve workers to the lowest supervisor.

In separating packets of duties into manageable parts, so that no individual's span of control need be too great, three types of division are commonly employed: (1) functional, (2) product or service, and (3) regional or geographical. The functional type of division has been discussed in connection with the principle of specialization. A company that has a radio manufacturing department and a television manufacturing department is using product division. Examples of service divisions are provided by a public utility company which has a lighting department and a heating department, or a bank that has an insurance department and a mortgage department.

When operations are widely scattered, the most effective plan is sometimes to set up a unit in each geographical area. In public utilities such as railroads, this is a natural way of assigning duties. Life insurance companies, too, often have regional divisions.

Many companies use a combination of these methods. Within a sales department (a functional division) there may be a western and an eastern sales office (regional divisions). Or the refrigerator division of an electrical products company (product division) may use the functional basis for separating its activities into manageable parts — engineering, manufacturing, sales, etc.

Some point out that there is danger in oversupervision as well as in undersupervision, that is, in having the span of control too short. At the top levels, the executive coordinates dissimilar positions. He should not coordinate too many positions simply because they are dissimilar. Account must be taken of the frequency with which new problems arise and other factors which influence the span of control. If, however, the executive is not given enough positions to coordinate, he may have time on his hands. Such a person may have a tendency to inject himself into operational decisions, undermining authority which has been delegated.

11. *The organization should be flexible, so that it can be adjusted to changing conditions.* The organization plan should stand up, in boom and in depression, in war and in peace, when new markets appear and when old ones disappear. The plan should permit expansion and contraction without disrupting the basic design. Good organization is not a straitjacket.

12. *The organization should be kept as simple as possible.* Too many levels of authority, as has been noted, make communication difficult. Too many committees impede rather than achieve coordination.

All of these principles (there are more than the dozen listed, but these are ones that are frequently referred to in discussions of organization) are based on the idea of leadership and delegation of authority. Complete authority is delegated by the board of directors to an individual, who is able to carry out his responsibilities by delegating authority to others.

BENEFITS OF GOOD ORGANIZATION

A few of the benefits of the application of these principles have been touched upon in describing the precepts. The following reiterate some of them, but include additional benefits that companies attribute to organization planning. Application of the principles

Disposes of conflicts between individuals over jurisdiction.

Prevents duplication of work.

Decreases likelihood of "run-arounds."

Makes communication easier through keeping the channels clear.

Shows promotional possibilities, which is useful in executive development. Organization charts and position descriptions show where a
man can expect to go, what qualifications are needed to fill a superior
job, what additional training is needed to prepare a man in one position for a superior post.

Provides a sound basis for appraisal and rating of individual performance and capabilities. If one knows what an individual is supposed
to be doing, it is then possible to measure how well he is living up
to the requirements of the job.

Aids in wage and salary administration. The analysis of duties for the
higher executives performs the same service as job descriptions for
those in the lower echelons.

Permits expansion with adequate control, and without killing off top
executives. Activities are administered in manageable units, so that
no one person has too heavy a load.

Permits changes to be made in the right direction as opportunities
present themselves. In the absence of a plan, changes are likely to
be made on the basis of expediency, with the likelihood of perpetuat-
ing original mistakes.

Increases cooperation and a feeling of freedom. Each person works best
with others when he knows for what he is responsible, to whom he is
responsible and the values of cooperative relationships with others.
A feeling of freedom comes when responsibilities are definite and
known and when delegation is actually practiced.

GROUP BEHAVIOR AND THE ORGANIZATION CHART*

Keith Davis

Apart from the clean lines on a company's organization chart and the concise statements in the job descriptions, there is a highly interesting complex system of social relationships known as the informal organization. This organization arises from the social interactions of people. It is significant to management because of its powerful influence on productivity and job satisfaction.

Like the formal organization, the informal one has basic functions or activities. As it performs them, it develops certain abuses or problems as a natural consequence of its actions. The problems may be called the reciprocals of the function, since they arise from the function, often in proportion to the degree in which it is performed.

For example, one of the basic functions of informal groups is communication. A reciprocal that unfortunately arises therefrom is rumor. Another function is social control of members. The reciprocal is undesirable conformity.

This type of analytical framework offers a useful way to examine the role of informal structures in our complex industrial society. In the discussion that follows, however, only one principal reciprocal of each function will be described. There are, of course, more than one.

The informal communication system is familiarly known as the grapevine, and rumor, the reciprocal of each, is defined as the injudicious or untrue part of the grapevine.

Rumor is a devastating disease that sweeps through an organization as fast as a summer storm — and usually with as much damage. Consequently, management must be prepared to deal with it, but must know how and what to do. It is a serious mistake to strike at the whole grapevine merely because it happens to be the agent which carries rumor. That approach would be as injudicious as throwing away a typewriter because of a misspelled word.

The best approach when dealing with rumor is to get at its causes — the preventive approach. Trying to kill the rumor after it has already started is a tardy, curative approach.

*Reprinted from *Advanced Management — Office Executive*, vol. 1, no. 6 (June 1962), with the permission of the publisher.

A NORMAL DEFENSE ACTION

A cooperative high-morale group has little rumor-mongering, for the simple reason that its members have little cause to start rumors. When people feel reasonably secure and they feel they are on the team, when they understand the things that matter to them, there are few rumors. But when people are poorly placed in the group, are emotionally maladjusted, or are inadequately informed about their environment, they are likely to be rumor-mongers. This is a normal defensive reaction in an attempt to make a situation more meaningful and secure.

But, in spite of all that can be done, rumors do start. Then what? In general, managers should try to stop the ones that are important enough to be of concern. These "big" ones should be stopped as early as possible, for research shows that once a rumor's general theme is known and accepted, then employees distort future happenings to conform to the rumor.

INTERPRETED AS CONFIRMATION

For example, if employees accept the "scuttlebutt" that there are plans to move the firm's offices to a new building, then every minor change thereafter will be interpreted as a confirmation of that rumor (even, say, when an electrician comes to repair a plug). If the rumor were dead, minor changes could be made without any employee-upset at all.

Naturally not all rumors should be fought, for that policy would be like Don Quixote fighting windmills. But the damaging ones must be dealt with. Rumors are stopped or weakened by getting out the facts in any way possible. Usually, face-to-face supply of facts is the most effective way, but a word of warning is in order. The facts must be given directly without first mentioning the rumor. When a rumor is repeated at this time, it is remembered just as well as the refutation!

Regardless of its importance, a rumor should be listened to carefully, because, even though untrue, it usually carries a message. One should ask: Why did that rumor originate? What does it mean? In every case, there is some cause which needs to be understood.

IT MAY MEAN SOMETHING ELSE

If, for example, a rumor says Joe is quitting, it may mean that his associates wish he would quit, or he wishes he could quit, or his wife is quitting her job, or something else, or nothing at all. The obligation is to examine the hodge-podge of rumors that pass by and try to get some meaning from them.

Maybe this approach is unrealistic for some of us in everyday life, but the idea can be illustrated with the case of the labor relations director who, during a strike, listened carefully to what the workers said management was going to do. He knew these were rumors, for management had not decided what to do. Nevertheless he listened, because the rumors gave him insight about worker attitudes toward management and about how far the workers would go.

A second function of informal organization is to provide social satisfactions. Informal organizations give a man recognition, status, and further opportunity to relate to others. In a large office an employee may feel like only a payroll number, but his informal group gives him personal attachment and status. With his group he is somebody, even though in formal structure he is only one of a thousand clerks. He may not look forward to posting 750 accounts daily, but the informal group can give more meaning to his day. When he can think of meeting his friends, eating with them, and sharing their jokes, his day takes on a new dimension that erases any disagreeableness or routine in his work.

Of course, these conditions can work in reverse: A group may not accept a worker, thereby making his work more disagreeable and driving him to transfer, or to be absent, or to resign. These are reciprocals of the social satisfaction function. However, the main reciprocal which tends to develop is role conflict.

The quest for group satisfactions often leads members away from organizational objectives and, hence, into a role conflict in which formal and informal roles are pulling against each other. For example, a motivated employee may want to be productive in his role of employee, but he may also want to be the less-productive "good Joe" in his role as a fellow worker with others — hence, two roles in conflict.

PERFECT HARMONY NOT FEASIBLE

Much of this role conflict can be avoided by carefully cultivating mutual interests with informal groups. The more the interests, goals, methods, and evaluation systems of formal and informal organizations can be integrated, the more productivity and satisfaction can be expected. However, there must always be some formal and informal differences. This is not an area where perfect harmony is feasible.

An interesting example of role conflict is one in which two electricians used an unusual situation to gain informal status with their peers and with a staff engineer — an attempt in which glory soon faded!

A young electrical engineer was assigned the job of mapping the underground cable system of a shipyard which, after five years of abandonment, had been taken over by a new chemical firm. No blueprints of the cable system were included in property transfer, and management was unable to discover any. The only visible evidence was locations where cables entered and left the ground.

Two plant electricians at the chemical firm had formerly worked at the shipyard, and the engineer went to them to see if they remembered any of the cable paths. Preliminary discussion and a tour of the grounds indicated that the electricians could be helpful, so the engineer started working with them regularly.

To establish rapport with the two electricians, the engineer frequently bought them morning and afternoon snacks, and engaged them in long bull sessions in walks around the grounds. He felt, too, that this practice jogged their memories and helped them recall the cable paths.

DELIGHTED WITH NEW STATUS

The electricians were delighted with their new status and importance, so much so that their memories of the cable paths seemed slower and slower, though still surprisingly accurate. Meanwhile, spurred by a completion date, the engineer worked even harder to be nice to them.

One day the engineer was with the electricians when an emergency occurred requiring knowledge of a cable location not yet found. One of the electricians, without thinking, walked over to his locker and unrolled the complete original set of blueprints of the electrical cable system re-marking as he found the cable in question, "Here it is Joe, right by the north end of number 7 shop." At this point, he looked up and saw the engineer five feet away!

A third function of informal organization is social control by which the behavior of others is influenced and regulated to help the group achieve its satisfactions. Social control is both internal and external. Internal control is directed toward making members of the group conform to its culture. In an accounting office, for instance, an employee wore a bow tie to work. Comments and "razzing" from other workers soon convinced him a bow tie was not an accepted style in the group, so thereafter he did not wear it.

External control is directed toward those outside the group, such as management, union leadership, or other informal groups. Pressures of external control can be quite strong, as when a walk-out strike occurs.

SUPPOSED EVILS OF CONFORMITY

Although social control is necessary, its undesirable reciprocal is conformity. Much has been written in fiction and non-fiction about the supposed evils of conformity, as it has developed within formal organizations. In both cases, writers have tended to assume that, since conformity existed in formal organizations, the formal organizations were the cause of it.

However, the informal organization appears to be an equal cause of employee conformity. Certainly the informal culture can be just as brutal in its demands for conformity as formal organizations can be. Evidence — the fads and fashions of teenage speech and conduct, and the work restrictions in the factory.

There are two types of conformity-action and attitude. Uniformity of action is called group standards. Standards are essential to coordinate large work groups, and where standards derive from the work requirements themselves, there seem to be no overtones of conformity. Only when standards are arbitrarily required does the charge of conformity arise. Although business and government certainly do have some arbitrary conformity, much of what appears to be conformity is simply a requirement of the work process itself, but is not understood as such by the employee. No human boss arbitrarily requires employees to conform.

MUCH EVIDENCE TO THE CONTRARY

In fact, business organizations are known for their encouragement of initiative and difference. They have been one of the strongest worldwide supporters of individuality. There is little evidence that conformity is a hallmark of business culture, as compared with government, church or labor unions. But there is much evidence to the contrary in the business record of innovation, research, and employee advancement.

One study of managers, for example, showed that those who were different (idiosyncratic) were regarded as superior administrators. Another study reported that managers who valued conformity least were rated most effective as managers.

A more serious matter is conformity of action away from work. Here, again, formal organizations do not seem to be the main influence.

The most serious conformity is of attitude. If attitude conformity can be induced, then man loses his individuallty, and he can be manipulated by unscrupulous leaders. Group requirements for attitude consistency are known as norms, and the group whose norms a person accepts is a reference group, whether he belongs to it or not. Informal norms and reference groups are a powerful force in work society. They consistently guide opinion and wield power contrary to the leadership for formal management or formal union.

The great danger of informal group conformity is not its dull loss of personal difference, which is bad enough, but rather that the members become subject to the willful control of the informal leader who can skillfully manipulate them for bad as well as for good.

The informal leader is a leader in just as strong a sense as a formal leader is, but without the controls and weight of responsibility which constrain the formal leader. In this fashion the informal group becomes a prime instrument of manipulators and inciters of conflict who move into the informal structures of society to influence people toward their selfish ends.

In short, people themselves may be the chief cause of their own conformity — rather than their bosses, as current writers would have us believe. Indeed, informal organizations can be just as autocratic, destructive, and conforming as formal ones. This possibility is to be expected: both groups are made up of people — often of the same people.

A fourth function of informal groups is to perpetuate their culture. This function helps preserve the group's integrity and values. As a reciprocal, there develops a resistance to change — a tendency to perpetuate the status quo and to stand like a rock in the face of change. What has been good is good and shall be good.

If, for example, job A has always had more status than job B, then job A must continue to have more status — and more pay — even though conditions have changed to make job A inferior to B by other standards. If restriction of productivity was necessary in the past with an autocratic management, then it is necessary now, even though the management is becoming participative.

BOUND BY CONVENTION

Although informal organizations are bound by no chart on the wall, they are bound by convention, custom, and culture. Whenever managers deal with change, they especially need to understand informal organization, because the resistance will be a key to the success or failure of the change. In fact, fear of change can be as significantly disrupting as change itself, because the former reproduces identical anxieties and reactions.

That an informal group is made up of persons with high I.Q.'s or advanced degrees does not necessarily mean the group will better understand and accept change. Often the opposite is true, because the group uses its extra intelligence to rationalize more reasons why a change should not be made.

The more intelligent the group is, the more reasons it can find for opposing a change. Intelligence can be used either for or against change, depending on how management motivates the group. Often, therefore, intelligent high-level groups cannot be sold new methods as easily as average groups can be.

To summarize, each of the key functions of informal organization brings with it certain abuses or problems as reciprocals. The work environment might be better without these reciprocals, but managers learned long ago that informal organization cannot be abolished, starved, or hidden under a basket. It is here to stay, and the reciprocals are part of the package.

All the manager can do is develop a mature understanding of informal organization and chart his course toward minimizing the abuse and maximizing the benefits. Informal groups can be blended with formal organizations to make an immensely workable system for getting the job completed

HOW MONEY MOTIVATES MEN*

Charles D. McDermid

Obviously, the first meaning of money lies in its power to buy satisfaction of the basic physiological needs — food, clothing, and shelter. Closely allied to these basic needs are certain acquired needs with a physiological basis, such as the need for tobacco. It is only after these fundamental drives have been relatively well satisfied that any major amount of money will be diverted towards other goods.

Next in the hierarchy of needs is the category termed safety, a major expression of which, in today's culture, is the need for financial security. Here money represents insurance against physiological deprivation and against the financial hazards of poor health, old age, and unemployment. Collective bargaining demands for security, as well as such common phenomena as buying life insurance and "putting away for a rainy day," are obvious examples of using money to satisfy safety needs.

Money can also facilitate satisfaction of the social needs, the third level in the hierarchy, but only indirectly. Thus one can purchase membership in a country club, but the actual exchange of friendship and love does not necessarily result. The biggest benefit of money at this level lies in freeing the individual from the insistent clamor of his physiological and safety needs so that he can attend to his social wants.

The situation is different in the case of the esteem needs. The American way of life has stressed money as the measure of status and achievement. Hence it has become most important to the satisfaction of esteem needs. The extent to which this is ingrained in our sense of values can be seen not only in one man's evaluation of another on the basis of his financial show, but even in the dependence of his concept of himself on the amount of money he makes. Many men, in other words, are willing to accept their salary as the indication of their worth. Compensation has become important on this level not only for what it buys, but also for what it means, both in judging one's self and one's neighbor.

What about self-realization at the peak on the need pyramid? Money is of little importance in gaining fulfillment at this level; it can do no more than remove obstacles to self-realization. Here the role of money is to satisfy the physiological and other needs so that the individual is free to devote his efforts to fulfilling his potential.

---

*Reprinted by permission from *Business Horizons*, Winter. Copyright 1960 by the Foundation for the School of Business, Indiana University.

From the preceding paragraphs it can be seen that money is efficient in satisfying needs at the lower levels since it can be quickly and directly converted into ways and means of satisfying individual wants. A great variety of foods, clothes, and shelter arrangements can be bought. But at higher levels in the hierarchy, the situation is more complicated. Man's striving for money, once his basic needs are satisfied, often becomes a substitute for the true satisfaction of his higher needs. It might be instructive at this point to examine how this happens, and what can be done about it.

Offering a money wage to an employee is based on much the same principle as dangling a carrot in front of a donkey. High wages are a reward for productive work. Conversely, withholding money by demoting or firing the employee is a form of punishment for poor work, much like the cancellation of a child's treat. This system of rewards and punishment is effective at lower need levels since the gratification of physiological and safety needs is largely dependent on buying outside sources of satisfaction. When a man is motivated by these needs, he can be controlled by the granting or withholding of money. But the source of satisfaction for higher needs lies within each individual. The man motivated by social or esteem or self-realization needs is not easily controlled by external rewards and punishments; consequently, money per se is a relatively weak motivating force. As D.M. McGregor puts it: ". . . direction and control are useless methods of motivating people whose physiological and safety needs are reasonably satisfied and whose social, egoistic, and self-fulfillment needs are predominant."[1]

People in many walks of life are motivated to work by incentives other than money. The dollar-a-year men in Washington, religious leaders, scientists and academicians, dedicated trade-unionists, and creative artists take pride in the significance of their work; they attach personal and social values to it. Within the large corporation, too, there are many who will respond as readily to work of intrinsic interest and value as to financial rewards, which are always extrinsic to any job.

This means two things to management:

1. Do *not* rely exclusively on further increases in wages and security benefits to motivate employees, once adequate wages and benefits have been established.
2. *Do* create conditions conducive to a man's satisfying his social and esteem and self-realization needs on the job.

For management the important conclusion to be drawn from the whole theory is that no one incentive is the only answer to motivating men on the job. Money is powerful, but its power is limited. Aiding group activities, creating opportunities, recognizing worth, encouraging

---

[1] D. M. McGregor, "The Human Side of Enterprise," in *Adventure in Thought and Action* (Cambridge: Massachusetts Institute of Technology, 1957), p. 28.

growth, and fostering individual expression can also promote employee effort, in some cases more effectively than money. It is the responsibility of management to understand those factors that motivate their men and to arrange conditions and methods of work so that employees can best achieve their own goals by directing their efforts towards organizational objectives.

PRACTICAL APPLICATION

This money-motivation theory can be used to evaluate any compensation device and to help determine how to maximize its motivational impact. Let us take, as an example, a management incentive plan. The questions basic to our study are:

How well is this management incentive plan attracting, retaining, and
    motivating superior men?
Is it successful? Are its returns greater than its costs to the corporation?
How can this management incentive plan be improved?

Specific hypotheses may be formulated from the money-motivation theory set out in the preceding paragraphs. It is obvious from the following list that all these hypotheses cannot be true at one and the same time. The aim here is to cover every possibility.

Positive motivation

Incentive awards primarily represent purchasing power to recipients (physiological need level).
Incentive awards primarily represent financial security to their recipients (safety need level).
Incentive awards primarily indicate the participants' belonging or participating or contributing to the corporate welfare (social need level).
Incentive awards primarily confirm one's own sense of achievement for a job well done (self-esteem need level).
Incentive awards primarily indicate recognition of one's contribution to the corporation (other-esteem need level).
Incentive awards primarily encourage the recipient to fulfill his potential (self-realization need level).

Negative motivation

Reducing or withholding incentive awards (for mediocre performance) increases the intensity of positive need gratification.
Reducing or withholding incentive awards (for mediocre performance) produces frustration effects inimical to the accomplishment of the plan's objectives.

All elements in the package — base pay, incentive plans, protective provisions, benefit programs, and perquisites — could be evaluated in their relationship one to another. Then if it were found that a given level of employees was primarily motivated by physiological needs, great emphasis could be placed on base pay; by safety needs, on protective provisions; by esteem needs, on perquisites.

Thus, through an understanding of what needs were motivating men and how money could be used to satisfy them, the compensation program could be so ordered as to achieve maximum motivation at lowest possible cost; the needs of each individual would best be met, and the attainment of corporate objectives best ensured.

THE MOTIVATION-HYGIENE CONCEPT AND PROBLEMS OF MANPOWER*

Frederick Herzberg

The Motivation-Hygiene theory of job attitudes began with a depth interview study of over 200 engineers and accountants representing Pittsburgh industry. (10) These interviews probed sequences of events in the work lives of the respondents to determine the factors that were involved in their feeling exceptionally happy and conversely exceptionally unhappy with their jobs. From a review and an analysis of previous publications in the general area of job attitudes, a two-factor hypothesis was formulated to guide the original investigation. This hypothesis suggested that the factors involved in producing job satisfaction were separate and distinct from the factors that led to job dissatisfaction. Since separate factors needed to be considered depending on whether job satisfaction or job dissatisfaction was involved, it followed that these two feelings were not the obverse of each other. The opposite of job satisfaction would not be job dissatisfaction, but rather *no* job satisfaction; and similarly the opposite of job dissatisfaction is *no* job dissatisfaction — not job satisfaction. The statement of the concept is awkward and may appear at first to be a semantic ruse, but there is more than a play with words when it comes to understanding the behavior of people on jobs. The fact that job satisfaction is made up of two unipolar traits is not a unique occurrence. The difficulty of establishing a zero point in psychology with the procedural necessity of using instead a bench mark (mean of a population) from which to start our measurement, has led to the conception that psychological traits are bipolar. Empirical investigations, however, have cast some shadows on the assumptions of bipolarity; one timely example is a study of conformity and non-conformity, where they were shown not to be opposites, but rather two separate unipolar traits (3).

METHODOLOGY

Before proceeding to the major results of the original study, three comments on methodology are in order. The investigation of attitudes is

*Reprinted by permission from *Personnel Administration*, January-February, 1964. Copyright 1964 by the Society for Personnel Administration, 485-87 National Press Building, 14th and F Streets, N.W., Washington, D.C. 20004.

plagued with many problems, least of which is the measurement phase; although, it is measurement to which psychologists have hitched their scientific integrity. First of all, if I am to assess a person's feeling about something, how do I know he has a feeling? Too often we rely on his say so, even though opinion polling is replete with instances in which respondents gladly respond with all shades of feeling when in reality they have never thought of the issue and are devoid of any practical affect. They respond to respond and we become deceived into believing that they are revealing feelings or attitudes. Secondly, assuming the respondent does have genuine feelings regarding the subject under investigation, are his answers indicative of his feelings; or are they rationalizations, displacements from other factors which are for many reasons less easy to express, coin of the realm expressions for his particular job classification, etc.? Those who have had experience with job morale surveys recognize these ghosts and unfortunately some have contributed to the haunting of companies. Thirdly, how do you equate feelings? If two persons state that they are happy with their jobs, how do you know they are equally happy? We can develop scales, but in truth we are only satisfying our penchant for rulers which do not get inside the experience and measure the phenomenological reality, but rather have significance wholly within our devices.

To meet these objections, the methodology of the original study was formulated. It included a study of changes in job attitudes in the hope that if attitudes change there is more likelihood that an attitude exists. Further, it focused on experiences in the lives of the respondents which contained substantive data that could be analyzed apart from the interpretations of the respondents. Finally, rather than attempt to measure degree of feeling, it focused on peak experiences and contrasted negative peaks with positive peaks; without being concerned with the equality of the peaks. Briefly, we asked our respondents to describe periods in their lives when they were exceedingly happy and unhappy with their jobs. Each respondent gave as many "sequences of events" as he could which met certain criteria including a marked change in feeling, a beginning and an end, and contained some substantive description other than feelings and interpretations.

A rational analysis of the "sequences of events" led to the results shown in the accompanying chart. For a more complete description of the methodology as well as the results, see *The Motivation to Work* (10).

The proposed hypothesis appears verified. The factors on the right that led to satisfaction (achievement, recognition for achievement, intrinsic interest in the work, responsibility, and advancement) are mostly unipolar; that is, they contribute very little to job dissatisfaction. Conversely, the dissatisfiers (company policy and administrative practices, supervision, interpersonal relationships, working conditions, and salary) contribute very little to job satisfaction.

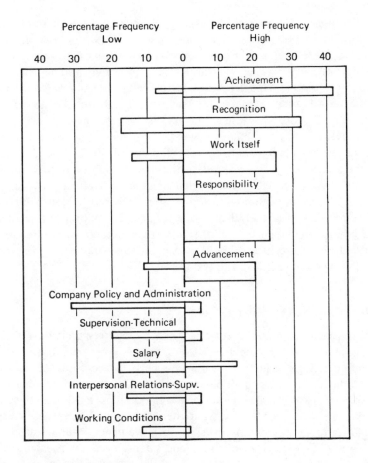

SATISFIERS AND DISSATISFIERS

What is the explanation for such results? Do the two sets of factors have two separate themes? It appears so, for the factors on the right all seem to describe man's relationship to what he does, to his job content, achievement on a task, recognition for task achievement, the nature of the task, responsibility for a task, and professional advancement or growth in task capability.

What is the central theme for the dissatisfiers? Restating the factors as the kind of administration and supervision received in doing the job, the nature of interpersonal relationships and working conditions that surround the job, and the amount of salary that accrues to the individual for doing his job, suggest the distinction with the "satisfier" factors. Rather than describing man's relationship to what he does, the "dissatisfier" factors describe his relationship to the context or environment in which he does his job. One cluster of factors relates to what the person does and the other to the situation in which he does it.

As usual with any new theory, a new jargon is invented, perhaps to add some fictitious uniqueness to the theory, although I prefer to think that these new terms better convey the meaning of the theory. Because the factors on the left serve primarily as preventatives, that is to prevent job dissatisfaction, and because they also deal with the environment, I have named these factors "the hygiene" factors in a poor analogy with the way the term is used in preventive medicine. The factors on the right I call the "motivators" because other results indicate they are necessary for improvement in performance beyond that pseudo improvement which in substance amounts to coming up to a "fair day's work."

In these terms we can recapitulate the major findings of the original study by stating that it is the hygiene factors that affect job dissatisfaction and the motivator factors that affect job satisfaction, with the further understanding that there are two parallel continua of satisfactions. I have only reported on the first study because of the required brevity of this paper. Corroboration can be found in the studies with the following references, (1), (2), (4), (13), (14), (15), (16).

SIGNIFICANCE OF HYGIENE FACTORS

Why? We next explore the reasons given by our respondents for the differential effects that the two sets of factors have on job attitudes. In brief, the hygiene factors meet man's need to avoid unpleasantness. "I don't like to be treated this way; I don't want to suffer the deprivation of low salary; bad interpersonal relationships make me uncomfortable." In other words they want their lives to be hygienically clean. The motivator factors on the other hand make people happy with their jobs because they serve man's basic and human need for psychological growth; a need to become more competent. A fuller commentary on these two separate needs of man are contained in the following publications, (5), (6), (7), (8), (10), (11), (12).

This theory opens wide the door for reinterpretations of industrial relations phenomena. To begin with, job attitudes must be viewed twice; what does the employee seek — what makes him happy; and then a separate question not deducible from the first, what does he wish to avoid — what makes him unhappy? Industrial relations that stress sanitation as their modus operandi can only serve to prevent dissatisfactions and the resultant personnel problems. Of course such attention to hygienic needs is important, for without it any organization, as we well know, will reap the consequences of unhappy personnel. The error of course lies in assuming that prevention will unleash positive health and the returns of increased productivity, lowered absenteeism, turnover, and all the other indices of manpower efficiency. One additional deduction from the theory which is supported by empirical findings should be added. The effect of improved hygiene lasts for only a short time. In fact man's avoidance needs are recurrent and of an infinite variety, and as such we will find that demands for improved salary, working conditions, interpersonal relations and so on will continue to occupy the personnel administrator without any hope of escaping the "what have you done for me lately."

There is nothing wrong with providing the maximum of hygienic benefits to the employee, as much as the society can afford (which appears to be more than the historic cries of anguish, which have always accompanied the amelioration of work hygiene would indicate). What is wrong is the summation of human needs in totally hygienic terms. The consequences of this onesided view of man's nature has led to untoward consequences of much greater import than the direct monetary costs of these programs to our organizations. The more pertinent effect has been on the psychological premises of industrial relations and its effect in turn on the self concepts of the employees.

Since hygiene is the apparent key to industrial success, the motivators are given but lip service, and attention to the challenge and meaningfulness of jobs is satisfied via the pious espousal of cultural noises. We are today familiar with the industrial engineering principle of leveling jobs down to the lowest common talent as it applies to the rank and file assembly operation. The same denigration of human talent at the managerial and professional level, the sacrificing of human performance and potentiality to insure that no one will fail or make for unpleasantness, is obscured by referring to the rank and file when acknowledging the lack of meaning in work. At these higher levels, the effects of the assembly line are accomplished by the overuse of rules and regulations, rational organizational principles and the insidious use of interpersonal *skills*. We find that more and more training and education is required to do less and less; more and more effort on surround and less and less substance on accomplishment. Pride in work, in successful accomplishment, in maximizing one's talent is becoming socially gauche or more tragically a victim of progress. We cry for nurturance of human talent and find that we have no place for most of it; human talent on the job has become as much of a surplus commodity as our wheat. And where are our personnel managers? Their problem is hygiene, not the creative function of maximizing human resources.

SIGNIFICANCE OF MOTIVATORS

The Protestant Ethic is being replaced by an Avoidance Ethic in our world of work, and those in charge of personnel utilization have almost totally directed their efforts to maintenance procedures. This is seen from the very beginning of employment in the practice of college recruitment on the campus, where each company sets up its own enticing tent, and selection is transformed into public relations, luring of candidates, and in fact the incredible situation of the candidate interviewing the interviewer.

Job attitude data suggest that after the glow of the initial year on the job, job satisfaction plummets to its lowest level in the work life of individuals (9). From a life time of diverse learning, successive accomplishment through the various academic stages, and periodic reinforcement of efforts, the entrant to our modern companies finds that rather than work providing an expanding psychological existence, the opposite occurs; and successive amputations of his self-conceptions, aspirations, learning, and talent are the consequence of earning a living. Of course as the needs and values of our industrial enterprises have become the template for all aspects of our lives, the university is preparing many young people by performing the amputations early, and they enter already primed for work as only a means of hygienic improvement; or for those still capable of enjoying the exercise of their human talents, as means of affording off the job satisfactions. If the number of management development programs is a valid sign, the educational system has done its job too well.

A reaction to retirement policies is beginning to set in as the personal consequences of organizational definitions of human obsolescence are being told. Prior to retirement, however, are 30 to 40 years of partial retirement and partial commitment to work for the too many who have not "succeeded" in terms of organizational advancement. From the first orientation to the farewell party, the history of work careers is a history of human waste. What a paradox we face. There is a shortage of talent in the country at a time when our problems are defined in planetary dimensions and to meet these circumstances we have evolved a system and a philosophy to use and motivate our talent that serves to decrease further this precious resource.

What alternatives are there? A spate of new research and literature is becoming available that is reacting to personnel and managerial psychology that has too long tried to emulate the vast and short term goals of the military. The new literature while encompassing diverse problems, exhortations, solutions, and conceptions seems to have the common theme of emphasizing the motivator needs of man and the necessity for the personnel function of industry to pause in its search for the Holy Grail of instruments, to become creative in finding ways to meet the motivator needs. Man is distinguished from all other animals in that he alone is a determiner. How strange that when it comes to the satisfactions of his special psychological growth needs he finds himself a victim of outside determinisms and helpless in affecting the way he is utilized in work. The short term economic "necessities" cannot justify the larger economic loss and the denial of human satisfaction that the restriction of human talent inevitably costs. I might add that many of the barriers to fuller utilization of manpower that are "justified" by economic reasons are, in reality, devices of fearful and inadequate managers who are not prepared to meet the challenge of managing adults. The philosophy of management which prizes such men is changeable. We need a goal of industry which includes the expansion of manpower utilization in addition to the expansion of productivity and profit. The acceptance of such a goal as basic will lead to the means for its implementation. Personnel cannot remain the one management function that only establishes objectives for which techniques and procedures are available.

REFERENCES

1. Fantz, R. Motivation factors in rehabilitation. *Unpublished doctoral dissertation, Western Reserve University Library,* Cleveland, 1961.
2. Gibson, J. Sources of job satisfaction and job dissatisfaction. *Unpublished doctoral dissertation, Western Reserve University Library,* Cleveland, 1961.
3. Guilford, J.P.; Christensen,;P.R., Bond, N. and Sutton, M. A factor analysis study of human interests. *Res. Bull.,* 53-11, Human Resources Research Center, San Antonio, 1953.
4. Hamlin, R. and Nemo, R. Self-actualization in choice scores of improved schizophrenics, *J. clin. Psychol.,* 18, 1962.
5. Herzberg, F. New approaches in management organization and job design. *Industrial Med. and Surgery,* November, 1962.
6. Herzberg, F. Basic needs and satisfactions of individuals. *Industrial Relations Monograph,* No. 21, Industrial Relations Counselors, Inc., New York: 1962.
7. Herzberg, F. Comment on the Meaning of Work. Proceedings of symposium of the Worker in the New Industrial Environment. *Industrial Med. and Surgery,* June, 1963.
8. Herzberg, F. The meaning of work to the individual. In, *Basic Psychology and Physiology of work,* edited by H. Hellerstein, C.C. Thomas Press, Ft. Lauderdale, In Press.
9. Herzberg, F. et al. Job attitudes: Research, and opinion. Psychological Service of Pittsburgh, 1957.
10. Herzberg, F., Mausner. B., and Snyderman, B. *The motivation to work.* John Wiley and Sons, New York: 1959.
11. Herzberg, F., and Hamlin, R. A motivation-hygiene concept of mental health. *Mental Hygiene,* July, 1961.
12. Herzberg, F., and Hamlin, R. Motivation-hygiene concept and psychotherapy. *Mental Hygiene,* July, 1961.
13. Lodahl, T. Patterns of job attitudes in two assembly technologies. *Graduate School of Business and Public Administration, Cornell University,* Ithaca, New York, 1963.
14. Saleh, S. Attitude change and its effect on the pre-retirement period. *Unpublished doctoral dissertation, Western Reserve University Library,* Cleveland, 1962.
15. Schwarz, P. *Attitudes of middle management personnel.* American Institute for Research, Pittsburgh, 1961.
16. Schwartz, M., Jenusaitis, E. and Stark, H. Motivation factors among supervisors in the utility industry. *Personnel Psychology,* 16, 1963.

THE HONOR SYSTEM*

James MacGregor

When Fran Manale reports for work at Alcan Aluminum Corp.'s rolling mill here, he doesn't punch a time clock. There aren't any.

There aren't any bells or whistles, either, to tell him when to take his breaks. If his mill operator's job begins to get him down, Mr. Manale can always relieve the monotony by switching jobs with another worker for an hour or two. And if he needs to visit his dentist or lawyer, he can do that on company time, too.

Inefficient? Not at all. Alcan's Oswego mill has an impressive record on several counts. Tardiness and turnover are almost nonexistent. Absenteeism runs about 2.5%, compared with an industry average of nearly 10%. Alcan won't disclose its productivity, but industry sources don't think plant manager Richard Dekker is exaggerating much when he boasts, "I'll match this plant against any in the industry on a cost-per-ton-produced basis."

Behind the Oswego mill's success is its "honor system" philosophy, Mr. Dekker says. It involves yanking out the time clocks and designing all production jobs to give workers unusual freedom and decision-making responsibility. Moreover, worker wages are guaranteed even during absences or layoffs, making them in effect salaried employes. Production workers are also on the same benefit programs as the white-collar workers.

MR. MANALE'S VIEW

"We're trying to eliminate all distinctions between blue-collar and white-collar employes," Mr. Dekker says. "We tell our workers they can do their jobs any way they think best as long as the machines keep running." Other Alcan officials admit to some initial skepticism, but they say Oswego's success is rapidly making them believers in honor systems.

Even Mr. Manale, a leader in several unsuccessful union organizing drives here, is becoming a convert. He still sports a Steelworkers' patch on his shirt pocket, but now he reflects that "the threat of a union keeps the company on its toes, but things have gotten so much better in the last couple of years I'm not as sure we really need one here."

*Reprinted with permission from *The Wall Street Journal*, May 22, 1970.

A number of other companies report similar success with efforts to boost productivity and reduce personnel problems by giving more decision-making power and individual responsibility to blue-collar workers. Among them are IBM, Texas Instruments, Motorola, an automotive valve plant of Eaton Yale & Towne and R.G. Barry, a footwear maker.

The trend is hardly widespread. No more than a few dozen companies are involved, primarily in nonunionized plants making light, technical equipment. But industrial psychologists and company officials say inquiries about their honor systems are increasing steadily, coming from such diverse sources as petroleum refineries and machine tool makers.

REMOVING THE IRRITANTS

Personnel experts say honor systems grew up in response to the dilemma of many a manufacturing operation: Even though wages and benefits have soared in recent years, absenteeism, turnover and employe grievances have continued to climb. Increases in automation haven't always produced corresponding increases in productivity, and sometimes they have led to an increasing number of costly employe errors.

"How motivated would you be if your job consisted of tightening five bolts with a torque wrench a thousand times a day, and if, in addition, mechanical devices called time clocks and whistles told you when to work, when to eat, when to stretch your legs and when to use the bathroom?" asks Frederick Herzberg, professor of industrial psychology at Case Western Reserve University and a leading consultant on employe motivation.

Mr. Herzberg believes most production jobs provide so little satisfaction for a worker that they should be automated out of existence. When that's not possible, the honor system approach can improve motivation by "removing irritants" like time clocks and by providing positive factors like identification with an employer and responsibility and discretion on the job, he says.

AN ANTIUNION PLOY?

Labor leaders contend that a more self-serving reason prompts companies to adopt honor systems. They assert the programs are put in to keep unions out. Indeed, Alcan's Oswego mill here has defeated five union drives in seven years. Malcolm Daisley, vice president for industrial relations of Eaton Yale & Towne, admits one reason for building a valve plant at Kearney, Neb. (where the union movement isn't strong) and putting it on an honor system was to help head off any incipient labor movement.

Workers at plants with the honor system usually have broader, more flexible job assignments and considerably more discretion as to how the work will be done than do workers in unionized plants. A machine operator may also perform routine machine maintenance and quality inspection of his own work; in a unionized plant, three men might be required for those duties. An Ohio union official claims these honor system practices can trim employment "up to 25% at any plant, which more than pays for the added benefits workers get but shortchanges the labor movement as a whole."

In Washington, a spokesman for the AFL-CIO says honor systems are still too rare to have serious implications for the labor movement. He also notes that some aspects of honor systems are long-time union goals, including guaranteed salaries and elimination of differentials in benefit plans for blue-collar and white-collar workers.

A few employers have gone a step beyond the basic honor system approach. Texas Instruments says it has achieved "significant increases in productivity" by organizing some workers into production teams and encouraging them to analyze production processes on their jobs. When they come up with suggestions, they work with supervisors and engineers to see if the ideas can be implemented.

"We tell our workers everyone has a responsible job he can use his mind on," says a personnel official. "Once they get over the initial shock of being asked for their opinions, they respond quite well. They often find things managers and industrial engineers aren't even aware of."

EVOLVING MODELS OF ORGANIZATIONAL BEHAVIOR*

Keith Davis

The affluent society of which John Kenneth Galbraith wrote a decade ago has become even more affluent.[1] There are many reasons for this sustained improvement in productivity, and some of them are advancing technology, available resources, improved education, and a favorable economic and social system. There is, however, another reason of key significance to all of us. That reason is management, specifically the capacity of managers to develop organizational systems which respond productively to the changing conditions of society. In recent years this has meant more complex administrative systems in order to challenge and motivate employees toward better teamwork. Improvement has been made by working smarter, not harder. An increasingly sophisticated knowledge of human behavior is required; consequently, theoretical models of organizational behavior have had to grow to absorb this new knowledge. It is these evolving models of organizational behavior which I wish to discuss; then I shall draw some conclusions about their use.

The significant point about models of organizational behavior is that the model which a manager holds normally determines his perception of the organizational world about him. It leads to certain assumptions about people and certain interpretations of events he encounters. The underlying model serves as an unconscious guide to each manager's behavior. He acts as he thinks. Since his acts do affect the quality of human relations and productivity in his department, he needs to be fully aware of the trends that are occurring. If he holds to an outmoded model, his success will be limited and his job will be harder, because he will not be able to work with his people as he should.

Similarly, the model of organizational behavior which predominates among the management of an organization will affect the success of that whole organization. And at a national level the model which prevails within a country will influence the productivity and economic development of that nation. Models of organizational behavior are a significant variable in the life of all groups.

---

*Reprinted with permission from *Academy of Management Journal*, March, 1968.
[1] John Kenneth Galbraith, *The Affluent Society* (Boston, Mass.: Houghton Miffin, 1958).

Many models of organizational behavior have appeared during the last 100 years, and four of them are significant and different enough to merit further discussion. These are the autocratic, custodial, supportive and collegial models. In the order mentioned, the four models represent a historical evolution of management thought. The autocratic model predominated 75 years ago. In the 1920s and 1930s it yielded ground to the more successful custodial model. In this generation the supportive model is gaining approval. It predominates in many organizations, although the custodial model probably still prevails in the whole society. Meanwhile, a number of advanced organizations are experimenting with the collegial model.

The four models are not distinct in the sense that a manager or a firm uses one and only one of them. In a week — or even a day — a manager probably applies some of all four models. On the other hand, one model tends to predominate as his habitual way of working with his people, in such a way that it leads to a particular type of teamwork and behavioral climate among his group. Similarly, one model tends to dominate the life of a whole organization, but different parts therein may still be pursuing other models. The production department may take a custodial approach, while supportive ideas are being tried in the office, and collegial ideas are practiced in the research department. The point is that one model of organizational behavior is not an adequate label to describe all that happens in an organization, but it is a convenient way to distinguish one prevailing way of life from another. By comparing these four models, we can recognize certain important distinctions among them.

THE AUTOCRATIC MODEL

The autocratic model has its roots deep in history, and certainly it became the prevailing model early in the industrial revolution. As shown in Figure 1, this model depends on power. Those who are in command must have the power to demand, "You do this — or else," meaning that an employee will be penalized if he does not follow orders. This model takes a threatening approach, depending on negative motivation backed by power.

In an autocratic environment the managerial orientation is formal, official authority. Authority is the tool with which management works and the context in which it thinks, because it is the organizational means by which power is applied. This authority is delegated by right of command over the people to whom it applies. In this model, management implicitly assumes that it knows what is best and that it is the employee's obligation to follow orders without question or interpretation. Management assumes that employees are passive and even resistant to organizational needs. They have to be persuaded and pushed into per-

Figure 1
Four models of organizational behavior

	Autocratic	Custodial	Supportive	Collegial
Depends on:	Power	Economic resources	Leadership	Mutual contribution
Managerial orientation:	Authority	Material rewards	Support	Integration and teamwork
Employee orientation:	Obedience	Security	Performance	Responsibility
Employee psychological result:	Personal dependency	Organizational dependency	Participation	Self-discipline
Employee needs met:	Subsistence	Maintenance	Higher-order	Self-realization
Performance result:	Minimum	Passive cooperation	Awakened drives	Enthusiasm
Morale measure:	Compliance	Satisfaction	Motivation	Commitment to task and team

Source: Adapted from Keith Davis, *Human Relations at Work: The Dynamics of Organizational Behavior* (3rd ed.; New York: McGraw-Hill, 1967), p. 480.

formance, and this is management's task. Management does the thinking, the employees obey the orders. This is the "Theory X" popularized by Douglas McGregor as the conventional view of management.[2] It has its roots in history and was made explicit by Frederick W. Taylor's concepts of scientific management. Though Taylor's writings show that he had worker interests at heart, he saw those interests served best by a manager who scientifically determined what a worker should do and then saw that he did it. The worker's role was to perform as he was ordered.

Under autocratic conditions an employee's orientation is obedience. He bends to the authority of a boss — not a manager. This role causes a psychological result which in this case is employee personal dependency on his boss whose power to hire, fire, and "perspire" him is almost absolute. The boss pays relatively low wages because he gets relatively less performance from the employee. Each employee must provide subsistance needs for himself and his family; so he reluctantly gives minimum performance, but he is not motivated to give much more than that. A few men give higher performance because of internal achievement drives, because they personally like their boss, because the boss is a "natural-born

[2]Douglas McGregor, "The Human Side of Enterprise," in *Proceedings of the Fifth Anniversary Convocation of the School of Industrial Management* (Cambridge, Mass.: Massachusetts Institute of Technology, April 9, 1957). Theory X and Theory Y were later popularized in Douglas McGregor, *The Human Side of Enterprise* (New York: McGraw-Hill, 1960).

leader," or because of some other fortuitous reason; but most men give only minimum performance.

When an autocratic model of organizational behavior exists, the measure of an employee's morale is usually his compliance with rules and orders. Compliance is unprotesting assent without enthusiasm. The compliant employee takes his orders and does not talk back.

Although modern observers have an inherent tendency to condemn the autocratic model of organizational behavior, it is a useful way to accomplish work. It has been successfully applied by the empire builders of the 1800s, efficiency engineers, scientific managers, factory foremen, and others. It helped to build great railroad systems, operate giant steel mills, and produce a dynamic industrial civilization in the early 1900s.

Actually the autocratic model exists in all shades of gray, rather than the extreme black usually presented. It has been a reasonably effective way of management when there is a "benevolent autocrat" who has a genuine interest in his employees and when the role expectation of employees is autocratic leadership.[3] But these results are usually only moderate ones lacking the full potential that is available, and they are reached at considerable human costs. In addition, as explained earlier, conditions change to require new behavioral models in order to remain effective.

As managers and academicians became familiar with limitations of the autocratic model, they began to ask, "Is there a better way? Now that we have brought organizational conditions this far along, can we build on what we have in order to move one step higher on the ladder of progress?" Note that their thought was not to throw out power as undesirable, because power is needed to maintain internal unity in organizations. Rather, their thought was to build upon the foundation which existed: "Is there a better way?"

THE CUSTODIAL MODEL

Managers soon recognized that although a compliant employee did not talk back to his boss, he certainly "thought back"! There were many things he wanted to say to his boss, and sometimes he did say them when he quit or lost his temper. The employee inside was a seething mass of insecurity, frustrations, and aggressions toward his boss. Since he could not vent these feelings directly, sometimes he went home and vented them on his wife, family, and neighbors; so the community did not gain much out of this relationship either.

It seemed rather obvious to progressive employers that there ought

---

[3]This viewpoint is competently presented in R.N. McMurry, "The Case for Benevolent Autocracy," *Harvard Business Review* (Jan.-Feb., 1958), pp. 82-90.

to be some way to develop employee satisfactions and adjustment during production — and in fact this approach just might cause more productivity! If the employee's insecurities, frustrations, and aggressions could be dispelled, he might feel more like working. At any rate the employer could sleep better, because his conscience would be clearer.

Development of the custodial model was aided by psychologists, industrial relations specialists, and economists. Psychologists were interested in employee satisfaction and adjustment. They felt that a satisfied employee would be a better employee, and the feeling was so strong that "a happy employee" became a mild obsession in some personnel offices. The industrial relations specialists and economists favored the custodial model as a means of building employee security and stability in employment. They gave strong support to a variety of fringe benefits and group plans for security.

The custodial model originally developed in the form of employee welfare programs offered by a few progressive employers, and in its worst form it became known as employer paternalism. During the depression of the 1930s emphasis changed to economic and social security and then shortly moved toward various labor plans for security and control. During and after World War II, the main focus was on specific fringe benefits. Employers, labor unions, and government developed elaborate programs for overseeing the needs of workers.

A successful custodial approach depends on economic resources, as shown in Figure 1. An organization must have economic wealth to provide economic security, pensions, and other fringe benefits. The resulting managerial orientation is toward economic or material rewards, which are designed to make employees respond as economic men. A reciprocal employee orientation tends to develop emphasizing security.

The custodial approach gradually leads to an organizational dependency by the employee. Rather than being dependent on his boss for his weekly bread, he now depends on larger organizations for his security and welfare. Perhaps more accurately stated, an organizational dependency is added atop a reduced personal dependency on his boss. This approach effectively serves an employee's maintenance needs, as presented in Herzberg's motivation-maintenance model, but it does not strongly motivate an employee.[4] The result is a passive cooperation by the employee. He is pleased to have his security; but as he grows psychologically, he also seeks more challenge and autonomy.

The natural measure of morale which developed from a custodial model was employee satisfaction. If the employee was happy, contended, and adjusted to the group, then all was well. The happiness-oriented morale survey became a popular measure of success in many organizations.

---

[4]Frederick Herzberg, Bernard Mausner, and Barbara Synderman, *The Motivation to Work* (New York: John Wiley and Sons, 1959).

Limitations of the custodial model

Since the custodial model is the one which most employers are currently moving away from, its limitations will be further examined. As with the autocratic model, the custodial model exists in various shades of gray, which means that some practices are more successful than others. In most cases, however, it becomes obvious to all concerned that most employees under custodial conditions do not produce anywhere near their capacities, nor are they motivated to grow to the greater capacities of which they are capable. Though employees may be happy, most of them really do not feel fulfilled or self-actualized.

The custodial model emphasizes economic resources and the security those resources will buy, rather than emphasizing employee performance. The employee becomes psychologically preoccupied with maintaining his security and benefits, rather than with production. As a result, he does not produce much more vigorously than under the old autocratic approach. Security and contentment are necessary for a person, but they are not themselves very strong motivators.

In addition, the fringe benefits and other devices of the custodial model are mostly off-the-job. They are not directly connected with performance. The employee has to be too sick to work or too old to work in order to receive these benefits. The system becomes one of public and private paternalism in which an employee sees little connection between his rewards and his job performance and personal growth; hence he is not motivated toward performance and growth. In fact, an overzealous effort to make the worker secure and happy leads to a brand of psychological paternalism no better than earlier economic paternalism. With the psychological variety, employee needs are dispensed from the personnel department, union hall, and government bureau, rather than the company store. But in either case, dependency remains, and as Ray E. Brown observes, "Men grow stronger on workouts than on handouts. It is in the nature of people to wrestle with a challenge and rest on a crutch . . . The great desire of man is to stand on his own, and his life is one great fight against dependency. Making the individual a ward of the organization will likely make him bitter instead of better."[5]

As viewed by William H. Whyte, the employee working under custodialism becomes an "organization man" who belongs to the organization and who has "left home spiritually as well as physically, to take the vows of organizational life."[6]

As knowledge of human behavior advanced, deficiencies in the custodial model became quite evident and people again started to ask, "Is there a better way?" The search for a better way is not a condemnation of

---

[5]Ray E. Brown, *Judgment in Administration* (New York: McGraw-Hill, 1966), p. 75.

[6]William H. Whyte, Jr., *The Organization Man* (New York: Simon and Schuster, 1956), p. 3.

the custodial model as a whole; however, it is a condemnation of the assumption that custodialism is "the final answer" — the one best way to work with people in organizations. An error in reasoning occurs when a person perceives that the custodial model is so desirable that there is no need to move beyond it to something better.

THE SUPPORTIVE MODEL

The supportive model of organizational behavior has gained currency during recent years as a result of a great deal of behavioral science research as well as favorable employer experience with it. The supportive model establishes a manager in the primary role of psychological support of his employees at work, rather than in a primary role of economic support (as in the custodial model) or "power over" (as in the autocratic model). A supportive approach was first suggested in the classical experiments of Mayo and Roethlisberger at Western Electric Company in the 1930s and 1940s. They showed that a small work group is more productive and satisfied when its members perceive that they are working in a supportive environment. This interpretation was expanded by the work of Edwin A. Fleishman with supervisory "consideration" in the 1940s[7] and that of Rensis Likert and his associates with the "employee-oriented supervisor" in the 1940s and 1950s.[8] In fact, the *coup de grace* to the custodial model's dominance was administered by Likert's research which showed that the happy employee is not necessarily the most productive employee.

Likert has expressed the supportive model as the "principle of supportive relationships" in the following words:

The leadership and other processes of the organization must be such as to ensure a maximum probability that in all interactions and all relationships with the organization each member will, in the light of his background, values, and expectations, view the experience as supportive and one which builds and maintains his sense of personal worth and importance."[9]

The supportive model, shown in Figure 1, depends on leadership instead of power or economic resources. Through leadership, management

---

[7]An early report of this research is Edwin A. Fleishman, *"Leadership Climate"* and *Supervisory Behavior* (Columbus, Ohio: Personnel Research Board, Ohio State University, 1951).

[8]There have been many publications by the Likert group at the Survey Research Center, University of Michigan. An early basic one is Daniel Katz et al., *Productivity, Supervision and Morale in an Office Situation* (Ann Arbor, Mich.: The University of Michigan Press, 1950).

[9]Rensis Likert, *New Patterns of Management* (New York: McGraw-Hill, 1961), pp. 102-103. (Italics in original.)

provides a behavioral climate to help each employee grow and accomplish in the interests of the organization the things of which he is capable. The leader assumes that workers are not by nature passive and resistant to organizational needs, but that they are made so by an inadequate supportive climate at work. They will take responsibility, develop a drive to contribute, and improve themselves, if management will give them half a chance. Management's orientation, therefore, is to support the employee's performance.

Since performance is supported, the employee's orientation is toward it instead of mere obedience and security. He is responding to intrinsic motivations in his job situation. His psychological result is a feeling of participation and task involvement in the organization. When referring to his organization, he may occasionally say "we" instead of always saying "they." Since his higher-order needs are better challenged, he works with more awakened drives than he did under earlier models.

The difference between custodial and supportive models is illustrated by the fact that the morale measure of supportive management is the employee's level of motivation. This measure is significantly different from the satisfaction and happiness emphasized by the custodial model. An employee who has a supportive leader is motivated to work toward organizational objectives as a means of achieving his own goals. This approach is similar to McGregor's popular "Theory Y."

The supportive model is just as applicable to the climate for managers as for operating employees. One study reports that supportive managers usually led to high motivation among their subordinate managers. Among those managers who were low in motivation, only 8 per cent had supportive managers. Their managers were mostly autocratic.[10]

It is not essential for managers to accept every assumption of the supportive model in order to move toward it, because as more is learned about it, views will change. What is essential is that modern managers in business, unions, and government do not become locked into the custodial model. They need to abandon any view that the custodial model is the final answer, so that they will be free to look ahead to improvements which are fitting to their organization in their environment.

The supportive model is only one step upward on the ladder of progress. Though it is just now coming into dominance, some firms which have the proper conditions and managerial competence are already using a collegial model of organizational behavior, which offers further opportunities for improvement.

---

[10]M. Scott Myers, "Conditions for Manager Motivation," *Harvard Business Review* (Jan-Feb., 1966), p. 61. This study covered 1,344 managers at Texas Instruments, Inc.

THE COLLEGIAL MODEL

The collegial model is still evolving, but it is beginning to take shape. It has developed from recent behavioral science research, particularly that of Likert, Katz, Kahn, and others at the University of Michigan,[11] Herzberg with regard to maintenance and motivational factors,[12] and the work of a number of people in project management and matrix organization.[13] The collegial model readily adapts to the flexible, intellectual environment of scientific and professional organizations. Working in substantially unprogrammed activities which require effective teamwork, scientific and professional employees desire the autonomy which a collegial model permits, and they respond to it well.

The collegial model depends on management's building a feeling of mutual contribution among participants in the organization, as shown in Figure 1. Each employee feels that he is contributing something worthwhile and is needed and wanted. He feels that management and others are similarly contributing, so he accepts and respects their roles in the organization. Managers are seen as joint contributors rather than bosses.

The managerial orientation is toward teamwork which will provide an integration of all contributions. Management is more of an integrating power than a commanding power. The employee response to this situation is responsibility. He produces quality work not primarily because management tells him to do so or because the inspector will catch him if he does not, but because he feels inside himself the desire to do so for many reasons. The employee psychological result, therefore, is self-discipline. Feeling responsible, the employee disciplines himself for team performance in the same way that a football team member disciplines himself in training and in game performance.

In this kind of environment an employee normally should feel some degree of fulfillment and self-realization, although the amount will be modest in some situations. The result is job enthusiasm, because he finds in the job such Herzberg motivators as achievement, growth, intrinsic work fulfillment, and recognition. His morale will be measured by his commitment to his task and his team, because he will see these as instruments for his self-actualization.

---

[11]Likert describes a similar model as System 4 in Rensis, Likert,*The Human Organization: Its Management and Value* (New York: McGraw-Hill, 1967), pp. 3-11.

[12]Herzberg *et. al., op. cit.*

[13]For example, see Keith Davis, "Mutuality in Understanding of the Program Manager's Management Role," *IEEE Transactions on Engineering Management* (Dec., 1965), pp. 117-122.

SOME CONCLUSIONS ABOUT MODELS OF ORGANIZATIONAL BEHAVIOR

The evolving nature of models of organizational behavior makes it evident that change is the normal condition of these models. As our understanding of human behavior increases or as new social conditions develop, our organizational behavior models are also likely to change. It is a grave mistake to assume that one particular model is a "best" model which will endure for the long run. This mistake was made by some old-time managers about the autocratic model and by some humanists about the custodial model, with the result that they became psychologically locked into these models and had difficulty altering their practices when conditions demanded it. Eventually the supportive model may also fall to limited use; and as further progress is made, even the collegial model is likely to be surpassed. There is no permanently "one best model" of organizational behavior, because what is best depends upon what is known about human behavior in whatever environment and priority of objectives exist at a particular time.

A second conclusion is that the models of organizational behavior which have developed seem to be sequentially related to man's psychological hierarchy of needs. As society has climbed higher on the need hierarchy, new models of organizational behavior have been developed to serve the higher-order needs that became paramount at the time. If Maslow's need hierarchy is used for comparison, the custodial model of organizational behavior is seen as an effort to serve man's second-level security needs.[14] It moved one step about the autocratic model which was reasonably serving man's subsistence needs, but was not effectively meeting his needs for security. Similarly the supportive model is an effort to meet employees' higher-level needs, such as affiliation and esteem, which the custodial model was unable to serve. The collegial model moves even higher toward service of man's need for self-actualization.

A number of persons have assumed that emphasis on one model of organizational behavior was an automatic rejection of other models, but the comparison with man's need hierarchy *suggests that each model is built upon the accomplishments of the other.* For example, adoption of a supportive approach does not mean abandonment of custodial practices which serve necessary employee security needs. What it does mean is that custodial practices are relegated to secondary emphasis, because employees have progressed up their need structure to a condition in which higher needs predominate. In other words, the supportive model is the appropriate model to use *because* subsistence and security needs are already reasonably met by a suitable power structure and security system. If a misdirected modern manager should abandon these basic organizational needs, the system would quickly revert to a quest for a workable

---

[14]A.H. Maslow, "A Theory of Human Motivation," *Psychological Review* (L,1943), 370-396.

power structure and security system in order to provide subsistence-maintenance needs for its people.

Each model of organizational behavior in a sense outmodes its predominance by gradually satisfying certain needs, thus opening up other needs which can be better served by a more advanced model. Thus each new model is built upon the success of its predecessor. The new model simply represents a more sophisticated way of maintaining earlier need satisfactions, while opening up the probability of satisfying still higher needs.

A third conclusion suggests that the present tendency toward more democratic models of organizational behavior will continue for the longer run. This tendency seems to be required by both the nature of technology and the nature of the need structure. Harbison and Myers, in a classical study of management throughout the industrial world, conclude that advancing industrialization leads to more advanced models of organizational behavior. Specifically, authoritarian management gives way to more constitutional and democratic-participative models of management. These developments are inherent in the system; that is, the more democratic models tend to be necessary in order to manage productively an advanced industrial system.[15] Slater and Bennis also conclude that more participative and democratic models of organizational behavior inherently develop with advancing industrialization. They believe that "democracy is inevitable," because it is the only system which can successfully cope with changing demands of contemporary civilization in both business and government.[16]

Both sets of authors accurately point out that in modern, complex organizations a top manager cannot be authoritarian in the traditional sense and remain efficient, because he cannot know all that is happening in his organization. He must depend on other centers of power nearer to operating problems. In addition, educated workers are not readily motivated toward creative and intellectual duties by traditional authoritarian orders. They require higher-order need satisfactions which newer models of organizational behavior provide. Thus there does appear to be some inherent necessity for more democratic forms of organization in advanced industrial systems.

A fourth and final conclusion is that, though one model may predominate as most appropriate for general use at any point in industrial history, some appropriate uses will remain for other models. Knowledge of human behavior and skills in applying that knowledge will vary among

---

[15]Frederick Harbison and Charles A. Meyers, *Management in the Industrial World: An International Analysis* (New York: McGraw-Hill, 1959), pp. 40-67. The authors also state on page 47, "The design of systems of authority is equally as important in the modern world as the development of technology."

[16]Philip E. Slater and Warren G. Bennis, "Democracy is inevitable," *Harvard Business Review* (March-April, 1964), pp. 51-59.

managers. Role expectations of employees will differ depending upon cultural history. Policies and ways of life will vary among organizations. Perhaps more important, task conditions will vary. Some jobs may require routine, low-skilled, highly programmed work which will be mostly determined by higher authority and provide mostly material rewards and security (autocratic and custodial conditions). Other jobs will be unprogrammed and intellectual, requiring teamwork and self-motivation, and responding best to supportive and collegial conditions. This use of different management practices with people according to the task they are performing is called "management according to task" by Leavitt.[17]

In the final analysis, each manager's behavior will be determined by his underlying theory of organizational behavior, so it is essential for him to understand the different results achieved by different models of organizational behavior. The model used will vary with the total human and task conditions surrounding the work. The long-run tendency will be toward more supportive and collegial models because they better serve the higher-level needs of employees.

[17]Harold J. Leavitt, "Management According to Task: Organizational Differentiation," *Management International* (1962), No. 1, pp. 13-22.

DISCIPLINE IN THE INDUSTRIAL SETTING*

Norman R. F. Maier

The question of discipline can be looked at from the point of view of the undesirable act that has already been committed, and then if there is a punishment provision, the person is made to pay a price. The concept of justice grows out of that point of view.

One can also look at discipline not in terms of the act that has been committed, but in terms of the future. One wants to prevent a recurrence of an undesirable act. Viewed in this way discipline functions as a deterrent. It can't change past behavior, but it can influence the future. If this is so, then the situation has improved.

In the writer's opinion, psychologists would, in general, agree that it is possible for discipline to act as a deterrent. It also seems that this would be consistent with common sense experience. One lives within the speed limits of a community because of the threat of punishment. The danger, however, is to assume that there are no other important effects.

Discipline can do a number of other things, and if it can be administered without accomplishing some of the undesirable effects that will be mentioned in this paper, then it is an excellent technique. The question is, can the undesirable effects be avoided?

UNDESIRABLE EFFECTS OF DISCIPLINE

The first such effect is that it may frustrate the individual. When one punishes a child instead of training him, frustration may result.

The characteristic behaviors of a frustrated individual are (1) hostility and hate; (2) childishness, known as regression; and (3) rigidity, called fixation. Each of these characteristics has been experimentally produced by means of discipline. It is common knowledge that a child who is punished for fighting is much more likely to fight in the future than the child that is not. Punishment, when it frustrates, provides the hostility that makes for future fighting.

This is not to say that discipline does not deter. It may well, but it may also do just the opposite. It may actually freeze, or fixate behavior

*Reprinted with permission from *Personnel Journal*, No. 4, 1965.

and in this way increase the very kind of behavior that one is trying to change. If it produces regression, we are blocking development since regression is the reversal of growth.

Another undesirable effect of discipline is that the person may make the wrong association or the wrong connection. In a classical experiment, a Chinese psychologist wanted to train cats to avoid rats. He placed a cat in a wired cage and then he introduced a rat. Just as soon as the rat made a pass at the cat, he threw a switch and gave the cat a good shot of electricity.

Now, what did cats learn under these conditions? With the large groups of cats tested, about a third of them learned to avoid rats. When exposed to a rat, they would go in the other direction. What about the other two-thirds? They still went after rats as before. However, half of them, instead of avoiding rats, avoided the cage. As soon as they were put in the cage, they would fight and try to get away from it. The remaining cats didn't avoid the cage, they didn't avoid rats; but they avoided rats in the box. In other words, although all of the cats were given the same training, they developed different responses.

When a man in an industrial situation is disciplined for violating a safety regulation, what does he learn? Does he merely learn that he shouldn't violate the safety regulations? Very often he learns that the foreman is unfair, unreasonable, a nasty person. Or he might connect the punishment not with the violation, but with getting caught. That is one of the most common results of discipline: it causes people to use their creative abilities to find ways to avoid getting caught.

NEGATIVE ASPECTS

A third aspect of discipline under suspicion is its nonconstructive approach to behavior. When an effort is made to control behavior by means of punishment, people are taught what *not* to do. This assumes that not doing things is the important value in behavior. With a philosophy of this kind the only virtuous people are dead ones. They break no rules. There is nothing for which they can be punished because they have done nothing wrong. And yet a dead man is completely worthless.

A person does not have to know how *not* to hold a golf club in order to play golf. Yet, when we discipline we, in effect, say thou shalt not do this and that. With negative training the person develops the feeling of being fenced in, something that is detrimental to free and constructive creative thinking.

Not only is punishment nonconstructive, it is actually suggestive. On one occasion the vice-president of personnel in a utility anticipated some problems in connection with a forthcoming strike. He realized that the strikers could do a lot of damage if they shot bullets through some of the cables. As soon as the strike was on, he announced that any one who shot a rifle bullet through a cable would be dealt with by the law. The company never had so many bullets shot through cables.

To illustrate further, let me ask you *not* to do something. Planting the suggestion not to notice how the roof of your mouth feels, actually leads to an awareness of it.

In one plant the author has visited, a sign over the time clock listed twenty-two possible violations, with the penalty stated next to each. One doubts whether any employee in that company could have thought of twenty-two ways in which to annoy the company. But in this case he didn't have to — it was all spelled out for him.

Finally, an unpleasant disciplinary climate sets up a depressing attitude which hangs like a cloud over all activity. A child who is forced to practice the piano may develop an unfactorable attitude toward music because it tends to be connected with the unpleasantness caused by the threats. The child is actually trained to dislike music because he hears it under unpleasant circumstances.

AVOIDING BAD SIDE EFFECTS OF DISCIPLINARY ACTION

The above discussion should not be interpreted to mean that all forms of discipline should be abandoned. The discussion has been about the bad side effects. One question is "How can these be prevented?" The second question is, "Are there other alternatives?" Is it possible that people can be taught how to do things without teaching them how not to do them?

The picture here is gloomy. Companies still have disciplinary actions. They set policies and they expect supervisory people to carry them out. When a man violates a safety practice, company regulations state a one week layoff. Now, what do supervisors do under these circumstances?

We experiment with a simulated role-playing situation in which a foreman thinks he catches a man working on top of a telephone pole without a safety belt. (Real foremen played the parts.) Thus, two individuals are involved. One is the repairman who allegedly has violated the safety regulations. He knows he has committed a violation, but he thinks he knows more about safety than the foreman. He has never fallen off a pole, and so he thinks he knows when to use a safety belt and when not. While the safety regulation never allows a man to take that kind of freedom, men take these liberties anyway.

HOW FOREMEN REACT WHEN CONFRONTED WITH VIOLATIONS

What do different foremen do under these circumstances? The foreman in our study was confronted with choices in a series of situations. If he saw that a man had violated a safety regulation, did he discuss it with him or not? (Diagram 1 shows this choice point as "A"). Twenty-five percent decided not to discuss the safety regulations. If they did discuss safety, they never raised the question of whether a violation had occurred on this occasion. When they took this approach, sixty-seven percent of the workers said that they would be more likely

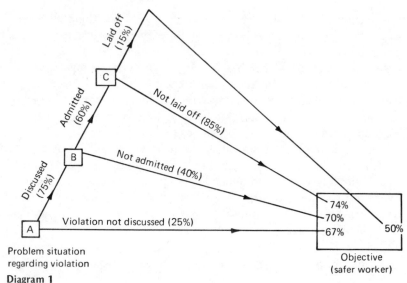

Problem situation
regarding violation

Objective
(safer worker)

Diagram 1
Guilt not established, penalty great (N = 154). *(From Danielson & Maier,* Personnel
Psychology, *1957, 10, 169-180)*

to use their safety belts as a result of this experience. (This percentage
is shown in the square on the right of the diagram.)

But suppose the foreman decided to discuss the safety violation. If
he discussed it, he progressed to the next choice point "B." At point
B, two alternatives are possible. The man might deny the violation and
escape punishment. Forty percent confronted with this violation denied
the violation and, of these, 70 per cent indicated they would be more
safe.) The other 60% admitted the violation. The foreman then had
to decide about punishment. This took him to choice point "C."

Now, if the worker admitted it, what happened? If he was not laid
off, even though he admitted the violation, seventy-four percent said
they would be more safe. If he was laid off after he admitted it, fifty
percent said they would be more safe, while a good many of the others
said they would be less safe.

Now, the interesting thing is that we can deal with this situation the
easy way (turn right at point "A" by going all the way to point "C")
or the hard way. When the punishment was given, it was less effective
than when the violation was ignored.

The foreman is in a very rough spot. Sixty percent of the workers
admitted that they committed a violation, and yet the foreman tended
not to lay these workers off. The chart indicates that only fifteen percent of the foremen laid the worker off. In other words, foremen
were not carrying out the orders of management.

When management discovers that their foremen are not enforcing
regulations, they put on pressure. The foreman now cooperates, but
if he starts laying off men he finds himself in difficulty. The company
runs an attitude survey which shows that foremen who lay workers

off get poor scores. Further, a man who is laid off may start a grievance. Then, after the grievance goes through several stages, the legal approach might be, "What's all the fuss about? How much will it cost to pay this man for the time he has been laid off? Let's pay him and get this thing settled." Thus the case is reversed.

On the other hand, foremen find that when they don't lay off workers, they expose themselves to being accused of discriminatory practice. To resolve the dilemma they come up with an elegant conclusion. "Never catch anybody." As a result, the company has to put in a separate safety organization because it can't depend on foremen. Now the foreman has been completely absolved from any obligation to look after safety.

MANY FOREMEN AVOID PUNISHING VIOLATORS

One can be concerned with the high percentage of foremen who didn't lay off a worker. And it is rather interesting to observe that the higher up in management you go, the more likely people are to lay off a violator. Down the line foremen learn the hard way — it's easier to stay out of trouble if you don't notice things.

The penalty in the experiment reported was a week, and the question of innocence or guilt was vague, unless the man admitted it. When the researcher asked the foremen why they didn't lay the man off, he obtained such reasons as "The penalty was too severe." "Well, we weren't sure." "The man admitted it in confidence."

To test the validity of such reasons, another research study was made. In this situation a man is found smoking in a "no-smoking" area. He is holding the cigarette, puffing away, and the foreman is looking right at him. The foreman lays him off on the spot. The prescribed penalty is a three day layoff for smoking in a restricted area.

Now, a person is assigned the role of the union steward whose task it is to see if he can get the foreman to reverse his decision. All of the facts are those favoring guilt. There is no question about a violation. The only argument the union steward has is that the man doesn't like to be laid off. He has a family — a layoff would create a hardship.

Table 1 shows that only about thirty-five percent of the foremen stick to their guns and give the man a three day layoff.

Another thirteen percent were unable to reach agreement. But, interestingly enough, here is a large group of foremen in-between; over fifty percent who actually back down. Some backed down by reducing the layoff, which technically was not permitted by the rules; others gave the worker a warning in place of a layoff; still others forgave the worker; and the rest agreed to talk to higher management and see if the rule couldn't be changed.

This is an amazing result considering that the guilt of the worker was obvious and there was no factual evidence that should force a foreman to back down. The only forces against the decision were the workers' feelings. And yet many foremen did back down and change their decisions.

Table 1
Guilt clear, penalty mild (N = 172)

Decision	Frequency (per cent)	Result in grievance
Full 3-day lay-off	34.9	45%
Reduced lay-off	4.6	
Warning	22.7	
Forgiven	7.5	
Consult higher management	8.7	2%
Consult workers	3.5	
Other	4.6	
No decision	13.4	43%

From Maier & Danielson, *Jour. Appl. Psychol.*, 1956, 40, 319-329.

We must face the fact that the people who are supposed to administer discipline don't like to do it, and that they try to find ways to avoid carrying out the assignment. Discipline comes easy only when done in anger.

The results of the grievances are also interesting. When one gives a man a layoff, he finds he has created another problem, especially when it leads to a grievance. The question then is no longer the issue of safety. It had to do with innocence or guilt. But the prevention of smoking, as a problem, drops out of the picture.

The writer remembers one case that went to grievance in a large factory when a man was caught smoking in a "no-smoking" area. It went through several stages of the grievance procedure. In this case, smoking was permitted on the balcony, and the man charged with smoking had one foot on the balcony, but his other foot was on the stairs.

We are confronted with a situation where the union argues that the man was on the balcony (one foot), and hence was allowed to smoke; the company argued he had one foot on the stairway, and hence he was not allowed to smoke.

This discrepancy then led to the question, "Where was most of his weight?" The union contended that he was leaning forward, which would put most of the weight on the balcony. The company contended that he was standing upright, which puts most of the weight on the step.

In the debate over such issues, the question of the prevention of smoking the original purpose of the regulation, ceases to become the issue.

"PEOPLE DON'T EXECUTE DECISIONS THEY DON'T LIKE"

In summary, it can be said that there are various effects of discipline. We have found that people don't execute decisions that they don't like. Even when they think a man deserves punishment, they do not like to do things that hurt people's feelings, especially when they like a person.

In industry, there is a further complication because regulations are decided at the top. The people who make the regulations don't have to police them. Subordinates are obliged to do this. The very supervisors who are most effective are the ones who are the most considerate of people. Such considerate supervisors are the very ones who are least inclined to carry out the kind of disciplinary action that is established at the top.

THE DYNAMICS OF MANAGEMENT OBJECTIVES*

Edward C. Schleh

If management is to obtain the best possible blending of the interests of the individual with those of the corporation, extreme care must be exercised in getting objectives down to the man concerned. Both the process of objective setting and the application of objectives to the individual must be realistic as they affect human beings, their individual motivations, their interests, their normal reactions. Since the purpose is to stimulate the man, these human factors are all-important in obtaining the greatest value from objectives. Many companies err in this area because they accept too easily the authoritarian approach which assumes simply that delegations come from above and are referred downward. Organizationally speaking, this is sound. Delegations are determined by the superior. If you want to make that delegation effective and most earnestly embraced by the subordinate, however, a whole series of principles of motivation must be observed.

OBJECTIVES SHOULD BE A STIMULUS

First of all, *any objective must be set in light of all known existing conditions.* The determination of these conditions includes an evaluation of past history, of competition, of the impact of other people in the enterprise on the man, and of any obstacles that may prevent his accomplishing results. When the conditions change, the objectives should change.

The superior should *set both basic and outstanding performance objectives for each result.* He would do this by first asking himself, "In light of all the conditions as I know them, what would be reasonable job performance on this particular result?" Reasonable job performance usually means the answer to this question: If you had an experienced man who understood the job well, what might be considered reasonably good performance for him (not outstanding and not poor)? Ordinarily, anyone who would be kept on the payroll over a period of time should be expected to attain a performance of this level. Determine specifically what the objective should be and state this as the basic performance objective (see Figure 1).

---

*From *Management by Results* by Edward C. Schleh. Copyright © 1961 by McGraw-Hill, Inc. Used by permission of McGraw-Hill Book Company.

Figure 1
Examples of objectives

Result area	Basic performance objective	Outstanding performance objective
1. Sales volume	$100,000	$140,000
2. Sales outlets	10 new outlets	16 new outlets
3. Development of a product	$150,000 profit in first 2 years after paying all development costs	$300,000 profit in first 2 years after paying all development costs
4. Cases completed	8 per day	11 per day
5. Meet schedules	90% of the time	98% of the time

A superior should then ask himself further, "In the light of all these same conditions, what would I consider to be an outstanding job?" In other words, define very good performance that could be achieved by a good man with high effort. A word of caution in this regard: "Outstanding" in this case would mean that the individual, by extra application or insight, would probably be able to reach this level. It should not be something almost unattainable out yonder. It should be attainable by a man doing a very good job under the conditions as envisioned for the coming year. This should then be set as the outstanding objective. You have determined the basic accomplishment expected of a man if he works well and in the right direction, and, in addition, you have set what he should shoot for in order to be recognized as outstanding. Do the same thing for each of the major results expected of him in the period.

Many executives make the mistake of setting only one figure for an objective. Ordinarily they have only a loose idea as to whether it would represent normal or outstanding accomplishment. Should the man work hard and apparently accomplish the objective with ease (which happens frequently when men are set up against specific objectives), a subtle change develops in the mind of the superior. He tends to minimize the accomplishment of the subordinate. He feels that his objective was too loose in the first place. Much of the stimulus is taken away from the employee in that he feels that he has been tricked. Should the man, however, have some difficulty in accomplishing the objective, there is a tendency to view the objective then as something to be striven for but not necessarily attained. Both the man and the superior begin to look at the objective as something that the man is not accountable for. One of the common errors managers make in setting objectives is that they do not set both the basic and the outstanding accomplishment expected for each item.

Another common error made by managers is to assume that objectives apply to the job and not to the individual. This error can spoil a good man as he enters a job. It is worthwhile having a man work against objectives even when he is comparatively new on the job (after his initial training period). However, *objectives for a new man should be set in light of his experience.* In other words, one of the conditions affecting the setting of objectives is the lack of experience of the man (on this particular job). On reflection it is perfectly logical that both the basic and the outstanding accomplishment expected of a beginner on a job would not be as high as that of an experienced man. Setting lower objectives for new men has important implications later on when determining their authority. Since authority should be set in light of objectives or accomplishment expected, the superior will then automatically consider authority for the beginner realistically.

Should you set the same objective for a beginner as you would for an experienced man, you may set the stage for failure. The man may do his best to achieve his objectives. In doing this he may step out of line and make errors which will cast a reflection on him for years to come, a situation with serious implications for the future for a young manager, say, who is in one of his early management positions. On the other hand, he may simply give up, knowing full well that it will be almost impossible for him to achieve these objectives. His superior permits this, since the man is new. The man then develops an unsatisfactory lack of accountability for objectives. He will be weakened for the future.

If a firm is large and has both staff and line people, it is helpful to *set the line objectives first.* Since these focus on the central service the enterprise is to provide, the basic company accomplishment is highlighted. After this, staff objectives should be set so that they are harmonious with those objectives set for the line. (Staff provides service functions aimed at helping the line do its job better.)

One of the most difficult phases of setting objectives is that of making each objective harmonious with others. A man who is working toward an objective may become impervious to the needs of other people in the firm. Objectives may accentuate "lone wolf" inclinations. Therefore, after all objectives have been set in a preliminary way, it is well to write them down and *cross-check to see that all objectives blend with each other.* The individual objectives for each man must be studied in their implication to see whether or not they will interfere with the objectives of other men. If so, adjustment should be made so that it is to the advantage of one man to help another.

Objectives should also be cross-checked upward so that the objectives of any man tie into those of his superior and eventually into the objectives of the enterprise. If this is done carefully, each echelon is allied with the echelons above. All are encouraged to work together toward an overall company objective. They are all on the same team and heading in the same direction. If a subordinate fails, the superior shares his failure. This cross check puts a great deal more strength behind any objective program. It sets up a basis for realistic accountability, tying all levels of the organization together effectively. Better communications are encouraged.

They become more realistic, as they are now part of a natural management flow. They are essential for the smooth working toward objectives.

A strong drive toward one particular result may lead to imbalance in the company. Very often there is an optimum level beyond which an achievement may actually be harmful to some other objective of the firm. In a plant, quality control carried too far may have detrimental effects on waste and on cost of production. In a procurement department, getting the material in on time may raise costs by not allowing time to get several bids. Each objective should be carefully scrutinized to determine the optimum point beyond which the objective might be detrimental to the achievement of other objectives. Setting the outstanding objective and giving no credit for accomplishment beyond it will minimize excessive pressure on any one result. To this extent such a limitation encourages further concentration on other objectives.

Another way to prevent imbalance is to set a counter-objective. For example, a purchasing agent may be held accountable for both a level of inventory and for down time due to lack of materials. Going too far on one generally affects the other. A built-in type of self-discipline is provided whereby the man can regulate himself. The need for constant checks by supervision is minimized, and the wise exercise of judgment by the purchasing agent is encouraged.

One loan company increased its volume of business (and profits) substantially by arbitrarily setting up a higher loss ratio. They were then able to accept much more of the business that came to the counter. They could do this profitably at a comparatively low cost, and as a consequence their net profits were more than enough to overcome the added credit losses they incurred.

People trained in precise figure work, such as engineering and accounting people, are inclined to feel that once objectives are set the job is done. Nothing could be farther from the truth. The prime value of an objective is in the stimulation of a man. The emotional impact on the man must, therefore, be carefully considered when objectives are installed. If objectives are to stimulate *the man*, he *must feel that the objectives are fair*. It is not enough that they are actually fair; what is important is that the man feels that they are fair. What makes him feel that they are fair? A man is usually much more sold on objectives if he participates in setting them. He understands them better and is better sold on their fairness. Resentment, opposition, and alibis generally develop if objectives are set above and simply handed down for compliance.

There is a difficulty, however. Essentially, objective setting is the job of the superior — it is the final expression of his delegation. How can you get the subordinate to set objectives and still avoid the violation of this superior-subordinate relationship? Ordinarily the following procedure works quite well: The superior should first discuss the general conditions under which the man will be working and in a broad way point out to the man the over-all expectation in company objectives. In a way he is pointing out the general track on which the total operation is running. It is also helpful for the superior to point out some of the places in the man's job where he thinks objectives might be especially worthwhile that year. He should then *ask the man* to take this information, carefully review his own sphere of action, and come back later *to suggest what he considers to be sound objectives* for himself. Ask him how he will shoulder his share of the total responsibility. Most men do not wish to be considered laggards. The man will often suggest much more difficult objectives for himself than his superior might otherwise have set. And note this! He will generally be more sold on their fairness than if someone else had forced him to accept these objectives.

An important additional benefit results from this method of setting objectives. Since a man has to go back and think through the objectives, he will think much more broadly than he would otherwise and plan ahead. He is usually careful to analyze his whole operation so that when he comes back with objectives he is fairly certain that he will be able to accomplish them. Before proposing objectives he will probably lay out a plan for reaching them. He becomes a broader man by the process, one who is able to plan ahead and think through problems without imposing them on his superior. Such a procedure places the planning function solidly on the subordinate's shoulders.

What if the man returns with objectives that are much higher than those his superior had been considering? There is a temptation for the superior to accept these higher objectives since the man himself set them. In most cases this would be a grave mistake. If the superior is still convinced that these objectives are higher than they should be, he should reduce them. This would be true either for basic or for outstanding performance or for both. A good way to do this is to tell the man, "I appreciate your interest in setting such difficult objectives, but I would be well satisfied if the following (lower) objectives were met. If you meet them, I'll still consider that you have done the job."

The impetus and drive that this approach gives to the man, and the confidence in the fairness of the superior, provide a strong stimulus. His general reaction is, "I can easily meet that." (Note the comment made earlier, that men are more stimulated by success than they are by failure.) Do not set tougher objectives for a man simply because he proposes them. If the subordinate shows in the discussion that the superior's first idea of sound objectives was really too loose, then it is perfectly all right to accept a higher objective. Since this is an easy rationalization for the superior, however, he should try to be very critical of this step before he takes it.

It is also helpful to ask the man to set percentage values for each of his objectives. The superior may then compare these with the percentages that he would have assigned and have a good basis for a discussion of the relative value of the different objectives. Both on the objectives and on the percentage values, however, the final decision still has to be made by the superior. Many managers find this participative procedure difficult to accept; they feel they are giving away some of their prerogative. Nothing is given away, because the man is still finally accountable for the accomplishment which has been agreed to by the superior. If the man should return with objectives that are too low, these would not be accepted. They would be used as a basis for a discussion with the man to build him up to accepting higher objectives.

It is very important that *the superior should adopt a positive attitude toward objective setting.* In other words, once objectives have been set, it should be tacitly assumed that they will be met. Otherwise a subordinate may develop a negative approach. He just can't meet them! This points up all the more the importance of setting reasonable objectives that can be met. Setting objectives that you assume will not be met or that would be extremely difficult to meet may very well take much of the steam out of the program. There is then a tendency for the man to "carp" too much and for the superior to be too quick to relieve a man of accountability because of some unusual condition. A part of the conditions under which objectives have been set should be the "normal" unpredictable occurrences that affect the job. It is assumed that the man will meet his objectives in spite of these conditions.

Many executives ask whether or not they should adjust objectives in the middle of the year should conditions change. Ordinarily the answer is no! Adjustments tend to weaken an objective program. However, there are some circumstances that may require an adjustment. These get right back to fairness to the individual. It is assumed that the normal give-and-take of a job is covered earlier in establishing the conditions. Objectives may be revised, however, if there is a radical change in the conditions assumed when setting the objectives. A mid-period review may be advisable to consider whether the conditions are actually as anticipated.

For example, one of these conditions might be the fact that a plant from which all products were to be sold in a given territory was burned down. It is quite obvious that no salesman could possibly sell high volume if he has few products to sell. His objectives may therefore be adjusted in light of the potential now available to him. The fact that competition was a little tougher than anticipated or that the economy went up or down 5 or 10 per cent should not change the objectives. Ordinarily, within these limits, objectives should hold for the year. The man is expected to carry the load for the company. Perhaps a 20 per cent drop in the potential may justify a change. If at the end of the year objectives prove to be wrong one way or the other, they may be adjusted or changed for the coming year. Any errors would be corrected then, because objectives would be reviewed for change anyway at the beginning of the year.

In some cases it may be perfectly sound to set sliding objectives in the beginning of the year and tie them to possible changes in key conditions. In a mail-order house a supervisor may have cost objectives tied to the number of orders sent in each week. If it is up, his cost objective is higher. If it is down, his cost objective is lower.

How could accomplishment on one objective be looked at versus accomplishment on another? Very frequently an employee on a job may feel that one objective is much more difficult or much more valuable and put a great deal of time into it. As a consequence, he may achieve accomplishments far beyond the outstanding objective for that particular item. However, he may not even reach the basic performance on one of the other objectives. The objective that he focused on may actually prove to be worth more money in that particular period. Should the supervisor balance off the very superior accomplishment on one objective against the below-normal accomplishment on another? Let us examine what would happen if this were done. If he permitted this, he would, in effect, be allowing the man to determine his own delegation without the consent of the superior. In subsequent years the man would also pick and choose among the objectives irrespective of the percentage weights that had been agreed to for each. Severe imbalance in the operation could result.

Failure to accomplish a given objective may also seriously impinge on the work of other people in the operation so that serious losses may be incurred and bottlenecks develop. For example, concentration on one type of product in a plant department in order to get long runs may cause too many back orders. On the other hand, unbalanced sales volume may easily cause shutdowns of entire lines in a plant. The man concerned may not feel accountable for these losses. In order to maintain balance *the superior should require at least basic accomplishment on all objectives in each period.* If he does not, he will lose control of the operation. Unusual accomplishment on one objective should almost never be accepted as excusing of lack of accomplishment on other objectives. Otherwise the superior will not be able to depend on the man for balanced accomplishment in the future. Lack of balance is one of the most costly errors in most operations.

GETTING THE NEW OBJECTIVE PROGRAM INTO OPERATION

Frequently, the first reaction of managers considering a management-objective program is that they do not have enough figures or data on which to set objectives. It seems impossible to determine accurately what objectives or measurements should be used. Fortunately it is not necessary to require perfection in your objective program at the outset. *Crude objectives or measurements* that are not completely accurate *are usable in getting the program started.* Experience will later prove where they are in error. You can make adjustments in the next period. They will still operate as a better stimulus than not having them.

At the start records may not seem particularly well adapted to the objective program. Parts of a job may be hard to measure. There is therefore a tendency to retreat from objectives because the whole position cannot be covered. It does not have to be. In the beginning, concentrate on one or two of the major results such as cost reduction, sales increase, waste reduction, better schedule performance, etc., if this is all that you can do in light of the records available. You will still get the man to concentrate on an item that is important and will get him accustomed to operating under a mode of operation based on objectives.

Initially it is a good idea to select those items for which measurements are readily available even though they are somewhat crude. It is not essential that every facet of the job be covered in the first year. A perfectly workable plan might set objectives for only part of the job in the first year. Men develop a better understanding of objectives and will usually get improvement without forcing any major long-range imbalance. In subsequent periods all major parts of the job should be covered as soon as possible, however, or you will probably push toward an imbalanced operation.

When executives first approach an objective program, they often become very enthusaistic about it and try to accomplish the ultimate in the first year. There is something about the analysis that precedes objective setting that opens up one's eyes to possible improvements. A new millennium of perfection seems quickly within reach. It is not that easy! *Do not demand the ultimate the first year.*

If a 15 per cent improvement in the operation is possible, a manager often feels that this should be the objective for the first year. Nothing could be farther from the truth. You are much better off encouraging a 4 per cent improvement (something you may never have obtained before) in the first period. Some managers may react against such a suggestion, feeling that 4 per cent is not as much as he ought to demand since 15 per cent is possible (but the 15 per cent will probably not appear fair to his subordinates). In the following year he may get 5 per cent more, and perhaps 6 per cent in the third year. Eventually he would probably be up beyond 15 per cent. But note this! His men will get in the habit of meeting objectives. This is essential! They will be encouraged to use their own initiative to plan ahead, and will be spurred on by success, a much more effective stimulus in any case than failure. Men will develop much more rapidly and the firm will accomplish more in the long run.

EXECUTIVE COMMUNICATIONS: BREAKING THE SEMANTIC BARRIER*

Stuart Chase

The modern executive lives in an increasingly complicated network of communication, with lines leading up, down, and sideways from his desk. He has to keep lines clear, not only to those below in the business hierarchy, but to whatever levels may be above. Some years ago, a New Jersey company called in a consultant to set up a so-called "vertical round table" — a discussion group designed to keep lines open between *seven* levels of management, from top drawer to assistant supervisor. (The experiment introduced them to each other for the first time, and worked out most helpfully.)

Important communication lines run outside the company, too, of course, to dealers, suppliers, consumers, government officials, and the general public — whose good will is so essential today.

Many excellent studies on the problems of communication have already been published. But there is a close relationship between communication and the lively young science of semantics, and executives interested in improving communication can take advantage of this new tool.

Semantics has been defined as "the systematic study of meaning." It deals mostly with words, but may include other methods of signaling, such as gestures, facial expressions, signs, and symbols. UNESCO has been working on a system of highway symbols (curves, side roads, danger, etc.) which can be understood in any part of the world, irrespective of the language spoken.

Semantics goes far beyond dictionary definitions. It attempts to evaluate what a speaker really means, as contrasted with what he says. To call a man a "horse-thief," in literal dictionary terms, is to accuse him of a serious crime. But when Jones greets Robinson with "Hullo, you old horse-thief!" his intention may be nothing but affection.

The goal of semantics is a better understanding inside our heads of what goes on *outside* them, and consequently a better adjustment to our environment. It can help us to clarify meanings in much the same way as a good pair of glasses can clarify a landscape to one suffering from astigmatism.

From the outside world come signals and messages in the form of light waves, shock waves, pressures. They follow nerve currents from eye, ear, fingertips, to the brain. What do they mean? If we interpret them incorrectly, we are in trouble. The sight of an oncoming car crossing into our lane can, in a sense, become a problem in semantics. So can the task of unscrambling such terms as "fair price," "reasonable profit," and "security risk." Insurance men, I understand, are having as much trouble defining "explosion" as the United Nations is having with "aggression."

The present author tried to bring the whole subject of semantics to a wider audience in 1938 with his book, *The Tyranny of Words.* Since then, there have been many books, monographs, lectures, and seminars devoted to semantics, and more than 100 colleges now give courses in the subject.[1]

Semantics takes its place beside a dozen other disciplines concerned with communication, ranging from the rigorous mathematical theory of Claude Shannon of the Bell Laboratories to studies in how to listen. Automation is the child of cybernetics, and cybernetics, developed by Dr. Norbert Wiener of M.I.T., is a branch of communication theory.

When I investigated the excellent communication system at Pitney-Bowes, Inc.,[2] I was doing a little semantic research to determine how the rank and file got their suggestions, grievances, and stories up to top management and how management got its stories down. There were at least five upward channels, and more than that downward.

One particularly interesting channel at Pitney-Bowes is the annual "Jobholders Meeting," which follows the stockholders meeting and takes a similar form. (The semanticist is shy of the word "same" since no two events are ever *precisely* the same.) Workers hear the president, treasurer, and other officers give an account of what has happened in the past fiscal year and predict the fortunes of the company for the new year. Questions are in order from the floor, and plenty come. "I see here on the balance sheet that all our patents are only worth one dollar. That doesn't seem right," says a machinist. This one gives the treasurer some minutes of acute mental activity!

ROADBLOCKS TO COMMUNICATION

Perhaps the major principle of semantics is to stop, look, and listen when a message comes in to be decoded by the brain and not let it trigger off an emotional response. If there is time, consider what this particular message means coming from this particular source.

[1] Semantics was introduced into the language by Lady Viola Welby in a book called *What Is Meaning?* published in 1903. In 1921, Ogden and Richards brought out their devastating *Meaning of Meaning*, which, among other things, turned the great philosophers from Aristotle to Hegel upside down, and shook them vigorously for verbal content. Alfred Korzybski, a Polish-American mathematician, published *Science and Sanity* in 1933, introducing what he called "General Semantics" — a discipline which emphasized psychological aspects of meaning.

[2] See "Communication Up, Down, and Sideways," *Reader's Digest*, September, 1952.

Equally important is the proper sending of messages. Will your words correspond well enough to the past experience of the hearer so that he can understand what you say? To use the terminology of Claude Shannon, will he decode what you encode? Without common experience stored in the memories of both speaker and hearer, the communication line is dead. "Foreigners" are not ignorant, they've just had different experiences. "Workers" (or "bosses") are not necessarily stupid; they, too, have had different experiences. If an Indian from the Amazon has never seen or felt snow, it is useless to talk to him about skiing.

How does one identify roadblocks on the communication line? Out of more than a dozen which have been classified, here are the six most common:

1. The confusion of words with things

Words are so cardinal in human affairs that we tend to assume that behind every word must stand a physical thing to which the word refers. Take the term "unemployment." It sounds pretty specific, but to the student of semantics, it is exceedingly indefinite. He might make a list of various kinds of unemployment, using an index notation like this:

$Unemployment_1$ is where a man has lost his job and is looking hard for another one.

$Unemployment_2$ is where a man has lost his job but is not looking for another one. His wife can balance the budget.

$Unemployment_3$ is where a man needs a job, is looking for a job, but is physically incapable of doing a job (unemployable).

$Unemployment_4$ is where a man is laid off for a month while the model is changed to the biggest, longest, most beautiful number the world has ever seen!

$Unemployment_5$ is where a man is working part time and is looking for another part-time job to pay the grocer.

No wonder honest statisticians, trying to figure the exact number of "unemployed" on a given day, are driven to distraction!

The executive with a little semantic training never forgets that *words are not things*. "Unemployment" is a word in our heads, with no precise *referent* out there in the world of space and time. It can be applied to a whole spectrum of referents.

The Empire State Building, on the other hand, is more manageable. We can point to it, see the clouds form around the TV mast, go up and kick its solid cornerstone, and agree on a physical thing to which the term "Empire State Building" refers. When we discuss the "architectural beauty" of the building, however, agreement may vanish and a hassle develop. Why? Because "architectural beauty" is a term in our heads, for which everyone has a somewhat different meaning.

2. The careless use of abstract words

This roadblock is close to the one above. An abstract term should not be used carelessly. Everyone interested in international affairs today is talking about "aggression." The British committed "aggression" in Egypt, the Russians committed "aggression" in Hungary, the Chinese committed "aggression" in Korea. A committee of the United Nations, however, after two years' intensive study, has been unable to define the term. The committee is in despair, but no semanticist is surprised. "Aggression" is an abstraction of a high order with severely limited usefulness. It has many meanings, on various levels. In international politics it has a "bad" meaning, but aggressiveness in business is quite different. We think well of an aggressive salesman, and we say a good executive should be alert and aggressive. But we don't like it when an executive displays "aggression" towards his associates.

Also up in the stratosphere are two formidable abstractions glowering at each other — "capital" and "labor." As all cartoonists know, one wears a plug hat, the other a kind of square cap popular with stone masons in the 1840's. These high abstractions can never come to terms; their combat is supposed to be eternal, and is formalized in the "class struggle" of Karl Marx. But the semanticist goes down the abstraction ladder to the real world. There he finds Company X in constant hot water with the unions, and Company Y not only living at peace with them, but using union shop discipline to produce better dividends. He also finds that "capital" is an increasingly muzzy term, now that the legal owners of most large corporations leave control to self-perpetuating managers who may own very little stock. This semantic exercise, incidentally, again demolishes the class struggle concept of Marx, which assumed a monolithic, unchanging "capitalism."

Abstract terms are necessary — indeed, we could not think without them — but we should be aware of their limitations, aware of the level they are on. When a politician sounds off about "liberty" — just liberty — the semanticist remembers the saying, "Your liberty to swing your arms ends where my nose begins." "Liberty" means little until we bring it down and ask: *liberty to do what?* Has a business man, for example, unlimited "liberty" to cut prices, or to enter into agreements in restraint of trade?

3. The confusion of facts with personal opinions

We meet this roadblock on every mental highway. Children should be warned about it at the age of ten, but seldom are. In Madison, Wisconsin, reporters for the *Capital Times* took a sidewalk poll, asking some 300 citizens: "What is a Communist?" A farmer in from the country gave a typical reply: "They're no good in my opinion. I don't know what they are." Observe that he had no facts, could draw no inferences, but did not hesitate to jump to the opinion level and deliver a moral judgment!

The correct way to get at the truth of an event is precisely the reverse. First gather the relevant facts, then draw logical deductions from them. Finally, if the occasion warrants, deliver your personal *opinions*.

When two men from the Department of Justice arrived one day at Pitney-Bowes, rumors might well have gone racing through the plant: "They're going to close us up!" Management, anticipating such rumors, immediately posted this notice on every bulletin board:

*All employees should assist the bureau's representatives in every
way . . . such investigations by the Department of Justice
have become almost routine throughout American industry.
They represent a necessary policing of our economic
system.*

Thus management substituted a true meaning for a wild one. Rumors, which may be as dangerous to a business firm as fire and go even faster, are often dizzy leaps to the opinion level. They can usually be extinguished by a flood of plain facts. The alert executive will get his facts on the notice board *before* the event, if he knows it is coming.

4. Judging people and events in terms of black or white

Sometimes this roadblock is called "either-or thinking," sometimes "two-valued thinking." Many situations are indeed black or white, without shades of gray. A man is alive or he is dead, for example. But the vast majority of our big social, political, and economic problems are many-sided, not just two-sided.

The either-or thinker says, "Those who are not with us are against us," and consigns India to the Communist camp. The semanticist recoils at such a conclusion. It is bad enough, he thinks, to cope with Russia and Red China without taking on the half-billion inhabitants of the "neutral" nations.

If an employer takes the position that *unions are bad*, period, he is inviting unnecessary trouble in the world of today. If, however, he takes the position that some *unions are badly led*, or *some union members are bad actors*, he will find life easier, for he is coming closer to the actual situation.

The bell-shaped frequency distribution curve is a useful offset to rigid two-valued thinking. If all the men in a given society are measured for height, and the figures charted, the curve will show a few seven-footers at one end, a few five-footers at the other end, and most of us in the middle. The case is similar for union members (or for employers) — the saints at one end, the so-and-so's at the other, and most of us in the middle. The curve represents the semantic multi-valued view, as against the two-valued view.

5. False identity based on words

This roadblock was the cause of great confusion in the days of Senator [Joseph] McCarthy. Anyone who disagreed with him risked being labeled a Communist, on the syllogism:

Communists are against McCarthy.
Spifkins is against McCarthy.
Therefore, Spifkins is a Communist.

"Things equal to the same thing are equal to each other" may be true of the words in a syllogism, but not necessarily of the actual situation. False identity can also be established by the old saying, "The enemy of my enemy is my friend." Similar reasoning would put the U.S. in the predicament of being Russia's friend when both censured the British for the invasion of Egypt.

Guilt by verbal association can also be shown in the classic case of the late Senator Taft. When he introduced his bill for public housing in 1947, he was attacked by certain real estate interests whose arguments boiled down to this syllogism:

Communists favor public housing.
Senator Taft has sponsored a bill for public housing.
Therefore, Senator Taft is following the Moscow line.

Following the same type of reasoning, a student of semantics could prepare another syllogism:

Communists favor apple pie.
Senator Taft favors apple pie.
Therefore . . . etc.

The trick is to find one characteristic, just one, shared by your victim and a common enemy, and then leap to the conclusion that *all* their characteristics are identical. Since all of us have literally thousands of characteristics — sex, weight, height, eye color, race, religion, occupation, aptitudes, attitudes, beliefs — it is child's play to find one shared by any two persons, or by a person and an organization. With this common bond established, guilt (or innocence) can be "proved," at least well enough to make the headlines. Indeed, with this monstrous logic it is possible to prove anybody guilty of anything.

6. Gobbledegook

The last semantic roadblock we shall investigate is the clouding of meaning by fancy words. On the campus it is known as "pedageese" — the pedageese of the pedagogues, a variety of protective coloration. The term "gobbledegook" was invented by the late Maury Maverick, Congressman from Texas, to describe the language of paper work in big government offices. Any big office is likely to come down with a severe attack.

A member of Parliament, A.P. Herbert, exasperated with bureaucratic jargon, once translated Nelson's immortal phrase, "England expects every man to do his duty," into standard big-office prose:

England anticipates that, as regards the current emergency, personnel will face up to the issues and exercise appropriately the functions allocated to their respective occupational groups.

An American office manager sent this memo to his chief:

Verbal contact with Mr. Blank regarding the attached notification of promotion has elicited the attached representation intimating that he prefers to decline the assignment.

Translation: Mr. Blank doesn't want the job.

On reaching the top of the Finsteraarhorn in 1945, M. Dolfuss-Ausset, when he got his breath, exclaimed: "The soul communes with the infinite in those icy peaks which seem to have their roots in the bowels of eternity."

Translation: He likes the view.

A Washington department announced:

Voucherable expenditures necessary to provide adequate dental treatment required as adjunct to medical treatment being rendered a pay patient on in-patient status may be incurred as required at the expense of the Public Health Service.

Translation: You can charge your dentist bill to the Public Health Service. Or can you?

To be fair to Washington, I should point out that the Federal Security Agency in 1950 made an intensive study of interoffice gobbledegook and issued an excellent report thereon, a report which every executive in business as well as government might well have on his desk.[3] It is not only instructive, but funny. For example:

The problem of extending coverage to all employees, regardless of size, is not as simple as surface appearances indicate . . . .
Though the proportions of all males and females in ages 16-45 are essentially the same. . .
Dairy cattle, usually and commonly embraced in dairying. . . .

These solemn statements, and many others found in the paperwork, enlivened the investigation.

SEMANTICS FOR THE EXECUTIVE

Semantics is no "monopoly" of heavy thinkers. It is for anyone to use who needs to keep his communication lines clear — and what business

---

[3]Hall and Grady, *Getting Your Ideas Across Through Writing*. Training Manual No. 7, 44 pages

man does not? It is common sense combined with a systematic study of how words behave at various levels and how meanings can be better sent and received.

Beardsley Ruml has observed: "Reasonable men always agree if they understand what they are talking about." "Always" may be a little strong, but we can safely settle for 95 per cent.

STIMULATING UPWARD COMMUNICATION*

Earl G. Planty and William Machaver

Managers, by and large, have been relatively quick to perceive the problems of downward communication. The growth and complexity of modern industry have placed pressure upon management at all levels to develop effective means of transmitting to lower echelons information that is vital to the continuing, efficient operation of the business.

Executives and supervisors recognize, too, that misinformation and the resulting misunderstanding lessen working efficiency. Sharing information with subordinates at all levels of the organization tends to diminish the fears and suspicions that we all sometimes have in our work and toward our employer; it affords the security and feeling of belonging so necessary for efficiency and morale. In general, it may be said that *downward* communication is an integral part of the traditional industrial organization and is readily accepted and made use of — more or less effectively — by management.

The neglected other half

Unfortunately, however, some managers tend to consider communication a one-way street. They fail to see the values obtained from encouraging employees to discuss fully the policies and plans of the company. They do not provide a clear channel for funneling information, opinions, and attitudes up through the organization.

There are many values, however, that accrue to those managers who listen willingly, who urge their subordinates to talk freely and honestly. Upward communication reveals to them the degree to which ideas passed down are accepted. In addition, it stimulates employees to participate in the operation of their department or unit and, therefore, encourages them to defend the decisions and support the policies cooperatively developed with management. The opportunity for upward communication also encourages employees to contribute valuable ideas for improving departmental or company efficiency. Finally, it is through upward communication that executives and supervisors learn to avert the many explosive situations which arise daily in industry.

If these advantages are to be achieved, we must realize that communication is dynamic. It must flow constantly up as well as down if it is to stimulate mutual understanding at all levels of the organization.

Faced as all industry is with the need for education in this complex and emotion-laden problem of upward communication, Johnson & Johnson and affiliated companies established a committee of operating executives to make a thorough investigation of the problems of upward communication. The personnel directors, a sales director, and two vice presidents in charge of manufacturing constituted the committee. They met, read, studied, interviewed specialists, argued the question among themselves, and then prepared the material which constitutes the body of the following report. Operating in panel style, they presented the report to the board of directors of the parent company, to the boards of affiliated companies, and to major operating executives, inviting their suggestions and criticisms.[1] Other committees similarly prepared themselves, presented reports, and invited discussions with middle and lower levels of management. Thus the report which follows represents practical recommendations dealing with the fundamentals and techniques of upward communication — a program developed by the joint effort of operating executives.

1. THE VALUE OF EFFECTIVE UPWARD COMMUNICATION[2]

A. Values to superiors

1. Many of management's best ideas are sown on cold and sour soil, not tilled and prepared in advance for the information. Where attitudes and feelings are transmitted freely upward, however, management is forewarned of possible failure and can better prepare the seed bed before its own ideas are broadcast. Upward communications tell us not only when our people are ready to hear our story, but also how well they accept our story when we do tell it. We have no better means than upward communication of knowing whether our downward communications have been believed.

2. If we are to gain understanding and full acceptance of our decisions, subordinates must be given the opportunity to participate in their

---

[1] The writers wish to acknowledge the assistance of the following members of the committee who presented the report: E.A. Carlson, Controller at Johnson & Johnson; J.T. Freeston, Assistant Personnel Director at Johnson & Johnson; J.F. Kiley, Vice President, General Line Field Sales Force at Johnson & Johnson; W.S. McCord, Director of Industrial Relations at Personal Products; C.V. Swank, Vice President in Charge of Manufacturing at Johnson & Johnson; and H.A. Wallace, Vice President in Charge of Manufacturing at Ethicon Suture Laboratories, Inc.

[2] The points outlined in this section were developed by the panel in reply to the moderator's question, "What values may we expect in business and industry from improved upward communications?"

making or at least to discuss the merits and defects of proposed actions. Social scientists tell us that employee understanding and loyalty do not come solely from hearing facts, even true facts. Appreciation and loyalty result from self-expression in a situation in which the subordinate feels there is personal sympathy toward him and his views. Therefore the superior should encourage subordinates at any level to ask questions and contribute their own ideas. Above all, he should listen, sincerely and sympathetically, with intention to use workable ideas that are proposed.

3. From upward communication we discover whether subordinates get the meaning from downward communication that is intended by the superior. It is highly unlikely that a subordinate left completely to his own interpretation will understand a directive or an action just as the originator intended it. In the first place, management may phrase its messages vaguely or ambiguously. Second, recipients interpret even the clearest communication in the light of their own biases and experience. Even though it may seem to us most logical that they should draw only one conclusion, we can never be sure what subordinates think unless we get them to relay back to us their interpretations and reactions to what we do and say.

4. Finally, effective upward communication encourages subordinates to offer ideas of value to themselves and the business. The need here is to devise and use every form of upward communication that will draw these ideas from all who are qualified to make them.

B. Values to subordinates

1. Upward communication helps satisfy basic human needs. All subordinates look upon themselves as having inherent worth at least as great as the personal worth of their superiors. This is true even if they feel their own inferiority in managerial ability or in some other skill. They still think, just as you and I do, that because they are individual human beings they have certain values and rights. This sense of personal worth is always injured when people do not get a chance to express their ideas — when they are merely told, without opportunity to comment or reply. This principle applies even if the telling is very well done. We respect our employees' dignity only when we allow, or better still invite, them to express their reactions to what is told — preferably before action is taken.

2. Employees who are encouraged to talk directly and frankly with their superiors get a release of emotional tensions and pressures which otherwise may find outlet in criticism to other members of the company and the community, or in loss of interest or efficiency. Some superiors feel that by listening to fanatics, crackpots, and neurotics they encourage their complaints. If complaints seem to arise from physical or mental ailments, treatment by a physician or psychiatrist may be necessary. But to the degree that the maladjustment lies in the man's work relations, listening to him may identify failures and sore spots in the organization that cause his problems. Moreover, it is well established

that the right kind of listening enables many individuals to understand and solve their own problems. For the *normal* individuals in industry, it is likely that the more you listen willingly to what employees are inclined to tell you, the less time you will in the future be called upon to give.

3. Unlike the organizational structure of the church, the school, the local and even the national government, industry in its organization is essentially authoritarian. This makes it even more necessary in industry than in, say, education or government that every opportunity be given subordinates to express their views freely and to make their influence felt. Many think that business cannot continue to exist as we know it today unless more and more ways are found to bring the essentials of democracy into the workplace. Fortunately, the principles of democracy do not require that such business functions as financing, expansion or curtailment of production, and hiring be decided upon by vote of the majority. However, the fact that by nature we must be authoritarian in some matters makes it imperative that we be more democratic in those business matters where employee participation is appropriate. Nothing is more fundamental to democracy than upward communication in which the ideas of subordinates are given prompt and sympathetic hearing followed by such action as is desirable.

II. BARRIERS TO UPWARD COMMUNICATION

Even though management may appreciate the need for effective upward communication, it may not translate this need into action. It becomes apparent at once that to swim up the stream of communication is a much harder task than to float downstream. The currents of resistance, inherent in the temperament and habits of supervisors and employees and in the complexity and structure of modern industry, are persistent and strong. Let us examine some of these deterrents to upward communication.[3]

A. Barriers involving business organization

1. The physical distance between superior and subordinate impedes upward communications in several ways. Communication becomes difficult

---

[3]Panel discussions with various groups revealed that until the obstacles to effective communications were clearly identified and accepted it was difficult to discuss techniques and methods profitably. A clear understanding of what impedes upward communications must precede removal of obstructions. In many cases an open channel is all we need for ideas and attitudes to flow upward. It was the thought of the syndicate that more could be gained by first emphasizing the removal of barriers than by first putting out enticements and formal devices for stimulating communication upward. Group meetings, written reports, and individual contacts become mere window dressing and will fail in their purpose if superiors have not first dispelled completely any feeling of disinterest or impatience with what their subordinates are telling them.

and infrequent when superiors are isolated so as to be seldom seen or spoken to. In large organizations executives are located in headquarters or divisional centers, at points not easily reached by their subordinates. In smaller organizations their offices are sometimes remotely placed, or they hold themselves needlessly inaccessible.

2. Complexity also delays communication up. Suppose there is at the employee's level a significant problem that eventually must be settled at the top. The employee tells his supervisor. They talk it over and try to settle it. This takes a day or two. Then it goes to the department head. He requires some time to hear the case, thinks about it a day or two, and then tells the divisional manager, who holds the case a week while he investigates, unwilling to bother the vice president with it. Since there may appear to be an admission of failure in passing the problem up, each level of supervision is reluctant to do so, thus causing more delay. By the time the problem reaches the top echelon, months may have elapsed since it first arose.

3. Movement of information through many levels dilutes or distorts it. Since each supervisor consciously or unconsciously selects and edits the information he passes up, the more levels of supervision, or filter stations, it passes through before it reaches the top, the less accurate it becomes. Also, in a large company with a hierarchy of management, contacts become fewer and more hurried as one ascends in the organization. A group leader contacts his workers more often than a president contacts his vice presidents.

B. Barriers involving superiors

1. The superior's attitude and behavior in listening will play a vital role in either encouraging or discouraging communication up. If the boss seems anxious to get the interview over with or appears to be impatient with his subordinate, or annoyed or distressed by the subject being discussed, this attitude will place an insurmountable communications barrier between them in the future.

2. A boss may fall into the familiar error of thinking that "no news is good news," whereas lack of complaint or criticism is often a symptom that upward communication is working in very low gear; or he may assume, often wrongly, that he knows what subordinates think or feel; or he may have such an exaggerated sense of duty that he feels it disloyal to listen to complaints, especially if made intemperately. This attitude tends to discourage employees with justifiable complaints from approaching their superiors.

3. We all have a natural defensiveness about ourselves and our actions. As managers, we are prone to resent and resist communications which indicate that some of our actions have been less than perfect. Where this attitude is evident, loyal workers who could be most helpful to us sometimes withhold information. In such cases communicating is of necessity done by the less loyal workers and the maladjusted. In other words, unless

we are willing to hear criticism freely, much we learn about our organization comes from those who are the least loyal to it.

4. Superiors often resist becoming involved with the personal problems of their subordinates. This resistance to listening may affect the subordinates' willingness to communicate up on other matters more directly related to the job. Moreover, job problems and personal problems are often closely linked, and it is difficult to discuss the one without the other.

5. One of the strongest deterrents to communication up is the failure of management to act on undesirable conditions previously brought to its attention. The result is that the workers lose faith both in the sincerity of management and in the value of communication.

6. Listening is time-consuming. Many executives feel that they are too involved with daily problems and responsibilities to provide adequate time for listening fully to their subordinates' ideas, reports, and criticisms. Nevertheless, many time-consuming problems could be minimized or eliminated if superiors were free to listen to their employees, for in listening they can discover solutions to present problems or anticipate causes for future ones. The subordinate who has free access to his boss can get the answers to many budding problems and thus eliminate heavier demands made when the problems have gotten complex, emotion-laden, and possibly out of control.

A man's philosophy of management determines the value he places upon communications and the time he gives to it. A manager who has freed himself of much of his routine responsibilities and is engaged in building individual subordinates and developing teamwork in his group will rank communications high in priority and will allow time for it, since it is the nerve center of such a leader's management. In contrast, the boss who acts alone, solves most of his department's problems himself, and lets the growth of subordinates take its own course may well be too busy to communicate.

C. Barriers involving subordinates

1. Communications down may run more freely than communications up because the superior is free to call in the subordinate and talk to him at will. The subordinate does not have the same freedom to intrude upon the superior's time. A man is discouraged from going freely over his boss's head or from asking appeal from his decisions by the line of authority that prevails in industry.

2. Neither the facilities available nor the rewards offered to the subordinate for upward communication equal those for messages downward. Management can speed the flow of information down by the use of company publications, in-plant broadcasts, meetings, bulletin boards, form letters, etc. By praise, promotions, and other signs of recognition management can reward subordinates who act upon communications down, as it can penalize those who fail to act. Few such facilities or

incentives for encouraging communications upward are available to the employee.

3. Communications from subordinate to superior cannot be prepared with as much care as those that move down. A sales manager, for example, may address a message to a dozen men — a message resulting from the combined thinking of his staff, strengthened by research, careful writing, editing, and visual aids. He and his staff are free to give that message far more time and thought than a salesman in the field can expend on a message back to the sales manager.

4. Because tradition, authority, and prestige are behind communications down, they flow more easily in that direction than do communications up. In communicating up, the subordinate must explain himself and get acceptance from one who has greater status and authority. The subordinate's difficulties are greater also because he is likely to be less fluent and persuasive than the man who communicates down to him.

The semantics barrier is likewise greater for the subordinate. His superior, probably having worked at one time on the subordinate's job, knows the attitudes, the language, and the problems of that level. On the other hand, the man who is communicating up faces the difficulty of talking to a person with whose work and responsibilities he is not familiar.

5. Like all of us, employees are emotional and prejudiced. Their feelings mix freely with their facts, creating further barriers to objective upward communications. Their observations and reports to management are prejudiced by their own personal habits and sentiments. The establishment of rapport through judicious listening will help the superior to understand and interpret what employees are trying to tell him. The superior, of course, must recognize and minimize his own prejudices and idiosyncrasies before he can do this.

6. Unless superiors are particularly receptive, subordinates generally prefer to withhold or temper bad news, unfavorable opinions, and reports of mistakes or failures. Because some managers are defensive about listening to bad news, those who like and respect them withhold information or minimize omissions and errors out of friendly motives; others keep back information from fear, dislike, or indifference.

THE BUDGETARY CONTROL FUNCTION*

Ernest I. Hanson

The process of budgeting and its product, the budget, are extremely use-ful in assisting management to fulfill its functions of planning, co-ordinating, and controlling enterprise activities. Although it is difficult to isolate these interdependent functions, they are usually so cate-gorized when portraying the budgetary process. This paper will focus on the control function. The conventional concept of control will be expanded as consideration is given to the factors which influence the nature of the responses of employees performing within the sphere of the budgeting process.

BUDGETS AND CONTROL: CONVENTIONAL CONCEPT

A budget is a formal statement by management of its plans for a given time period which will be used as a guide during that period. The view of the budget as a blueprint for action gives rise to the typical role attributed to it in the control function. It is portrayed as a type of "yardstick" against which performance is measured. An evaluation of this measurement then determines what corrective action is necessary.

Without management's implementing the yardstick qualities of the budget through measurement, the budget is not considered to be useful as a control device. The control process starts after the budget has been adopted. A diagrammatic representation of this control function is shown in Exhibit 1.

The representation of the budget as a desired state follows from the fact that it is a management plan designed to provide direction to the entity concerned. Since effective planning requires the existence of entity objectives, it is apparent that the fulfillment of corporate plans will move the enterprise nearer to its over-all goals.

The conventional concept of control is not complete. It is incomplete since it explains control through budgeting as a mechanistic, responsive action without recognizing that it is to some degree a self-governing action. Responding to measured differences between budgeted and actual performances, the corrective actions will always be applied after perfor-mances creating the differences have taken place. The corrective actions can in no way control these past activities.

*Reprinted with permission from *The Accounting Review*, April, 1966.

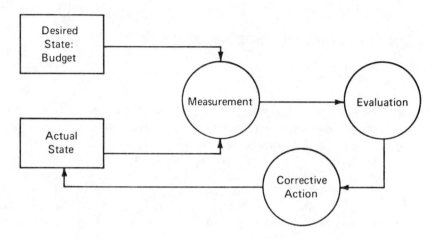

Exhibit I

BUDGETS AND CONTROL: EXPANDED CONCEPT

The typical control concept does delineate the objective of the control process, namely, to carry out plans with a minimal divergence between budgeted and actual activities. In addition to the sporadic corrective actions, there are certain attributes of the control process which operate continuously to bring about congruity between the planned and actual performance. The formulation of a more comprehensive concept requires the explicit recognition of these self-governing characteristics.

The expanded concept considers the fact that the control function necessarily involves the direction of people. Accordingly, it is appropriate to view the business enterprise within which budgeting takes place

. . . as a miniature society in which traditional social controls over the individual appear in sharp focus. The organization draws upon the accumulated learning and experience of the individual, who brings to it certain socially inculcated attitudes that encourage a satisfactory accommodation to the organization's major values and expectations.[1]

The additional areas of control which become relevant with this perspective of a business organization may be categorized as follows:

1. The nature of authority and the budget.
2. The degree of employee identification with budget goals.
3. The degree of attainability of budget goals.

[1] Robert V. Presthus, "Toward a Theory of Organizational Behavior," *Administrative Science Quarterly*, 3 (June, 1958), p. 49.

These intangible aspects of control precede the measurement and evaluative activities of the conventional model. They are complementary to the responsive and corrective actions focused on in the typical concept. These attributes are functioning at all times to reduce divergencies between actual performance and desired performance.

THE NATURE OF AUTHORITY AND THE BUDGET

Authority is the power to make decisions which guide the actions of another. Authority establishes superior-subordinate relationships. A business organization, a system of structured interpersonal relationships, contains many of these superior-subordinate relationships.

Custom may be the most important basis for the acceptance of the superior-subordinate role by the respective parties.[2] The many authoritative situations that an individual confronts, and accommodates to, prior to entering a business organization possibly explain why this relationship is accepted within an enterprise as a matter of custom.[3] In any event, deference to authority is one of the "socially inculcated attitudes" brought into the organization by an individual.

An important condition for the creation of an authoritative relationship is that the superior's decisions be communicated to subordinates. Without communication effective authority does not exist. Since the budget is a formal statement of management's plans, its role in the control function is evident. It is a vehicle used to convey the wishes of management. The budget acquires an authoritative aspect once it is communicated to those to whom it pertains. The customary tendency to defer to authority suggests that the individuals to whom the budget is communicated will undertake appropriate actions to meet the budget requirements. Authority, therefore, is a major control mechanism in a business firm. A budget, as it achieves authoritative characteristics, thus also serves as an effective control mechanism.

This conception of the budget as a control device remains completely detached from the manner in which it is administered. The budget is often pictured as a pressure device. In contrast, the reasoning developed thus far leads to a different conclusion. The budget acts as a *pressure-reducing device* since it provides individuals with a knowledge of actions necessary in order for them to meet the approval of their superiors.

THE DEGREE OF IDENTIFICATION WITH BUDGET GOALS

The communication of budget requirements to an individual does not assure that his responses will be entirely in accord with those desired,

---

[2]Herbert A. Simon, *Administrative Behavior*, 2d ed. (The MacMillan Company, 1957), p. 130.
[3]Presthus, op. cit., p. 57.

even given the tendency to defer to the authoritative nature of the budget. There is a reciprocal aspect to authority such that a subordinate may choose not to abide by the communicated budget.[4] There is a continuum of responses available, some of which are clearly more appropriate than others in meeting the budget requirements. The more closely an individual identifies himself with budget goals, the more appropriate will be his responses to the budget. Another significant aspect of the control function, then, centers on the degree of identification with budget goals.

There are numerous procedures available which serve to increase employee identification with budget objectives. One procedure directly associated with budgeting is the use of a participative budgeting process.[5] Meaningful involvement in the budgeting process at the lower operating levels is a useful principle to employ in the planning function of a budgetary system. Those who are going to have the responsibility for the performance of certain cost and profit centers should be fully involved in the planning of the expected performances.

The control aspects of participative budgeting are equally as important as its planning advantages. By becoming involved in the creation of the budget, the members of the organization associate themselves more closely with and become better acquainted with the budget goals. Thus, the participative process, which precedes the execution of plans, works as a control mechanism once the budget is implemented since it encourages identification with the budget objectives.

The existence of an evaluation system is an additional influence affecting the identification with budget goals. Under the conventional concept of the control function, the measurement and evaluation of performance provide the basis for formulating corrective actions. Inherent in this process, however, is an element of control influencing the actions of employees as they perform. This is noted in the following remark:

> . . . there is another, more subtle way in which cost reports
> influence performance, and indeed influence the very performance
> being reported on. Advance knowledge of the fact that a report on
> performance is going to be prepared can be an important stimulus
> to good performance on the part of the person being judged.[6]

Many of the procedures thus develop employees' identification not only with budget objectives but also with all organizational goals. A

---

[4]Chester I. Barnard, *The Functions of the Executive* (Cambridge, Mass.: Harvard University Press, 1938), p. 163.

[5]For a consideration of the applicability of participation to different types of business environments see Selwyn Becker and David Green, Jr., "Budgeting and Employee Behavior," *The Journal of Business,* October 1962, pp. 392-402; and Andrew Stedry, "Budgeting and Employee Behavior: A Reply," *The Journal of Business,* April 1964, pp. 195-202.

[6]Robert N. Anthony, "Cost Concepts for Control," *The Accounting Review,* April 1957, p. 233.

company's selective recruiting and hiring process must contain some judgment as to how well a potential employee's interests and motivations will mesh with the organization's needs and objectives. Training programs, whether of the formally structured type or of the continuous on-the-job type, are designed to hasten one's inculcation of the enterprise's values. The involvement of the individual in peripheral company activities, such as participation in company recreational functions, also serves to strengthen the identification process.

An organization's system of rewards and penalties fulfills a function of maintaining an individual's identification with company goals, or perhaps, even increasing the degree of identification by a more direct means than the procedures discussed up to now. Examples of positive sanctions available to a business entity include periodic pay raises, commissions, pensions, stock options, promotions, and bonuses. Negative sanctions include pay cuts or no increases, demotions or no advancement, and the possibility of losing the job.

The authoritative nature of the budget and the receptiveness of employees to communicated budget goals are important factors controlling the action-responses to a budget. Yet these items are not enough if the objective of control is to reduce the divergencies between actual and desired performances.

THE DEGREE OF ATTAINABILITY OF BUDGET GOALS

A third critical area involves the attainability of the budget goals. If budget standards are not reasonably attainable, there may be much inefficient and frustrating employee performance. On the other hand, budget standards that are too easily attainable are also impractical. To obtain efficient and productive performance, budget goals must be attainable and yet challenging.

Since the attainability of budget goals is significant, a sound system of control must include mechanisms designed to prevent too unfavorable a gap from developing. One mechanism, a participative budgeting process, has already been discussed. Two other techniques are flexible budgeting and establishing a range of performance levels for each goal.

A flexible budget is intended to provide attainable goals regardless of the operating level. Under a fixed budget, attainability of goals becomes meaningless as soon as the operating level varies from the level assumed.

Creating a range of expected performances for any given level is another budget approach. One author has suggested gradations of excellent, good, fair, and poor in the expected levels of performance.[7] Obviously, some performances within this range are more desirable than others. Yet this

[7]Chester H. Sneider, "Setting Operating Goals and Measuring Achievements," *N.A.A. Bulletin*, July 1958, p. 27.

multi-goal approach does act as a hedge against the creation of a situation wherein the individual is faced with a single unattainable goal.

Closely related to the importance of attainable budget goals is the concept of responsibility accounting. An individual should not be expected to achieve certain budget objectives unless he has the responsibility for whatever performances are necessary to reach the goals. The absence of such responsibilities may cause the budget requirements to appear unattainable. Formulating a budget in terms of responsibility centers therefore helps to increase the effectiveness of the budgeting control function. This means the budget system must be individually tailored to each organization.

Also relevant to this discussion is the suggestion that more frequent comparisons of actual and budgeted performance should be made and communicated to the employees.[8] The objective of such a recommendation is to obtain information so that budget goals may be adjusted, if necessary, to keep them rigorous yet achievable. Success in achieving goals generally leads to a rising aspiration level and failure to a lowering aspiration level.

SUMMARY

The objective of any control system is to reduce to a minimum the difference between actual conditions and desired conditions. The conventional concept of the budgeting control system emphasizes the process whereby management's attention is directed mainly to differences which have arisen. This concept, however, fails to give express recognition to the intangible and self-governing elements which serve to reduce the number and the magnitude of these differences.

The budget itself controls as soon as it achieves its authoritative characteristics through approval by high management and communication to subordinates. All factors which increase employee identification with budget goals are control elements. These include a participative budgeting process, advance knowledge of performance evaluations, hiring and training programs, involvement in extra-organizational activities, and a system of sanctions. Attainability is a third attribute of good control by budgetary means. For this purpose, flexible budgets, multi-goal performance levels, and responsibility accounting are leading methods of implementation. To the extent that authority, identification, and attainability are properly applied, the effectiveness of budget control should be increased.

[8]Becker and Green, op. cit., p. 402.

MANAGEMENT THOUGHT AND PRACTICE

Part IV begins with a history of the management movement. This article shows that modern management began with the industrial revolution and has continually been extended and refined. The second article, by William G. Scott, traces the development of classical, neoclassical, and modern theories of organizations.

In the next two articles Louis A. Allen explains how to best use line-staff relationships and committees. L. F. Urwick then offers a resounding defense of some earlier contributors to management thought.

In a lighter vein, Louis Fried suggests that managers often are involved in games which may work to the detriment of the organization. C. Northcote Parkinson explains in the next article how organizations can become buried in their own paperwork.

The powerful reasons for the growth of industrial bureaucracies are then discussed by Eugene V. Schneider.

Peter T. White next describes some esoteric applications of computers, and J. Stanford Smith suggests that man and computer have entered into a new partnership that will produce outstanding results. Next, Justin G. Longenecker explains how systems analysis has become a basic point of view for the management theorist and practitioner.

In his article, Raymond E. Miles explains the human resources concept, a type of approach that has become fundamental in modern management theory.

Finally, George Kozmetsky tells us his futuristic views of what management will be like in the next century.

HISTORY OF THE MANAGEMENT MOVEMENT*

Anonymous

A little more than a century ago, Michael Faraday, the noted British physicist, managed to gain audience with a group of high government officials, to demonstrate an electro-chemical principle, in the hope of gaining support for his work.
After observing the demonstration closely, one of the officials remarked bluntly, "It's a fascinating demonstration, young man, but just what practical applications will come of this?"
"I don't know," replied Faraday, "but I do know that 100 years from now you'll be taxing them."

From the demonstration of a principle to the marketing of products derived from that principle is often a long, involved series of steps. The speed and effectiveness with which those steps are taken are closely related to the history of management, the art of getting things done. Just as management applies to the wonders that have evolved from Faraday and other inventors, so it applied some 4,000 years ago to the workings of the great Egyptian and Mesopotamian import and export firms . . . to Hannibal's remarkable feat of crossing the Alps in 218 B.C. with 90,000 foot soldiers, 12,000 horsemen and a "conveyor belt" of 40 elephants . . . or to the early Christian Church, with its world-shaking concepts of individual freedom and equality.

These ancient innovators were deeply involved in the problems of authority, division of labor, discipline, unity of command, clarity of direction and the other basic factors that are so meaningful to management today. But the real impetus to management as an emerging profession was the Industrial Revolution. Originating in 18th-century England, it was triggered by a series of classic inventions and new processes, among them John Kay's Flying Shuttle in 1733, James Hargreaves' Spinning Jenny in 1770, Samuel Crompton's Mule Spinner in 1779 and Edmund Cartwright's Power Loom in 1785.

The industrial metropolis. Power from steam, rather than wind or water, accelerated industrial developments. Use of coke in iron production also had far-reaching effects. But the cost of steam engines or machines to pump water, weave fabrics and saw wood was so high that "manufactories"

---

sprang up all over England; privately financed, they engaged in the hiring of individual artisans who could perform skillfully, but who could not afford the equipment on their own. The factory owner soon found himself faced by managerial problems of planning and coordinating at a level far beyond any previously established in the business world. Frequently he found himself at the hub of a growing industrial metropolis.

The advent of railroads and steamboats touched off still further changes, as did the new Bessemer process, that prodigious contribution toward the development of the two giants of mid-19th century industry: steam and steel. The machine to make the machine was another vital contributor to the changing pace of industry.

During this lively industrial period, Charles Babbage lived and worked in England. A mathematical scientist and intellectual theorist, his interests led him toward two surprising anticipations of modern management: 1) To speed mathematical calculation, he invented a forerunner of today's electronic computer. 2) In researching the methods of many factories, he also observed underlying "principles" which seemed to be at work. This premise led to important propositions upon which Frederick W. Taylor and his successors later built the edifice of scientific management: namely, that *definite concepts of management exist;* that *they can be determined by experience;* and that *they can be broadly applied through the interchange of this experience.*

Fayol's contributions. While industrial changes were vigorously transforming England itself during Charles Babbage's lifetime (1792-1871), the Industrial Revolution was making slower headway in France, not having started until the 1830s. As French industry later matured and industrial problems developed, a remarkable new management pioneer emerged: Henri Fayol.

"I brushed right by the grime-smeared, disheveled miner near the pit, saying brusquely that I was looking for Mr. Fayol."

"'I'm Fayol,' replied the rough-looking apparition. 'What do you want?'"

Henri Fayol (1841-1925) was no desk-chair theorist, but a practical mining engineer who spent more than 50 years in the study and practice of management. Many of the management principles used today, particularly those concerning top management and administration, grew out of the work of this man who had such an intimate acquaintance with the lower levels of industrial society.

Although other pioneers contributed to the developing theses, Fayol eventually articulated the principles in a manner that was widely recognized. His tenets: *1) Specialization must be a factor. 2) Responsibility is a corollary of authority. 3) Unity of direction is necessary, with one head and one plan for each activity. 4) Unity of command must be established, with each person reporting to only one boss.*

Lydall F. Urwick, James D. Mooney, Chester I. Barnard, and many other management pioneers and writers have amplified these four basic principles and added significantly to them.

Management and society. In the 1850s, the Industrial Revolution's influence began spreading to the German Confederation of Independent States. Walther Rathenau (1867-1922), an idealist and a politician, became deeply interested in management problems. Like Fayol, he was a practicing manager; but, unlike Fayol, he was not interested in the daily management of an industrial plant.

Instead of probing inwardly at the administrative processes under his direction, he elected to look to the community and the world around him, evaluating management in terms of society and all human organization. He saw the world as a single industrial and intellectual mechanism divided only superficially by arbitrary political frontiers on the one hand, and by internal class distinctions on the other. His greatest aim was to eliminate all unnatural barriers that hindered development of both the potential, wealth-creating capacity of industry and the ordered advancement of mankind.

The United States made certain technological advances during the early stages of the Industrial Revolution, notably with Eli Whitney's Cotton Gin. However, the real transformation of America into an industrial community took place largely after the Civil War and was based upon the English model.

With the increase of competition after the Civil War, American engineers began to look for ways to improve plant efficiency. The first sustained effort was made by Frederick Winslow Taylor (1856-1915) with his intensive and systematic studies to find out how much men could accomplish when given the proper tools and materials. His experiments in the Eighties and Nineties ranged from carefully timed trials of various shovel sizes for yard gangs handling large tonnages of coal and ore at Bethlehem Steel to tests determining the best cutting speeds and feeds for boring mills at the Midvale Steel Company.

Though Babbage had, unknown to Taylor, recorded the time required for certain pin-manufacturing operations at least 50 years earlier, Taylor's contributions went much further than mere timing. His real contribution lay in evaluating the combinations of human skills, tools and practices that would result in the highest productivity.

Scientific method. An engineer and production man, as well as executive and consultant, Taylor was the most influential of the management pioneers. Known as a Classicist in management theory, he dealt primarily with formal organization. Most interested in functional foremanship, he systematized mainly at the foreman's level, whereas Henri Fayol had worked from the top of the pyramid down.

Taylor's most widely recognized contribution was his application of *scientific method* to the solution of factory problems. From his analyses, he evolved orderly sets of principles to replace the trial-and-error methods then in use.

While Taylor was busy crystallizing management thought and laying the foundation for management techniques which were to lift the United

States to the highest standard of living in the world, a contemporary was pioneering in a different direction. He was Henry Laurence Gantt (1861-1919), a close associate for many years.

Gantt, while holding many of the same management views as Taylor, became more deeply concerned with the man behind the machine. Later, as a consultant, he paid major attention to the human element in productivity and approached the concept of *motivation*, as we understand it today. In his paper called "A Bonus System of Rewarding Labor," he underscored this viewpoint, with far-reaching effects on compensation problems and methods. He placed great stress on the common interests of employer and employee, later expanding his philosophy that "to teach and to lead" would become the management technique of the future, replacing the prevailing technique, "to drive."

Increasingly, his interests focused on management's broad obligations to society. In 1919, his thought-provoking book "The Parting of the Ways" urged management to return to a philosophy of greater social concern, a philosophy which gained increasing acceptance in the Thirties and has been strongly influential ever since.

Although Mary Parker Follett (1868-1933) was a philosopher, historian and political scientist, she had a profound effect upon the management field, especially in the areas of personnel and group relationships. Her paper on management served as a point of convergence for the broad channels of philosophy evolved by Fayol, Taylor and Gantt, expressing the conviction that scientific method could be applied to problems in human relations.

The motion study. Frank Bunker Gilbreth (1868-1924), like Gantt, was enormously interested in human beings and human effort. Combining this concern with a prodigious capacity for organizing details, he developed the motion study as a basic management technique. Working with his wife, Dr. Lillian Gilbreth, who has continued his work since his untimely death, he stressed the importance of employees as individuals. He painstakingly investigated the effects of attitude, opportunity and environment on productivity. A further contribution of the Gilbreths — anticipating by nearly 40 years what is today known as systematic management development — was their "three-position plan of promotion," first proposed in 1916.

Another contemporary deeply concerned with social purpose in management was Henry S. Dennison, who died in 1952. He exemplified Mary Parker Follett's contention that business organization is not a separate entity, but that rules and principles are necessary wherever men struggle to cooperate.

The 1930s and 1940s, with men such as Elton Mayo and the Hawthorne experiments, saw an ever awakening interest in human relations. Attitudes of management focused on the human factor even more strongly than in the period influenced by Gantt — so much so that the factor of "human relations" became over-emphasized. The pendulum swung all the way from the early austerity associated with the management function to a kind of "permissiveness" in which the extremists felt that management's prime responsibility was "to keep people happy."

Since the 1940s, the trend has been toward a middle ground that is half-way between permissiveness and the old concept of austere "scientific management." Studies by men like Likert and McGregor in the 1950's tended to show that happiness and high morale did not necessarily make for the highest, most efficient productivity. Concurrently, the perfection of such new tools as computers and other sources of definite information have brought increasing emphasis on decision-making as a rational process. Today, mathematical and rational methods are being applied where previously human judgment, experience and pure hunch had to be employed in the absence of more complete facts. At the same time, managers realize that data-processing and other tools are only complementary to the management process of getting things done through people.

Deluge of theories. While management Classicists like Taylor concerned themselves mainly with production, and Neo-Classicists like Gantt and the Gilbreths with the human element, and while other major pioneers were evolving significant concepts of management, a third body of theorists has been trying to crash the gates. This body is composed of theorists whose approach may be serious and dedicated, but whose definitions only serve to muddy the picture. Professor Harold Koontz, of the University of California, expressed it this way in a recent article in the *Journal of the Academy of Management,* under the title "The Management Theory Jungle":

The noteworthy absence of academic writing and research in the formative years of modern management theory is now more than atoned for by a deluge of research and writing from the academic halls. What is interesting and perhaps nothing more than a sign of the unsophisticated adolescence of management theory is how the current flood has brought with it a wave of great differences and apparent confusion. From the orderly analysis of management at the shop-room level by Frederick Taylor and the reflective distillation of experience from the general management point of view by Henri Fayol, we now see these and other early beginnings overgrown and entangled by a jungle of approaches and approachers to management theory.

Professor Koontz, who is also President of the Academy of Management, clarified the six "Major Schools" of management theory, stating his experienced opinion that trying to effect a further breakdown would only result in a tangled undergrowth through which no practical manager could hack his way. To go into the theories of each of the six is beyond the scope of this article. However, it should be pointed out that the important factor is not *which* of the major theories a manager embraces as much as it is *how well he understands what course he is following and what his own objectives are.*

ORGANIZATION THEORY:
AN OVERVIEW AND AN APPRAISAL*

William G. Scott

Man is intent on drawing himself into a web of collectivized patterns. "Modern man has learned to accommodate himself to a world increasingly organized. The trend toward ever more explicit and consciously drawn relationships is profound and sweeping; it is marked by depth no less than by extension."[1] This comment by Seidenberg nicely summarizes the pervasive influence of organization in many forms of human activity.

Some of the reasons for intense organizational activity are found in the fundamental transitions which revolutionized our society, changing it from a rural culture, to a culture based on technology, industry, and the city. From these changes, a way of life emerged characterized by the *proximity* and *dependency* of people on each other. Proximity and dependency, as conditions of social life, harbor the threats of human conflict, capricious anti-social behavior, instability of human relationships, and uncertainty about the nature of the social structure with its concomitant roles.

Of course, these threats to social integrity are present to some degree in all societies, ranging from the primitive to the modern. But, these threats become dangerous when the harmonious functioning of a society rests on the maintenance of a highly intricate, delicately balanced form of human collaboration. The civilization we have created depends on the preservation of a precarious balance. Hence, disrupting forces impinging on this shaky form of collaboration must be eliminated or minimized.

Traditionally, organization is viewed as a vehicle for accomplishing goals and objectives. While this approach is useful, it tends to obscure the inner workings and internal purposes of organization itself. Another fruitful way of treating organization is as a mechanism having the ultimate purpose of offsetting those forces which undermine human collaboration. In this sense, organization tends to minimize conflict, and to lessen the significance of individual behavior which deviates from values that the organization has established as worthwhile. Further, organization increases stability in human relationships by reducing uncertainty regarding the nature of the system's structure and the human roles which are inherent to it. Corollary

---

*Reprinted with permission from *The Journal of the Academy of Management*, April, 1961.

[1] Roderick Seidenburg, *Post-Historic Man* (Boston: Beacon Press, 1951), p. 1.

to this point, organization enhances the predictability of human action, because it limits the number of behavioral alternatives available to an individual. As Presthus points out:

Organization is defined as a system of structural interpersonal relations . . . individuals are differentiated in terms of authority, status, and role with the result that personal interaction is prescribed. . . . Anticipated reactions tend to occur, while ambiguity and spontaneity are decreased.[2]

In addition to all of this, organization has built-in safeguards. Besides prescribing acceptable forms of behavior for those who elect to submit to it, organization is also able to counterbalance the influence of human action which transcends its established patterns.[3]

Few segments of society have engaged in organizing more intensively than business.[4] The reason is clear. Business depends on what organization offers. Business needs a system of relationships among functions; it needs stability, continuity, and predictability in its internal activities and external contacts. Business also appears to need harmonious relationships among the people and processes which make it up. Put another way, a business organization has to be free, relatively, from destructive tendencies which may be caused by divergent interests.

As a foundation for meeting these needs rests administrative science. A major element of this science is organization theory, which provides the grounds for management activities in a number of significant areas of business endeavor. Organization theory, however, is not a homogeneous science based on generally accepted principles. Various theories of organization have been, and are being, evolved. For example, something called "modern organization theory" has recently emerged, raising the wrath of some traditionalists, but also capturing the imagination of a rather elite *avant-garde.*

The thesis of this paper is that modern organization theory, when stripped of its irrelevancies, redundancies, and "speech defects," is a logical and vital evolution in management thought. In order for this thesis to be supported, the reader must endure a review and appraisal of more traditional forms of organization theory which may seem elementary to him.

In any event, three theories of organization are having considerable

---

[2] Robert V. Presthus, "Toward a Theory of Organizational Behavior," *Administrative Science Quarterly,* June, 1958, p. 50.

[3] Regulation and predictability of human behavior are matters of degree varying with different organizations on something of a continuum. At one extreme are bureaucratic type organizations with tight bonds of regulation. At the other extreme are voluntary associations, and informal organizations with relatively loose bonds of regulation.

This point has an interesting sidelight. A bureaucracy with tight controls and a high degree of predictability of human action appears to be unable to distinguish between destructive and creative deviations from established values. Thus the only thing which is safeguarded is the *status quo.*

[4] The monolithic institutions of the military and government are other cases of organizational preoccupation.

influence on management thought and practice. They are arbitrarily labeled in this paper as the classical, the neoclassical, and the modern. Each of these is fairly distinct; but they are not unrelated. Also, these theories are on-going, being actively supported by several schools of management thought.

THE CLASSICAL DOCTRINE

For lack of a better method of identification, it will be said that the classical doctrine deals almost exclusively with the *anatomy of formal organization*. This doctrine can be traced back to Frederick W. Taylor's interest in functional foremanship and planning staffs. But most students of management thought would agree that in the United States, the first systematic approach to organization, and the first comprehensive attempt to find organizational universals, is dated 1931 when Mooney and Reiley published *Onward Industry*.[5] Subsequently, numerous books, following the classical vein, have appeared. Two of the more recent are Brech's, *Organization*[6] and Allen's, *Management and Organization*.[7]

Classical organization theory is built around four key pillars. They are the division of labor, the scalar and functional processes, structure, and span of control. Given these major elements just about all of classical organization theory can be derived.

1. *The division of labor* is without doubt the cornerstone among the four elements.[8] From it the other elements flow as corollaries. For example, *scalar* and *functional* growth requires specialization and departmentalization of functions. Organization *structure* is naturally dependent upon the direction which specialization of activities travels in company development. Finally, *span of control* problems result from the number of specialized functions under the jurisdiction of a manager.

2. The *scalar and functional processes* deal with the vertical and horizontal growth of the organization, respectively.[9] The scalar process refers to the growth of the chain of command, the delegation of authority and responsibility, unity of command, and the obligation to report.

The division of the organization into specialized parts and the regrouping of the parts into compatible-units are matters pertaining to the functional

---

[5] James D. Mooney and Alan C. Reiley, *Onward Industry* (New York: Harper and Brothers, 1931). Later published by James D. Mooney under the title *Principles of Organization*.

[6] E. F. L. Brech, *Organization* (London: Longmans, Green and Company, 1957).

[7] Louis A. Allen, *Management and Organization* (New York: McGraw-Hill Book Company, 1958).

[8] Usually the division of labor is treated under a topical heading of departmentation, see for example: Harold Koontz and Cyril O'Donnell, *Principles of Management* (New York: McGraw-Hill Book Company, 1959), Chapter 7.

[9] These processes are discussed at length in Ralph Currier Davis, *The Fundamentals of Top Management* (New York: Harper and Brothers, 1951), Chapter 7.

process. This process focuses on the horizontal evolution of the line and staff in a formal organization.

3. *Structure* is the logical relationships of functions in an organization, arranged to accomplish the objectives of the company efficiently. Structure implies system and pattern. Classical organization theory usually works with two basic structures, the line and the staff. However, such activities as committee and liaison functions fall quite readily into the purview of structural considerations. Again, structure is the vehicle for introducing logical and consistent relationships among the diverse functions which comprise the organization.[10]

4. *The span of control* concept relates to the number of subordinates a manager can effectively supervise. Graicunas has been credited with first elaborating the point that there are numerical limitations to the subordinates one man can control.[11] In a recent statement on the subject, Brech points out, "span" refers to ". . . the number of persons, themselves carrying managerial and supervisory responsibilities, for whom the senior manager retains his over-embracing responsibility of direction and planning, co-ordination, motivation, and control."[12] Regardless of interpretation, span of control has significance, in part, for the shape of the organization which evolves through growth. Wide span yields a flat structure; short span results in a tall structure. Further, the span concept directs attention to the complexity of human and functional interrelationships in an organization.

It would not be fair to say that the classical school is unaware of the day-to-day administrative problems of the organization. Paramount among these problems are those stemming from human interactions. But the interplay of individual personality, informal groups, intraorganizational conflict, and the decision-making processes in the formal structure appears largely to be neglected by classical organization theory. Additionally, the classical theory overlooks the contributions of the behavioral sciences by failing to incorporate them in its doctrine in any systematic way. In summary, classical organization theory has relevant insights into the nature of organization, but the value of this theory is limited by its narrow concentration on the formal anatomy of organization.

NEOCLASSICAL THEORY OF ORGANIZATION

The neoclassical theory of organization embarked on the task of compensating for some of the deficiencies in classical doctrine. The neoclassical school is commonly identified with the human relations movement.

---

[10] For a discussion of structure see: William H. Newman, *Administrative Action* (Englewood Cliffs: Prentice-Hall, Incorporated, 1951), Chapter 16.

[11] V. A. Graicunas, "Relationships in Organization," *Papers on the Science of Administration* (New York: Columbia University, 1937).

[12] Brech, *op. cit.*, p. 78.

Generally, the neoclassical approach takes the postulates of the classical school, regarding the pillars of organization as givens. But these postulates are regarded as modified by people, acting independently or within the context of the informal organization.

One of the main contributions of the neoclassical school is the introduction of behavioral sciences in an integrated fashion into the theory of organization. Through the use of these sciences, the human relationists demonstrate how the pillars of the classical doctrine are affected by the impact of human actions. Further, the neoclassical approach includes a systematic treatment of the informal organization, showing its influence on the formal structure.

Thus, the neoclassical approach to organization theory gives evidence of accepting classical doctrine, but superimposing on it modifications resulting from individual behavior, and the influence of the informal group. The inspiration of the neoclassical school was the Hawthorne studies.[13] Current examples of the neoclassical approach are found in human relations books like Gardner and Moore, *Human Relations in Industry*,[14] and Davis, *Human Relations in Business*.[15] To a more limited extent, work in industrial sociology also reflects a neoclassical point of view.[16]

It would be useful to look briefly at some of the contributions made to organization theory by the neoclassicists. First to be considered are modifications of the pillars of classical doctrine; second is the informal organization.

Examples of the neoclassical approach to the pillars of formal organization theory.

1. The *division of labor* has been a long standing subject of comment in the field of human relations. Very early in the history of industrial psychology study was made of industrial fatigue and monotony caused by the specialization of the work.[17] Later, attention shifted to the isolation of the worker, and his feeling of anonymity resulting from insignificant jobs which contributed negligibly to the final product.[18]

Also, specialization influences the work of management. As an organization expands, the need concomitantly arises for managerial motivation and

[13] See: F. J. Roethlisberger and William J. Dickson, *Management and the Worker* (Cambridge: Harvard University Press, 1939).

[14] Burleigh B. Gardner and David G. Moore, *Human Relations in Industry* (Homewood: Richard D. Irwin, 1955).

[15] Keith Davis, *Human Relations in Business* (New York: McGraw-Hill Book Company, 1957).

[16] For example see: Delbert C. Miller and William H. Form, *Industrial Sociology* (New York: Harper and Brothers, 1951).

[17] See: Hugo Munsterberg, *Psychology and Industrial Efficiency* (Boston: Houghton Mifflin Company, 1913).

[18] Probably the classic work is: Elton Mayo, *The Human Problems of an Industrial Civilization* (Cambridge: Harvard University, 1946, first printed 1933).

coordination of the activities of others. Both motivation and coordination in turn relate to executive leadership. Thus, in part, stemming from the growth of industrial specialization, the neoclassical school has developed a large body of theory relating to motivation, coordination, and leadership. Much of this theory is derived from the social sciences.

2. Two aspects of the *scalar and functional* processes which have been treated with some degree of intensity by the neoclassical school are the delegation of authority and responsibility, and gaps in or overlapping of functional jurisdictions. The classical theory assumes something of perfection in the delegation and functionalization processes. The neoclassical school points out that human problems are caused by imperfections in the way these processes are handled.

For example, too much or insufficient delegation may render an executive incapable of action. The failure to delegate authority and responsibility equally may result in frustration for the delegatee. Overlapping of authorities often causes clashes in personality. Gaps in authority cause failures in getting jobs done, with one party blaming the other for shortcomings in performance.[19]

The neoclassical school says that the scalar and functional processes are theoretically valid, but tend to deteriorate in practice. The ways in which they break down are described, and some of the human causes are pointed out. In addition the neoclassicists make recommendations, suggesting various "human tools" which will facilitate the operation of these processes.

3. *Structure* provides endless avenues of analysis for the neoclassical theory of organization. The theme is that human behavior disrupts the best laid organizational plans, and thwarts the cleanness of the logical relationships founded in the structure. The neoclassical critique of structure centers on frictions which appear internally among people performing different functions.

Line and staff relations is a problem area, much discussed, in this respect. Many companies seem to have difficulty keeping the line and staff working together harmoniously. Both Dalton[20] and Juran[21] have engaged in research to discover the causes of friction, and to suggest remedies.

Of course, line-staff relations represent only one of the many problems of structural frictions described by the neoclassicists. As often as not, the neoclassicists will offer prescriptions for the elimination of conflict in structure. Among the more important harmony-rendering formulae are participation, junior boards, bottom-up management, joint committees, recognition of human dignity, and "better" communication.

---

[19] For further discussion of the human relations implications of the scalar and functional processes see: Keith Davis, *op. cit.*, pp. 60-66.

[20] Melville Dalton, "Conflicts between Staff and Line Managerial Officers," *American Sociological Review*, June, 1950, pp. 342-351.

[21] J. M. Juran, "Improving the Relationship between Staff and Line," *Personnel*, May, 1956, pp. 515-524.

4. An executive's *span of control* is a function of human determinants, and the reduction of span to a precise, universally applicable ratio is silly, according to the neoclassicists. Some of the determinants of span are individual differences in managerial abilities, the type of people and functions supervised, and the extent of communication effectiveness.

Coupled with the span of control question are the human implications of the type of structure which emerges. That is, is a tall structure with a short span or a flat structure with a wide span more conducive to good human relations and high morale? The answer is situational. Short span results in tight supervision; wide span requires a good deal of delegation with looser controls. Because of individual and organizational differences, sometimes one is better than the other. There is a tendency to favor the looser form of organziation, however, for the reason that tall structures breed autocratic leadership, which is often pointed out as a cause of low morale.[22]

The neoclassical view of the informal organization.   Nothing more than the barest mention of the informal organization is given even in the most recent classical treatises on organization theory.[23] Systematic discussion of this form of organization has been left to the neoclassicists. The informal organization refers to people in group associations at work, but these associations are not specified in the "blueprint" of the formal organization. The informal organization means natural groupings of people in the work situation.

In a general way, the informal organization appears in response to the social need — the need of people to associate with others. However, for analytical purposes, this explanation is not particularly satisfying. Research has produced the following, more specific determinants underlying the appearance of informal organizations.

1. The *location* determinant simply states that in order to form into groups of any lasting nature, people have to have frequent face-to-face contact. Thus, the geography of physical location in a plant or office is an important factor in predicting who will be in what group.[24]

2. *Occupation* is a key factor determining the rise and composition of informal groups. There is a tendency for people performing similar jobs to group together.[25]

3. *Interests* are another determinant for informal group formation. Even though people might be in the same location, performing similar jobs, differences of interest among them explain why several small, instead of one large, informal organizations emerge.

[22] Gardner and Moore, *op. cit.*, pp. 237-243.

[23] For example: Brech, *op. cit.*, pp. 27-29; and Allen, *op. cit.*, pp. 61-62.

[24] See: Leon Festinger, Stanley Schachter, and Kurt Back, *Social Pressures in Informal Groups* (New York: Harper and Brothers, 1950), pp. 153-163.

[25] For example see: W. Fred Cottrell, *The Railroader* (Palo Alto: The Stanford University Press, 1940), Chapter 3.

4. *Special issues* often result in the formation of informal groups, but this determinant is set apart from the three previously mentioned. In this case, people who do not necessarily have similar interests, occupations, or locations may join together for a common cause. Once the issue is resolved, then the tendency is to revert to the more "natural" group forms.[26] Thus, special issues give rise to a rather impermanent informal association; groups based on the other three determinants tend to be more lasting.

When informal organizations come into being they assume certain characteristics. Since understanding these characteristics is important for management practice, they are noted below:

1. Informal organizations act as agencies of *social control.* They generate a culture based on certain norms of conduct which, in turn, demands conformity from group members. These standards may be at odds with the values set by the formal organization. So an individual may very well find himself in a situation of conflicting demands.

2. The form of human interrelationships in the informal organization requires *techniques of analysis* different from those used to plot the relationships of people in a formal organization. The method used for determining the structure of the informal group is called sociometric analysis. Sociometry reveals the complex structure of interpersonal relations which is based on premises fundamentally unlike the logic of the formal organization.

3. Informal organizations have *status and communication* systems peculiar to themselves, not necessarily derived from the formal systems. For example, the grapevine is the subject of much neoclassical study.

4. Survival of the informal organization requires stable continuing relationships among the people in them. Thus, it has been observed that the informal organization *resists change.*[27] Considerable attention is given by the neoclassicists to overcoming informal resistance to change.

5. The last aspect of analysis which appears to be central to the neoclassical view of the informal organization is the study of the *informal leader.* Discussion revolves around who the informal leader is, how he assumes his role, what characteristics are peculiar to him, and how he can help the manager accomplish his objectives in the formal organization.[28]

This brief sketch of some of the major facets of informal organization theory has neglected, so far, one important topic treated by the neoclassical school. It is the way in which the formal and informal organizations interact.

---

[26] Except in cases where the existence of an organization is necessary for the continued maintenance of employee interest. Under these conditions the previously informal association may emerge as a formal group, such as a union.

[27] Probably the classic study of resistance to change is: Lester Coch and John R. P. French, Jr., "Overcoming Resistance to Change," in Schuyler Dean Hoslett (editor) *Human Factors in Management* (New York: Harper and Brothers, 1951) pp. 242-268.

[28] For example see: Robert Saltonstall, *Human Relations in Administration* (New York: McGraw-Hill Book Company, 1959), pp. 330-331; and Keith Davis, *op. cit.,* pp. 99-101

A conventional way of looking at the interaction of the two is the "live and let live" point of view. Management should recognize that the informal organization exists, nothing can destroy it, and so the executive might just as well work with it. Working with the informal organization involves not threatening its existence unnecessarily, listening to opinions expressed for the group by the leader, allowing group participation in decision-making situations, and controlling the grapevine by prompt release of accurate information.[29]

While this approach is management centered, it is not unreasonable to expect that informal group standards and norms could make themselves felt on formal organizational policy. An honestly conceived effort by managers to establish a working relationship with the informal organization could result in an association where both formal and informal views would be reciprocally modified. The danger which at all costs should be avoided is that "working with the informal organization" does not degenerate into a shallow disguise for human manipulation.

Some neoclassical writing in organization theory, especially that coming from the management-oriented segment of this school, gives the impression that the formal and informal organizations are distinct, and at times, quite irreconcilable factors in a company. The interaction which takes place between the two is something akin to the interaction between the company and a labor union, or a government agency, or another company.

The concept of the social system is another approach to the inter-actional climate. While this concept can be properly classified as neo-classical, it borders on the modern theories of organization. The phrase "social system" means that an organization is a complex of mutually interdependent, but variable, factors.

These factors include individuals and their attitudes and motives, jobs, the physical work setting, the formal organization, and the informal organizations. These factors, and many others, are woven into an overall pattern of interdependency. From this point of view, the formal and informal organizations lose their distinctiveness, but find real meaning, in terms of human behavior, in the operation of the system as a whole. Thus, the study of organization turns away from descriptions of its component parts, and is refocused on the system of interrelationships among the parts.

One of the major contributions of the Hawthorne studies was the integration of Pareto's idea of the social system into a meaningful method of analysis for the study of behavior in human organizations.[30] This concept is still vitally important. But unfortunately some work in the field of human relations undertaken by the neoclassicists has overlooked, or perhaps discounted, the significance of this consideration.[31]

---

[29] For an example of this approach see: John T. Doutt, "Management Must Manage the Informal Group, Too," *Advanced Management*, May, 1959, pp. 26-28.

[30] See: Roethlisberger and Dickson, *op. cit.*, Chapter 24.

[31] A check of management human relations texts, the organization and human relations chapters of principles of management texts, and texts on conventional organization theory for management courses reveals little or no treatment of the concept of the social system.

The fundamental insight regarding the social system, developed and applied to the industrial scene by the Hawthorne researchers, did not find much extension in subsequent work in the neoclassical vein. Indeed, the neoclassical school after the Hawthorne studies generally seemed content to engage in descriptive generalizations, or particularized empirical research studies which did not have much meaning outside their own context.

The neoclassical school of organization theory has been called bankrupt. Criticisms range from "human relations is a tool for cynical puppeteering of people," to "human relations is nothing more than a trifling body of empirical and descriptive information." There is a good deal of truth in both statements, but another appraisal of the neoclassical school of organization theory is offered here. The neoclassical approach has provided valuable contributions to the lore of organization. But, like the classical theory, the neoclassical doctrine suffers from incompleteness, a short-sighted perspective, and lack of integration among the many facets of human behavior studied by it. Modern organization theory has made a move to cover the shortcomings of the current body of theoretical knowledge.

MODERN ORGANIZATION THEORY

The distinctive qualities of modern organization theory are its conceptual-analytical base, its reliance on empirical research data and, above all, its integrating nature. These qualities are framed in a philosophy which accepts the premise that the only meaningful way to study organization is to study it as a system. As Henderson put it, the study of a system must rely on a method of analysis, ". . . involving the simultaneous variations of mutually dependent variables."[32] Human systems, of course, contain a huge number of dependent variables which defy the most complex simultaneous equations to solve.

Nevertheless, system analysis has its own peculiar point of view which aims to study organization in the way Henderson suggests. It treats organization as a system of mutually dependent variables. As a result, modern organization theory, which accepts system analysis, shifts the conceptual level of organization study above the classical and neoclassical theories. Modern organization theory asks a range of interrelated questions which are not seriously considered by the two other theories.

Key among these questions are: (1) What are the strategic parts of the system? (2) What is the nature of their mutual dependency? (3) What are the main processes in the system which link the parts together, and facilitate their adjustment to each other? (4) What are the goals sought by systems?[33]

---

[32] Lawrence J. Henderson, *Pareto's General Sociology* (Cambridge: Harvard University Press, 1935), p. 13.

[33] There is another question which cannot be treated in the scope of this paper. It asks, what research tools should be used for the study of the system?

Modern organization theory is in no way a unified body of thought. Each writer and researcher has his special emphasis when he considers the system. Perhaps the most evident unifying thread in the study of systems is the effort to look at the organization in its totality. Representative books in this field are March and Simon, *Organizations,*[34] and Haire's anthology, *Modern Organization Theory.*[35]

The parts of the system and their interdependency. The first basic part of the system is the *individual,* and the personality structure he brings to the organization. Elementary to an individual's personality are motives and attitudes which condition the range of expectancies he hopes to satisfy by participating in the system.

The second part of the system is the formal arrangement of functions, usually called the *formal organization.* The formal organization is the interrelated pattern of jobs which make up the structure of a system. Certain writers, like Argyris, see a fundamental conflict resulting from the demands made by the system and the structure of the mature, normal personality. In any event, the individual has expectancies regarding the job he is to perform; and, conversely, the job makes demands on, or has expectancies relating to, the performance of the individual. Considerable attention has been given by writers in modern organization theory to incongruencies resulting from the interaction of organizational and individual demands.[36]

The third part in the organization system is the *informal organization.* Enough has been said already about the nature of this organization. But it must be noted that an interactional pattern exists between the individual and the informal group. This interactional arrangement can be conveniently discussed as the mutual modification of expectancies. The informal organization has demands which it makes on members in terms of anticipated forms of behavior, and the individual has expectancies of satisfaction he hopes to derive from association with people on the job. Both these sets of expectancies interact, resulting in the individual modifying his behavior to accord with the demands of the group, and the group, perhaps, modifying what it expects from an individual because of the impact of his personality on group norms.[37]

Much of what has been said about the various expectancy systems in an organization can also be treated using status and role concepts. Part of modern organization theory rests on research findings in social-psychology

---

[34] James G. March and Herbert A. Simon, *Organizations* (New York: John Wiley and Sons, 1958).

[35] Mason Haire (editor), *Modern Organization Theory* (New York: John Wiley and Sons, 1959).

[36] See Chris Argyris, *Personality and Organization* (New York: Harper and Brothers, 1957), esp. Chapters 2, 3, 7.

[37] For a larger treatment of this subject see: George C. Homans, *The Human Group* (New York: Harcourt, Brace and Company, 1950), Chapter 5.

relative to reciprocal patterns of behavior stemming from role demands generated by both the formal and informal organizations, and role perceptions peculiar to the individual. Bakke's *fusion process* is largely concerned with the modification of role expectancies. The fusion process is a force, according to Bakke, which acts to weld divergent elements together for the preservation of organizational integrity.[38]

The fifth part of system analysis is the physical setting in which the job is performed. Although this element of the system may be implicit in what has been said already about the formal organization and its functions, it is well to separate it. In the physical surroundings of work, interactions are present in complex man-machine systems. The human "engineer" cannot approach the problems posed by such interrelationships in a purely technical engineering fashion. As Haire says, these problems lie in the domain of the social theorists.[39] Attention must be centered on responses demanded from a logically ordered production function, often with the view of minimizing the error in the system. From this standpoint, work cannot be effectively organized unless the psychological, social, and physiological characteristics of people participating in the work environment are considered. Machines and processes should be designed to fit certain generally observed psychological and physiological properties of men, rather than hiring men to fit machines.

In summary, the parts of the system which appear to be of strategic importance are the individual, the formal structure, the informal organization, status and role patterns, and the physical environment of work. Again, these parts are woven into a configuration called the organizational system. The processes which link the parts are taken up next.

The linking processes. One can say, with a good deal of glibness, that all the parts mentioned above are interrelated. Although this observation is quite correct, it does not mean too much in terms of system theory unless some attempt is made to analyze the processes by which the interaction is achieved. Role theory is devoted to certain types of interactional processes. In addition, modern organization theorists point to three other linking activities which appear to be universal to human systems of organized behavior. These processes are communication, balance, and decision making.

1. Communication is mentioned often in neoclassical theory, but the emphasis is on description of forms of communication activity, i.e., formal-informal, vertical-horizontal, line-staff. Communication, as a mechanism which links the segments of the system together is overlooked by way of much considered analysis.

One aspect of modern organization theory is study of the communication

---

[38] E. Wight Bakke, "Concept of the Social Organization," in *Modern Organization Theory*, Mason Haire (editor), (New York: John Wiley and Sons, 1959) pp. 60-61.

[39] Mason Haire, "Psychology and the Study of Business: Joint Behavioral Sciences," in *Social Science Research on Business: Product and Potential* (New York: Columbia University Press, 1959), pp. 53-59.

network in the system. Communication is viewed as the method by which action is evoked from the parts of the system. Communication acts not only as stimuli resulting in action, but also as a control and coordination mechanism linking the decision centers in the system into a synchronized pattern. Deutsch points out that organizations are composed of parts which communicate with each other, receive messages from the outside world, and store information. Taken together, these communication functions of the parts comprise a configuration representing the total system.[40] More is to be said about communication later in the discussion of the cybernetic model.

2. The concept of *balance* as a linking process involves a series of some rather complex ideas. Balance refers to an equilibrating mechanism whereby the various parts of the system are maintained in a harmoniously structured relationship to each other.

The necessity for the balance concept logically flows from the nature of systems themselves. It is impossible to conceive of an ordered relationship among the parts of a system without also introducing the idea of a stabilizing or an adapting mechanism.

Balance appears in two varieties — quasi-automatic and innovative. Both forms of balance act to insure system integrity in face of changing conditions, either internal or external to the system. The first form of balance, quasi-automatic, refers to what some think are "homeostatic" properties of systems. That is, systems seem to exhibit built-in propensities to maintain steady states.

If human organizations are open, self-maintaining systems, then control and regulatory processes are necessary. The issue hinges on the degree to which stabilizing processes in systems, when adapting to change, are automatic. March and Simon have an interesting answer to this problem, which in part is based on the type of change and the adjustment necessary to adapt to the change. Systems have programs of action which are put into effect when a change is perceived. If the change is relatively minor, and if the change comes within the purview of established programs of action, then it might be fairly confidently predicted that the adaptation made by the system will be quasi-automatic.[41]

The role of innovative, creative balancing efforts now needs to be examined. The need for innovation arises when adaptation to a change is outside the scope of existing programs designed for the purpose of keeping the system in balance. New programs have to be evolved in order for the system to maintain internal harmony.

New programs are created by trial and error search for feasible action alternatives to cope with a given change. But innovation is subject to the limitations and possibilities inherent in the quantity and variety of

---

[40] Karl W. Deutsch, "On Communication Models in the Social Sciences," *Public Opinion Quarterly*, 16, (1952), pp. 356-380.

[41] March and Simon, *op. cit.*, pp. 139-140.

information present in a system at a particular time. New combinations of alternatives for innovative purposes depend on:

(a) the possible range of output of the system, or the capacity of the system to supply information.
(b) the range of available information in the memory of the system.
(c) the operating rules (program) governing the analysis and flow of information within the system.
(d) the ability of the system to "forget" previously learned solutions to changed problems.[42] A system with too good a memory might narrow its behavioral choices to such an extent as to stifle innovation. In simpler language, old learned programs might be used to adapt to change, when newly innovated programs are necessary.[43]

Much of what has been said about communication and balance brings to mind a cybernetic model in which both these processes have vital roles. Cybernetics has to do with feedback and control in all kinds of systems. Its purpose is to maintain system stability in the face of change. Cybernetics cannot be studied without considering communication networks, information flow, and some kind of balancing process aimed at preserving the integrity of the system.

Cybernetics directs attention to key questions regarding the system. These questions are: How are communication centers connected, and how are they maintained? Corollary to this question: what is the structure of the feedback system? Next, what information is stored in the organization, and at what points? And as a corollary: how accessible is this information to decision-making centers? Third, how conscious is the organization of the operation of its own parts? That is, to what extent do the policy centers receive control information with sufficient frequency and relevancy to create a real awareness of the operation of the segments of the system? Finally, what are the learning (innovating) capabilities of the system?[44]

Answers to the questions posed by cybernetics are crucial to understanding both the balancing and communication processes in systems.[45] Although cybernetics has been applied largely to technical-engineering problems of automation, the model of feedback, control, and regulation in all systems has a good deal of generality. Cybernetics is a fruitful area which can be used to synthesize the processes of communication and balance.

3. A wide spectrum of topics dealing with types of decisions in human systems makes up the core of another important process in organizations.

---

[42] Mervyn L. Cadwallader, "The Cybernetic Analysis of Change in Complex Social Organization," *The American Journal of Sociology*, September 1959, p. 156.

[43] It is conceivable for innovative behavior to be programmed into the system.

[44] These are questions adapted from Deutsch, *op. cit.*, 368-370.

[45] Answers to these questions would require a comprehensive volume. One of the best approaches currently available is Stafford Beer, *Cybernetics and Management* (New York: John Wiley and Sons, 1959).

Decision analysis is one of the major contributions of March and Simon in their book *Organizations.* The two major classes of decisions they discuss are decisions to produce and decisions to participate in the system.[46]

Decisions to produce are largely a result of an interaction between individual attitudes and the demands of organization. Motivation analysis becomes central to studying the nature and results of the interaction. Individual decisions to participate in the organization reflect on such issues as the relationship between organizational rewards versus the demands made by the organization. Participation decisions also focus attention on the reasons why individuals remain in or leave organizations.

March and Simon treat decisions as internal variables in an organization which depend on jobs, individual expectations and motivations, and organizational structure. Marschak[47] looks on the decision process as an independent variable upon which the survival of the organization is based. In this case, the organization is viewed as having, inherent to its structure, the ability to maximize survival requisites through its established decision processes.

The goals of organization. Organization has three goals which may be either intermeshed or independent ends in themselves. They are growth, stability, and interaction. The last goal refers to organizations which exist primarily to provide a medium for association of its members with others. Interestingly enough these goals seem to apply to different forms of organization at varying levels of complexity, ranging from simple clockwork mechanisms to social systems.

These similarities in organizational purposes have been observed by a number of people and a field of thought and research called general system theory has developed, dedicated to the task of discovering organizationed universals. The dream of general system theory is to create a science of organizational universals, or if you will, a universal science using common organizational elements found in all systems as a starting point.

Modern organization theory is on the periphery of general system theory. Both general system theory and modern organization theory study:

1. the parts (individuals) in aggregates, and the movement of individuals into and out of the system.
2. the interaction of individuals with the environment found in the system.
3. the interactions among individuals in the system.
4. general growth and stability problems of systems.[48]

[46]March and Simon, *op. cit.,* Chapters 3 and 4.

[47]Jacob Marschak, "Efficient and Viable Organizational Forms" in *Modern Organizational Theory,* Mason Haire (editor), (New York: John Wiley and Sons, 1959), pp. 307-320.

[48]Kenneth E. Boulding, "General System Theory — The Skeleton of a Science," *Management Science,* April, 1956, pp. 200-202.

Modern organization theory and general system theory are similar in that they look at organization as an integrated whole. They differ, however, in terms of their generality. General system theory is concerned with every level of system, whereas modern organization theory focuses primarily on human organization.

The question might be asked, what can the science of administration gain by the study of system levels other than human? Before attempting an answer, note should be made of what these other levels are. Boulding presents a convenient method of classification:

1. The static structure — a level of framework, the anatomy of a system; for example, the structure of the universe.
2. The simple dynamic system — the level of clockworks, predetermined necessary motions.
3. The cybernetic system — the level of the thermostat, the system moves to maintain a given equilibrium through a process of self-regulation.
4. The open system — level of self-maintaining systems, moves toward and includes living organisms.
5. The genetic-societal system — level of cell society, characterized by a division of labor among cells.
6. Animal systems — level of mobility, evidence of goal-directed behavior.
7. Human systems — level of symbol interpretation and idea communication.
8. Social system — level of human organization.
9. Transcendental systems — level of ultimates and absolutes which exhibit systematic structure but are unknowable in essence.[49]

This approach to the study of systems by finding universals common at all levels of organization offers intriguing possibilities for administrative organization theory. A good deal of light could be thrown on social systems if structurally analogous elements could be found in the simpler types of systems. For example, cybernetic systems have characteristics which seem to be similar to feedback, regulation, and control phenomena in human organizations. Thus, certain facets of cybernetic models could be generalized to human organization. Considerable danger, however, lies in poorly founded analogies. Superficial similarities between simpler system forms and social systems are apparent everywhere. Instinctually based ant societies, for example, do not yield particularly instructive lessons for understanding rationally conceived human organizations. Thus, care should be taken that analogies used to bridge system levels are not mere devices for literary enrichment. For analogies

---

[49]*Ibid.*, pp. 202-205.

to have usefulness and validity, they must exhibit inherent structural similarities or implicitly identical operational principles.[50]

Modern organization theory leads, as it has been shown, almost inevitably into a discussion of general system theory. A science of organization universals has some strong advocates, particularly among biologists.[51] Organization theorists in administrative science cannot afford to overlook the contributions of general system theory. Indeed, modern organization concepts could offer a great deal to those working with general system theory. But the ideas dealt with in the general theory are exceedingly elusive.

Speaking of the concept of equilibrium as a unifying element in all systems, Easton says, "It (equilibrium) leaves the impression that we have a useful general theory when in fact, lacking measurability, it is a mere pretense for knowledge."[52] The inability to quantify and measure universal organization elements undermines the success of pragmatic tests to which general system theory might be put.

Organization Theory: Quo Vadis? Most sciences have a vision of the universe to which they are applied, and administrative science is not an exception. This universe is composed of parts. One purpose of science is to synthesize the parts into an organized conception of its field of study. As a science matures, its theorems about the configuration of its universe change. The direction of change in three sciences, physics, economics, and sociology, are noted briefly for comparison with the development of an administrative view of human organization.

The first comprehensive and empirically verifiable outlook of the physical universe was presented by Newton in his *Principia.* Classical physics, founded on Newton's work, constitutes a grand scheme in which a wide range of physical phenomena could be organized and predicted. Newtonian physics may rightfully be regarded as "macro" in nature, because its system of organization was concerned largely with gross events of which the movement of celestial bodies, waves, energy forms, and strain are examples. For years classical physics was supreme, being

---

[50]Seidenberg, *op. cit.,* p. 136. The fruitful use of the type of analogies spoken of by Seindenberg is evident in the application of thermodynamic principles, particularly the entropy concept, to communication theory. See: Claude E. Shannon and Warren Weaver, *The Mathematical Theory of Communication* (Urbana: The University of Illinois Press, 1959). Further, the existence of a complete analogy between the operational behavior of thermodynamic systems, electrical communication systems, and biological systems has been noted by: Y.S. Touloukian, *The Concept of Entropy in Communication, Living Organisms, and Thermodynamics,* Research Bulletin 130, Purdue Engineering Experiment Station.

[51]For example see: Ludwig von Bertalanffy, *Problem of Life* (London: Watts and Company, (1952).

[52]David Easton, "Limits of the Equilibrium Model in Social Research," in *Profits and Problems of Homeostatic Models in the Behavioral Sciences,* Publication 1, Chicago Behavioral Sciences, 1953, p. 39.

applied continuously to smaller and smaller classes of phenomena in the physical universe. Physicists at one time adopted the view that everything in their realm could be discovered by simply subdividing problems. Physics thus moved into the "micro" order.

But in the nineteenth century a revolution took place motivated largely because events were being noted which could not be explained adequately by the conceptual framework supplied by the classical school. The consequences of this revolution are brilliantly described by Eddington:

From the point of view of philosophy of science the conception associated with entropy must I think be ranked as the great contribution of the nineteenth century to scientific thought. It marked a reaction from the view that everything to which science need pay attention is discovered by microscopic dissection of objects. It provided an alternative standpoint in which the centre of interest is shifted from the entities reached by the customary analysis (atoms, electric potentials, etc.) to qualities possessed by the system as a whole, which cannot be split up and located — a little bit here, and a little bit there. . . .

We often think that when we have completed our study of one we know all about two, because "two" is "one and one." We forget that we have still to make a study of "and." Secondary physics is the study of "and" — that is to say, of organization. [53]

Although modern physics often deals in minute quantities and oscillations, the conception of the physicist is on the "macro" scale. He is concerned with the "and," or the organization of the world in which the events occur. These developments did not invalidate classical physics as to its usefulness for explaining a certain range of phenomena. But classical physics is no longer the undisputed law of the universe. It is a special case.

Early economic theory, and Adam Smith's *Wealth of Nations* comes to mind, examined economic problems in the macro order. The *Wealth of Nations* is mainly concerned with matters of national income and welfare. Later, the economics of the firm, micro-economics, dominated the theoretical scene in this science. And, finally, with Keynes' *The General Theory of Employment Interest and Money*, a systematic approach to the economic universe was re-introduced in the macro level.

The first era of the developing science of sociology was occupied by the great social "system builders." Comte, the so-called father of sociology, had a macro view of society in that his chief works are devoted to social reorganization. Comte was concerned with the interrelationships among social, political, religious, and educational institutions. As sociology progressed, the science of society compressed. Emphasis shifted

[53]Sir Arthur Eddington, *The Nature of the Physical World* (Ann Arbor: The University of Michigan Press, 1958), pp. 103-104.

from the macro approach of the pioneers to detailed, empirical study of small social units. The compression of sociological analysis was accompanied by study of social pathology or disorganization.

In general, physics, economics, and sociology appear to have two things in common. First, they offered a macro point of view as their initial systematic comprehension of their area of study. Second, as the science developed, attention fragmented into analysis of the parts of the organization, rather than attending to the system as a whole. This is the micro phase.

In physics and economics, discontent was evidenced by some scientists at the continual atomization of the universe. The reaction to the micro approach was a new theory or theories dealing with the total system, on the macro level again. This third phase of scientific development seems to be more evident in physics and economics than in sociology.

The reason for the "macro-micro-macro" order of scientific progress lies, perhaps, in the hypothesis that usually the things which strike man first are of great magnitude. The scientist attempts to discover order in the vastness. But after macro laws or models of systems are postulated, variations appear which demand analysis, not so much in terms of the entire system, but more in terms of the specific parts which make it up. Then, intense study of microcosm may result in new general laws, replacing the old models of organization. Or, the old and the new models may stand together, each explaining a different class of phenomenon. Or, the old and the new concepts of organization may be welded to produce a single creative synthesis.

Now, what does all this have to do with the problem of organization in administrative science? Organization concepts seem to have gone through the same order of development in this field as in the three just mentioned. It is evident that the classical theory of organization, particularly as in the work of Mooney and Reiley, is concerned with principles common to all organizations. It is a macro-organizational view. The classical approach to organization, however, dealt with the gross anatomical parts and processes of the formal organization. Like classical physics, the classical theory of organization is a special case. Neither are especially well equipped to account for variation from their established framework.

Many variations in the classical administrative model result from human behavior. The only way these variations could be understood was by a microscopic examination of particularized, situational aspects of human behavior. The mission of the neoclassical school thus is "micro-analysis."

It was observed earlier, that somewhere along the line the concept of the social system, which is the key to understanding the Hawthorne studies, faded into the background. Maybe the idea is so obvious that it was lost to the view of researchers and writers in human relations. In any event, the press of research in the microcosmic universes of the informal organization, morale and productivity, leadership, participation, and the like forced the notion of the social system into limbo. Now, with the advent of modern organization theory, the social system has been resurrected.

Modern organization theory appears to be concerned with Eddington's "and." This school claims that its operational hypothesis is based on a macro point of view; that is, the study of organization as a whole. This nobility of purpose should not obscure, however, certain difficulties faced by this field as it is presently constituted. Modern organization theory raises two questions which should be explored further. First, would it not be more accurate to speak of modern organization theories? Second, just how much of modern organization theory is modern?

The first question can be answered with a quick affirmative. Aside from the notion of the system, there are few, if any, other ideas of a unifying nature. Except for several important exceptions,[54] modern organization theorists tend to pursue their pet points of view,[55] suggesting they are part of system theory, but not troubling to show by what mystical means they arrive at this conclusion.

The irony of it all is that a field dealing with systems has, indeed, little system. Modern organization theory needs a framework, and it needs an integration of issues into a common conception of organization. Admittedly, this is a large order. But it is curious not to find serious analytical treatment of subjects like cybernetics or general system theory in Haire's *Modern Organizational Theory* which claims to be a representative example of work in this field. Beer has ample evidence in his book *Cybernetics and Management* that cybernetics, if imaginatively approached, provides a valuable conceptual base for the study of systems.

The second question suggests an ambiguous answer. Modern organization theory is in part a product of the past; system analysis is not a new idea. Further, modern organization theory relies for supporting data on microcosmic research studies, generally drawn from the journals of the last ten years. The newness of modern organization theory, perhaps, is its effort to synthesize recent research contributions of many fields into a system theory characterized by a reoriented conception of organization.

One might ask, but what is the modern theorist reorienting? A clue is found in the almost snobbish disdain assumed by some authors of the neo-classical human relations school, and particularly, the classical school. Re-evaluation of the classical school of organization is overdue. However, this does not mean that its contributions to organization theory are irrelevant and should be overlooked in the rush to get on the "behavioral science bandwagon."

Haire announces that the papers appearing in *Modern Organization Theory* constitute, "the ragged leading edge of a wave of theoretical

---

[54] For example: E. Wight Bakke, *op. cit.*, pp. 18-75.

[55] There is a large selection including decision theory, individual-organization interaction, motivation, vitality, stability, growth, and graph theory, to mention a few.

development."[56] Ragged, yes; but leading no! The papers appearing in this book do not represent a theoretical breakthrough in the concept of organization. Haire's collection is an interesting potpourri with several contributions of considerable significance. But readers should beware that they will not find vastly new insights into organizational behavior in this book, if they have kept up with the literature of the social sciences, and have dabbled to some extent in the esoterica of biological theories of growth, information theory, and mathematical model building. For those who have not maintained the pace, *Modern Organization Theory* serves the admirable purpose of bringing them up-to-date on a rather diversified number of subjects.

Some work in modern organization theory is pioneering, making its appraisal difficult and future uncertain. While the direction of this endeavor is unclear, one thing is patently true. Human behavior in organizations, and indeed, organization itself, cannot be adequately understood within the ground rules of classical and neo-classical doctrines. Appreciation of human organization requires a *creative* synthesis of massive amounts of empirical data, a high order of deductive reasoning, imaginative research studies, and a taste for individual and social values. Accomplishment of all these objectives, and the inclusion of them into a framework of the concept of the system, appears to be the goal of modern organization theory. The vitality of administrative science rests on the advances modern theorists make along this line.

Modern organization theory, 1960 style, is an amorphous aggregation of synthesizers and restaters, with a few extending leadership on the frontier. For the sake of these few, it is well to admonish that pouring old wine into new bottles may make the spirits cloudy. Unfortunately, modern organization theory has almost succeeded in achieving the status of a fad. Popularization and exploitation contributed to the disrepute into which human relations has fallen. It would be a great waste if modern organization theory yields to the same fate, particularly since both modern organization theory and human relations draw from the same promising source of inspiration — system analysis.

Modern organization theory needs tools of analysis and a conceptual framework uniquely its own, but it must also allow for the incorporation of relevant contributions of many fields. It may be that the framework will come from general system theory. New areas of research such as decision theory, information theory, and cybernetics also offer reasonable expectations of analytical and conceptual tools. Modern organization theory represents a frontier of research which has great significance for management. The potential is great, because it offers the opportunity for uniting what is valuable in classical theory with the social and natural sciences into a systematic and integrated conception of human organization.

---

[56]Mason Haire, "General Issues," in Mason Haire (editor), *Modern Organization Theory* (New York: John Wiley and Sons, 1959), p. 2.

THE LINE-STAFF RELATIONSHIP*

Louis A. Allen

Inadequate working relationships between line and staff departments are one of the most potent sources of friction and inefficiency in many companies. Frequently staff people are confused and uncertain as to what they are supposed to do and what right they have to do it. Just as often, line managers look upon staff specialists as unnecessary impediments in the otherwise simple and efficient administration of production operations.

Unfavorable effects are usually obvious. Decision-making is often slowed to a feeble walk in the unending hassle between line and staff. There is constant jockeying for position and authority. Important deadlines may be missed. And coordination is often inadequate.

The picture is not all black, however. In many companies, staff and line work together as an integrated team. As a result, line management is supported by a highly effective group of experts who are on call to help with the complicated problems that arise in the highly technical operation of modern industry.

Even where line and staff differences are most troublesome, there is no question about the necessity of staff. Basically, the problem is one of how staff and line can learn to work together in helping the company achieve its goals. But preliminary to the solution of this problem is an understanding of what line and staff mean and what they do.

DEFINING LINE AND STAFF

Every company is organized for a specific purpose. This may be to make, invent, or sell a product or service, or any combination of these. But whether it be production, sales, research, or finance, the line component is the one that has direct responsibility for accomplishing the objectives of the enterprise. Organizationally, the line is the chain of command that extends from the board of directors through the various delegations and redelegations of authority and responsibility to the point where the primary activities of the company are performed. The line, then, refers to those departments that have the power to initiate and carry through to conclusion the basic activities of the company.

*Reprinted with permission from *Management Record*, September, 1955.

"Line" is identified by the objectives of the company. Since the line is directly responsible for accomplishing the objectives of the company, it follows that line elements can be identified most accurately in terms of these objectives.[1]

To the extent that objectives of companies differ, line activities also differ. For example, a steel company has as its primary objectives the manufacture of quality steel products and their sale at a profit. The line functions in this instance are production and sales.

An oil company is organized to develop sources of crude oil and natural gas, to manufacture petroleum products and by-products, to market these products, and to operate transportation facilities. The line departments are production, manufacturing, transportation, and marketing.

In a department store chain success depends as much upon buying as selling. Both the buying or purchasing and the sales functions are line.

Some functions are line in one company, staff in another. There is little uniformity as to what is line and what is staff from one company to another. For example, one eastern company is organized primarily to manufacture and sell machinery. Engineering the product and providing service to customers are important, but only as a means of selling more effectively. Consequently, in this case, manufacturing and sales are line. Engineering operates in an advisory capacity to the line, and the service function supplies parts, training and assistance to the franchised dealers who service the machines. It is noteworthy that in the organizations of the franchised dealers, sales and service are the line functions.

These same functions receive different emphasis in an aircraft manufacturing company. Here the enterprise can succeed only if it continually invests a good share of its effort in the complex problems of design and engineering of new aircraft, and the testing, servicing and modification of the aircraft it sells. In this organization, the line departments are engineering, manufacturing, sales and service.

The finance function is considered staff in many companies; in others it is line. In a typical manufacturing company, for example, the finance department operates as a specialized staff department, with responsibility for financing, accounting, and reporting or budgeting and control of expenditures. The performance of these duties is a staff service to other units of the company and does not involve the exercise of authority by the finance department over line departments. Necessary uniformity as to accounting, budgeting and reporting procedures is secured through company policy and procedures, which are issued by top line management.

---

[1] See "Organization Planning," *Management Record*, October, 1954, p. 372.

In some companies, however, finance is line. In an eastern manufacturing company, for instance, about half of the company's business comes from products which are leased to customers instead of being sold outright. Because most lessors pay their rental on a usage basis, the accounting group within the finance department is directly concerned with a substantial amount of the company's income. Finance is therefore set up as a line operation, with authority to make final decisions as to leasing arrangements, in the same fashion that manufacturing and sales have the last word in their functions.

Research is line in some companies, staff in others. Again, the reason for the difference can be found in the objectives of the company. In a typical case, research is responsible for providing advice and recommendations aimed at the improvement and maintenance of products and the development of new products. Manufacturing and sales are the line departments in this case.

Another company, however, considers research of equal importance with sales and manufacturing in achieving its objectives. This company believes its future success depends upon a steady flow of new products and processes. Therefore, it has established research as a line department and gives its research director a place comparable to that of the directors of manufacturing and sales.

Some functions are both line and staff in the same company. A function may be both line and staff in the same company. For example, in a decentralized business, the chief executive officer may need specialists in sales and production to advise him on matters of over-all planning, policy making and control. Sales and production thus are specialized staff departments at the corporate level. However, within the operating divisions of this same company, sales is responsible for marketing and distributing the product. At this point it is line. Since production handles the manufacturing in the plants, this function is also line at the operating level.

WHAT STAFF IS

Once a line manager's job grows beyond a certain size, he needs help to perform it properly. Staff refers to those elements of the organization which provide advice and service to the line. Actually, staff is best thought of in terms of a relationship. When one *position* exists primarily to provide advice and service to another, it is in a staff relationship. And if the work of a *department* is predominately that of advice and service to one or more other departments, it is classified as a *staff department.* Staff includes all elements of the organization which are not line.

It is to be noted that a line, or chain of command, runs from the top to the bottom of each staff department, just as it does within each line component. Some positions within the staff department may exist primarily to provide advice and service to other positions within the same department. In this case there is an internal staff and line relationship. For example, in the personnel department in one company the line runs from the manager to the section heads of management development, labor relations and compensation. The personnel department also has a personnel research section which conducts library research and surveys for the management development, labor relations and compensation sections — not for the company as a whole. The personnel research section is staff to the line of the specialized staff department. In the same way, an assistant to the personnel manager is staff to him.

Part of the confusion in identifying staff and in determining its proper relationship to line stems from the failure to recognize that managers need help of two different kinds and that two types of staff provide this help.

Personal staff refers to the positions created primarily to aid the manager in carrying out those parts of his job he cannot, or does not wish to, delegate to others. These *reserved responsibilities,* which the manager performs personally may include over-all planning for his function, policy making and interpretation, coordination, human relations and control.[2]

Specialized staff helps the line by performing work that requires *special skills* or more *objectivity* than the line can normally be expected to possess. This may include help with accounting, personnel, engineering, purchasing, medical and other problems. Work of this type is so highly specialized that it can be delegated as a separate function to the appropriate specialist.

Personal staff

Personal staff may consist of three kinds of assistants:[3]

- Line assistants
- Staff assistants
- General staff assistants

Line assistants. The line assistant assists his chief in the whole range of his duties, except where a more limited delegation is made. He helps the principal to manage the function; that is, he assists with over-all planning, organizing, direction, coordination and control. Although the line assistant is in the direct chain of command, he is staff to his superior because he exists only to advise, counsel and act *for* his principal. The line assistant has no responsibility apart from that of his principal; therefore, he has none to redelgate.

---

[2]See "The Art of Delegation," *Management Record,* March, 1955, p. 92.

[3]For a detailed discussion of assistants and how they can be used most effectively, see "The Uses of Assistants," *Management Record,* May, 1955, p. 174.

Staff assistants. The staff assistant is also commonly known as the "assistant to." He usually serves in a much more restricted fashion than does the line assistant. The staff assistant is differentiated from the line assistant in that he has no authority over other employees, except in the case of special assignments. Neither does he take over the department in the absence of his principal.

The work of the staff assistant varies widely from one company to another. He may be anything from a glorified secretary to a vice-president. His duties may range from opening the mail and answering the telephone to sitting in on board of directors meetings of subsidiary companies with power to speak for the president of the company.

Staff assistants may also be called "administrative assistants," "special assistants," and "executive assistants," depending upon the kind of work that they actually do.

General staff assistants. Some companies use a general staff, which is an adaptation of army practice. This is, in reality, a group of staff assistants functioning at a high level. These staff assistants usually serve as advisors to top management in specified areas. The general staff is used in addition to the regular corporate specialized staff.

Specialized staff

In contrast to personal staff, the specialized staff advises and serves all line and other staff departments in a functional capacity. For instance, the staff finance department reporting to the president is available not only to advise and serve him, but also to serve other departments that need help in financial matters. The specialized staff thus becomes a reservoir of special knowledge, skills and experience which the entire organization can use. The specialized staff has two identifying characteristics:

1. It has no authority over other parts of the organization. The specialized staff advises and serves; it does not direct.
2. It can be used by all line and staff units of the organization, within the limits of company policy or practice. The activities of each specialized staff department are restricted to one specialized area or function. This differentiates it from the personal staff, which exists primarily to help one executive in carrying out his reserved responsibilities.

The specialized staff assists the line and other staff functions in two ways. First, it performs advisory activities — providing advice, counsel, suggestions, and guidance. Second, it performs service activities — specified work *for* the line, which may include making decisions that the line has asked it to make.

Advisory activities. Specialized staff managers are, by definition, best qualified to advise the line and other staff managers in matters having to do with their specialties. The advice offered by staff may be of several different kinds.

Staff may offer planning advice to managers by undertaking study, research, analysis and the development of alternative courses of action. These can be of invaluable assistance to the line manager who has to make a final decision. This advice may include planning objectives, policies and procedures which will apply to and govern the operations of the line departments. It may cover the explanation and interpretation of objectives, plans and policies to line and other staff departments.

Staff may offer advice as to how decisions can best be put into practice. It may advise the line on planning performance controls. This advice may include assistance in establishing standards or yardsticks, determining the best methods of measuring work in progress, analysis of actual performance compared with the standard, and reporting findings to responsible executives.

Service activities. Staff may perform service activities by carrying out specified work *for* the line. For example, the personnel department may recruit, select, and employ people for the line and other staff departments. The purchasing department may buy materials and supplies for the line. Finance may install accounting, budgetary and reporting systems for the line organization.

It is to be noted that in each case where staff performs a service for the line, authority for performing that service and final decisions as to how it is to be done rests with the line. For example, the accounting department, if it is staff, does not direct the line to conform to standardized accounting procedures necessary for the compilation of a consolidated balance sheet. Such procedures are authorized by the president, who gives either explicit or implied authority to the accounting department to install *for him* the accounting system that will best serve the objectives he has set forth. The personnel manager who recruits college graduates, and who may even hire them, is acting only at the express request of the line departments he serves.

IMPROVING LINE-STAFF RELATIONSHIPS

Study of company organization brings to light frequent instances of friction and conflict between line and staff. What is at the root of the difficulty? Both line and staff have their viewpoints.

The line viewpoint

Line managers most often have these complaints about the staff organization:

- Staff tends to assume line authority

- Staff does not give sound advice
- Staff steals credit
- Staff fails to see the whole picture

Staff assumes line authority. Line managers are generally keenly aware of their responsibility for results and profits. While they recognize that the staff man is necessary and valuable, they frequently resent what he does, or what they think he is trying to do, because they feel it encroaches upon their duties and prerogatives.

For example, in one company the plant manager had just finished negotiating a contact with a labor union. The central staff labor relations manager had been present all through the proceedings, ostensibly to guide and assist the plant manager in the negotiations.

The plant manager was not complimentary about the staff man's participation. "He knew just what he wanted, and he tried every way he knew to get me to go along. He would have made concessions to the union we didn't have to make at this plant and that we couldn't live with. I know some other plants in the company had to give in on those points, but there is no reason why we should."

Staff does not give sound advice. Many managers complain that the counsel and advice staff offers is not always fully considered, well balanced, and soundly tested. In many companies, staff is considered "academic" or "ivory tower." Responsibility for this attitude can sometimes be laid squarely on staff people. For one thing, since staff is not held accountable for ultimate results, some staff managers show a tendency to propose new ideas without thinking them through or testing them. For another, staff specialists sometimes become enthusiastic advocates of ideas or programs because they work well in other companies. They do not always determine whether these ideas are adapted to the operating conditions of their own organization.

The sad fact is that sometimes the staff man is not well enough acquainted with operating conditions or processes in his own company to be able to identify the limiting factors. For instance, in one company the executive development director attended a seminar in which he heard accounts of the effectiveness of the committee method of executive appraisal. He made an enthusiastic recommendation to two division managers that they install this system in their plants. He did not understand why his idea met with a cold reception until he realized, several months later, that both divisions had many small treating plants with fifteen or twenty people and one or, at the most, two supervisors. As a result, committee appraisal was highly impractical.

Staff steals credit. Another common complaint is the tendency of staff to assume credit for programs that are successful and to lay the blame on line when they are not

Staff people usually have a strategic advantage because they are closer to the top line manager and have more frequent access to him. In the nature of things, if a division manager accepts his staff industrial engineer's recommendation for installation of a methods improvement program, he will consult with him frequently on how best to go about it. Since the staff man has his chief's ear, he will be able to inject his own opinions and judgments as to why the program does or does not work. As one production superintendent said, "When things go wrong, those staff engineers make sure we're behind the eight ball. But when things click, every staff man in the shop rushes in to take credit."

Staff fails to see the whole picture. Line managers frequently point out that staff people tend to operate in terms of the limited objectives of their own speciality rather than in the interests of the business as a whole. The difficulty here seems to be that the staff man becomes so involved in his own area that he fails to relate it to the task of the line and to the over-all objectives of the company.

The staff viewpoint

Complaints in the staff-line relationship are not entirely one-sided. Many staff men have complaints about the line. These usually center about the following:

- Line does not make proper use of staff
- Line resists new ideas
- Line does not give staff enough authority

Line does not make proper use of staff. In many companies, the advice and help of staff is sought only as a last resort. The line manager possibly prefers to run his own show and does not want to call in a specialist. He may be reluctant to place his actions in public view so they can be criticized. Again, he may distrust the motives of staff, and feel they are trying to usurp his authority. Whatever the cause, staff specialists usually believe that their potential value is minimized if they are only called in when a situation is so far out of hand as to be hopeless.

Most specialized staff managers feel that they should be consulted during the planning stages of a program that involves their own area of specialty. This enables them to anticipate problems and to recommend precautionary measures. As one safety engineer put it: "If I'm called in before machinery or equipment is ordered, I can help specify safety features that the maintenance and purchasing people aren't aware of. It's my business to keep up with our special requirements and new developments in safety engineering. Most times I get in on the show only after accidents have happened."

Line resists new ideas. Many staff men feel that line management tends to be shortsighted and resistant to new ideas. Staff men are usually alert to the newest thinking and innovations in the field of their specialties. The public relations man may be enthusiastic about open-house programs; the personnel man may be convinced that psychological testing is a panacea for many of the ills of the plant; the industrial engineer may be certain that statistical quality control is the cure-all for low quality.

Line management, however, is often cautious and slow to accept new ideas. One industrial engineer who was advocating the use of work sampling and meeting with a great deal of resistance from the plant superintendent summed up this point of view when he said, "They preach 'wait and see' while we're wasting thousands of dollars a day. We'd do better with a little gumption and less caution."

Line does not give staff enough authority. A common theme in the staff manager's complaint is lack of authority. As one industrial engineer said: "We're paid to be experts. Most of us know a lot more in our specialty than line people. But we haven't got the authority to make it stick."

Many staff managers feel that if they have the best answer to a problem, they should be able to enforce the solution on the line man involved. To their way of thinking, knowledge is authority, and there is not much point in throwing organizational barriers between the man who knows and the job that has to be done.

Solutions

The answer to better teamwork between staff and line seems to lie, first, in an understanding of their basic relationship. Company experience indicates that the following important points must be observed if effective teamwork is to exist.

1. The units that are designated as line have ultimate responsibility for the successful operation of the company. Therefore, line departments must be responsible for operating decisions.
2. Staff elements contribute by providing advice and service to the line in accomplishing the objectives of the enterprise.
3. Staff is responsible for providing advice and service to appropriate line elements when requested to do so. However, staff also is responsible for proffering advice and service when it is not requested, but where the staff believes it is needed.
4. The solicitation of advice and acceptance of suggestions and counsel is usually at the option of the line organization. However, in some instances it must be recognized that only the top level of the organization has this option and that top management's decision with respect to

the use of staff advice or service is binding throughout lower levels. For instance, if the president decides that all purchasing will be handled by the staff procurement department, an operating department is not at liberty to contract for its own purchases of safety shoes. These decisions may be expressed in company policies or procedures, or they may be conveyed informally.

5. Line is responsible for giving serious consideration to advice and offers of service made by staff units, and should follow the recommendations if it is in the company's best interest to do so. However, except in those cases where the use of staff advice and service is compulsory and subject only to appeal to higher authority, it is not mandatory that the advice of staff be followed. Except as noted above, line managers should have authority to modify, reject or accept such advice.

6. Both line and staff should have the right to appeal to higher authority in case of disagreement on staff recommendations. However, this right to appeal should not be permitted to supersede the line's responsibility for making immediate decisions when required by the operating situation.

How staff can do a better job

How can the staff specialist do a better job in terms of these relationships? Many companies find that the following points help facilitate and improve staff operations.

Operate in terms of policies and objectives of the company as a whole. Written statements of company policy have an important bearing on staff-line relationships. These statements of what the company believes and intends to live by provide guides to both line and staff people over which the staff exercises a watchdog kind of control. In many cases the staff executive is responsible for interpreting these policies with, of course, the final decision resting with the chief executive officer in cases of dispute. Understanding by both line and staff executives of their responsibilities for the development of and adherence to the company policies tend to eliminate much of the friction that can easily develop between line and staff. The objectives of staff departments should be aimed at helping the company accomplish its purposes, and not devoted to the specialized goals of the staff department itself.

For example, the company may not need a program of psychological testing because tests are not capable of identifying the special kinds of talent the company requires. Statistical quality control may not be indicated because the company is trying a new market in which gross tolerances are permissible and in which price is far more important than precise machining. To be able to operate in such terms, the staff man first has to see the over-all picture. He needs to know what the company is trying to accomplish in terms of operations, costs and sales. Then he needs to be able to subordinate his personal and professional interests to the welfare of the company as a whole.

Encourage and educate line to use staff effectively. A line manager cannot use a staff specialist effectively unless he knows what that specialist can do for him. The staff man has the responsibility of letting the line know what he has to offer.

In some companies, this is done through training conferences. Each staff manager appears before conference groups of line and other staff personnel and describes his function to them. He points out how he can be helpful in solving specific problems, and answers questions that may come up.

In other companies, staff managers make a point of talking with line managers individually about their operations. The staff man uses this opportunity to outline his own activities and to introduce any ideas he may have as to how he may be useful to the line operator.

Recognize and overcome resistance to change. One of the important reasons for line opposition to ideas presented by staff is the psychological factor of resistance to change. People tend to resist ideas that threaten to change their way of doing things. The fact that a change is even suggested seems to imply that the old way was not good enough.

It is not so commonly recognized that people are even more set against changes that threaten disturbance or alteration in personal relationships. For example, a maintenance supervisor may be moderately opposed to a suggested change in his job responsibilities. He has always been responsible for the installation of new equipment and he does not want to give it up, even though he is being given responsibility for the lubrication program in its place. However, if the change means that he will also have to move to another part of the plant and work with another group of people, his resistance is likely to be greatly intensified.

Staff specialists can anticipate and overcome this natural resistance to proposed changes. Many companies have found these points helpful:

1. Determine to what extent the proposed change will affect personal relationships. Is the staff man advocating a major, sweeping change which will affect the social patterns established in the group? If so, the traumatic effect and accompanying resistance can be diminished if the change is broken into smaller, more numerous moves which will make gradual adjustment possible.

2. When major changes are involved which will modify the relationships between a manager and the people who work for him, opposition from the manager will be minimized if he participates in the preliminary planning. Then, when announcement of the change is made, the principal directly affected can make it as a working partner with the staff, and not as an unwilling associate. In effect, this gives the line manager an opportunity to make the idea his own.

3. People who will be affected by the change will accept it better if:

● The change is tied in as closely as possible with their personal goals and interests, their jobs, families, and futures, and if they are convinced it will make their own work easier, faster or safer.
● They have an opportunity to offer suggestions, ideas and comments concerning the change as it affects them — provided they are convinced these suggestions are sincerely wanted and will be given serious consideration.
● They are kept informed of the results of the change.
● They are able to check on how well they are doing in terms of the change.

4. Acquire technical proficiency. The primary reason for the existence of staff is that it is highly informed and capable in a specialized field. It follows that the staff specialist, if he is to merit respect and to do his work properly, must be an expert. He needs a detailed and extensive knowledge of his field, and he needs to be able to convey this knowledge and information convincingly to others.

Technical proficiency in a staff man implies more than specialized knowledge. It also requires that the specialist have a knowledge of the company and its operations. The more he knows of line problems and operations, and those of other staff specialties, the better he can develop effective recommendations in his own area.

How line can make better use of staff

The effectiveness of the line manager depends to a large extent upon how he makes use of staff services. The line manager who wants to make most advantageous use of the staff services at his disposal will find the following points of value:

1. Make maximum use of staff. The more the line man makes use of staff, the better acquainted the specialists will become with his problems and his way of working. Many line executives find that it is only common sense to make habitual use of staff. In effect, the line manager has on retainer a consultant who can help him perform better.
2. Make proper use of staff. Lost motion, duplication and personal irritation often occur because the line manager hasn't made up his mind what advice or service he needs before he calls in the specialist.

In one case, for example, a plant manager asked the purchasing agent to secure data on the comparative costs of a pusher bar conveyor installation as compared to the existing crane and magnet operation. After the purchasing agent had completed his study at considerable time and effort, the plant manager told him: "We haven't got the money for new equipment. I guess what I really wanted to know was how to operate that crane with two men instead of three." He then called in the industrial engineer to make a new study for him.

3. Keep staff informed. Line managers frequently take action directly affecting staff activities without notifying the staff people concerned. For example, in one company the executive vice-president and the manager of one of the operating divisions decided to install a fully automatic assembly line in one plant of the division. This necessitated the use of many more maintenance and technical people over a period of years, together with several additional engineers. The personnel manager found out about the new plan only after the work was completed and a request for additional people came through. Instead of having an opportunity to train and upgrade people from within the company over a period of months, he was forced to hire the additional staff from the outside.

Many companies have found that time and effort spent in training and educating managers in proper line-staff relationships is an excellent investment. Evidence seems to show that this is a direct means of improving teamwork, increasing the productive capacity of members of management and reducing friction in personal relationships.

MAKING BETTER USE OF COMMITTEES*

Louis A. Allen

If the man-hours spent in committee meetings every working day were added end to end they would undoubtedly total time, and to spare, to run a company the size of General Motors. Attending committee meetings is probably one of the most popular avocational pursuits in American business today. This does not mean, however, that all who attend committee meetings are in favor of them. The range of reaction from positive to negative encompasses a good deal of honest bewilderment.

The president of a Philadelphia company of 10,000, for example, was exasperated at his inability to find executives in their offices when he called. The secretary's explanation was invariably "He's in committee." Determined to find out what kind of administrative complex he had fathered, the president instituted a study of the committee system in his company. From high to low, he found 286 committees functioning for one reason or another. Some managers were members of ten and twelve committees, and literally spent more than half their working time in meetings.

This may be an extreme example. However, to many managers, committees are an unending source of frustration. "If I need a policy decision and the problem gets into a committee, I give up," said one Chicago executive, sales manager for a food company. "Committees are an organized means of passing the buck. The only reason we have them is that some of our top people can't make up their minds and they want a committee to do it for them."

While this viewpoint is prevalent, it is by no means universal. And even where individual executives complain bitterly about the inefficiency of the system, committees still seem to roll along as implacably as a juggernaut.

A great many companies swear by committees as an indispensable tool of management. "We have eight decentralized divisions, and forty plants, and we are located in five foreign countries as well as the United States," said the president of an equipment company with headquarters in New York City. "I can't be personally acquainted

*Reprinted with permission from *Management Record*, December, 1955.

with every issue that comes up, so I rely on committees to give me advice and to help me decide. Without our committee system this company would come apart at the seams."

In spite of the firmly established position of committees and the hot debate as to their merit. *The Conference Board* has found in its current study on organization planning that few companies have made a serious analysis of their use of committees. The role of the committee remains only partially evaluated; so, whether or not maligned, it is usually misunderstood.

DEFINITION OF COMMITTEE

Committees are usually relatively formal bodies, with a definite structure. They have their own organization. To them are delegated definite responsibility and authority. A committee is usually given a specific job to do. For example, it may review budgets, formulate plans for new products, or make policy decisions. Or the committee may only have power to make recommendations and suggestions to a designated official. But whatever its task, it is generally given the authority or power it needs to carry it out.[1]

The character and composition of committees is often spelled out in the bylaws or the administrative procedures of the company. Committees usually have a fixed membership. In most cases members are appointed, although, sometimes, as with the board of directors, they may be elected. Membership in a committee is never a casual matter; for example, people don't become members because they happen to join a department, as is true of membership in staff meetings.

In their deliberation, committees usually follow definite rules and procedures, which are often written. But if unwritten, the rules are no less binding. Most committees specify that only the regular members on their designated representatives may vote. Some committees can function if a quorum is in attendance; others must wait until the full membership is present.

Some companies state that their committees are "informal." This is a relative term. Even the most "informal" of committees usually conform to the above criteria. The fact that members may gather in a company plane en route from one city to another or around the luncheon table does not detract from the prescribed membership or method of conduct or area of responsibility of the group.

Definition of a committee is difficult because there are many different kinds of committees and the concept of a committee varies widely from one company to another. However, in terms of the criteria outlined above,

---

[1] See "Organization Planning," *Management Record*, October, 1954, p. 402.

an acceptable definition might be: *A committee is a body of persons appointed or elected to meet on an organized basis for the consideration of matters brought before it.*

WHEN SHOULD COMMITTEES BE USED?

A committee almost invariably is created to carry out responsibilities that would otherwise be delegated to a single individual. Most companies agree that committees are used properly only when individuals in regular, established positions cannot adequately carry out a specific responsibility. It follows that, under certain circumstances, the committee must have inherent capabilities that enable it to operate more effectively than one person.

What unusual properties are found in a committee? Committees have inherent advantages in some situations because people in groups react differently from people as individuals. Group dynamics give the committee certain potential advantages over an individual acting alone.

Pooled knowledge and judgment. A committee is an effective method of bringing the collective knowledge and judgment of a number of people to bear on a problem. One company, in analyzing committee participation, found that the average committee of seven people has over 150 years of composite experience. Representing, as it does, varied viewpoints and backgrounds, this pooled knowledge and judgment may be an invaluable asset when focused on complex problems. In addition, the committee has another closely related characteristic.

Group pressure. The individual members of the group exert pressure or censorship on the ideas, suggestions, comments and judgments of other members. The more loyalty one member feels toward other members of the committee, the more he wants to be liked and respected by them, and, consequently, the more he will tend to conform to this group pressure. The net result may be favorable or unfavorable.

Many executives point out that the very act of pooling and integrating ideas and viewpoints within the group often results in a product that is greater than the sum of the individual contributions. A few executives with outstanding analytical ability or a sense of timing or keen judgment may raise the level of participation of the whole group. A natural question here is: why not throw the problem to such an outstanding individual and let him handle it by himself? The response is that even the outstanding person doesn't have all the answers. If he gets off the beam, or if he is too much influenced by personal prejudices, group pressure will tend to bring him back into line.

This brings up the danger inherent in group pressure. Some specialists claim that this censorship may bring an exceptionally able individual down to the level of a mediocre group. If such an individual's thinking goes beyond the group, or if he shows more imagination than the group can assimilate, or, in fact, if he is very much beyond the capabilities of the group in any way, group pressure may tend to make him conform. Many experienced committee chairmen who have dealt with this situation point out, however, that under proper leadership the group can be encouraged to reconsider ideas it cannot at first assimilate so that eventually the same ideas are reproposed by other members and finally prevail because of their intrinsic merit.

Enforces participation. A third characteristic of group action is that it tends to enforce participation. A major source of resistance to new policies and projects by those who are delegated responsibility for carrying them out is lack of participation on their part at the planning stage. The person who is called upon to suggest, criticize, and make recommendations concerning a policy or project is likely to be motivated to carry it out wholeheartedly. This participation is especially important in decisions which will be binding on all parts of the organization. Many companies find that when department heads who will be affected have an opportunity to participate before the final decision is made, there is better understanding and greater acceptance than will prevail if the decision is by edict.

Obviously, the committee is not the only means of securing this participation. There may be other and more effective opportunities in the normal process of supervision. The chief merit of the committee in this respect seems to be that it makes participation mandatory on the part of members of the committee who are also key people who will be affected by a given decision.

HOW ARE COMMITTEES USED?

Committees are most commonly used for the following purposes:

Coordination. When it is necessary to integrate and unify varying points of view, which cannot conveniently or effectively be coordinated by individuals, the committee may be of value in bringing all those concerned together. For example, an eastern chemical company depends largely upon research to provide new products in a competitive market. To determine the feasibility of proposed new products, it is necessary to integrate and unify the ideas and suggestions of the managers of such functions as research, engineering, production, sales, finance and purchasing. At one time the manager of research attempted to coordinate his work by personal visits and discussions with other functional heads. However, he found there were always loose ends, no matter how many personal contacts he made. From this experience, the company concluded that the most effective and economical way to coordinate new product development is through committee meetings which offer opportunity for presentation and resolution of differing points of view.

Advice. Committees may exercise a staff role[2] by providing advice to a specific individual or to the organization at large.

The committee acts in a personal staff role when it restricts its advisory activities to one executive, who may or may not be a member of the committee. It may act in the role of specialized staff when it offers expert counsel and service in one specialized area to the entire organization, as well as to the line principal involved.

Many companies find that committees tend to overlap and duplicate the services available from normal staff agencies when they are used in this fashion. And committees usually have potential handicaps when they act in an advisory capacity. From a procedural viewpoint, a committee is a poor means of gathering and analyzing facts. This usually requires mobility, independent study and investigation. In some companies, the advisory committee has its own staff, or fact-gathering apparatus, in which case the committee acts to review and evaluate the data placed before it.

A committee may be used to advise and counsel a top executive in policy formulation. This has the obvious advantage of pooled knowledge, experience and judgment. It also is a means of bringing out and resolving varying viewpoints so as to ensure a workable policy that will be accepted by those who must put it into effect.

Committees also may provide advice on controls, or the measurement and evaluation of results. Control requires the establishment of standards, recording of current progress, analysis and reporting of variances and exceptions, and appropriate managerial action and follow-up. The committee functions most effectively when it receives reports of progress and variances from fact-gathering and reporting agencies. The committee members study these reports *before* the committee meeting. They devote their meeting time to review and discussion of the data and formulation of recommendations, which are forwarded to the accountable line executive. Committees rarely take control action. This responsibility is usually pinpointed in the line.

Decision-making. Committees sometimes serve as decision-making bodies. This is usually confined, however, to high-level committees. There are those who assert that decision-making should rarely if ever be the responsibility of committees below the level of the board of directors. In other words, committee decision-making seems to be accepted as a sound procedure only when it is not desirable to make a single individual responsible or accountable for the decision. For example, the members of the board of directors share responsibility for making over-all policy decisions and are accountable to the stockholders. In a large manufacturing company, a financial policy committee, comprised of members of the board of directors, decides financial policies. In another company,

[2]See "The Line-Staff Relationship," *Management Record,* Sept, 1955, p. 346.

an executive compensation committee, made up of department vice-presidents, makes final decisions on salary matters for all personnel in specific salary grades.

DANGERS IN THE USE OF COMMITTEE

Some companies have eliminated committees entirely. Others have instituted studies of committee action which have resulted in radical surgery on the committee system. One company, for example, cut down the number of management committees from eighty to twelve; another cut back from two hundred to twenty-four. When this type of curtailment is possible in a well-run, profitable and rapidly expanding company, it is obvious that serious abuses of the committee system are taking place. Company experience shows the following danger points as most prevalent.

1. *Committees encourage managers to shirk or evade decision-making responsibilities.* If a manager has an opportunity to carry a problem to a committee, he may seize upon this as a means of avoiding the necessity for making up his own mind, or to escape the consequences of an unpopular decision. If the chairman of the committee is the accountable person, he can fall back upon the committee as an alibi or scapegoat. If the committee as a whole is held accountable (a nice administrative feat), accountability is so diffuse as to be impossible of assignment.[3] Some managers utilize the committee as a means of avoiding the laborious and difficult process of logical thinking that leads to a sound decision. "I'll bring it before the committee," often serves as an excuse rather than as an acceptable means of administrative action.

2. *Slows decision-making.* Company experience demonstrates that committee action is almost invariably slow and unwieldy, compared to individual decision-making. In some cases this seriously handicaps management of the enterprise. In one company, for example, practically every matter that came to top management had to have the blessing of a committee before the president would make a decision. It was only after a newly styled product was so delayed by committee action that it came out a month behind a similar product of a competitor that the company swept out the overlapping and cumbersome committee system and established straight-line channels for prompt decisions.

The very mechanics of calling people together and providing for discussion is time consuming. And when the managers who are members of the committee are forced to ignore important day-to-day matters to attend a meeting, this compounds the difficulty. There are other

---

[3]"The Art of Delegation," *Management Record*, March, 1955, p. 90.

mechanical difficulties. Absenteeism, lack of preparation before meetings, and substitutions in membership all slow down decision-making.

3. *May serve to mask ineffective management.* Many companies find that committees are most popular with managers who are inadequate in their own right. The committee thus serves as a crutch. Since there are likely to be at least a few capable people on the committee, it is able to come to a better decision than an ineffective individual. At the same time, decisions made on the basis of committee participation are likely to be successful to the extent that they have the full support of those members of the committee who participated in the decision. In some cases, committee support is knowingly given an individual by management because there is no capable individual available to do the job. In many instances, however, committees are set up by managers who want to conceal their own weaknesses.

MAKING BETTER USE OF COMMITTEES

Many companies have demonstrated that proper procedures can help cut down the time required for committee meetings, improve the resultant action, and make committees a useful agency of management, rather than a doubtful and much bedeviled administrative gimmick. Such companies usually point to the importance of the following factors:

1. *The committee should have a clearly stated purpose.* A great many committees meet without any clear idea as to what they are supposed to consider. A wage and salary committee, in one company, for example, discusses anything from approval of salary ranges and salaries (its rightful province) to suggestions on how the job evaluation system could be improved — which is a responsibility of the personnel department. The overlap is both wasteful and confusing. Companies that have a systematic approach to the use of committees usually find that this danger can be avoided by setting out a charter in writing for each committee. This specification usually outlines some or all of the following:

- Function and scope of the committee
- Responsibilities
- Authority
- Organizational relationships

2. *Members of the committee should be carefully selected.* Generally, it is wise to have the members of the group of equal status. One of the most common failings of committee action is that one man, who is superior in position to the other members, is able to sway the thinking of the group because of his position. If the members of the group are expected to discuss and contribute on an equal basis, they should be of

similar organizational rank. The manager will think twice before he opposes his vice-president; the vice-president may be uncomfortable if he has to disagree with the chairman of the board. Many companies find, however, that differences in rank are not so critical if the committee members chosen represent different departments.

Some individuals are constitutionally incapable of effective committee action. With subordinates, they are domineering; with superiors, they are obsequious; and with peers, they are quarrelsome. Proper selection of committee members requires a nice judgment as to personality differences, ability in expression, as well as status.

3. *The committee chairman should understand his proper role.* Primarily, the chairman's job is that of expediting and facilitating the progress of the meeting. An executive sometimes wants to use a committee to advise and counsel him, and at the same time to participate as its chairman. When this is the case, he needs to be a highly skilled discussion leader if he is to get the best the group has to offer, rather than an expression of what the group thinks he wants to hear.

The committee chairman's job is to encourage others to express themselves, to settle differences, and to add a touch of humor when the going is rough. He is an arbiter, a peacemaker and an expediter. He should not be a special pleader, an advocate of one point of view or a judge of the opinions being expressed. In practice, the chairman usually finds that he is more the servant of the group than its leader. He does what needs to be done to get maximum cooperation and participation. His job is to get members of the group to think, not to think for them.

4. *The committee should be of proper size.* If the group is too large, many of the members will not have adequate opportunity to express their viewpoints. A large committee with many vocal members may become chaotic. The more people he has to contend with, the more difficult it is for the chairman to keep the discussion moving in productive channels. When the group is too small, it becomes difficult to secure a well-rounded viewpoint. And there is more of a tendency for the members to take sides on every point that comes up. Specialists usually recommend from five to nine as best for the average committee meeting.

5. *There should be adequate preparation for the committee meeting.* If committee meetings are to be productive, little time should be wasted on "make ready" and clerical details during the meeting itself. The chairman should be provided with adequate clerical and staff assistance, so that he can furnish all available factual data for each member before the meeting starts. Or the chairman or secretary of the group can review the data at the beginning of the meeting. Most companies find it is a waste of time to ask the group to volunteer basic facts and background information during the meeting.

Many committee chairmen recommend that the following steps be taken before every committee meeting:

● Notice of the meeting should be sent out as far in advance as possible. Many feel that at least a month's notice will enable people to schedule trips and appointments before or after the committee meeting and thus help to conserve their time. A week is considered an absolute minimum except in cases of emergency.

● Give as much information as possible about the meeting as far in advance as possible. A properly prepared agenda will give the members of the committee an opportunity to think about the subject matter, make inquiries, read and study pertinent data and reports.

● Set an exact beginning and ending time for the meeting. This will help the members to arrange schedules, and make it convenient for secretaries to hold telephone calls until the meeting is over.

6. *Follow a logical procedure in conducting the meeting.* Many chairmen limit their leadership to statements such as "Well, what do you think about it?" and "Let's go on to something else." If the time of the committee members is to be invested most wisely, many experienced committee chairmen recommend that some sequence of logical thinking be followed to carry the discussion in an orderly fashion to a logical conclusion. A sequence which has repeatedly yielded good results is the following:

● Review of the pertinent facts by the chairman
● Analysis of the problem in terms of what caused it, if this has not already been brought out, and determining how committee members feel about it
● Suggested solutions
● Group decision or recommendation

The important requirement is that the entire group think together on each step of the sequence. This builds up the necessary background and makes a logical decision possible.

In some companies, the consensus of the meeting is secured by majority vote. Others require concurrence by all members. Still others accept the recommendation of the majority, but record the viewpoints of the dissenters.

7. *Adequate follow-up is necessary.* If the committee presents a recommendation or comes to a decision, appropriate means are necessary to ensure that the intent of the committee is carried out. Usually this is accomplished by making the chairman, secretary or a committee member responsible for whatever follow-up action is required. In all cases, minutes of the committee should be prepared and distributed to each

member and to designated members of company management. Some companies require that minutes be prepared and distributed no later than the third working day after the meeting is held.

6. *The work of the committee should be constantly evaluated.* Many companies have periodic reviews of the work of each committee. They determine if it is operating effectively in terms of the purpose for which it was established and whether that purpose is still valid. If this type of control is not instituted, committees often become self-perpetuating. They may waste time, clog administrative channels and take managers from more important work.

ORGANIZATION AND THEORIES ABOUT THE NATURE OF MAN*

L. F. Urwick

In the September number of the Journal, James L. Gibson paraphrased Anthony Downs, saying that "the organization man of to-day is suspicious, distrustful, jealous, deceitful, self-centered, apathetic and immature. He is intolerant of differences, unable to communicate in depth with his fellows, and short-sighted. In short, here is a man whose integrity and moral fibre should be seriously questioned."[1] And he finished his article, "If it is concluded that such behaviour is a necessary concomitant of organizations, I for one will count it a cost" (p. 245).

He "urged organization theorists and practitioners to express explicitly their assumptions about the nature of man" (p. 234). And he included this writer among "classical organization theorists" who "owe an intellectual debt to Max Weber" (p. 236). May the writer at this point insert a word of personal explanation? He has never read Max Weber. He did not create "big business." That development of finance capitalism was largely an American invention. He agrees with Gibson that "the bureaucratic form of organization was (and is) prominent in business practice" (p. 237). But that may be, not because anyone put it there deliberately, but because it is inescapable if systems of human collaboration are developed beyond a certain size. It is certainly found in all governments larger than the Greek city states, in armies and in most forms of human cooperation that develop beyond the face-to-face leadership of a small handful of individual "followers."

In the United States, of course, bureaucracy is a "dirty" word to many individuals. It stands for the strains and inefficiencies associated with government. Some of its characteristics are, however, present, even where face-to-face leadership is still possible, as in an orchestra. A large orchestra has subdivision and specialization of tasks — the wind instruments and the strings. Sometimes these groups develop intergroup rivalries and tensions; the second violins can't get along with "that bloody drummer." An orchestra has "standard practice instructions" — the score. It has personal leadership — the conductor. It is only when all these "influences" are melded, and each individual player is highly trained, that you get a distinguished rendering of a great piece of music. All concerned are united in the

---

*Reprinted with permission from *Academy of Management Journal*, March, 1967.

[1] James L. Gibson, "Organization Theory and the Nature of Man," *Academy of Management Journal*, IX, No. 3 (Sept., 1966), pp. 233-245.

common aim of making a success of the performance. Each member of the orchestra is, for the time being, first a musician and only second-arily an individual. The term "member" is not without significance.

A great modern enterprise, be it governmental, military, or economic, is as many times more difficult to integrate than an orchestra as there are separate "bits" not within sight and sound of each other. Indeed, it is a hundred or a thousand orchestras in different rooms, different build-ings, different plants, different cities, different countries, perhaps half-a-world apart — all trying to play the same score. The surprising thing is that men succeed in doing it as well as they do, not that there are strains and tensions accompanying their efforts to do it.

The situation is a completely novel problem: it is hardly a quarter of a millenium since the beginning of the modern technological revolution. And 250 years is a watch in the night in terms of human evolution. As Thorstein Veblen once wrote,

Most of those civilizations or peoples that have a long history have from time to time been brought up against an imperative call to revise their scheme of institutions in the light of their native instincts, on pain of collapse or decay. . . . But history records more frequent and more spectacular instances of the triumph of imbecile institutions over life and culture, than of peoples who have by the force of instinctive insight saved themselves alive out of a desperately precarious institutional situation, such, for instance, as now faces the people of Christendom.[2]

It is perhaps not irrelevant that that sombre passage was first published in March, 1914.

Three decades and two world wars later, after the Hawthorne Experi-ments, Elton Mayo and his colleagues, T.N. Whitehead and F.J. Roethlis-berger, were saying very much the same thing. Mayo wrote, "The so-called social sciences . . . do not seem to equip students with a single social skill that is usable in ordinary human situations. Sociology is highly developed, but mainly as an exercise in the acquisition of scholarship. Students are taught to write books about each others' books. . . . If our social skills had developed step by step with our technical skills there would not have been another European war."[3] Whitehead cautioned mankind, saying, "Whether he realizes it or not, the [modern industrial] executive is in danger of directing a formed society from without; a society that will evolve defence mechanisms and sentiments of antagonism if its social living appears to be in danger of interruption." This is an entirely new problem. "Never before have large numbers of men been re-quired to guard their society by means of an explicit social understanding;

[2]Thorstein Veblen, *The Instinct of Workmanship and the State of the Industrial Arts* (New York: MacMillan, 1914).

[3]Elton Mayo, *The Social Problems of an Industrial Civilization* (Boston, Mass.: Harvard University, Graduate School of Business Administration, 1945), pp. 20, 23.

for never before has a complex society dedicated its energies to unending technological progress."[4] And Roethlisberger added, "In the area of social skill there seems to be a wide gulf between those who exercise it — the actual administrators — and those who talk about it."[5]

Yet, despite the urgency of the situation, more than half the energies of those professionally devoted to the study of organization in the United States seem to be devoted to undermining the work of their predecessors rather than to building upwards on the foundations already laid.

Gibson's demand that "organization theorists and practitioners should express explicitly their assumptions about the nature of man" (p. 234) is, of course, as he very well knows or should know, a reactionary demand. It is an assertion that we can know nothing worth knowing about how human cooperation works until we have a complete psychology of group behavior. Individual psychology is a long way from being an exact science. Social psychology and sociology have scarcely begun to be sciences in any true meaning of the word. This demand is simply a means of throwing doubt on the slight progress we have made on *one* aspect of how human institutions work.

Nor is this demand necessary. It is a demand that elementary anatomy should explain the biochemistry of the human nervous system, which it has not yet done completely after four hundred years. And his demand is based on double talk, on the dual usage of the word "organization" in American practice, that is the use of "the" or "an organization" as a synonym for an institution as a whole. Earlier writers, in what Gibson describes as "the classical" or "mechanistic" tradition, weren't using the term organization in this meaning at all. They were using it of one aspect or function of the total problem of arranging human systems of collaboration, that aspect or function which was concerned with the arrangement of work. Insofar as they considered the people aspects of organization, they considered them under other terms such as coordination, control, leadership, morale. Because a child is sometimes described colloquially as "a little anatomy," we don't criticize anatomists because they aren't child psychologists. Classical organization theory was not and has never claimed to be a complete scientific description of how social systems work.

Nor was it "the objective of Taylor and his associates," as Gibson states, "to reduce the contribution of each workman to the smallest, most specialized unit of work possible" (p. 235). To try to find out exactly what you are asking people to do is *not* the same thing as assigning a task to a man neatly calculated to turn him into a moron. This criticism of Taylor's work is inaccurate. The subdivision of labour as a principle

[4]T.N. Whitehead, *Leadership in a Free Society* (London: Oxford University Press, 1936), pp. 79, 91.

[5]F.J. Roethlisberger, *Management and Morale* (Cambridge, Mass.: Harvard University Press, 1942), p. 138.

was a logical consequence of mechanized industry and was so stated by Adam Smith eighty years before Taylor was born:

The greatest improvements in the productive powers of labour, and the greatest part of the skill, dexterity, and judgment, with which it is anywhere directed, or applied, seem to have been the effects of the division of labour.[6]

The writer, and he counts himself a humble follower of Frederick Winslow Taylor, carried through a reorganization of office work in 1924-25 based on the principle of "job enlargement," though, of course, at that date, he had never heard of the term.[7] It seemed to him just common sense in dealing with people. The apprehensive old fuddy-duddy who had devised the soul-destroying routine which was displaced had also never heard of Taylor. He was merely afraid of giving people jobs which involved any training.

This kind of comment about "scientific management" simply ignores Taylor's constant preoccupation with up-grading men, whether workers or foremen.[8]

In order to design organization, as earlier students of management understood and used the term, it is not necessary to have a complete and scientifically defensible theory of human behavior. In fact it is only necessary to make one reasonably simple assumption about human behavior, that human beings cannot be expected to cooperate effectively for any common purpose unless both they and those who guide the system know what they, as individuals, are expected to do and when. Or, to put the same proposition in slightly different terms, the key to organization as earlier students understood the term is communication. An organization chart is a wiring diagram.

The late Chester Barnard probably did more to add to men's insight about organization than any other writer in this century. He stated this same point time after time in his famous *The Functions of the Executive.* "The possibility of accomplishing a common purpose and the existence of persons whose desires might contribute motives for contributing towards such a common purpose are the opposite poles of the system of cooperative effort. The process by which these potentialities become dynamic is that of communication." He returns repeatedly to the point that communication is the key to cooperation: "the essential executive functions . . . are, *first*, to provide the system of communication,"[9] and so on.

---

[6]Adam Smith, *The Wealth of Nations* (London: Oxford University Press, World's Classics, 1904), 1, 5. First published 1776.

[7]L. Urwick, *Organizing a Sales Office* (London: Victor Gollancz, 1928; Pitmans, 1938), p. 162.

[8]F.W. Taylor, *Scientific Management* (New York: Harper and Bros., 1947), "Shop Management" (1903), pp. 142, 143.

[9]Chester I. Barnard, *The Functions of the Executive* (Cambridge, Mass.: Harvard University Press, 1938), pp. 89, 217. See also pp. 82, 91, 94-5, 106, 113, 175.

Haire says, "Whenever we try to plan what an organization should be like, it is necessarily based on an implicit concept of man."[10] Simon and March say, "Propositions about organizations are propositions about human behaviour, and imbedded in every such proposition, explicitly or implicitly, is a set of assumptions as to what properties of human beings have to be taken into account to explain their behaviour in organizations."[11]

But elsewhere Simon has observed, "It hardly seems necessary to add that the sum total of facts we have accumulated about human behavior in organizations is still a pail of water in an ocean of ignorance."[12] So, if we are to follow his lead we must all move back to square 1, and executives facing actual problems of organization are, as far as his guidance is concerned, condemned to the unpropitious exercise of trying to swim in a bucket.

If one wishes to emphasize the word "behaviour" it is, of course, arguable that ultimately it is impossible to be exact about organization without a complete and scientifically valid analysis of human greatnesses, follies, loves, and hates covering all the races of man through all time—in fact the accumulated stories of history, philosophy, politics, semantics, and a dozen other "disciplines," since the world began. But, if one wishes to be practical and to accumulate a little insight into a disordered world, surely it is more "common-sensible" to start with what one can study with some hope of objective insight — the system of communication, and in short, to agree with Barnard. For that system does not depend primarily on persons. It is a system of communication between offices or positions, which are, for the time being, occupied by individual people, just as a telephone exchange is manned at one time by Miss Smith and at another time, possibly on the same day, by Miss Jones. This is, it is true, impersonal. Miss Smith or Miss Jones is more likely to reply "Operator speaking" to an inquiry, than "This is Mary Smith" or "Eliza Jones." And this impersonality can degenerate into inhumanity. But the point the writer wishes to make is that impersonality is much better than too personal a system. An undertaking dominated by personalities means an organization based on nepotism and "blue-eyed boys."

That large-scale undertakings do issue in strains and stresses is undeniable. But why? The writer would suggest that one other fact about human behaviour of which we are reasonably sure is that behaviour is, at least in large part, though with many failures and exceptions, determined by the culture into which a child is born and in which it

---

[10]Mason Haire as quoted by Gibson, *Academy of Management Journal*, p. 245.

[11]James G. March and Herbert A. Simon, *Organizations* (New York: John Wiley and Sons, 1958), p. 6.

[12]Harold F. Koontz (ed.), *Toward a Unified Theory of Management* (New York: McGraw-Hill, 1964), p. 80. Herbert Simon is quoted.

is brought up. One of the leading living sociologists in the United States has made the point that the culture of the United States is founded on a contradiction. Thus W. Lloyd Warner writes,

In the bright glow and warm presence of the American Dream all
men are born free and equal. Everyone in the American Dream has
the right, and often the duty, to try to succeed and to reach the top.
Its two fundamental themes and propositions, that all of us are equal
and that each of us has the right to the chance of reaching the top,
are mutually contradictory, for if all men are equal there can be no
top level to aim for, no bottom one to get away from, there can be
no superior or inferior positions, but only one common level into
which all Americans are born and in which all of them will spend
their lives. We all know such perfect equality of position and
opportunity does not exist. [13]

Need we look further for the underlying cause of what Gibson describes as "the pressure-packed and anxiety-ridden culture of the times"? (p. 245) If we put this reality alongside Veblen's sombre warning quoted earlier, as to the difficulty of adjusting customary ideas to changing circumstance, is it not obvious that the United States is offering to its citizens a hope which, in 999 cases out of every 1000, is bound to be falsified by events? Every child is brought up in the "American dream." But, as the size of undertakings grows, the pyramid narrows. There is less and less room at the top. There are more and more frustrated people, more and more grown-up children whose Horatio Alger-dream has turned to ashes.

That big business has raised the material standards of the American people out of all recognition is irrelevant. This is an advantage enjoyed more or less by everyman. But everyman is also a unique personality, an individual. He often has a wife, who frequently watches his progress in prestige more closely than he does. And who can blame her? Her man has the interest of the job and its accompanying social satisfactions. Particularly as her children grow up and away from her, she has only the waning interest of the man and such social satisfaction as she can distil vicariously from his place in the world.

To this incessant pressure we must add the fact that less than two centuries ago the United States was largely a nation of subsistence farmers, splendidly independent and needing no more than an occasional town meeting to regulate such affairs as they had in common. American citizens have been nurtured in a dislike of authority and a prevalent belief that it is morally undesirable for one man to exercise power over another. Americans are, as a people, unwilling to place any obstacle in the way of a man who is trying to reach the top, however unethical and socially undesirable his methods of doing so may be.

[13]W. Lloyd Warner, *Social Class in America — The Evaluation of Status* (New York: Harper and Row, 1960), p. 3. Originally published by Science Research Associates, Chicago, 1949.

A people thus conditioned to individualism and tolerance of the unethical practices by which some men pursue personal ambition have been
rather suddenly forced, by the rapid evolution of the large-scale business
undertaking under unified control, into a social framework where the very
virtues of three generations ago are handicaps. Is it surprising if they are
sometimes confused and ambiguous, that many individuals exhibit the un-
attractive characteristics which Gibson has listed? A completely new social
ethic, a philosophy adapted to organization forms to which individuals
are unaccustomed, takes time to evolve and to become the norm. It is
much to their credit that their clearest thinkers have already pointed the
way. Professor Peter Drucker, for instance, in his *The Practice of Management,* mentions integrity more than fifteen times as *the* quality essential
in a manager.[14] The moral fibre is there. What is missing in many instances
is awareness of how it can be applied to a new situation.

The solution will not be found by studying how people, caught in this
cultural dilemma, this dichotomy between ideas persisting from a handi-
craft culture and the realities of large-scale scientific production, behave
today, however many PhDs are awarded for such inquiries. Their current
behaviour is inevitably a reflection of a situation in which their social concepts have lagged behind their material achievements. Rather, a solution
will come, as Veblen suggested half a century ago, from "taking thought
how best to conduct industrial affairs and the distribution of livelihood in
consonance with the technical requirements of the machine industry."[15]
To be one player in a nation-wide or world-wide collection of orchestras
calls for an attitude towards music different from that of the solitary
fiddler at a village fair.

[14]Peter F. Drucker, *The Practice of Management* (New York: Harper and Bros.,
1954), pp. 147, 157(4), 158 (3), 196 (2), 345 (2), 348 (2), 349 (3), 378. The figures
in brackets show the number of times the word "integrity" appears on the page.

[15]Veblen, *op. cit.*

GAMES MANAGERS PLAY*

Louis Fried

The insights into social relationships suggested by Dr. Eric Berne's *Games People Play* indicate that a similar look at the world of management might be stimulating. The games identified in this sphere have been analyzed in a clinical manner to describe the players' overt activities and their covert or internally rationalized motives for their actions.

The "stone tablets" policy

The player assumes that past policy decisions should not be questioned regardless of their applicability to current conditions. He feels that if top management wanted to change the "commandments," it would do so.

The payoff. The player obtains a feeling of security from the stability of these policies "engraved in stone." He also attributes omniscience to management, investing it with godlike (or father-image) characteristics. This permits him to evade responsibility for errors so long as he obeys policy.

The crash program

This is a multiplayer game with two basic types: the Crasher (who initiates the crash program) and the Crashee (who has to perform the work of the program). The Crasher has often procrastinated to the point where only a special effort can solve the problem. This may be a deliberate effort to set himself up in a position to make a heroic contribution to the firm.

The Crash Program is related to another game called "Beat the Budget" in that it provides an opportunity for the manager of an understaffed function to raise an alarm that will permit him to indiscriminately ignore previous budget constraints. Instead of reporting that his function could not properly operate at the original level, he operates within the budget until his situation is critical and then demands the Crash Program.

The Crashee, too, can use the program to make a heroic contribution. He can also use the program as an excuse for games like Workhorse.

*Reprinted by permission of *Management Services*, November-December. Copyright 1967 by the American Institute of CPAs. As condensed in *Management Review*, September, 1968, published by the American Management Association, Inc.

The payoff. The Crasher can benefit from the notice of his superiors or by giving vent to his sadistic impulses. He also can free himself from constraints or convince himself that he can, by this effort, make up for previous negligence or error. Unfortunately, the Crash Program almost always costs more than the properly planned activity would have cost.

The Crashee may use the program to make an impression on his superior. He may also use it against the Crasher by faking his effort. This way he doubles his payoff by looking like a heroic worker while sabotaging the program to strike back at the Crasher's sadism.

Hot potato (HOPO)

This is the well-known game of passing the buck. It is often played in conjunction with Stone Tablets, Delayed Reaction Decision, or Consensus. HOPO flourishes in any area of weak authority or where conflicting lines of authority exist.

HOPO has a subgame called Recrimination in which, rather than just passing the hot potato, the players actively accuse each other of being at fault. Recrimination is not only a good smoke screen but, by using a technique of misdirection, can also consume a great deal of time. This dulls the original keen interest in locating the real source of a problem. There is also some chance that, given enough time, the problem will disappear.

The payoff. The player obviously hopes to advance by selectively taking credit for successes while avoiding the blame for failures.

Consensus

The executive interviews members of his staff on a question and as many of his superiors as he can safely approach. He then publishes the results of his survey as a "consensus" decision.

The payoff. The player is able to hide from responsibility behind a communal "we decided" when stating policy or decisions.

The delayed reaction decision

This game requires two players, a superior and a subordinate. The superior delays making urgent decisions until circumstances force his subordinate to act. The superior can then adopt the decisions if the results are good or blame the subordinate if the results are bad.

The subordinate plays his version, which might be titled, "You get your job." At the sign of a delay by his superior, the subordinate forces events and creates an atmosphere in which action appears necessary. He then acts and gambles on the outcome.

The payoff. The payoff to the superior is obviously a chance to stay out of trouble by sidestepping responsibility. Numerous executives of limited talent maintain a hold on top positions through skillful use of this game.

The payoff for the subordinate is multivalued. He may be seeking an outlet for masochistic impulses, in which case he will specialize in wrong decisions. On the other hand, he may be trying to make himself indispensable to a weak superior. This particular subordinate's end of the game could be titled "Eager Beaver."

Workhorse

The player of this game works at least six days a week and never less than nine hours per day. He finds excuses to come to work on holidays and never takes a vacation. He makes sure to be at work before his superior arrives and after he leaves. He triple-checks everything he does.

The payoff. Workhorse is not played for advancement. The Eager Beaver may play a game that looks like Workhorse, but he, being consciously after advancement, merely tries to create an impression without working.

The actual Workhorse player really works. The game is played for payoffs that vary with the motivation. Generally, however, the Workhorse player is a frightened under-achiever. He occupies a position beyond his normal capability and must therefore work much harder than average to do his job. The payoff for this player is survival in the firm.

Beat the budget

The object of this game is to manipulate the budget to accomplish a given purpose. Techniques are extremely varied. Subgames range from Martyr to Empire.

The Martyr player seeks advancement by demonstrating his ability to save the firm's money. This performance may lead to total disregard for accomplishing his stated purpose in a satisfactory manner. Martyr players try to find methods that are "cheaper but just as good" rather than do the originally defined task. This may — and usually does — result in unsatisfactory or inadequate performance. However, until such results are discovered, the player is a hero. When the results are discovered, he may play Martyr and claim credit for saving the firm's money.

Bright Boy. This player takes advantages of the timing relationship between budgets and short-run projects by using a method of flexible budgeting. The essence of the game is to budget after the project is completed. When the budget is exceeded on major projects, then Bright Boy can make his excuses palatable by pointing to his excellent past record of project budget comparisons.

The Empire player spends to the limit of his budget and beyond if circumstances will permit. If he approaches the end of a budget period with funds unspent, he finds some way to dispose of these funds.

Empire players are probably greater gamblers than Martyrs. The Empire player tries to assure himself successively larger budgets by his technique. The Empire game was a favorite during the cost-plus-fixed-fee government contract days and is still popular in R&D-oriented firms.

The payoff. Martyr and Empire represent two different routes to advancement. In fact, the Martyr may even go so far as to suggest elimination of his own job in the hope of advancing.

Bright Boy, on the other hand, is usually a game of survival rather than of advancement.

Musical chairs

This is an executive game for one player. The basic method is to use reorganization as an excuse for poor organizational performance. If a functional area of the firm has problems that do not seem to permit a rapid solution, then the player moves his supervisors into positions with which they are entirely unfamiliar. Naturally, each supervisor must learn the duties of his new position. This learning process takes time, during which the original problem cannot be cured. With luck, the problem may disappear.

But sometimes the transplanted supervisors create more problems by taking the move seriously and trying to modify the new areas before they're thoroughly familiar with them. On the other hand, there's always the remote possibility that some supervisor may solve the problem.

The payoff. Chairs is played to gain time and, to a lesser degree, on the long-shot hope that it may solve a problem. It's ordinarily used only when an executive can think of no immediate solution to problems.

Intramural politics (INTRAPOL)

This is the big game and all members of management (willing or otherwise) must play it. The previously mentioned games are all used in addition to these briefly described by their titles: Rumor, Crown Prince, Inside Track, Three-Way Parlay, and Gang-Up.

The payoff. INTRAPOL is generally played for advancement but may be played for survival. The heavy players are often identifiable by nervous characteristics, club trophies and handy supplies of dyspepsia preventives.

PARKINSON ON PAPERWORK*

C. Northcote Parkinson

Krupp, the giant German steel organization, centers on Essen. Before World War II it had 150 plants in a rather tight group around the town. This was fine for control, convenient for transportation, but in time of war it became a bombardier's dream. The result was that the Royal Air Force came over and wiped the plants out flat. By accident or uncanny precision, they left the head office unscathed. This brought forth a fascinating phenomenon.

Here was Krupp, not producing a thing. As soon as it tried it was bombed again. Yet the head office remained majestically in the center of its empire, its staff of 2,000 observing in practice what I have maintained in theory. They kept on working as busily as before.

I suspect these conditions might have left them *more* busy than before, but this apparently was not proved.

But it did confirm a theory that I have been playing with: that any organization with a head office staff of 1,000 people (and Krupp's was twice that) is administratively self-sufficient. It can keep busy by reading its own memoranda. It can live upon the paper it produces.

Krupp today is a very efficient firm. It must have learned a lesson for its head office staff has been cut to 250 executives, and company policy is to hold to that figure regardless of how the company grows. There are already 200,000 people on the payroll, and a new administration center is under way. But the directors, in their enlightenment, are providing office space for 250 executives and no more.

OVER-HIGH

In America, administrative managers are also learning lessons about the over-high overhead of paperwork. They are giving long-overdue attention to this subject, and I congratulate them.

In this area it is commonly thought that management can find a source of profit, derived not from increased sales or decreased production costs, but simply from lower overhead.

But you must remember that the cost of paperwork does not bear a constant ratio to an organization's output. It tends rather to rise in

*Reprinted with permission from *Administrative Management*, April, 1966. ©Kelly Girl Service, Inc

accordance with the law of nature to which I have modestly attached my name. One aspect of this law concerns the way in which rewards — salary, prestige — go to the man with the larger number of subordinates.

Friends of mine in the temporary-personnel industry have sought to explain this increase in terms of ordinary experience. Work, they remind us, is subject to seasonal fluctuations of climate and weather; the problems of transportation and industrial dispute; the sessions of politics, education and law, and the anomalies of the Christian, Moslem and Hindu calendars. The work load varies thus from week to week, spasms of activity being followed by periods of idleness, the latter made more frequent by the incidence of bottlenecks, delay over one thing holding up everything else. The permanent staff is established at the highest level to cope with the peak load, and is relatively idle at other times, the idleness being disguised partly by management and partly by the staff.

Up to a point I regard this as an accurate picture of what happens and, indeed, of what has always happened. In an agricultural society, the fluctuations of the work load are even more dramatic. The husband-man has to wait for the season just as the sailor has to wait for the tide, and a soldier has to wait for a war. And history is full of devices for dealing with the problem.

If you reduce the hours of work, telling people that because there is relatively little to do, they can arrive at 9 a.m. instead of 7, there is trouble when you revert to the old timetable. "But we never come until 9," comes the protest. "It's an ancient custom, we always leave at 4." So the supervisor finds work for the people to do. The Army and and Navy have many experts in this field. They find such work as scrubbing the decks and polishing the brasswork. In the cavalry, it used to mean cleaning out the stables. In commerce, it means checking inventory and balancing accounts to the last half-penny.

ELASTICITY

Originally the working day went from dawn to dusk, which automatically reduced a winter's day. The inventors of artificial light made it possible to work round the clock, with the result that working hours were fixed at an arbitrary number, overtime becoming the only element of elasticity.

But the problem remains of how to keep people occupied when there is little for them to do. This problem is sometimes solved by management, but more often by the employees themselves. The fact is, however, that pseudo-work has a demoralizing effect. It is more than a waste of money, it is the cause of inefficiency when the next peak of activity is reached. People who have been doing everything by the slowest method cannot be galvanized overnight into a different and quicker routine. Our policy should be to reduce the permanent staff, relating it to the minimum workload, while using temporary staff to deal with periods of peak activity. This is what the Post Office does every Christmas.

Alongside the *fluctuating* workload you have the problem of the *increasing* workload. You'd have *this* problem even if the workload didn't fluctuate — first, because of organizational growth from mergers and the like; second, because of new head-office control techniques, and third, because of the comparative importance attached to costs as applied to things, and costs as applied to time. The total volume of paper to be processed is affected by these factors, and it is this total volume, I suggest, that we should want to reduce.

The first of my points should be relatively familiar to any knowledgeable administrator.

So should the second, but permit me to observe that an administrator, in a seat of power near the computer, is possessed of a tool of control with which to assert himself — and all his instinct, an historic instinct, is to use it to the full. He can do what for centuries was impossible. He can exact the fullest information and issue the most detailed instructions; and the effectiveness of his control can be measured in tons of paper comprising statistics, reports, accounts, regulations, extrapolations, exhortations and advice. It is a very potent factor in the situation.

Now to my third point: the emphasis on things as opposed to time. The historic obsession of any administrator is with equipment, goods, machines and tools. This attitude dates from the period when wages were low and equipment relatively expensive. *Things* matter because they can be shown on the credit side of a balance sheet, subject to depreciation but nevertheless an asset. *People* appear only on the debit side as a continued expenditure. So the great aim is to check the inventory and detect pilfering of things like carbon paper and envelopes.

EXAMPLES

Does anyone think that these three factors exist only in my mind? I have already cited the example of the Krupp organization. Here is another — known perhaps to some of you [see "The Quiet Trend to Risk Taking," *AM*, July '65], but I will venture to repeat it — of a British chain store, known as Marks & Spencer, dealing mainly in clothing. The story begins when the chairman of the board visited a small branch in a provincial town on a Saturday afternoon, rather late, and found the staff absorbed with things called catalog cards. The chairman looked round, saw they were all busy and asked, "What are you doing?" They said, "Oh, we are filling in catalog cards." And he said, "What for?" They said, "Well, that is what you do with catalog cards. There is nothing else you can do with a catalog card — just fill it in, you see." When he looked at the document he couldn't see that it served any useful purpose. It got him thinking: were the cards really necessary? Then he started looking at other paper they were handling and asked whether a lot of that was really necessary. The final result was to eliminate approximately 20 million pieces of paper.

Marks & Spencer did this on three principles which remain basic to its administration policy: (1) Trust the local manager. (2) Trust the girls behind the counter, (3) Trust the customer. Anyone can now bring anything back to any branch of the firm and get a refund without argument — or paperwork. This is not a matter of benevolence but a result of discovering what paperwork costs. It is cheaper to give the money back and have done with it, than to process complaint forms, circulate them round and initial them at different levels.

I recite finally the example of British hospitals. I am careful not to say American hospitals, which I am sure are different in every way. British hospitals are peculiar institutions in which two traditions combine, that of the convent and the British Army. The monastic tradition (which involved the idea that the sisters and nurses weren't paid, or if they were paid, certainly no economic wage) was crossed with the British Army's passion for the rectitude of accounts and the checking of stores. In the Armed Forces you must have either the *item* or a *signature*.

This is the first rule of war. Well, you get this army tradition of checking the stores superimposed on the traditions of the convent. This means that nobody has until very recently tried to cost a nurse's time. As for the patients, they can bleed to death while the staff busily counts the blankets and the chamber-pots.

The discovery that the nurses' time spent in counting the equipment is worth more than the missing chamber-pot is a very recent one indeed in hospital practice. They will eventually discover that it is better to have an agreed pilfering rate, any departure from which will, of course, be *harshly criticized.*

RELATIONSHIP

I have dealt with various factors in paper work. I must emphasize that these factors are inter-related. The attempt to over-control kills all initiative on the circumference of the organization. It also kills all leisure at the center. The paper arrives in a quantity directly related to the degree of centralization being attempted. The staff must be large enough to cope with the flood (if only to file it). And the paper has a tendency to breed and multiply.

It starts off with someone saying, "Now we want a report, yes we want to know how many towels were used in the firm's lavatories last month." And out goes the decree. But the man who asks for it doesn't say, "I just want it for *last* month" and finish. He says, "I want a report." Twenty years later it will still be coming in. And the people who handle it then, carried away with artistic genius, will have added more and more questions with more and more elaboration, and so the overhead rises and rises.

This is, of course, one aspect of making work artifically in slack time. Any office acquires a life of its own, a personality, a tradition, a will to survive and a will to grow.

"I want the statistics on absenteeism," you say. Before long the absenteeism statistics section will need more clerks, more filing cabinets and more space for the filing cabinets, and the statistics required will become more elaborate. "Is absenteeism," they ask each other, "more characteristic of male or female, old or young, married or single, Protestant or Catholic, or Freemasons or Elks? Is it related to climate or latitude, or height above sea level? Is it affected by the moon or the sun or the baseball results?" The possibilities ramify but nothing is done to abolish absenteeism. Nothing at all.

Why, if you abolished it, you would kill the section, which has by now become a department. In much the same way when government sets up an anti-pornographic department, it perpetuates pornography as well as the department. No rodent control officer ever wishes to eliminate rats. He wants to continue a picturesque struggle against them. So it happens that an inflow of paper is more easily started than stopped.

Finally we must note that the paper flood has another effect. The administrative manager is himself pinned to his desk by the mere weight of correspondence. He has no opportunities to discover what is going on. He is defeated by his own office routine, and it is this paper flow which prevents the manager from discovering how little of the paper is really necessary after all. The fortunate manager who has succeeded in emptying his OUT tray is at the point where his day's work *ought* to begin.

CAUSES OF THE RISE OF INDUSTRIAL BUREAUCRACY*

Eugene V. Schneider

If bureaucratic organization has triumphed in industry, it is because bureaucracy has met certain needs inherent in large-scale production. What are these needs, and why have they resulted in bureaucracy?[1]

1. In general, bureaucracy seems to develop in any type of social organization which experiences considerable growth in size, especially if this growth is a long-term trend. The case of industry fulfills this condition for the growth of bureaucracy. Industrial expansion has not been based on a myriad of small establishments but, typically, on gigantic individual units or clusters of giant units. This pattern of growth has resulted, as we have seen, from the demands for efficiency, from the need to use central sources of power, and from the resultant superior profitability of large-scale enterprises. Today, as in the past, existing large-scale units tend to continue to grow in size, and large-scale production continues to invade areas formerly dominated by small-scale production. At least up to the present, this has been a well-nigh irreversible process. Only rarely has the opposite occurred, that is, the breaking up of the large-scale enterprise into small productive units.

As the size of industrial units has increased, the task of administration has increased in something like a geometric progression. The large-scale procurement of raw material, the necessity for hiring and training large numbers of managers, experts, and workers, the need to coordinate the activities of large numbers of men and machines, and the necessity for disposing of a great quantity of finished products — all these pose administrative problems of a vast scope. The solution of these administrative problems demands a corps of trained experts, centralized planning and control, efficient communication between various parts of the organization, discipline, and a complicated system of record keeping. In each of these respects, bureaucracy offers great advantages. It provides for specialized offices and a rigid system of central supervision. It provides

*Reprinted from *Industrial Sociology* by Eugene V. Schneider. Copyright 1957 by McGraw-Hill Book Company. Used with permission of McGraw-Hill Book Company.

[1]Weber, *From Max Weber: Essays in Sociology*, pp. 209-211; Marshall E. Dimock, *Bureaucracy and Trusteeship in Large Corporations*, Temporary National Economic Committee Monograph 11, Government Printing Office, 1940, chaps. V and VI; Alvin W. Gouldner, *Patterns of Industrial Bureaucracy*, Free Press, Glencoe, Ill., 1954.

means for enforcing discipline. It provides channels of communication, through which information and orders can flow. So great are these advantages that it seems doubtful whether a continuous large-scale industry could have developed, or could continue to exist, except within the bureaucratic framework.

2. The development of specialization in industry (that is, a very fine and increasing division of labor) has increased the need for bureaucracy in our system of production. Undoubtedly, specialization is possible within many different types of social organizations; for example, it occurs in the family. But bureaucracy offers certain advantages for the development of a particularly elaborate system of specialization. One advantage is that bureaucracy creates offices, with carefully defined spheres of operation. Specialization can, so to speak, be hung on the peg of the bureaucratic office.

Furthermore, the sharp separation of the bureaucratic office from all other nonindustrial roles coincides with the needs of industry. Industrial specialization demands single-minded devotion to the task at hand and the sloughing off of other roles during working hours.

Finally, the fact that bureaucratic offices are circumscribed by rules dovetails neatly with the needs of industrial specialization which depends upon elaborate rules as to the rate, quality, and precision of work.

3. Large-scale industrial production depends on the application of expertness and technical knowledge to the specialized task. This is true as much for the operation of a complex machine as for the conducting of a complicated experiment in a research laboratory or the administering of a managerial office. In fact, the ability to supply special scientific or technological knowledge to a given task is another factor in the superiority of the industrial system over other productive systems. Bureaucracy offers great advantages for the utilization of the expert and of specialized knowledge. For one thing, the bureaucracy, which is itself a rationalized social organization, helps to create the proper attitudes in its members for the application of rational knowledge and techniques. Furthermore, because the bureaucracy is divided into offices and positions which demand the full time and attention of those who fill them, there is the opportunity for becoming really expert at one job. This holds as much for the scientist in the laboratory as for the worker at a press. By way of contrast, we may consider how relatively little expertness could be achieved at any one task by the guild workingman who manufactured an entire suit of clothing. Bureaucracy is the natural habitat of the expert.

4. The development of a mechanized technology in industry has hastened the development of a bureaucratic social organization. Mechanization inevitably increases specialization and therefore, in the manner noted

above, the need for bureaucracy. Also, mechanization demands the coordination of human activities; there must be a steady supply of raw materials for the machines, various mechanized tasks must be integrated so that a smooth flow of work is maintained, uniformity in the finished products must be ensured. Such coordination demands not only careful and rational planning but also a rigorous system of discipline, both of which can be best attained under a bureaucratic form of organization. Furthermore, the bureaucracy provides opportunity for the efficient organization of production into departments such as procurement, production, inspection. For instance, successful regulation of the activity of the machine tender, both as to rate and quality of work, demands a rigid chain of command and discipline. Finally, only bureaucracy seems to be able to match the ever finer division of mechanized tasks with equally finely defined roles; both the machine process and bureaucratic organization seem to be almost infinitely divisible. It is hardly accidental then that the machine age is also the bureaucratic age.

5. The marriage of industry and bureaucracy is also founded on the need of industry for long-range planning, for rational calculation for the future. Industry needs long-range planning in order to meet future orders, in order to have adequate and proper types of raw materials on hand, in order to ensure itself of proper types of labor, in order that machines and plants may not suffer periods of idleness. Long-range planning is also needed in order that research on new products may be undertaken, in order that capital may be accumulated at a proper rate and invested wisely, in order that payrolls may be met. In fact, modern industry is founded on rational planning no less than on the machine technology. But if long-range planning is to be a success, a type of social organization is demanded in which the actions of individuals are controllable and predictable, in which the power of management to control the use of raw materials and machines is unchallenged. A type of organization is needed in which the power of human whim or fancy to disrupt a plan is reduced to a minimum. It will hardly be necessary to point out what advantages bureaucracy offers in this respect.

6. Finally, though by no means of least importance, industry finds in bureaucracy a means for creating and maintaining a continuous and rigid discipline over its personnel at all levels. The need of industry for the coordination of many diverse tasks, the need for fitting human activity to the highly rational and often monotonous routine of the machine, the need for long-range planning — all these demand a close supervision of work, a rigid obedience to rules, and the suppression of many natural human impulses.

These needs bureaucracy can meet in a number of ways. It will be recalled that, in a bureaucracy, the worker as well as the official is separated from ownership of raw materials or machines or other facilities. This means that both worker and official are economically dependent on the bureaucracy, and consequently are necessarily submissive to the demands of the organization. Furthermore, the fact that a bureaucracy assigns certain tasks to certain offices or positions, and surrounds each office or position with rigid rules, means that the quality and quantity of the performance of each worker or official can be determined, and properly rewarded or punished. Finally, the rigid lines of authority in the bureaucracy mean that responsibility for the performance of a task can be definitely located; someone must assume responsibility for deficiencies and failures, or receive credit for successes.

We may say, then, that the bureaucracy more nearly meets the needs of industry than any other type of social organization. The reason for this, as Max Weber said, [2]

has always been its purely technical superiority over any other form of organization. The fully developed bureaucratic mechanism compares with other organizations exactly as does the machine with the tool.

More specifically, Weber found the superiority of the bureaucracy in its[3]

precision, speed, unambiguity, knowledge of the files, continuity, discretion, unity, strict subordination, reduction of friction and of material and personal costs.

Undoubtedly, there are also social and cultural factors in the spread of bureaucracy in American industry. For instance, the development of mass markets, the development of rapid means of communication, the leveling of social classes have all, in various ways, played a part in the development of bureaucracy. However, the main reasons for the triumph of bureaucracy in industry seem to be inherent in the inner compatibility of bureaucracy and large-scale production.

It would be erroneous to suppose, however, that bureaucracy has failed to meet resistance in industry. Certain areas in industry have eluded the grasp of bureaucracy. For instance, there are certain informal groups in industry whose organization and aims are often diametrically opposed to those of the bureaucracy.

[2]Weber, *From Max Weber: Essays in Sociology*, edited and translated by H.H. Gerth and C. Wright Mills, Oxford University Press, New York, 1946, p. 214, by permission.

[3]*From Max Weber: Essays in Sociology*, p. 214. By permission.

READING 44

BEHOLD THE COMPUTER REVOLUTION*

Peter T. White

An even more graphic lesson awaited me at the Massachusetts Institute of Technology. The associate dean of engineering took me to a desk equipped with a TV screen, a keyboard, and a so-called light pen all connected to the same computer.

"Take the pen and draw on the screen," he said. "Lines of light will appear on the screen, in the path of the pen. Please draw a child's set of building blocks. When you are satisfied, press this key — your drawing will be stored in the computer's memory."

I was creating a model, so to speak, of a set of blocks. It was in the form of information stored in the computer, representing algebraic formulas based upon lines and curves. No need to worry about the mathematics, though; the computer's program took care of that.

"Now watch," said the dean. "I can command your blocks to become larger or smaller. I can change their shapes. And rotate them, to view them in different perspectives. I can arrange them as I like; I can erase them." He did all that, moving the light pen, pressing keys. I had never seen a fancier toy.

COMPUTER MODELS HELP DECISION MAKERS

"In the same way," said the dean, "we can create a model of something we really want to build. A school building perhaps, or a traffic interchange. Then we type in information on the physical site, on design requirements, and human considerations, on many factors affecting our project. The computer calculates these, and we can modify the model accordingly — add parts, delete parts, change some.

"We look at various stages of modification. We measure the effects and the costs. We are simulating things that might happen — to find the best choice, to make the best decision."

* * *

What if computer-equipped authority, insufficiently restrained, should turn hyperinquisitive someday? If every purchase one makes, down to the

---

*Reprinted with permission from the *National Geographic*, November, 1970.
NOTE: ✳✳✳ indicates the deletion of material by the editor.

last 10-cent newspaper, is recorded by a computer, showing where it was made and at what time; if millions of telephone conversations can not only be recorded daily but instantly scanned to pick out key words considered alarming by the surveillance officers. . . . The implications surpass the horrors of George Orwell's *1984.*

Dr. Jerome B. Wiesner, Provost of MIT, has said that the computer's potential for good, and the danger inherent in its misuse, exceed our ability to imagine. Wouldn't that be the worst it could do — to become an instrument of tyranny, propelling mankind into a new Dark Age?

Flying north over the snowy fields of New England, I thought of the best it might do. It might induce men to take a fresh look at the world. Let's call this the systems view, and let me explain how it was explained to me.

To make a useful computer model of a complicated process at work, one must first gather a mass of facts about that process. About the life cycle of the lobster. About the growth and decay of the cities. About the dynamics of the American economy, for the model now being built for the governors of the Federal Reserve System.

The finished model should help one decide what to do if one wants more lobsters, or healthier cities, or a healthier economy. But the greatest value of the model lies not in such specific guidance, but in the insight one gains in making the model, in what one learns while going after the factors that make up a complicated, ever-changing process.

In short, the common way of thinking in terms of simple cause and effect — the Newtonian, mechanistic view — is replaced by new awareness: of many causes, constantly producing varied effects, in what really are highly complicated and dynamic systems.

MAN AND COMPUTER: THE NEW PARTNERSHIP*

J. Stanford Smith

Almost from the day that the first electronic computer began operating in 1946, the computer has been recognized as a potentially revolutionary invention.

Self-appointed prophets told us that either Utopia or Armageddon was upon us: we would either be freed of the hard labor of thought, or the thinking machines would enslave us. But 15 years of experience with information systems built around the computer indicate that both these fantasies are unlikely to come true.

Instead, we seem to be entering an era in which man, and his information system, in a new partnership, can undertake much more complex tasks than ever before — to make human society more productive, and to make life more satisfying.

SWIFT PROGRESS

In the past 10 or 15 years, computer speeds have increased by a factor of 1000 to 1. Costs of computation have gone way down, on the order of 400 to 1. Memory capacity is up 1000 to 1.

Few technologies have experienced such swift progress. As a measure of the present commitment to electronic information systems — there are now over 40,000 such systems installed on a worldwide basis, with an if-sold value of almost $20 billion. Those numbers are expected to more than double by 1975.

But raw numbers tell us little about the tremendous human achievements this represents, and the impact of the information systems on our everyday life.

AT WORK IN INDUSTRY

On their television screens, the people have seen the banks of computers involved in the launching of space probes to the moon and planets. This symbolizes, for the citizen, the impact of information systems on modern science and engineering.

Engineers now use information systems as a matter of course in the design of products of a much more mundane nature than the exotic

*Reprinted with permission from *The General Electric Forum*, Winter, 1967-68.

space vehicles and military systems. From making steel to designing jet engines to controlling the blend of ingredients for cake mixes — computers are involved in making the common artifacts of life.

Manufacturers use information systems for production control, inventory scheduling, and factory planning. There are some observers who feel that one underlying reason for the unusually long and even growth of the U.S. economy in the past seven years has been the use of computers by individual businesses in inventory control.

Market analysis, order scheduling and follow-up, and so on have made the computer useful in marketing. And the bookkeeping drudgery of payroll and billing tasks has been transferred largely to electronic information systems.

CATERING TO VARIED PREFERENCES

It is interesting to note that early prophets predicted the reduction of humans to statistics by computer accounting. Instead, it has worked the other way. Electronic systems now enable companies to offer individual employees a much wider variety of payroll and benefit plans tailored to individual needs. And business concerns can cater to a wide variety of tastes and preferences among their customers. With manual bookkeeping, this was simply impossible.

These common tasks of mathematical application in business — design, simulation, production scheduling, inventory control, market analysis, payroll, and customer records — will continue to be the biggest use of computers in the period ahead.

But more subtle and far-reaching uses of electronic information systems are beginning to assume major importance. Let me cite four of them.

UNDERSTANDING NATURAL PHENOMENA

One is the new insights computer-mathematical techniques are granting to physical, biological, and social scientists. Once-mysterious natural phenomena are yielding their secrets as scientists see new patterns in massive amounts of data.

Perhaps the most familiar of these activities, to the public, is the analysis of data on weather. In like manner, electronic information systems are helping man find new understanding of the dynamics of the stars and planets — and of the atom and the living cell. Even social phenomena such as population growth and political and economic behavior are yielding to computer-aided study.

DEVELOPING BUSINESS AND GOVERNMENT POLICY

The second increasingly important use of information systems is in policy decision-making, both in government and in business.

Managerial decision-making will always involve human judgment, but new concepts and computer-oriented techniques have been developed that both suggest and evaluate a wider variety of options than the manager could seriously consider heretofore. The added feature of risk analysis enables the manager to measure the degree of risk involved in a variety of strategies.

Econometric models, for the whole national economy as well as individual companies, enable policy-makers to "run through the computer" combinations of policy decisions, to see what impact they would have — not only on the economy as a whole, but also on significant parts of it.

REDUCING THE TECHNOLOGY GAPS

When computers were first introduced in the business world, it was feared that (because of the expense) they would only be useful in the very big corporations. Similar complaints have been sounded about a "technology gap" between the United States and Europe, partly because of the U.S. lead in computer capacity.

But events are proving otherwise. Ingenious use of small computers and, even more, the development of time-sharing information services, have now brought computer-power within easy, economical reach of businesses of all sizes, both in the United States and abroad. Now it appears that the electronic information system may be the "great equalizer" — enabling smaller companies and smaller economies to match their larger competitors in productivity and technological development.

Time-sharing enables dozens of people to use a computer at the same time, through separate keyboards — and share the cost among them. The keyboards can go anywhere a telephone line can reach. There's no need for people to wait in line for computer time. They can sit at the nearest terminal (often in their own office), type their problems, and get immediate answers.

General Electric opened the first time-sharing information service centers in Phoenix and New York City in 1965. Now the Company has more than 25 time-sharing systems operating on a commercial basis in the United States, and is opening them in Europe, Canada, and Australia. More than 50,000 individuals are now tied in with this service.

Thus, small, as well as large, companies, governmental units, schools, and colleges now have instantaneous access to advanced techniques for computation, testing, modeling, simulation, data storage and retrieval, and problem-solving by way of time-sharing information service centers.

COMPUTERS IN EDUCATION

Perhaps the most exciting new possibility is the widespread training of college students, and even of secondary-school students, in the use of computers. The well-educated man of the 1970s will use computers as comfortably as he now uses books and telephones. This is already true of students at Dartmouth College. As Professor Kemeny reports, about 80 per cent of Dartmouth's undergraduates have had personal experience in operating a computer, using the highly practical computer language called BASIC.

I talked with a couple of juniors at Dartmouth the other day. They had been using computers from their first days at college. And they were surprised that this is not done at every college; they took computer training and computer availability for granted, like libraries and cafeterias.

After ten years of observing the information revolution, I completely subscribe   to a 1967 statement of the President's Science Advisory Committee:

The handicap of a lack of understanding and skill in the use of computers is extremely severe in all areas in which data analysis is vital, in learning as well as in practice — in business, in the social sciences, in psychology, in geology, in the health sciences, for example. In a very real sense, students who have not learned to use computers are badly equipped for the postbaccalaureate world. [1]

Going further, experience with computers should be part of every liberal education for the same reasons that humanities students are obliged to take science courses. One cannot fully understand the emerging culture without a first-hand knowledge of electronic information systems.

A QUIET REVOLUTION

Thus the information systems built around the electronic computer are, in such a short time, creating their quiet revolution in human society. They are already taking on the mathematical drudgery of operating a large, industrialized economy. They are making business firms, governments, educational institutions and national defense operations much more efficient.

Beyond that, they are helping us find new insights into natural phenomena. They are bringing new certainty into the processes of policy-making. They are accelerating the growth of small companies and small economies, no less than the large. As these techniques become familiar to a new generation of students, the partnership between man and his information systems will become an ever more creative force for progress at all levels of human society. Our challenge is to make this amazing new 20th-century technique available to every business, government, school, and profession that can benefit from its capabilities.

---

[1] Report of the President's Science Advisory Committee "Computers in Higher Education," page 9. U.S. Government Printing Office, February, 1967. For a free copy of the full text, write: Information Service Dept., General Electric Co., P.O. Box 620, Schenectady, N.Y. 12305.

SYSTEMS: SEMANTICS AND SIGNIFICANCE*

Justin G. Longenecker

References to systems are sprinkled through current writings of management theorists and the language of today's managers. Any individual conversant with recent developments knows something about systems analysis, information systems, open systems, marketing systems, feedback systems, social systems, weapon systems, and computer systems.

A reader must wonder at times whether systems terminology is merely a type of jargon contrived by the younger breed of managers and writers. Is the systems concept a new and useful concept, or is it simply a matter of semantics? This article indicates that it is probably a little of both.

THE SYSTEMS CONCEPT

A system is a group or combination of component parts arranged in such a way as to constitute a unified whole. A case, hands, spring, face, stem, and other parts are fastened together to form a watch which keeps time and provides this information to the user. If the parts were simply placed unassembled in a cup, they would not be a watch. The idea of order, plan, or meaningful arrangement is significant.

There are obviously many different types of systems — the machine, the human body, the business organization. There are also solar systems, defense systems, governmental systems, philosophical systems, and so on. Scientists have found the systems concept intriguing because of the nexus it provides among different scientific disciplines.[1]

The systems concept in traditional management theory

Any type of management utilizes the systems concept in at least rudimentary form. By its very nature, a business organization is a type of system, relating people and functions in some meaningful way.

Managers have long dealt with the problems of interrelationships of parts even though they lacked a systems terminology. Such labels as "organizing," "teamwork," and "coordination" describe an approach that

---

*Reprinted with permission from *S.A.M. Advanced Management Journal,* April, 1970.
[1]See, for example, Kenneth E. Boulding, "General Systems Theory — The Skeleton of a Science." *Management Science,* April 1956, pp. 197-208.

is inherently similar to that implied by systems theory. To coordinate the work of subordinates, for example, a manager is concerned with efficiently meshing their respective contributions.

An awareness of this traditional usage of the underlying systems concept makes one suspicious of the present systems lexicon. Does systems theory merely impose a new set of labels on age-old problems of organizational relationships? On the surface, it seems to offer little new except semantics. Before dismissing the movement as mere jargon, however, we must examine some of its unique features and emphases. Even though systems theory is not entirely novel, it may strengthen or improve traditional thinking about organizations and their performance.

INTEGRATION OF SUBSYSTEMS

Managers place varying degrees of emphasis on the interrelationships of parts. At one extreme, managers concentrate upon the efficient functioning of individual parts. Any attention to interrelationships is secondary. Department managers display this attitude when they focus upon their own departmental problems and overlook their contributions to other parts of the firm. Any neglect of important relationships results in some degree of inefficiency.

The systems concept is useful because of its strong emphasis upon these interrelationships. These interrelationships are stressed as being of primary importance. The role of management is seen as the management of interrelationships. This emphasis avoids some of the pitfalls of a "components" mentality in which departments work out their own relationships in a haphazard manner.

SOCIAL PROBLEMS

Traditionally, we have examined community and other social problems one at a time. There were traffic problems, garbage disposal problems, smoke abatement problems, educational problems, juvenile delinquency problems, housing problems, law enforcement problems, and so on. Private citizens, business firms, other private organizations, and public agencies did what they could to deal constructively with these various problems. Many of the solutions were ingenious, and the public welfare was greatly enhanced by the public and private efforts to deal with these matters of mutual concern.

The usual approach in all of these programs, however, was to treat each problem as an isolated problem. As long as social relationships and community life were simple, this approach was satisfactory. But economic growth, increasing population, congestion, and an increasing mutual interdependency of the citizenry revealed flaws in the simple, direct, and effective approaches of the past. Smog, for example, was caused by domestic trash burning and auto exhausts as well as by industrial smokestacks. Control of juvenile delinquency and other crime required consideration of housing, education, and law enforcement programs.

To some extent, these interrelationships were recognized all along. But an increasingly complex society made more explicit acknowledgment necessary if viable solutions were to be achieved. Current experimentation and developments in the solution of social problems suggest the direction that we are moving in applying systems concepts.

One example of the numerous studies and programs in this area is a research project of Dr. Isidor Chein of New York University. Dr. Chein has developed a model to estimate effects of housing projects and social welfare programs on juvenile delinquency.

The model contains some 45 social and economic factors, ranging from income and educational background to the density of the teenage population and the adequacy of living units in 2,000 New York City neighborhoods. The incidence of delinquency is measured against the number, type, and degree of public housing, neighborhood projects and similar social programs. In this way Dr. Chein has a model which can give him a statistical idea of what happens to the juvenile delinquency rate as more public housing is built or a mix of social programs is implemented.[2]

In 1965, four aerospace companies started systems studies for the State of California dealing with problems of crime, control of wastes, information flow in government, and transportation. Litton Industries contracted with the government of Greece to apply the systems approach to the economic development of Crete. In 1968, TRW, Inc., subjected Cleveland's urban problems to systems analysis.

Cancer research laboratories have employed the systems approach in their search for a cancer vaccine. As of 1969, laboratories throughout the U.S., and some abroad, were performing their research as a giant team under the coordination of National Cancer Institute virologist Dr. Frank J. Rauscher.

For the first time, the technique of systems analysis developed in the aerospace industry is being focused on a single goal in a major health project.[3]

THE OPEN SYSTEM

Although systems theory recognizes both open and closed systems, it is particularly relevant to open systems. All living systems are open systems by virtue of their interaction with their environment. Business organizations receive inputs from their environment (labor, materials, and so on)

[2]Robert W. Sarnoff, "The Social Uses of Computer Forecasting," *Michigan Business Review*, Vol. 21, No. 2, March, 1969, p. 28.

[3]"Hunt for Cancer Vaccine Closes In," *Business Week*, No. 2098, November 15, 1969, p. 68.

and send outputs (products, services, pollution) into their environment. They thus constitute a type of open system. Development of systems theory, therefore, focuses attention upon a firm's boundary relationships.

The emphasis upon external relationships is a healthy emphasis because of the tendency of business management toward preoccupation with internal affairs. Inside the firm, problems of production, cost control, personnel grievances, budgeting, information flow, and sales management are sufficient to require the major attention of the firm's executive team. Problems related to the external world are less demanding and often unrecognized until it is too late. A clear understanding of significant developments in the firm's relationships with the outside world demands a great sensitivity toward these relationships and a careful analysis of changes.

Ford's phenomenal success with the Mustang, in sharp contrast to its dismal failure with the Edsel, rested upon an accurate appraisal of forces in the marketplace. Likewise, the leadership of Henry Ford II and the Ford Motor Company in attacking the problem of hard-core unemployment through the National Alliance of Businessmen reflects an awareness of environmental change. The action of Ford and other business firms involved in this program recognizes the nature of the need and the rising expectations of our society that business should contribute to the solution of this major social problem.

It is obviously true that the terminology of systems theory need not be used in order to develop an increased awareness of the firm's environment. The open system idea of systems theory, however, encourages and reinforces steps in this direction.

MANAGEMENT SCIENCE

Coupling of the systems concept with the methodology of statistics and mathematics has permitted the development of management science and its application to decision making. One of the hallmarks of operations research is its analysis of business problems in the light of the total organization. The tools of operations research are used to optimize results on an organization-wide or company-wide basis.

The importance of the systems viewpoint in operations research is evident in the following comment upon its unique nature:

But management has always sought to acquire all the facts, a knowledge of all alternatives, and the probable impact of action decisions taken. What is new, then, about operations research? The answer lies in the broadness of perspective, in the interdisciplinary, scientific approach to a problem, and in the set of mathematical and statistical tools brought to bear upon the solution of problems.[4]

[4]H.N. Broom, *Production Management*, Revised Edition (Homewood: Richard D. Irwin, Inc., 1967), p. 98.

Note the emphasis upon the breadth of perspective involved in operations research. An attempt is made to optimize overall operations, and this sometimes requires suboptimization for particular departments or divisions.

Systems thinking, then, provides the basic rationale for a management scientist. He solves business problems in terms of the total system, avoiding the fragmented solutions that resulted previously. Scientific management has been with us for almost a century, but the development of operations research methodology during the past two decades demanded a systems viewpoint.

SUMMARY

The systems theorist uses some very old concepts with strikingly new labels. He talks about "inputs," "feedback," and "suboptimization," whereas the traditional manager used "planning" and "coordination" to achieve similar goals of effective teamwork. To some extent, therefore, the differences are semantic.

Even though these basic similarities exist, systems theory provides valuable concepts and emphases for current management thought and practice. In particular, it provides the following contributions to understanding and analysis:

1. A strong emphasis upon significant interrelationships within a business firm, counteracting tendencies toward a provincial concern with one's own department or segment of the total business.
2. An extension of this emphasis upon interrelationships into a macro setting, permitting a more realistic evaluation of complex social problems.
3. A stress upon the open nature of business systems, thus focusing attention upon the firm's relationships with its environment.
4. A basic rationale for the management scientist as he applies the tools of operations research to the solution of business problems.

Systems concepts, therefore, offer a blend of something old and something new. Their valuable and distinctive contributions may be used more comfortably and understandingly by one who has an appreciation of their ancestry.

READING 47

THE AFFLUENT ORGANIZATION*

Raymond E. Miles

A few years ago economist John Kenneth Galbraith marched through the china shop of classical economics, deliberately shattering cherished possessions right and left.[1] His attack was not bull-like, but precise, and he took special aim at the greatest treasure of all — scarcity. His purpose was to demonstrate that the modern dilemma in our society is not how to conserve limited resources but, rather, how to deal with, develop, and distribute our unrecognized abundance.

It is time, in my opinion, for a similar march through the antique-lined aisles of management thought. For what is true in the macroworld of our total economy seems also to hold in the microworld of the business organization. The typical company, I believe, suffers from an inability, or perhaps an unwillingness, to handle its own affluence. The challenge to modern management is not to control and conserve but, rather, to create an environment in which its already abundant resources can be utilized.

To carry my parallel a step further and to sharpen the point of my criticism, let me again refer to Galbraith. He suggested that our abundance, while dramatically large, is uneven. He pointed out first the portly posterior of the private sector of our economy, and then the relative emaciation of the public sector. In an example perhaps only slightly more timely in 1958 than today, he suggested that the specific task facing our economy is how to shift some of our investment dollars and creative talent away from tail fins and toward schools, hospitals, parks, and so forth.

Similarly, in the modern organization, there is an unevenness to the recognition and utilization of abundance. With dollar resources and machines, there is typically an unfettered drive to maximize employment and return. But the people sectors of the organization — its human resources — remain underdeveloped and underemployed. Constraints — some necessary, others structured on habit and myth — exist at every level. The individual organization member is seldom challenged to develop, or allowed to use, his full capabilities. Departmentalization too

*Reprinted from *Harvard Business Review*, May-June, 1966. ©1966 by the President and Fellows of Harvard College; all rights reserved.

[1]*The Affluent Society* (Boston, Houghton-Mifflin Company, 1958).

often grows along lines which serve as barriers to, rather than opportunities for, uncovering and utilizing the talents of department members.

Finally, traditional limits on the ways and means by which the organization can serve society and itself are too often accepted without question. The failure to explore these boundaries frequently places artificial constraints on the growth and development of the organization, and thus restricts the amount of challenge and opportunity available to its membership.

It is important to emphasize that the challenge to organizations to reappraise their human investment is not made on purely moralistic grounds. Galbraith's argument for a better balance between the public and private sectors of our economy reflected eminently practical economic principles — for both the short and the long run. Similarly, the call for modern organizations to reexamine the constraints binding up their human resources is based on economic concepts rather than welfare concepts, although an argument can be made on the latter grounds. It is simply a demand that managers carry out the entrepreneurial function that is theirs both by acquisition and default. Fulfilling this role, managers at every level have a basic economic obligation to recognize and to make more meaningful use of the skills, talents, and creativity of the people whom they direct.

Before attempting to develop these points, one further and important parallel linking the analysis of the affluent society with the analysis of the affluent organization should be considered. Many of the charges which Galbraith made concerning our economy were not entirely original; they had been made before and had gone largely unheeded. One crucial value of his message, however, was its timeliness. He levied his criticisms at a time when, in the face of tremendous potential, our hesitancy and uncertainty were forcing the economy to hobble along at a needlessly slow pace. Galbraith's message was two-pronged. He suggested that not only can we ill afford to continue to ignore our abundance but also, because we are affluent, we can well afford the risk involved in attempting to enjoy it.

Again, what is true in the larger system of the economy is also true in the subsystem of the firm. Charges that organizations are failing to realize their potential have also been made before with similarly small effect. But the abundance that exists in organizations today is both a challenge and an opportunity. It is a matter of debate whether organizations can, without serious costs, continue indefinitely to ignore their human assets. The point is that they need not. Most, in my opinion, are affluent enough to afford the gamble. This is, it seems to me, a most opportune moment for organizations to rekindle the entrepreneurial flame and to take some reasoned risks in an effort to tap and utilize their human resources.

In the balance of this article, I will attempt to strengthen the above points, and to provide answers to some of the more obvious questions.

The discussion will reveal why I believe organizations are rich in human resources, what the constraints at various levels are which currently limit the use of these resources, and, perhaps most important, why I feel organizations can and should now take the risk to make use of these resources.

ORGANIZATIONAL ABUNDANCE

Formal organizations, I believe, have almost always been more richly endowed with human resources than they have recognized. In this sense, affluence is not a uniquely modern phenomenon — only the magnitude has changed.

The very nature of formal organizations forces them to ignore some portion of their human resources. To organize, in fact, means to attempt rationally to structure both the external and internal environments of a group. The organization must select from its external environment certain goals or targets — that is, it must define the tasks which it will seek to perform and thus limit its total pattern of interaction with the system in which it operates. It must then seek to structure its membership in an effort to bring some assortment of talents and skills to bear on the tasks which it has chosen to perform. It follows that an organization can decrease or enhance the value of its human resources, whatever their absolute level, by the skill with which it both uncovers meaningful tasks to be performed and seeks out and arranges the existing and potential talents of its members to accomplish them.

Unseen costs

Good management calls for locating the proper balance between efforts, on the one hand, to draw out and utilize human resources and, on the other hand, to limit and order the contributions of organization members in the interest of coordination and control. Since human talents and skills take on measurable value only when they are actually applied to meaningful tasks, however, the costs of ignoring these resources are not immediately visible. The typical organization thus too often places far more weight on the side of stability and control than on that of development and utilization.

The direction in which management tends to lean is illustrated in the recent comment of a business school alumnus, speaking to a group of degree candidates: "Once you get on the job," he stated, "you can forget everything you learned here. The company will teach you what it wants you to know."

When the talents of the bulk of the organization's membership are minimal, when their interests are shallow and parochial, and when their concerns are shortsighted and entirely self-centered, the losses caused by excessive structure and control may not be too large. However, when the capabilities of the organization's members grow and their interests expand, the costs involved in failing to draw out their talents and to find valuable outlets for them also grow. Furthermore, these costs have grown dramatically in recent years. This is because the riches have continued to pile up at a growing rate while the recognition of them has remained at a consistently low level.

Unfulfilled needs

Organizations grow rich as society grows rich. Each new generation is larger than the last because it enjoys better food and better medical care. It knows more because its total educational opportunities are greater at school and at home (although Dad may have a little trouble helping Junior solve his homework problems in the new math).

Not only is each new generation bigger and brighter than its predecessors, but it is also more alert, more sophisticated, and more concerned with the world around it. The modern generation has been bent by the winds of change pushing against all of our social institutions. It wants and expects more from all phases of life — *purpose, meaning,* and *challenge* are its bywords — and it is not at all certain that a career in business will satisfy these needs.[2] Obviously, these capabilities, interests, and concerns range from very high to very low, but the mean has moved up, as it inevitably does over time.

Moreover, newer generations are moving into organizations whose current members are already concerned over lack of opportunity and challenge. Among managers, the chance to contribute meaningfully — to make use of their talents in goal setting and decision making — is frequently listed as their least fulfilled need.[3] Further, managers at all levels tend to view their own resources as largely untapped, and their creativity and concern as constrained by their own superiors. They view their jobs as similar to those of their own subordinates, demanding primarily "other-directed" traits.[4] In their own minds at least, they are boss-like people in subordinate-like jobs.

Down the hierarchy, workers frequently place the chance both to contribute and to do meaningful work near the top of their list of needs.[5] They dream initially of escaping the confines of their organizational role

---

[2] See Peter Drucker, "Is Business Letting Young People Down?" HBR November-December 1965, p. 49.

[3] See Lyman W. Porter, "Job Attitudes in Management: I. Perceived Deficiencies in Need Fulfillment as a Function of Job Level," *Journal of Applied Psychology,* December 1962, p. 375.

[4] See Lyman W. Porter, *Organizational Patterns of Managerial Job Attitudes* (New York, American Foundation for Management Research, 1964).

[5] See Rensis Likert, *New Patterns of Management* (New York, McGraw-Hill Book Company, Inc., 1961), p. 50.

and striking out on their own. These dreams, however, diminish over time. The family grows, the obligations accumulate and the chance — if it ever was there — may be recognized as lost. The worker "adjusts" to his lot by lowering his own ambitions and transferring them to his children.[6] His adjustment is in the direction of increasing indifference toward his job (the necessary portion of his life), and the channeling of his interest and enthusiasm into his hobbies, his clubs, his community (the voluntary portion of his life).[7]

The need to contribute and to play an important part is stronger in some than in others. For some, of course, this need is partly fulfilled by moving up the organizational ladder. For others, the demands of their present jobs may be seen as too large, and they may even long for the security of a less challenging environment. Nevertheless, it appears that managers at every level consistently underestimate the ambitions and enthusiasms of their subordinates for a chance to contribute.[8]

Untapped resources

The typical company "wastes" its human resources, I believe, for what appear to the organization to be three good reasons. First, top management often does not realize that these resources exist. Second, even if management is aware of the existence of such resources, it is not at all clear how to go about creating an environment in which they could be more fully utilized; therefore, it is easier to go along with tried and true methods of management. Finally, the very process of unleashing talent is challenging and threatening; top management is not at all certain how this talent could be guided or when, where, and if it should stop. The mere thought of innovating in this direction is unsettling and disconcerting, for there appear to be real constraints on the amount of creativity, concern, and enthusiasm which the typical organization is equipped to handle.

The fact that organizations typically doubt the existence of untapped resources of creativity and concern among their membership is well documented. Superiors at every level may acknowledge the loyalty, efficiency, and dependability of their subordinates, but they usually have doubts

---

[6]See Ely Chinoy, *Automobile Workers and the American Dream* (Garden City, New York, Doubleday & Company, Inc., 1955), especially pp. 1-6, 20-21, 110-122; and Robert H. Guest, "Work Careers and Aspirations of Automobile Workers," in *Labor and Trade Unionism,* edited by Walter Galenson and Seymour Martin Lipset (New York, John Wiley and Sons, 1960), p. 319.

[7]See Robert Dubin, "Industrial Research and the Discipline of Sociology," in *Proceedings of the 11th Annual Meeting* (Madison, Wisconsin, Industrial Relations Research Association, 1959), p. 152.

[8]See Likert, *op. cit.*

about their ability to exercise judgment, creativity, and responsibility.[9] The interesting point is not that these attitudes exist in the minds of managers, but that they exist without proof.

In reviewing with groups of managers their assumptions about their subordinates' capabilities, I have frequently asked them how they arrived at the opinion that those below them were generally incapable of exercising responsible self-direction and self-control. The usual answer was that they had never seen their subordinates exercise judgment, creativity, and responsibility. The predictable follow-up question, "Have they ever been given the chance to demonstrate these capabilities?" usually has drawn little more than a bemused grin.

On other occasions, particularly in training sessions with groups of managers, I have frequently posed problems whose only viable solution demanded that lower level members of a hypothetical work group be allowed to exercise judgment and self-control. Only rarely have the training groups adopted solutions of this sort. Instead, the managers have tended to argue that the problems are unworkable. They have opted for the safe course, and refused to gamble even when not taking a reasoned risk meant total failure of the group to achieve its task.

In view of this demonstrated behavior, it is natural to ask: What would managers do if they were presented with unquestionable evidence of the existence of talents and capabilities among their subordinates far in excess of job demands? Would they take the same reasoned risks necessary to invest these human resources for productive gain which they might be willing to take with other types of resources? I am convinced the answer would too often be *no* — a well-reasoned *no* perhaps, but still a *no*.

Moreover, this response would be quite understandable. Management training has typically not placed high priority on uncovering human resources, nor has it stressed methods by which these resources can be developed and utilized. In fact, management thinking has too often taken the position that people in organizations are necessary but probably more trouble than they are worth.

Further, not only has management thinking and training taken this tack, but the organizational environment itself reinforces this view. Since managers more often than not regard their subordinates as problem causers, rather than problem solvers, little effort is made to find new outlets for their talents. In the modern and affluent organization, managers may reasonably take the position: "Even if these abilities exist, how would I make use of them — what would I do with them?" It is thus much easier to deny their existence than to deal with them.

---

[9]See, for example, Mason Haire, Edwin Ghiselli, and Lyman W. Porter, "Cultural Patterns in the Role of the Manager," *Industrial Relations*, February 1963, p. 95.

PREVAILING CONCEPTS

As suggested, this view reflects conventional management thought and training, which over the past 30 years has been made up of varying proportions of two different organizational approaches; both, however, are based on standard procedures and routines.

Industrial engineering

With its roots in the "scientific management" movement of Taylor, Gilbreth, and Gantt, this traditional approach has always stressed simplification, specialization, and routinization. Following this approach, a small number of related tasks requiring similar skills are brought together to form a job which can be quickly taught and easily learned. Methods study attempts to simplify task performance, and once a sound method is uncovered, efforts are made to get each job holder to perform according to standard procedures.

Explicit in this traditional industrial engineering approach is the assumption that someone other than the job holder is best able to devise the "proper" way to do the job. Standard procedures and routines are designed to help the production worker to do his job without being required to exercise judgment — in fact, these are generally designed explicitly to prevent the exercise of judgment. This approach envisions a neat job definition which makes clear and precise what the employee is and, equally important, what he is not to do.

Human relations

This movement grew up as a partial solution to the problems caused by the application of the traditional industrial engineering model. Researchers in the 1920's and 1930's decided that organizational members come to their jobs with certain social and ego needs which they seek to fulfill in their work environment. Workers appeared to respond, not always rationally but with apparent enthusiasm, to management efforts to make them feel they were an important and useful part of the organization.

The human relations approach was built on these findings. Its premise was that management could make the environment more tolerable, and the manager's life easier, by such practices as giving workers recognition for good performance, listening to their complaints and problems, and involving them in minor and routine work decisions.

The crucial point is that neither the traditional industrial engineering approach nor the human relations approach emphasizes any requirement on the part of the manager to develop and make use of his subordinates' resources outside of those routine skills called for in their jobs. Both approaches stress what *the manager must do with or for his subordinates.*

They do not urge the manager to find out *what his subordinates can do for him and the organization.*

The offshoot is that when faced with any problem of organizational or job design, the typical manager's first impulse is to block out standard procedures and routines and then to set out to limit the exercise of individual self-direction and self-control in the interest of organizational stability and coordination. He may suggest policies emphasizing fair treatment and involvement of his subordinates in minor decision making, but only if such activities can be accomplished within the framework of the closely controlled organizational structure and process.

HUMAN RESOURCES APPROACH

It has only been in the last decade or so that management scholars have begun to develop concepts which stress and put some operational meaning into the definition of the manager's primary role as a developer and utilizer of human resources. This human resources approach begins with the assumptions that people can contribute far in excess of the usual demands of their jobs and that they are, in fact, generally willing and anxious to contribute.

The logical outgrowth of this set of assumptions is that job assignments must be broadened. However, this broadening must go beyond the limits frequently associated with current "job enlargement" practices. It must not be something which management, in line with the human relations view, does for its employees in order to increase job satisfaction. Rather, it must occur as the manager, for the specific purpose of utilizing the full range of human resources, attempts to create an environment that challenges his subordinates to work up to their full capabilities.

The human resources approach has not yet been fully developed, and it is possible that it never will be. This is because it is essentially a dynamic conceptualization of the organization as a growing organism — one that is continually innovating and adjusting in an effort to tap its own resources. Nevertheless, some general principles have been formulated.

For example, this approach stresses that, within broad limits, organizational subunits ought to be allowed to decide for themselves the information they want and need in order to carry out their assignments. Similarly, all subunits ought to be allowed to participate in setting their own goals and evaluating their own performance for their own guidance. (Note: subunits do these things anyway. This model merely suggests that these informal "adjustments" be legitimized and utilized.)

Moreover, the human resources approach suggests that the organization must be creative and generous in distributing the rewards of improved performance.

Finally, this model redefines the manager's role, de-emphasizing the functions of unilateral decision making and control, and stressing the functions of developing and coordinating.

Goal setting, in this approach, is a joint process; primary control is exercised by the person or group carrying out the assignment, and the manager's role is that of facilitating goal accomplishment by removing the barriers limiting the group's performance. As a general rule, the more important the problem or the solution, the more crucial it is for the manager to tap the full range of resources of his group in solving the problem.

BUILT-IN CONSTRAINTS

Beyond these general concepts, the human resources model offers the manager no specific list of things to do. It does not have the apparent definiteness of either the traditional industrial engineering approach or the human relations approach. And this, of course, is one of the reasons that it has failed to gain wider acceptance.

On the manager

Perhaps even more important, however, is the fact that the human resources approach provides no answer to the question suggested earlier: What will the manager do with these resources once they are developed? The typical organization is not geared to handle these resources. Can it adjust? Will these resources, if recognized, not pose a threat as well as a challenge? These questions have been raised repeatedly in discussions with groups of managers. Seldom, however, has the problem of organizational constraints been so dramatically illustrated as in the following recent experience:

A young woman, who was a very capable, bright and efficient supervisor, was describing her most pressing current problem. She recounted her experiences with one of her subordinates who was also young, bright, and capable. After only a few weeks on the job, the subordinate had completely mastered her original assignment and was finishing her task well short of the prescribed work day. She quickly began to use her unused work time to examine the total work process in the unit, and to discuss with the supervisor her ideas for improving the operation.

The supervisor acknowledged that she initially brushed off these suggestions as half-baked ideas typical of a new employee, but finally, after having been trapped into listening one day, was forced to admit the value of at least one suggestion. This idea was put into operation jointly by the superior and subordinate and, in fact, proved to be of major benefit; further, it allowed the subordinate to accomplish even more in an even shorter period. Predictably, the process continued. The subordinate was back almost daily with further suggestions, most of them well worth considering.

The supervisor's plea to me at this point was an anguished, "What am I to do? I'm spending a fourth of my time simply working with this subordinate, planning and implementing improvements in the work process. How long can this go on?"

To the outsider, this supervisor's anguish may appear incongruous. Is this not the very nature of her job — developing and utilizing all the resources available to improve performance? But to the young woman involved, the question "How long can this go on?" is indeed meaningful. She, as was her subordinate originally, is bound up in reports, routines, and procedures on which the larger organization places higher priority than on innovation and subordinate development. To this supervisor, whose unit is surrounded by such organizational constraints, the subordinate represents a dual threat: (a) to her own personal status — the subordinate will soon know as much about the unit's operation as she does — and (b) to the stability of the unit itself — the creative subordinate is as disruptive to stable operations as she would be if she were laggard in her performance.

The goal of any given unit within a larger organization prescribes a certain area of operation and a certain set of demands which the supervisor alone cannot enlarge. Unless the boundaries of the department can be expanded, along with the jobs of its members, the manager not only has little incentive to develop his subordinates, but may be strongly motivated to ignore their skills and abilities.

On the organization

Blue-collar workers have often been accused of operating under the myth that there is only a certain "lump of labor" to be done, and that when this runs out, some or all of the work group will be laid off or dismissed. Restrictive work rules and "stretch out" strategies are often cited as observable evidence of this kind of thinking. However, the young supervisor's reaction in the previous example and management's reaction in general to the human resources approach suggest that this myth may, in fact, not be a myth. In many organizational subunits there *is* only so much work to be done; when this is accomplished, people *are* laid off.

Furthermore, managers' reactions reinforce my opinion that make-work and stretch-out are as much a characteristic of the managerial level as they are of the blue-collar level in many organizations. Consider these two examples:

● A large organization recently revised a portion of its structure "to provide better centralized control." Its new systems and procedures allowed the organization to bypass certain units within the management hierarchy, thus resulting in the same work being done in two places. Although months have passed since the changes were instituted, the organization has not yet attempted to eliminate this duplication of effort and to realign its resources efficiently. Instead, it has allowed this make-work to continue, concerning itself only with keeping the bypassed units "out of harm's way" to prevent them from fouling up the system.

● In a service organization, one of its subunits put forth a proposal which would have greatly increased that department's contribution to the overall operation, and would also have expanded and improved the services offered by the total organization. The proposal, which was admittedly challenging and called for major rethinking, was "considered" for over a year — just long enough, in fact, for a competing organization to move into the field.

The logical solution to problems such as those posed above is for the total organization to adopt the human resources approach. The organization would then undertake the primary role of developing and utilizing the resources of its subunits, just as the supervisor discussed in an earlier example undertook this role, although somewhat reluctantly, with her subordinate. Lump-of-labor thinking, make-work, and stretch-out would become increasingly unnecessary as the organization seeks to employ fully the resources of each subunit.

A brief summary

Risking redundancy in the interests of clarity, let me briefly summarize here in an effort to drive home my point.

The human resources approach challenges the manager to attempt to recognize, develop, and apply the full range of resources of each of his subordinates. One of the major problems with this approach, however, is that it works! People do develop and grow — they grow right out of their initial assignments. This problem tends to solve itself when a particular unit is faced with a large and challenging set of tasks to perform. The members of the unit simply grow into more demanding jobs with added challenge and added reward.

If, however, a unit is tied to a narrow and undemanding set of tasks and goals, its members may find their growing capabilities are unutilized and unrewarded. Both the manager and his subordinates want and expect their resources to be profitably employed by the larger organization, and they quickly become frustrated and lose interest when this does not occur.

Organizations, therefore, cannot fully accept this approach unless they are willing constantly to challenge traditional goals and approaches, to probe and explore new areas in which they can invest their resources and serve society. And this is precisely what some innovative organizations are doing. The movement of computer builders into the field of education is a striking example. Similarly, the operation of Job Corps centers by private firms has proved successful, in terms of both public service and private gain. Perhaps an even more dramatic example is the acceptance by an aerospace firm of a state contract to study crime patterns and law enforcement procedures.

The opportunities for organizations to expand the investment of their resources in profitable service to society seem to me largely unexplored. Instead of merely giving dollars to society in the interest of public relations, perhaps organizations can seriously examine their own resources and invest them in community services. Organizations not only can provide such resources efficiently, but can achieve profitable returns on their investment.

REASONED RISKS

When talking with groups of managers, I am usually asked ¬t this point to be more specific as to the critical areas in which organizations can invest their human resources. My reply is simply that I don't pretend to know what resources exist in any particular organization or vhat profitable use can be made of these resources.

I could not have told the meat-packing industry 30 years ago what amazingly profitable resources existed in the portions of their products previously discarded. What's more, the industry's leaders did not expect anyone to tell them. They were willing to spend sizable sums to find out what was there and how it could be used. Similar examples can be drawn from every industry. Banking, steel, even modern railroads, all are re-evaluating their material assets and seeking new avenues of investment. I am equally convinced that human resources exist in unsuspected quantities, and can be developed and profitably invested by taking creative, but reasonable, entrepreneurial risks.

Will it work?

But what if this approach does not work? What if, instead of accepting the challenge, the organization's members exploit their broader autonomy to their own gain? What if, instead of exercising responsible concern and self-control, subunits and individuals neglect their objectives or overstep the bounds of reason? What if people at lower levels prove incapable of exercising judgment, creativity, and self-direction? What if the organization's limits cannot be expanded? Is the manager not abrogating his responsibility? Won't the whole organization collapse?

In my judgment, such fears are basically unfounded. The growing body of evidence concerning the usefulness of the human resources approach is quite encouraging. More importantly, while the approach has not always been measurably successful — for reasons which will be touched on shortly — it has never failed. At least, tnere is no evidence that the sort of disaster which managers fear has ever occurred. The worst that an organization can count on is that things will not improve. In that event, they will probably go on about the same as before.

Disaster does not occur for the simple reason that people will not let it occur. The manager frequently finds that his subordinates respond much as he is certain he would respond to a similar opportunity to use his own resources — responsibly and creatively. Subordinates do not attempt to usurp the manager's prerogatives. In fact, the manager is frequently better informed as to what is going on than before. He finds that he is consulted before any important moves are made, just as he would consult his superior. And, surprisingly, the manager finds that his subordinates may even initiate reports on their own performance.

These responses are clearly not uniform or inevitable. Some individuals and some units may prove incapable of going very far beyond their present level of performance. Others may resist innovation and, at least initially, prove fearful of challenge. A few, in fact, may behave in a fashion detrimental to the organization. But these responses are present in any traditionally managed organization.

There is a crucial question implicit here for both organizations and societies: Shall we structure our total system to control the few who would destroy it, or for the benefit of the many who can and will operate and improve it?

Finally, in any discussion of the nature and magnitude of the risk involved in attempting to utilize human resources, few organizations are ever faced with a clear-cut go/no-go situation. While no one would suggest that the reshaping of a total organization be attempted overnight, experimental situations can be structured. Decentralized units, for example, can be operated on a "pilot plant" basis while innovative management methods are tried out. Risk can thus be minimized. However, a word of warning must be sounded. If the investment is too small, few benefits are likely to accrue. There must be a meaningful commitment on the part of the management hierarchy to give the human resources approach a real opportunity to prove itself.

'Fat cats' only?

A manager recently explained to me his views toward some of the concepts implicit in the human resources approach. He stated in no uncertain terms that "only a 'fat' company can afford to decentralize, and only a 'fat' manager can afford to delegate authority and control." In his view, only those companies running at the head of the pack — those with good performance and good profits — can afford to allow their subunits to exercise broad discretion, and to experiment with new approaches for investing their own departmental resources. Similarly, he contended, only those managers whose units are operating well can afford to loosen up and allow subordinates greater autonomy. He emphasized his views by noting that those firms which are usually cited as progressive in managerial terms are all "fat cats" in their fields.

In some ways it is hard to argue with this manager's views. In fact, I agree with his thinking in part, since it is my opinion that most organizations today are fat, and can well afford the risk of innovation in developing and utilizing human resources. But, at the same time, I cannot agree with his perception of when organizations can afford to gamble along these lines. Here, it seems quite possible that he is confusing cause and effect.

While the evidence is not at all clear, it appears equally possible that the fat organizations — the innovators in progressive management — may well have gotten fat by just these techniques. Or, at least, it seems plausible to argue that they may well have remained fat by continuing to develop and utilize their human resources.

These two arguments appear even more convincing when we consider how organizations grow. Theories of growth are many and varied, but it is frequently argued that organizations grow primarily by finding new outlets for their resources — e.g., new markets for their products, new fields for investment of their funds, and new applications for their technology. Is it not also possible that organizations grow as they recognize unutilized human capabilities — their underemployed human resources? One economist has offered a biological analogy that suggests just this: growth pressure, in part, emanates from within as the organization develops the managerial capability to take on new tasks.[10]

It is thus reasonable to argue that progressive firms can afford to be progressive simply because they have been, and continue to be, progressive. They have in the past recognized their resources and sought to employ them, and in so doing have created new resources. Recognizing their affluence, they have not balked at taking reasoned risks in trying innovative concepts, theories, and approaches. A little doubt and uncertainty are the partners of innovation, but the name of the game is risk.

Moreover, the results are more often than not rewarding. Perhaps you have heard this currently circulating story:

A group of economic advisers to the President are frantically pouring over national income data in an effort to determine the impact of the 1965 tax cuts. After several anxious moments, one of the strongest advocates of the tax cut policy straightens up in amazement and announces, "My God, gentlemen! It actually worked."

Whether or not that story is true, I recently watched a similar scene enacted by a group of managers. One of the members was describing to his incredulous colleagues how he had put into practice certain of the human resources concepts described in this article. In a tone tinged with pride and surprise, he announced, "By God, fellows, it actually worked!"

ONE FINAL POINT

I have repeatedly suggested that organizations can and should take the risk involved in developing and utilizing their human resources. I have

[10]Edith Penrose, *The Theory of the Growth of the Firm* (New York, John Wiley & Sons, Inc. 1959), pp. 51-54, 67-87.

not, however, dealt with the question: What happens if they do not take this risk?

The answer is not easy to frame. On the one hand, the modern, affluent organization will likely survive — in the short run at least — even if it follows a highly conservative course in terms of developing and investing its human assets. It may even continue to exist in reasonable comfort, unaware of the waste involved in following this approach.

On the other hand, an organization that continues to adopt this conservative posture cannot claim to be well managed. Good management implies growth and development through the efficient utilization of all available resources. The well-managed organization is not the one that hides behind the myth of scarcity. It is the one that recognizes it has both abundant resources and opportunities for employing them, and it accepts the entrepreneurial challenge of profitably matching its resources and opportunities in the service of society.

REFLECTIONS OF A 21ST CENTURY MANAGER

George Kozmetsky

The end of the 20th century was duly marked by global celebrations. But for a relatively small group of Americans there were special satisfactions in entering the year 2001. They were the managers of various enterprises — in business, government and industry — whose careers extended all the way back to the late 1960s. Now in their fifties, they could look back on a period of extraordinary change. The manager's responsibilities had changed drastically while the composition of industry itself was marked by numerous stages of transformation.

Back in the early 1970s, they recalled, managers began to recognize new kinds of organizations. For convenience, these developing organizations were known as *nonroutine industries.*

Those nonroutine industries were made up of units of government, industry and education engaged in nonrepetitive or "nonroutine" pursuits. The education industry itself was a leading nonroutine industry. The defense and space industries were certainly nonroutine industries, and so were large segments of the medical, electronics, oceanography and "urban problem" industries. So were many areas of government.

The new industries had certain common characteristics. Often, for example, they were working on problems that required new orders of solutions. No textbooks held the answers to questions that arose in planning and building livable megalopolies, exploring the reaches of space or controlling the environment. Frequently, answers had to be improvised. The temporary solution to the problem of air pollution in Los Angeles, for example, was typically makeshift and typically "messy." When the pollution index struck a certain level, motorists were required to pull over to the curb and turn off the engine. As pollution grew worse, power plants were required to switch from diesel fuel to natural gas. Solutions to many such problems, ranging from garbage disposal to land pollution, were frequently patchwork and "messy," offensive to anyone who liked solutions to be "clean" and permanent.

Nonroutine industries were also technologically based; their products were the end result of much labor and thought by scientists, engineers and other technical and professional talents. Even as early as 1969, 70 percent of the available scientists and engineers were hired by the "nonroutine" industries.

*Reprinted with permission from *Bell Telephone Magazine,* March-April, 1969.

Another characteristic of the new industries was that the number of units they produced was not very large. Sometimes, in fact, the "unit" consisted only of a program or a plan. If the "units" were products, they ranged from one-of-a-kind to small production runs. The computer industry, for example, produced only 14,300 units in 1968, after 20 years of existence as an "industry." In contrast, the old mass-production auto industry turned out 10 million units.

Still another characteristic of the emerging industries was that their new products or proposals often required the cooperation and coordination of segments of government, education and industry. Problems associated with urbanization, for example, involved a large amount of interaction among public and private organizations. So did problems related to transportation, space exploration and health.

The rise and spread of such new industries gradually changed the nature of the manager's tasks.

In the old, mass-production industries, the manager was principally a supervisor of specialists. To his office came the experts in his company, the professionals in such fields as accounting, personnel, marketing, finance and production. But in the nonroutine industries, the manager had a different set of appointments. His office visitors were men in government, university professors, the many scientists and engineers within his own company, and numerous outside consultants.

More and more, it appeared, the manager of a nonroutine industry was not merely the supervisor and motivator of an assortment of talents; he was also a man with the ability to break across the artificial barriers among disciplines and professions. His experiences in education and government, as well as in business, enabled him to locate and tap expertise on short notice. He was, in fact, a manager of intellectual *resources.*

The ability to manage intellectual resources assumed overwhelming importance in the decades of the 1970s and 1980s. By then, education had unquestionably become America's leading industry, requiring a vast number of skilled managers. In 1980, college enrollments were three times higher than in 1970, and they advanced even faster in later decades. (In the year 2000, for example, the University of California had 275,000 students, compared with 99,000 in 1969, and that was fairly typical of the larger educational units. Education was a lifelong process of virtually all of America's 400 million people.)

Even as early as the 1970s, it had become quite common for a manager to leave The Company after five or six years in the demanding top echelons. Sometimes he went off to serve in government; often he joined a university. But in any kind of organization he was marked by his ability to tap intellectual resources, in the interest of solving problems and creating new knowledge.

The university was the ideal place for honing his abilities as a manager. The campus was obviously rich in intellectual resources. It offered him the chance to bring together different disciplines in an informal atmosphere and get them to work on a particular problem. The solutions they found — often unusual — could perhaps be applied in a few years to some industry, just as space technology and techniques had been adopted by industry in the 1960s.

Of course, the manager who could shuttle easily among government, industry and educational organizations was not particularly new. Such managers appeared noticeably in the 1960s. People like John Gardner, Robert McNamara, George Romney, Daniel Moynihan, Sol Linowitz, Dean Rusk, Orville Freeman and McGeorge Bundy were merely a few of the managers who could move gracefully — and successfully — from campus to a foundation, from business to government. Behind them were hundreds of lesser-known managers with similar adaptability. Increasingly, the business manager in most demand was one who could skillfully bring together experts of government and education into the planning stages of a project, drawing on *their* intellectual resources. But as the one-of-a-kind projects so typical of the nonroutine industries became more common in the 1970s and 1980s, the manager's tenure with a particular organization was significantly shorter than it was in the 1960s.

The need for managers of intellectual resources was intense, even in the 1960s. The shortage of such managers would have been worse, however, if the nation had not embarked on the era of manned space flight. With that era came the rise to prominence of the interdisciplinary scientists.

What America needed and got in that period was an increasing number of Leonardo da Vincis — people who could work across the sciences; people who could comprehend the subtleties of cellular biology and at the same time design the mechanical apparatus needed to keep living organisms alive and normally adjusted to the hostile environment of space. In addition, these same individuals were expected to manage and integrate their portion of the operation with the longer range objectives.

At the same time, a number of corporations — particularly those in the mass-production or routine industries — were themselves busily training future managers, even if they sometimes failed to realize the fact. It was occasionally noted, even in the 1960s, that systems experts quickly learned many of the essential details of running a company in the process of analyzing systems and structuring problems. As problem-solving by computer became more general in the 1970s, the systems experts were logical candidates for top management. It was they, after all, who could superbly perform what was to become the manager's chief function — the structuring of problems. And so, between the space programs and management training by computer, America had developed at least a stopgap supply of managers for the 1970s and 1980s. By this time, too, the leading university business schools had modernized their programs and were training many managers for the new-style enterprises.

One of the particularly vexing problems for nonroutine industry managers in this period involved an essential segment of their intellectual resources — the scientists and technicians. In the 1970s, most technically trained people had become even more mobile than managers.

The tenure of technically trained people on a project often lasted for just a few years. As soon as their specialized knowledge was exhausted, they found it necessary to acquire some other specialty — for their specialties — were often usable for one project only.

For all the talk about shortages of engineers and scientists in the 1960s, for example, there began to appear a kind of occupational unemployment; like actors, scientists found themselves "at liberty." When England found it couldn't compete in atomic energy and in the aircraft industries, the requirements for technical people were cut back 50 percent. Job switches and "brain drains" became common.

Motivating people to do their best in short-term projects was particularly trying for managers in the 1970s. In those years, however, enormous strides were made in understanding how people store and process information internally — in other words, how they think. The psychology developed from research in that area also was applied to problems of human behavior; and by the 1980s, knowledge of learning and motivation was as advanced as were chemistry and biology in the 1960s. By the end of the century managers in both routine and nonroutine industries were superior motivators.

The motivation question affected entire organizations, of course. Back in the 1960s, corporations were becoming aware of what was popularly called "social responsibility." Many companies quickly laid claim to the virtue; others said they had it all along. In any case the question became increasingly academic as corporate policies and activities seemed increasingly to involve the public interest. By the 1980s and 1990s the largest corporations squarely identified their goals with social objectives, and the manager became concerned with developing industrial strategies that would mesh with the goals of raising the quality of life. The motivating force behind his company, as he saw it, was the need to furnish people with the things that gave full meaning to life. Philosophical questions found a permanent place on the agenda of board meetings, and the chairman was as concerned about them as about return on investment.

On the eve of year 2001, a manager could take some satisfactions in the ways that some of the fears of the 1960s and 1970s had disappeared.

In those years, he recalled, there had been widespread concern that automation would create disastrous problems of chronic unemployment. When it developed that computers could not only think but could also frame questions better than most humans, there was further alarm. And when automated equipment began to produce automated equipment — in effect, a machine with the human power of reproduction — there was something akin to terror. Was man becoming obsolete?

In retrospect, the fears were groundless. The machines were actually helping to open up new opportunities and force the continuous upgrading of tasks.

Some of the biggest changes of all had occurred within the old mass-production industries. A third of all working people were in these industries by the year 2000, and virtually all could be considered supervisors or middle-managers. The 40- and 35-hour work week had disappeared many years before; supervisors and maintenance workers were in the automated factory only four hours each day. A typical factory had six shifts, five days weekly.

The managers at middle levels handled actual operations of the factory. They turned their tactical problems over to self-organizing computers, which in turn put the solutions into automatic operation — subject, of course, to the middle-manager's veto.

The top manager had an enormous amount of authority, compared with the top manager of the 1960s. All lines on the organization chart led to his office. The trend really started in the 1960s with the centralization of certain operations like payroll and billing, that was made possible by computers. As computer applications spread during the 1970s, companies recentralized authority and control. By the year 2000, the top manager and the machines were directly responsible for virtually all decision-making. The authority of middle managers was severely limited.

A high percentage of the top manager's time was devoted to strategic planning. He was concerned with the day-to-day operations of the company only to the extent of monitoring performance — to make certain that decisions were in line with his company's goals and policies.

Top managers had ample time for such strategic planning. Committee meetings and routine briefings had long been eliminated. The chief executive carried out communications with a voice-writer, color TV-telephone and computer display board. In strategic planning, he concentrated on formulating specialized management principles which would eventually be built into the computer; the computer could then offer solutions to specific problems in line with management principles and company goals.

When he wasn't planning, the manager was studying. His administrative aide (upgraded from secretary) helped assemble research and study sources.

His study efforts were considered an essential part of his daily chores. For in the nonroutine industries, a manager needed a deep knowledge of the natural sciences, the arts, the social sciences and the physical sciences. All in all, ne needed to keep abreast of 10 different fields in detail, and he needed a good conceptual knowledge of 90 others.

Other things had changed for the manager too. Communications had removed the necessity for most face-to-face meetings, and communicating itself was much briefer. And the proliferation of governmental authorities, with their overlapping jurisdictions, finally gave way in the late 1970s to a balance of federal and regional authorities, making communicating with government easier.

Solutions to problems were still tailor-made, but they were no longer "messy." With government, industry and education working toward the common goals of improving the quality of life, conflict of interest — that had made for patchwork solutions in the 1960s — had been largely eliminated.

Not all problems had been ironed out in the last third of the 20th

Century, of course. The knowledge explosion, for instance, was never really tamed. Despite the compression and fast transmission of data in forms other than the old printed word, managers had still to find a way to keep completely current, because knowledge kept doubling at ever faster rates. The typical manager in the year 2000 was more or less resigned to the idea that he would never know all he needed to know.

But, on the whole, for the manager, the satisfactions in reaching the 21st Century far outweighed any yearnings for simpler times. His skills had played no small part in easing burdens so that people had more meaningful control over their lives, enabling them to manage their own destinies.